Houses of the Interpreter:
Reading Scripture, Reading Culture

Houses

of the

Interpreter

Reading Scripture,
Reading Culture

David Lyle Jeffrey

Provost Series

Ᏸ

Baylor University Press
Waco, Texas USA

This volume is the forty-first published by the Markham Press Fund of Baylor University Press, established in memory of Dr. L. N. and Princess Finch Markham of Longview, Texas, by their daughters, Mrs. R. Matt Dawson of Waco, Texas, and Mrs. B. Reid Clanton of Longview, Texas.

Cover photo: The Vagabond/Prodigal Son by Hieronymus Bosch (c. 1450–1516) Museum Boymans van Beuningen, Rotterdam, The Netherlands

Cover design: Pamela Poll

All artwork, cover and interior, has been provided by Bridgeman Art Library.

Library of Congress Cataloging-in-Publication Data

Jeffrey, David L., 1941–
    Houses of the interpreter : reading scripture, reading culture / David Lyle Jeffrey.
        p. cm. — (The provost series)
"A Markham Press Fund Publication."
Includes bibliographical references and index.
    ISBN 0-918954-89-4 (alk. paper)
    1. Bible—Criticism, interpretation, etc.—History. 2. Christianity and the arts—History. I. Title. II. Series.

BS500.J44 2003
    220.6′09—dc22

                                                          2003013783

Printed in the United States of America on acid-free paper

Contents

PART THREE
Scripture in a House of Mirrors

Preface and Acknowledgments

I count it an honor to have been asked to prepare a volume of collected essays for the Provost Series at Baylor University Press. The Provost under whom this series was conceived is the same who hired me to Baylor. Donald D. Schmeltekopf's leadership over a dozen years has been instrumental in transforming the University, both in terms of its academic achievement and its vision for Christian scholarship. It is a privilege to have been invited to become part of such an intellectual community.

My assignment in this series has been to gather from past writings, as well as those current and unpublished, a representation of the fundamental lines of enquiry which have preoccupied me for more than three decades. Though my career has been lived out almost exclusively in secular universities, these lines may be retraced to prior and undergirding theological curiosity: the central and abiding interest of my intellectual life has been the cultural history of biblical interpretation. I have long been fascinated not merely by the conversation of diverse interpreters of Scripture in our own age, but with the manifold riches of interpretation of these texts by the universal church down through the centuries. Biblical tradition, from Torah to Talmud and from the New Testament to T. S. Eliot, is only partly the stuff of commentaries, sermons, and books of theology. In many cultures, it is also the living life of the arts. For me, thinking about how sculptors, musicians, poets, and painters have "read" the Bible, and about how their understanding of some texts has in turn deepened ecclesiastical understanding of Scripture (occasionally even the development of dogmatic theology), has been a source of unending pleasure as well as spiritual edification. I have discovered (and hope my students and readers may also) that whole sections of the Bible can leap to life in an unprecedented way when we look for and listen to the minds of the ages at work on texts we thought we had understood well enough but probably had not.

I have also learned that historically the really great readers of Scripture include fewer trained theologians than one might expect. This was at one time disconcerting for me because of a persistent hope that the free church tradition in North America, so sorely in want of a more deeply consistent and intellectually coherent biblical theology, might recover resources for better theological thinking from the treasury of foundational interpreters. While I still believe these sources to be invaluable, indeed essential (and the reader of these pages will see that) it has also come to me to recognize that they cannot be by themselves a sufficient basis for our recovery of a coherent biblical theology today. The understanding of the un-ordained, the laity, needs also to be gathered up and most carefully reflected upon in the light of Scripture itself.

Accordingly, in the final essays in this volume I make a layman's attempt at introducing lay criticism as well as lay understanding (mostly from the arts) into a theological reflection concerning the authority of Scripture. It is still my hope that by entering into a wider conversation with the full church—against and across time—that we in the free church in America today may learn to eschew not only the intellectual pride which we are so proud to disdain, but also the prideful anti-intellectualism for which, sadly, we have become notorious. By insisting, as so often we do, on our own subjective present experience as the primary referent for our reading of Scripture, we actually cease to read Scripture. By refusing the textual understanding of brothers and sisters down through the ages, we cut ourselves off from the work of the Holy Spirit in human history. These things are not merely a matter for intellectual embarrassment; they are, or ought to be, a matter of spiritual shame.

The essays which follow grow at least as much out of the blessed discovery that we are not the only standard of Christian spiritual understanding as they do from the joy of academic and intellectual discovery. I have included articles of literary criticism, literary and art history, scriptural exegesis, historical theology, and theological reflection. But there are also personal essays here, a word-study (a slightly less truncated version of one of the many I wrote for the *Dictionary of Biblical Tradition in English Literature*), and even two review articles. Part one includes theological consideration on the matter of how we read the Bible, the first two chapters having originated recently as conference talks here at Baylor. The central section is theological reflection from the arts; these essays were published during the 1970s and 1980s, though I have revised and updated each for this volume. Part three begins with a brief article on Lewis as a reader of Great Texts, composed at the behest of Todd Copeland, editor of the *Baylor Line;* it is followed by a lecture on C. S. Lewis as a reader of the Bible which Provost Schmeltekopf invited me to give when I first visited Baylor in February 2000. This section concludes with recent efforts in lay theology designed with the church at least as much as the university in mind.

Acknowledgments are in order. Chapters 6 and 7 originated in extremely lively debate with the late D. W. Robertson, Jr. of Princeton University, my professor and dissertation advisor. Though Robertson most emphatically did not share my Christian faith, his own lifelong determination to give an accurate account of the influence of scriptural interpretation upon medieval poetry has remained for me an exemplar of high intellectual integrity. In disciplines of the mind or ferocity for truth, few I have met could match him. He initially opposed my dissertation topic out of sheer dislike for Franciscan spirituality, but after he had read my preliminary long essay he directed the whole thing with an even-handed scrutiny. (As well, chapter 6, which parses a paper I did for him in a graduate seminar during my first autumn in Princeton, was my first journal publication.) Chapter 7 came years later, as a paper invited for a colloquium at Princeton on the occasion of Robertson's retirement. There were many fine papers that day from distinguished colleagues and former students. The Guest of Honor was generally quiet; only once did he rise to protest and engage a speaker in debate, and if I felt it coming it was because I knew he disliked intensely the biblicism he associated with John Wyclif and he wished to spare Chaucer any "taint" of it whatsoever. Yet there are few honors that have come my way which I value so much as the spirited criticism that has followed from being taken seriously—and treated fairly—by that great yet reclusive southern intellectual. Even the *Dictionary of Biblical Tradition in English Literature* (1992) owes something of its inception both to our debate and my persistent sense of obligation to the encyclopedic learning he exemplified.

Most other chapters in this volume began in my own classroom. Almost every research idea I have had was prompted by the effort to understand something more deeply for the sake of teaching more clearly. The essay on Bosch's "Haywain" triptych represents a process in which I have always been the chief beneficiary: from a classroom at the University of Rochester it came to be a paper given in Holland at the invitation of the art historian H. R. Rookmaker of the Vrije Universiteit. I then redrafted and submitted it to the distinguished historian Lynn White, Jr., then editor of *Viator*, who graciously accepted it. The other of its readers was E. H. Gombrich, art historian at the Warburg and Courtaulds Institute in London. Gombrich expressed a reservation about one aspect of my interpretation of the central panel. I was foolish enough to persist against that capacious expertise with my own conclusion, and I let the paper go to print as accepted. Later, the medievalist V. A. (Del) Kolve made complimentary use of my article, but it turned out that he had reservations on the same point as did Gombrich years earlier. I have at last taken the measure of their learned criticism and am happy for this belated opportunity to amend my earlier reading and, by way of reworking this section in the light of subsequent study, to express gratitude for their true colleagueship.

The articles on worship language and on theological truth each began as talks in response to requests from churchmen, the first by a pastor in the United Church of Canada; it was given to a lay audience and later published at the initiative of Jon Pott, editor of the *Reformed Journal*, who had seen a copy of the talk as circulated, unbeknownst to me, in typescript. The last chapter is the result of an invitation to address a conference of the Society for the Book of Common Prayer, an audience both of clerics and lay leaders in the Anglican Church; this one I have left in the extended sermon form in which it was delivered as the closing session of that conference.

All of my life I have benefited from fair and principled teachers. Some of them gave me grades; all the good ones gave me that which is far more valuable: thoughtful criticism. It is in this gift that not only colleagues and editors, but also several among my own students have gone on to be my teachers also. Such as I am able to bring to my classroom is at least as much a tribute to their collective love for truth as any ongoing diligence on my own part. I wish to mention in respect to these essays in particular my indebtedness to John V. Fleming, Russell Peck, Dominic Manganiello, Alden Smith, Michael Treschow, Phillip Donnelly, Di Gan, Helen Lasseter, Yi Li, Edith Humphrey and, for so long a perseverant and watchful eye and heart, Katherine Beth Jeffrey. In such company, indeed, one knows the real good of the intellectual life.

In dedicating this volume to the growing Christian intellectual community at Baylor University, I wish to be understood as including all those of the Baylor line who, though of another era, continue to be present in the conversation of their students and who, in one way or another, have read charitably, taught honorably, and ceaselessly sought after truth.

Thy statutes have been my songs in the house of my pilgrimage.

(Psalm 119:54)

PART ONE

Scripture in the House
of Theology

Chapter One

How Firm a Foundation . . . ?

Omnis ergo qui audit verba mea haec et facit ea, assimilabitur viro sapienti,
qui aedificavit domum suam super petram . . .

Matthew 7:24, Vulgate

It occasionally happens among Christians that a passage of Scripture comfortably familiar from childhood comes back much later to haunt us with an unfamiliar severity. This can especially be so when rereading those teachings of Jesus typically first encountered in "sword drill" verses and Sunday School songs.

"The wise man built his house upon the rock. . . . The foolish man built his house upon the sand . . ."—I can still hear the rollicking meter and anticipate the final, thunderous clap and clomp which nearly shook down the lights of our Baptist church when "the house on the sand went flat."

But before me now, in a considerably more tentative middle age, is the whole text, the concluding sentences of the toughest teaching in the Sermon on the Mount:

> Not everyone who says to Me, 'Lord, Lord,' shall enter the kingdom of heaven, but he who does the will of My Father in heaven. Many will say to Me in that day, 'Lord, Lord, have we not prophesied in Your name, cast out demons in Your name, and done many wonders in Your name?' And then I will declare to them, 'I never knew you; depart from Me, you who practice lawlessness!' Therefore whoever hears these sayings of Mine, and does them, I will liken him to a wise man who built his house on the rock: and the rain descended, the floods came, and the winds blew and beat on that house; And it did not fall, for it was founded on the rock. But everyone

who hears these sayings of Mine, and does not do them, will be like a foolish man who built his house on the sand: and the rain descended, the
floods came, and the winds blew and beat on that house; and it fell. And
great was its fall. (Matt 7:21–27)

Now, the cheerful singing of my childhood notwithstanding, I have to admit
that I have been one of those who from the time I learned that song until
now have said "Lord, Lord" quite a lot and heard his sayings many times but
have put them into obedient practice far less often than counts in this tough
text as "wise." When now I read or remember that last sentence (v. 27), it is
not the church hall lights that get to shaking.

Anyone who teaches for a living notices further that it is the matter of
authority which immediately sets the teaching of Jesus apart for his first
hearers: "And so it was, when Jesus had ended these sayings, that the people were astonished at His teaching, for He taught them as one having
authority, and not as the scribes" (Matt 7:28–29). Attempting both to
acknowledge and assuage my guilt when teaching this passage to the mostly
cheerful pagans in my erstwhile secular university, I have sometimes mis-
chievously paraphrased this last as "He taught them as one having authority, not like *our* professors." The students' typically generous laughter
indicates their appreciation of both points: they have already learned about
the gap between first-order and second-order discourse, and, without being
taught it, that many who practice the second kind, in their second-hand
fashion and self-interestedness, have lost what little authority they might
once have had. As with the scribes in Jesus' day, lost authority has become
a fact of contemporary life—in our universities as in other public institutions. Even in the church.

Teaching now at a historically Christian university still rooted in the
Baptist tradition, I have found the loss of authority in general an occasion for
frequent reflection. Recently, as a background for our consideration of the
modern British novel (from Joyce and Wilde to Rushdie and Julian Barnes)
my students and I read and reflected upon Hannah Arendt's *Between Past
and Future: Eight Exercises in Political Thought.* Famously in this book Arendt
declared that, as a viable concept, "authority has vanished from the modern
world."[1] She defines authority as that which implies obedience in a context
of freedom, not of coercion. What Arendt concludes about modernity is that
foundations, or tradition, have little or no power to constrain either anarchic
impulse or pragmatic temporizing; we have divorced ourselves from mutual
obligations to objective, mind-independent realities wherever possible. As a
lamentable result, we know a great deal about power and very little of
authority.

Confusion of authority with power persists with a vengeance in our puta-tively postmodern world. But when we still speak of "authority figures" we dutifully echo Freud, and typically mean to identify persons whose tacit or explicit standards, or censure, are perceived to constrain or critique our abso-lute personal freedom. That is, we are not much different from early moderns like Samuel Butler (1835–1902), author of the (appropriately enough) posthumously published semi-autobiographical novel, *The Way of All Flesh*.[2] Butler's rebellion against his parson father and his father's religion is, sum-marily, the story of his life. For him, rebellion grew readily into hatred, first for his father and his faith, then for even those prominent intellectuals whose resistance to Christianity he first shared and whose favor he often shamelessly curried (e.g., Sydney Smith, John Ruskin, Matthew Arnold). In the end, Butler even turned on his greatest hero, Darwin, with such vehemence as to prompt one of his biographers to observe of him what could be said of many moderns, that "his attitude in fact was as authoritarian and narrow as his father's, only exercised upon a different set of prejudices."[3]

Rebellion against authority, symbiotic passion that it is, remains an almost intractable feature of our fallen condition. But in our time it has come to be regarded as a virtuous condition, even the signature of what it means to be authentically modern. The Death of the Father (Freud) and Death of the Author (Barthes) and the Death of God (Nietzsche) are, after all, projections of a single impulse—a desire for the elimination of any authority which might constrain or inhibit our personal freedom, perhaps especially our sexual freedom, but also our "freedom" to make "truth" what we want it to be. That the concept of truth thus suffers from the same syn-drome as the concept of authority is clear enough.

Truth is, effectively, authority, and nowhere more explicitly synonymous than where biblical religion is the context. This is so obviously the case in a proto-Reformation reflection such as John Wyclif's *De Veritate Sacrae Scripturae* (*The Truth of Holy Scripture*) that translators are understandably divided as to whether *Veritate* in the title should be rendered "Truth" or "Authority."[4] In Wyclif's understanding, these were in respect of Scripture practically indistinguishable in the term.

Among the Reformers a century after Wyclif were Luther and Tyndale, for whom resistance to ecclesiastical and magisterial authority was construed as obligation to still higher authority, or truth, which the institutional church was, with some warrant, no longer perceived as serving. Inter-mediation of the authority of the Church in restriction of access to the sources of the Church in Scripture had become at last an exercise of raw, sometimes brutal power. Resistance here, too, became rebellion (and divorce), and because it was "of the Church," its implications were far-reaching indeed. To the degree to which the Reformation celebrated the shift from the authority of the institutional Church to the authority of the individual (*"Hier stehe ich"*) it liberated an individualism previously unknown and unanticipated. But this too, in its turn, has occasioned further confusions of authority and power.

Protestants in general have usually presented individualism—even in biblical interpretation—as pretty much an unmitigated good. John Bunyan's conviction that the Bible by itself is far better mental furniture than the entire libraries at Oxford and Cambridge without it became a sentiment both shared (and narrowed) among his evangelical and Baptist successors; his conviction that freedom to interpret Scripture by and for himself was the purest form of access to the truth was to be no less warmly embraced by that wing of the Reformation most successful in America.[5]

Now, with radical individualism and the autonomous interpretation of Scripture having grown to proportions of anti-authoritarianism, general biblical illiteracy, and theological incoherence no Tyndale or Bunyan could have imagined, there is at last some evidence that Christians in the evangelical tradition are willing to reconsider the role of authority in relation to biblical interpretation. What was already clear enough to a thoughtful Puritan like Richard Baxter is apparent now to the most modest reflection of anyone who is willing to think about it: loss of authority of the Church, *de jure*, has led inexorably, on these lines, to the *de facto* loss of authority of Scripture.[6] To put it as plainly as possible, the hackneyed adage among some adversaries of the faith, that Christians can make any verse of the Bible mean anything they want it to, is almost perfectly mirrored in the proclamation of some believers that the highest religious good is their right to interpret Scripture in whatever way they see fit.[7] When an insistence on absolute interpretative independence is coupled, as increasingly it is, with an almost staggering loss of biblical literacy amongst its champions, then the actual authority of Scripture can become so negligible as to make any claim to a biblical foundation either comic or tragic depending upon your point of view.

All of these factors make the governing ideas about biblical interpretation and the life of the Church before the Reformation of timely interest for Protestant Christians. For Catholics on the other hand, a recent outpouring of scholarship on biblical exegesis in the early Church is a retracing of steps, and it has led to a dramatic revival in biblical scholarship and biblical teaching.[8]

In fact, as Pope John XXIII, Vatican II, and most recently Pope John Paul II himself made clear in his encyclical letter *Veritatis Splendor* (*The Splendor of Truth*), it is by means of such careful rehabilitation of the teaching of Scripture in the historic Church that the Catholic magisterium of today has become so remarkably articulate about the centrality of Christ, "the decisive answer to every one of man's questions,"[9] for "it is he who opens up to the faithful the book of the Scriptures and, by fully revealing the Father's will, teaches the truth about moral action."[10] Whatever we choose to make of it, while many evangelicals were doing their utmost to be "seeker-sensitive" and, in the Church of the Blessed Power-point Projector, "moving on" to a kind of piety-lite, prominent Catholic biblical scholars and theologians were retracing their own way back to the fork in the road. It was they who saw more clearly, ironically, the necessary interconnectedness of the authority of Scripture and the authority of the Church.[11]

For the group of *Ressourcement* theologians of whom de Lubac was a member, it is essential to understand that the road first forked for Catholics not at the Reformation but earlier.[12] In the rise to preeminence of scholastic theology with Bonaventure and Aquinas in the thirteenth century, and the subsequent shift away from the direct study of Scripture to a more abstract philosophical theology and the analytical study of systems of reflection on the Gospels such as Peter Lombard's *Sententia* (*Sentences*) of the twelfth century, Catholic theology had moved away from the scriptural rock to a less secure, though intellectually impressive, philosophical foundation. By the nineteenth century, if one may speak metonymically, Aquinas ruled. Whereas medievalists like de Lubac, Louis Bouyer, M. D. Chenu, and Jean Daniélou might thus have been expected to follow in the dominant neo-Thomist tradition of their guild, they surprisingly joined forces with Henry Brouillard and the younger Hans Urs von Balthasar to go back well beyond the thirteenth century to the early church and patristic writers in particular. What they discovered there was a vitality in relationship to Scripture itself which renewed for them also the life of the liturgy.

The key to the intimacy of Scripture and worship in the early church and in the Fathers was clearly the vital place of spiritual exegesis in their practice as readers of the Bible. Here is how it is explained by Bouyer:

> Spiritual exegesis, which is supposed by the whole liturgy, is an exegesis dominated by two principles. The first principle is that the Bible is the Word of God, not a dead word, imprisoned in the past, but a living word addressed immediately to the man of today taking part in the celebration of the liturgy. The second principle is that the Old Testament is illumined by the New, just as the New only discloses its profundity once it is illumined in the Old. We must be still more specific: the bond between the two is determined by allegory in the precise sense given to that term by antiquity.[13]

The rehabilitation of allegory in the hermeneutic of the *Ressourcement* biblical scholars, so far from displacing the foundation of the literal and historical sense of Scripture, gives back to history the charged sacramental resonance it had for Augustine, Ambrose, and the early church. De Lubac cites authorities from Clement of Alexander to Scotus to show that for the whole tradition:

> [Scripture] is neither an exposition of abstract doctrine, nor a collection of myths, nor a manual of the inner life. It has nothing atemporal about it. [. . .] Divine revelation has not only taken place in time, in the course of history: it also has a historic form in its own right. It is contained within a *res gesta: a thing that has been accomplished.*[14]

The allegorical sense, rooted in history and seeking no referent apart from God's action in history, simply points all of that history to Christ. Allegory is preeminently the application of Scripture's meaning to the life of the Church, moving through the ages, looking unto the end, awaiting the Bridegroom. What was needed for a true revival in contemporary worship, de Lubac reasoned, was not so much continual dogmatic insistence upon Thomist and post-Tridentine formulations as a return to the source, Scripture itself, and a reestablishment of continuity with the pilgrim company of its great interpreters.

Accordingly, when de Lubac published his four-volume *Exégèse médiévale* (*Medieval Exegesis*) in 1959, it was truly an epoch-making moment, even as Fr. Joseph Lienhard, S.J. has suggested, for the "life of the Church" in the fullest sense.[15] Among other things *Medieval Exegesis* continued de Lubac's rehabilitation of one great ancient interpreter of the Bible whom Catholics had long dismissed as heretical, a rehabilitation begun with his earlier *Histoire et Esprit* (*History and Spirit*).[16] Origen (ca. 185–254), first supported and later opposed vehemently by St. Jerome (yet always supported by Gregory Nazianzus, and John Chrysostom) was as much through misinformation as anything else condemned by the Second Council of Constantinople (in 553). This dismissal was sufficient to perpetuate his oblivion until de Lubac's careful and remarkable rectification of the misinformation and hence judgmental misunderstanding. It turns out that works were sometimes attributed to Origen which in fact were written by someone else. Worse, all along and "much more often, Origen [has been] copied, summarized, amplified, adapted, or plagiarized, sometimes in the most massive way"[17] by persons whom political skills had made more successful and yet who were only too glad to have secretly an advantage in interpretative acuity borrowed without acknowledgment from the out-of-favor Origen. Thus, an early scholar of Scripture whom de Lubac shows to have been extraordinarily insightful, powerfully instructive, and almost overwhelmingly orthodox, by reason of the dishonest appropriation of many successors, was doubly maligned and obscured. The story, painstakingly yet beautifully documented by de Lubac, is broadly instructive.

In volume 1, de Lubac sets out to show us, however, something of still greater significance, namely, that the interpretation of Scripture *in communio* was the principal educational activity in the life of the pre-Scholastic Church. Before the twelfth century there was no such thing as systematic theology—*all* theological erudition was concentrated on biblical exegesis. Hermeneutics, the establishment of method and coherent ruling principles for interpretation, became the basis of organization for all other systems of education. This is particularly evident in the cathedral schools of the twelfth century which were midwife to the rise of Christian universities. Hugh of St. Victor, who was first an exponent of Scripture, made principles of biblical interpretation (grounded in Augustine's *De doctrina Christiana* [*On Christian Doctrine*]) foundational both to his theology of the sacraments (*De sacramentis*) and his philosophy of education (*Didascalicon*); in Hugh, each are in turn so natural an application of hermeneutics as to make the modern Christian educator regret our loss of what our medieval forebears called *disciplina*. For Augustine, the Christian life itself was "the discipline of Christ," a student was a disciple to "the Lord's discipline," the teacher to the "discipline of the Church," to "evangelical and apostolic discipline." This set the standard. De Lubac does not overstate the matter when he writes that all the great theologians "acknowledged that it would be sheer vanity to suppose that one could become holy without submitting oneself to 'disciplina,' or that one could achieve sanctity by resisting the 'goad of discipline.'"[18] The word evoked both good morals and practical virtues perfected by mutual submission, *in communio*, to the teaching of Christ. In his twelfth-century *Didascalicon*,[19] Hugh applied the term to the divisions and methods of academic study—now far removed from their foundation in the principled reading of Scripture—and here the term has stuck. That is, at least in our "academic disciplines" there persists some notion, however diminished, of self-transcending interpretative authority. It is often harder to find such a commitment to *disciplina* in our contemporary churches.

For Bonaventure and Aquinas, the terms "sacred Scripture" and "Theology" were still to be regarded as synonymous. With them as for St. Augustine, knowledge of the faith amounted to knowledge of Scripture. This did not imply a narrow view of Scriptures, but the contrary: as with the various levels of interpretation (generically "historical," "moral," "allegorical," and "anagogical"), pluralism is justified where all interpretation is, in the

final analysis, directed at the same object—a text possessed by and authoritative for all. Polysemeity is Scripture's way of mediating God's abundant truth
to the myriad members of the Body; it is, as Aelred of Rievaulx says, therefore "capable of harboring innumerable modes of thought."[20] But all find
their coherence in the whole together, the common Body, the Church independent of any merely synchronous manifestation of it. The "four senses" are
thus Scripture's way of mediating what happened once in time to all times
and all places spiritually, and it is the Church reading Scripture attentively
together, against and across time, which keeps the errata of any given
moment—its politics and fallen, self-justifying motives—from eclipsing the
authority of the Truth for all time.

The famous "four senses of Scripture" thus may be acceptably understood, as by Rabanus Maurus in his commentary on Galatians, as having just
two greater aspects: historical interpretation and spiritual understanding (cf.
Gal 4:22–27). In the thirteenth century, for Alexander of Hales, the three
spiritual senses are "understood and comprehended under the literal sense,"
and only predicated upon it. Volume 2 of *Medieval Exegesis* is dedicated to
showing how this great pedagogical schema was worked out in the teaching
of the pre-printing press Christian Church. Clearly and exhaustively, de
Lubac magnificently learned that recollection shows how the foundation of
early Christian exegesis is the text as history; how building up from that
foundation allegory becomes the "sense of the faith" or self-understanding of
the Church as the Body of Christ; how the moral understanding is not only
a matter of practical ethical instruction but of charismatic, mystical experience; and that, finally, anagogy, the "upward leading" sense of the text is the
framework of the Church's eschatological intuition.

It is worth reflecting upon that, among Protestants in the English-
speaking world at least, after the Bible itself, the best-known and most influential textual authority has been an allegory. John Bunyan's *Pilgrim's Progress*
was designed by its author as a means of teaching the meaning of biblical history for the life of the individual Christian in the here and now. That meaning, for Bunyan, takes shape in the inner life of the reader through a process
of vicarious and spiritual transposition: each Christian, even as Bunyan's protagonist, will to some considerable degree recapitulate in his or her inner life
the biblical history of human salvation, that emancipatory journey from
bondage, made possible by grace, which may be traced from the story of
Exodus on through Canaan to the New Jerusalem in the book of Revelation.

Early in Christian's representative journey, not long after he has set out
from the city of Destruction, he is directed to the House of Interpreter. Once
there he knocks repeatedly on the door and is eventually received by his host

with a promise to be shown that which will be "profitable" to him. What he gets, through his tour of several rooms, is a series of seven "examples" of edification such as were sought in contemporary Puritan hermeneutics. From the portrait of Evangelist to the man in the iron cage, each of these is presented as allegory in the strict doctrinal sense, but in fact they encompass also the moral sense of earlier Catholic exegesis (e.g., the dusty parlor) and the anagogical as well (the man who dreamed of the Judgment). They are not acknowledged as several senses, however, but rather presented as simply the operation of one "spiritual sense." Interpreter is probably to be understood here as the Holy Spirit,[21] whose function is to provide individual guidance through an essentially perspicuous Scripture. For Bunyan this guidance is necessarily infallible.

What Interpreter first shows Christian is the "picture of a very grave person [hung] up against the wall." As Bunyan's description makes plain, the image is of the authoritative expositor Evangelist. Strikingly, the features of the portrait have an older iconographic lineage:

> It had eyes lifted up to heaven, the best of books in its hand, the law of truth was written upon its lips, the world was behind its back; it stood as if it pleaded with men, and a crown of gold did hang over its head.

Like other saints, and in particular like St. Paul, the person in the portrait can beget children (1 Cor 4:15), and travail in birth with children (Gal 4:19). But "his *work* is to know and unfold dark things to sinners."[22] The suspended nimbus of gold caps, as it were, a conception of the Evangelist as sanctified prophet, able unambiguously to declare the perspicuous Word.

In the very next episode, the pilgrim Christian loses his own burden at the foot of the Cross. But the burden of finding the one right spiritual sense of Scripture—its unambiguous, unequivocal perspicuity—has not so readily rolled off the back of Evangelist and his successors. Rather, the pressure to collapse all spiritual senses toward one (often narrow) doctrinal exposition of the literal level has occasioned, in evangelical tradition, a perilous proclivity to declare apodictic certitude where it may not in fact exist. The pressure to declare precisely of a given Scripture the answer to the question "what does it mean?" was even from the beginning a burden for honest preachers of Puritan descent. Bunyan's contemporary John Owen, in his book *Of the Divine Originall, Authority, Self-evidencing Light, and Power of the Scriptures*, was constrained to protest that at the level of doctrinal exposition the assertions of any preacher "conclude to a *probability* only, and are suited to beget *firme opinion* at best, where the principle intended to be evinced is *de fide*, and must be delivered with faith divine, and supernatural." But few enough among Owen's modern successors have been willing to jeopardize the aura of absolute authority—even perhaps the aura of infallibility—that tended to crown their own certitude in the pulpit. The words of Truth, after all, were in singular fashion writ upon their lips.

One advantage which accrues to the older way of reading Scripture spiritually is the expectation of a plurality of witnesses to the one Spirit. Just as, at Pentecost, no individual language took precedence over others as a translation of the divine Word (Acts 2:1–12), so also with the possible registers of meaning in a given passage: no one valid register of meaning excludes the others. Consequently, allegory, though properly concerned with the doctrinal value of the text, had continuously to be balanced against the tropological or moral understanding ("How, then, shall we live?") as well as the anagogical potential of each passage ("Where is our story taking us?").

As we have seen, the anagogical register of meaning refers us to eschatology, to the "life of the blessed to come" and thus to our whole grand narrative, the *historia humanae salvationis*. Since of that closure no human expositor can declare a final understanding, much at this level must remain mystery and foreshadowing. An obligatory tentativeness, as well as a disposition to expect "levels" or "layers" to Scripture meaning more rich than any exposition can hope to summarize, leads the faithful interpreter to a certain modesty before the text. This modesty, I believe, ought to be more general among us. In such communities of interpretation the question of a given text is less insistently "What does it mean?" than "What, in the shared understanding of the Body of Christ, might it mean?" The subjunctive in the second question is not then merely a technical expectation of polysemeity, but a deep spiritual intuition that no singular exposition, let alone any "private" interpretation (2 Pet 1:21–22) can be comprehensive enough to exclude the understanding of other faithful readers—that is, obedient "doers" of the Word. What *can* most certainly be understood is the invitation to a straightforward "doing" of the Word, putting its precepts into practice. To this typically transparent sense of the text, all Christians are accountable.

I do not mean to suggest, therefore, that the text of Scripture is simply protean, or that Bunyan's Interpreter—as he understood it, the Holy Spirit as personal instructor to the reader in all matters of doctrine—has not both scriptural warrant and virtuous practice in the history of the Church. I do mean to suggest that there are other "Houses of the Interpreter" in which the manifold rooms of Christian instruction contain portraits and parchments in conversation with each other down through the ages, and that these several voices, in their own reflection of the Holy Spirit, are of great value to us. I mean also to suggest that if our contemporary Evangelists are to unshoulder the grievously heavy burden of subjectively derived or populist authority, and the equally burdensome evidence of disjunction between hearing the Word and doing it among their hearers, then we need to return reflectively to the fork in our own road concerning the outworking of scriptural authority in the reading practice of all kinds of Christians. It has become easier in some quarters to focus on contested views of "right doctrine" than on the universal obligation of discipleship—putting Christ's unambiguous teachings into practice.

Magister, magisterium—the teacher and the community of interpretation from which each teacher derives a greater authority: here is an idea about the Church in its largest sense, and hence about the normative trajectory of faithful contributions to our understanding of Scripture which is well worth tracking once again. Individualistic interpretation always runs the risk of being shallow, for it is necessarily partial. The same applies to fashionable, or merely subcultural interpretation. Interpreting in conversation with the wider Church—reading the Sermon on the Mount, for example, with Augustine, Chrysostom, and Martin Lloyd-Jones—can by its inculcation of *disciplina* lead to much deeper, better grounded reading and practice in any of us.

As is well known, the parables of Jesus can invite us to identify ourselves (often unexpectedly) with a character we may find unflattering. For many evangelicals steeped as we are in the love of confessional autobiography and the language of grace, the Prodigal Son is all too predictably "our" stand-in, and we have come to find him less unflattering than we ought. But it may be that we have squandered our own inheritance in quite another way than we have typically imagined. Nor ought we too readily to comfort our conscience that the elder brother is beset by his own domestic prejudices. We can do little about that. Our own pressing need is to stop trying to feed on the chaff and slop so inadequate for our nourishment, and to arise and return to our Father's house. It is, after all, a house of many rooms, and of many faithful readers who can instruct us concerning what the Spirit has been saying to the churches for a very long time. We need that, as a minimal check upon our own often shallow preoccupations.

For the sake of its constraint of excessive individualism alone, earlier exegesis is of value for evangelicals; for a rehabilitation of authority both for Scripture and for its community of interpretation in the Church, it is of value for every Christian. Not the least reason for this is the insistence in much of that exegesis on "doing" the Word. The foundation alone for both

Church and Scripture, that rock of wisdom which is the actual teaching of Christ, seems sometimes in grave risk of being ignored in these trendy times, and not only by our scribes and Pharisees. As we scrabble to build our various edifices upon easier and easier stuff, we should maybe think again of the old Sunday School song in its full scriptural context. In the end, that second kind of house still goes "splat."

(2001)

Chapter Two

Masterplot and Meaning in Biblical Narrative

Now all these things happened unto them for examples: and they are written for our admonition, upon whom the ends of the world are come.
1 Corinthians 10:11 KJV

This history not only declares that which appears on the face of it, but announces something more far-reaching, whence it is called an allegory. And what has it announced? Nothing less than all things now present.
St. John Chrysostom, *Commentarium in epistulam ad Galatas* 4:24

Grand narrative, it seems, has proven more resilient than its recent detractors imagined. When, in 1979, Jean François Lyotard announced the birth of postmodern consciousness as the coming of an age in which there no longer could be any culturally sustaining masterplot,[1] many of those most distressed to think he might be right had a vested interest of some sort in the grand narrative of classical and biblical literary tradition. Their favorite works of literature lived and moved and had their intellectual being within the ethos circumscribed by a masterplot. Superficially, such folk had less to fear than they thought. Lyotard's anomie was occasioned not by the reflective anxieties of a post-Christian, but rather of a post-Marxist age. For Marxism, true to its Hegelian underpinnings, is itself a meta-narrative; the goal of its dialectical development through history, the heavenly kingdom on earth of the classless utopia, is a secularized and materialized revision of the dominant Christian grand narrative. Unfortunately, by the late 1970s and 1980s, it was all too apparent to most Marxist intellectuals that the classless society had become just as illusory as the Christian heaven or kingdom of God which they had rejected before it. Stung, embittered, they turned inward in paroxysms of alienation, narcissism, and the pursuit of privatized fantasy or narrow political advantage.

The institutional power of the French intellectuals of the *poste-garde* in particular, and their American and European imitators secondarily, has been such that in the last two or three decades more effort has been spent on semiotics and revisionary gender politics than on the reading of traditional and culturally foundational works themselves. Few would want to argue that all of this has been wasted time. Still fewer, however, will be likely to spend more time chronicling it a decade hence.

Here then, as scholars lodged "between past and future," we are at a moment from which a kind of stocktaking prospect seems both possible and propitious. Inevitably, of course, such reflection takes us back to basics, to questions about structure as well as style, about projected worldview, as well as *Rezeptionsgeschichte*.[2] The excursus I propose here is preliminary. Nevertheless, I hope you will come to agree with me that a basic literary reflection is not, in our present historical context, without its merits. At the very least it will help us further our appreciation of why it is that, postmodernists of Lyotard's persuasion notwithstanding, ethnic and religious groups in a multicultural context insist upon the maintenance of their own cultures' grand stories, even seeing them as essential to cultural survival. Further, it may help us intuit why it is that those cultures with a firm grip on their own native grand narratives have often the clearest appreciation of the signal differences in worldview signified by the structure and resulting historiography of others. Islamic historiography affords one pertinent example: in Islam, history has unfolded as a series of incomplete realizations of an ideal kingdom in the past: the Medinan reign of the Prophet is the Golden Age to which the aspirant desires to return, so far as this may be possible. The goal of Islamic historiography is to teach the individual that his duty "is to transcend himself and his natural condition in order to become akin to the ideal man whose perfect example is the Prophet Muhammad." The Islamic myth, even in its typical modern guise, is one of incorporation and symbolic return.[3] That which resists incorporation and return is intractably alien and infidel; among purists, to the degree that the impurity of others threatens to pollute or structurally challenge the ideal it may—even must—be opposed with holy warfare.

Narrative Structure, Historiography, and Worldview

To state the obvious in a more literary way: the structure of formative narratives, as much as their style, bespeaks a *Weltanschauung*, a worldview.[4]

This elementary insight tends to escape us when we are dealing with a familiar or representative grand story from our own linguistic culture. Even in cases where (as in biblical studies in the West) the grand story is formatively naturalized, though not native, the putatively obvious can go so long unremarked that at last no one conjures with its decisive importance for *meaning in history*, either in the then-and-there of the original work or the here-and-now of its culturally contextualized interpretation. But when we come to epic or otherwise foundational literature in a truly alien culture, we are much more likely to notice immediately how not style alone, but still more deeply, structure expresses a worldview.

China affords another example—pertinent because its grand narrative patterns are ancient yet persist in modern literature as well as in historiography. *Journey to the West*, a sixteenth-century epic by Wu Cheng'en, has until recently been best known to Westerners (if they know it at all) through the Peking Opera redaction, "The Monkey King." An earlier and mostly unavailable translation by Jenner has been superceded by the translation of Anthony Yu and has now begun to attract a much wider literary audience.[5] In this pilgrimage epic of one hundred chapters, the pilgrim protagonist Tang Seng is modeled on an actual Buddhist priest and translator, Xuanzang, also known as the Dharma Master, who had died a millennium earlier. Tang Seng is aided by an acrobatic trickster Sun Wukong (the Monkey King) and other disciples as he makes his quest to find the True Scriptures. The little band of pilgrims journeys through episode after episode, conquering bandito *arhats*, symbolic of vices that would beset the pilgrim, and make their way to the "West"—India or Nepal—where Tang is successful in acquiring the True Scriptures. This takes ninety-seven chapters. Possessed at last of this foundation-building text Tang and his sidekicks return in only three chapters to the East (China), "where the nine nines are complete, the demons are all destroyed," and, "after the triple threes are fulfilled the Way returns to its roots." Summarily, in chapter 100, "the journey back to the East is complete and the five immortals achieve nirvana."[6]

As in all epic and romance, the structure here is key to meaning.[7] The point in *Journey to the West* is that one travels outward in search of that which will enrich or add value to what always remains the only possible home. The myth here is even more strongly one of return, and enrichment not so much of the individual as of one's national home and its people is the realized goal of a successful journey. Journeys to the West in search of wisdom are a cultural and literary motif in the Orient; they recur again and again. When wise men came from the East, following a star and seeking a Wisdom more luminous than their own to worship, they seem to have been living out a characteristic oriental impulse; having seen the Wisdom they sought, they presented gifts and "departed for their own country another way" (Matt 2:12)—i.e., they returned home, bearing their knowledge with them.

In Chinese culture the paradigm for such narratives and the sense of obligation they confer is called *luoye guigen*—and implies the inevitability of return to China: "you must go home again." To fail to return to one's source prompts great community anxiety and loss of honor: *zancao-cugen* ("assimilation") or *tong hua* ("the elimination of racial and cultural heritage") is an occasion of the deepest shame. Accordingly, resistance to "homecoming" remains a dark shadow force in the Chinese worldview, even, to some degree, among diaspora Chinese Christians.[8]

If we are struck by this grand narrative structure—or repetitions of the masterplot in modern Chinese, Korean, or Japanese literature[9]—it is likely because it seems to Westerners somewhat counterintuitive. The characteristic form of such narrative in Western Christian cultures involves a journey out from and beyond one notion of civilization almost entirely in order to found another. It is a voyage in which, in certain crucial respects, the initial civilization is left behind, emigrated from, in pursuit of a certain emancipation of the spirit that becomes possible only when that which is Old is transcended or transformed in the light of a New vision. There is at least the suggestion that to return to the precise beginning, even if enriched by foreign treasure, is not possible without losing precisely what in the new understanding was most valuable. Or to put it in Tom Wolfe's way, for such folk as ourselves, "You can't go home again."

In Western cultures after the incorporation of Christianity it is an additional feature that reaching the new land, the better city, is dependent not merely on the acquisition and mastery of certain kinds of knowledge (*gnôsis*) but upon a fundamental change of heart, a turning of the will in conscious preference for a new good (*metanoia*), hence choosing a new identity.[10] But it is instructive, I think, to consider the way in which the pilgrimage story of the Western epic narrative has developed through and away from narrative forms that were originally much more like the circular Chinese pattern. The *Iliad* and *Odyssey* of Homer are, taken together, the prominent example. Together these epics comprise a journey out from the Greek homeland and, after suitable conquest and discovery, an emphatic return home. In the battle at Troy, the Greeks are represented in various ways as achieving a conquest of the vices attached to wrath; manly *aretê* ("honor") is accumulated through a lifetime of deeds of bravery coupled with actions of self-restraint. Yet the overall meta-narrative does not conclude, as we might at first expect, with the cremation and burial of the heroic Hector at the end of the *Iliad*. Rather, for full closure to occur there must be added a vicarious return journey. In Homer it produces fully as long a narrative as the first; the *Odyssey* also is in twenty-four books, the return home is symmetrical with the journey out in its scope, the ardors of eros are weighted equally in importance with the agony of conquest and, in their challenges, they prove equally essential for the acquisition of *aretê*.[11]

In the episodes of the *Odyssey* the now mostly female antagonists are in their own way symbolic of the lure to settle elsewhere, a lust for evasion of all the responsibilities that home entails. Shacked up with Kalypso, the goddess who promises him immortality in exchange for sexual servitude, Odysseus can only bring shame upon himself. When he responds to the invitation of Wisdom (Athena) to leave her and set out for Ithaca, his becomes a pilgrimage in search of renewed *aretê*. His voyage is instructive, pedagogical, and finally exemplary, a trope of the progress from unwisdom to wisdom. *Nostos* ("nostalgia," i.e. longing for one's tribal home) is of the essence of the protagonist's motivation. Despite myriad sexual misadventures, the journey is circular; it culminates in confirmation of the old, original marriage and thus a reaffirmed identity in the city from which the pilgrim has set out (Ithaca). In Homer also then, the greatest liability for the pilgrim is temptation to settle down along the way (e.g., Nausikaa and the Phaiakians), to fall into complacency or anaesthetic evasion (Kirke and Kalypso). In short, the worldview projected from Homer's double epic is not entirely unlike that which we find in *Journey to the West*.

With Vergil we enter into new territory and stay there. His pilgrim protagonist, Aeneas, journeys out from a Troy that can no longer be home; his is the exile of "losers," of the defeated, and his pilgrimage is true wandering. In the deepest possible sense it is a journey out of the past, away from a history that is bankrupt, toward a future history yet unwritten. What Leonardo da Vinci captures so memorably in his drawing of Aeneas with his old father Anchises on his back is a universal, yet revolutionary truth. The pilgrim unable to return bears his past with him, but not all the way. With the death of Anchises the past recedes irrevocably, and with it Aeneas's yearning for rootedness in history deepens; there is pathos in his joyful discovery in the temple of Dido of those wall paintings in which the terrible destruction of Troy is revisited to remember that there was some honor for the Trojans too.[12]

The journey of Aeneas has all the standard features of Greek epic narrative, including the destructive second order affections so familiar to a reader of the *Odyssey*. Here too such lesser affections, no matter how appealing, must also be overcome in order for the journey to continue (Dido). But this is not a "journey home." The arc is broken off. As such, the *Bildungsroman* moral shifts away from the older focus, having less to do with self-restraint and self-knowledge. Rather, a much stronger sense of manifest destiny is the moral here. The journey culminates in a *new* marriage, rather than reaffirmation of an old marriage, and announcement of imperial civic purpose: "Romans, remember! Govern; rule the world!"[13] (*Aeneid* 6.851; my translation). In the *Aeneid* there is considerable strengthening of the idea that the end justifies the means. A New City is founded, a civilization now of winners. The poem exudes a tone of triumphalism as well as a strongly historicist worldview—a strong theory of historical progress. The honor of a complete life is expressed not precisely as *aretê*, or even *fama* (though that is desirable) but as the achievement of that civic virtue the Romans called *pietas*, with its close proximity to patriotism and nationalistic pride. The most exalted love is love of country: *amor/Roma/amor*.

Roman epic narrative, though heavily dependent upon Homeric epic narrative and even to some degree upon the expectations a reader's familiarity with that narrative creates, is thus also a fundamental challenge to it at the most basic level. One is almost tempted to say that the *Aeneid* is the first "tale of two cities." Almost, because of course that very phrase calls up a biblical historiography and with it, especially in the Roman context, Augustine's later riposte to the Roman grand narrative in which he superimposes upon it another masterplot, one drawn from his biblical sources.[14] But let us not hasten too quickly into the rhetorical and historiographical *tour de force* of the brilliant North African theologian. For our purpose at hand it is the canonical New Testament Scriptures themselves with which we have principally to reckon, and that in respect of the structure they imply or project into Hellenic and Mediterranean expectations, shaped as they were in part by the Hebrew Scriptures—and in part, I think we should acknowledge, by Greek and Roman epic narrative.[15] All of this, I want to suggest, still bears upon the question of "history" in relation to biblical interpretation.

Meaning and History

It is possible to employ the word "history" in several senses. Among these we may include (a) what happened; (b) what is alleged to have happened (reportage, witness); (c) the narrative memory (usually transgenerational) of what happened; (d) attempts at historical or scientific retrieval of documentary evidence; (e) academic speculation concerning what "might" or "most probably" did or did not happen; and even (f) *ex post facto* revision of received witness for some pressing political or personal purpose (e.g., new historicism). There is thus an intractable sense in which everything of received history is received by faith.

Yet another and supervening dimension must be reckoned with by intellectuals and layfolk alike, and we recognize it in the form of the tacit (less often explicit) question already alluded to: "What is the meaning in history?" In modernity in the West, this last and richer question had yielded to a subsequent and purely rhetorical interrogation borne out of a neo-positivist skepticism concerning in part the possibility of reliable (i.e., verifiable) answers to the other questions: "Can anything of the past be an authority for us today?" As the world becomes secularized or modernized (perhaps "Americanized") there has grown up a general popular perception that to this question the pragmatic answer must be "no."[16] But this deeply reflexive negative answer about the authority of the past is certainly not one concerning which the Christian Church could hope to remain neutral: the Scriptures upon which we ground our faith are undeniably "of the past." Thus, with respect to the textual sources of authority in the Church, preeminently Scripture, a general cultural indifference to history weighs heavily against the typical preoccupations of biblical scholars concerning historicity. It also predisposes—though that is subject for another occasion—to an ethically counterproductive obsession with future speculation.

Authority in the forms of remembering, I think we can say, is something with which the Church as a community ought still most properly to be concerned. In the adage sometimes attributed to Augustine, "we are what we remember." If God's emancipatory action in delivering Israel from bondage is what at its core defines orthodox Judaism, so God's central redemptive action in Christ Jesus is the common memory which defines the Church. This is not to say that there are no other parts of the biblical story important to memory in both traditions. Rather, it is to say that the central memory, narratively articulated, of an emancipatory experience of God in history, transforming history, is the matrix in which these other stories are embedded and in terms of which they make sense of a diversity of possible particular readings and parallel experiences. Secondary stories acquire additional profundity when seen in the light of the central undergirding narrative or masterplot from which derives their (and our) common identity. (I say "common," and stress it, because any authentically biblical identity must be that, communal, all the anarchic individualism of modernity/postmodernity notwithstanding.)

Now it is generally to be observed, I think, that the centering memory of a community's past (roots)—that is, the *concensus gentium* of a given people concerning what their shared history *means*—is typically found as a literary construct rather than a laundry list of evidentially corroborated facts.[17] Thus, for the Roman sense of meaning in their early post-Etruscan history one sensibly gives more weight to the *Aeneid* than, say, to a catalogue of archaeological findings, however valuable in their own right these may be for certain narrower kinds of possible discovery. A shard of pottery or even a strand of hair may tell us something we could not otherwise know. But for an intelligible witness to questions of meaning and religious substance (truth, value, authority) one turns elsewhere. It is in such texts as Vergil's narrative of exile, pilgrimage, new immigrant foundations and subsequent cultural conquest that we get at the really formative truths about early Roman history; this hardly anyone doubts. That such a commonsensical trust in the purport of the literary texts does not now pertain when we turn from the criticism of classical texts to biblical criticism is obvious. Presumably, questions about the authority projected by the Roman past are far less troubling to us than questions about the authority projected by the narratives of biblical history.

From a purely literary (but also, I think, anthropological) point of view, it is possible to say that a fervent preoccupation with listings of documentary evidence, a "scientific" retrieval of facts, is a pretty certain sign that what was once a living tradition is running out of gas. (To study the Bible "scientifically"—either to subvert or to uphold its veridical relation to history, may well be to engage *ipso facto* in a rejection of the meaning of history as the Bible's authors themselves understood it. This does not mean that the activity is worthless; it may mean that the activity is worth much less either for or against the historical truth upon which the Church depends than its practitioners on either side imagine.)

British sociologist Anthony Giddens has reasonably contended that what we call postmodernism is really just a working out of the consequences of modernity.[18] This, surely, is confirmable in the history of biblical scholarship over the last couple of centuries. Moreover, it may be confirmed on both sides of the debate about the Bible's authority. C. S. Lewis, for example, lamented both the literalism of fundamentalists in America and the literarily obtuse grunt-work of Bultmannians in the United Kingdom almost in the same breath.[19] Quite reasonably, it seems to me, Lewis regarded the antagonists on both sides as bad readers of the basic narratives. On both sides, he might have added, the obsession with evidentialism is an attempt to substitute facticity for faith. By contrast, what the vast majority of intelligent readers of the Bible have always assumed about grand narrative texts such as Deuteronomy 6, Psalm 78, and Hebrews 11, is that they reflect little or no concern with the establishment of data or, in any modern empiricist sense, "historical certitude." They simply—and reasonably—have assumed reliability in the witness to history, received this witness as "parable" (*mashal*—Ps 78:2) or prefiguration (*typoi*—1 Cor 10:11), and moved on to the question "what shall we then do?" That is, for them, as evidently for the biblical writers themselves, the question which most matters concerns the *authority* of the past. To refer to received history as a metaphor, a *mashal* (or as an "example for us today"), is not in any sense to diminish or call into question matters of fact; it is, in fact, to reveal more confidence in the essential truth of biblical history than could ever be warranted by archaeological evidence or a documentary hypothesis.

The passages to which I have just alluded are pivotal remembrances of history-as-to-meaning both for biblical narratives and for other narratives where the Bible is a foundational text. They remind us that the hermeneutic underpinnings of specific acts of interpretation are not often reducible to matters of method, or even of ideology more or less philosophically conceived. There is a deeper structure to worldviews, almost invariably referred to as "history" as the ancients rather than we moderns might define it, and it is invariably narratively encoded in forms or genres that are conventionally regarded as literary rather than historical. The power of shared memory, so constituted, is such that it has consequences for many things that might at first seem unrelated to the core narrative—theories of education, for example. As both the eighteenth-century novel of education (the *Bildungsroman*) and the Christian dream-vision pilgrimage texts it supplants makes clear, Western literature and, we might add, historiography, has been an ongoing tussle between classical Roman and biblical notions of what it is, and of what value it is, to "re-member" the past.[20]

It will be further apparent that core narratives, those commonly held to characterize community identity, imply definite attitudes toward the past. Typically (as for example in biblical and other oriental core narratives), this attitude will be one of profound respect. But this norm is not without exceptions. What we call modernity, with all of its consequences, implies a categorical contrary to this traditional regard for the past. This is apparent in modernity's defining moments. The French Revolution, for example, is nothing if not a dismissal of the reigning grand narrative. The American Revolution affords another example of an emphatic rejection of the past.

What ensues in these events, undeniably, is a powerful myth of new beginnings. Old things have passed away, all things become new. Yet even in the comparatively recently formed secular "grand narrative" we can see looming certain consequences for traditional approaches to biblical history. A sharply accentuated disdain for prior history, almost Vergilian in its firmness, and, in America especially, determination to make the frontier and future history supplant it, goes hand in hand with an inherent distrust of the authority of the more distant past—eventually perhaps a disregard for any authority that is not both contemporary and "popular." It is small wonder that, to the chagrin of their grandparents, North American evangelical congregations of this generation possess little more of biblical knowledge, that is, biblical history in the plainest sense, than they do of the secular history

which, more notoriously, they have also forgotten. But is the biblical scholarship of today, for all of our preoccupation with the questions of biblical
history, doing very much to offset this nearly incalculable loss of biblical history in the shared memory of the Church? Or is it, on both sides, merely
abetting the fading from memory and imagination alike of the actual content of biblical narrative? For the erasure or fading away from present
Christian consciousness of centering memory—in all its richness of texture
and narrative detail—constitutes a loss of authority for the biblical past far
more devastating in its implications than the obscure dubieties of academics
about this or that textual correspondence or correlation.

Biblical Meta-Narrative and Historiography

Happily, the readers of this essay need no review of Old Testament narrative. Permit me therefore to recall again something elementary: the narrative motif of exile and pilgrimage. Throughout the Hebrew Bible it recurs as
a concomitant of the persistent dialectic of bondage and freedom. Strangers
and sojourners are aliens whether in captivity or on the road: their Exodus is
above all emancipatory narrative, their famous names (*shêmot*) are all associated with a journey outward bound, and it is no accident that their supreme
deity is identified directly with emancipation: "I am the Lord your God,
who brought you out of the land of Egypt, out of the house of slavery. You
shall have no other gods before Me" (Exod 20:2–3 NASB). This foundational
passage suggests a deep connection of law and liberty in the Jewish biblical
imagination. But careful reading of the biblical texts shows that this view of
civic order is typically more effective when culture and identity are obliged
to be a moveable feast. The tabernacle, not the temple, is the perdurable
symbol thus of sanctuary for the writer of Hebrews (chs. 9–10) even as it was
in the book of Exodus and continues to be in Revelation (21:1–3; 22).
Vayikra el Moise ohel mo'ed ("Now the LORD called to Moses, and spoke to
him from the tabernacle of meeting"; Lev 1:1): one worships; one moves on;
and the symbols of communion and community move along with the faithful travelers.

Storytelling along the way is mandatory because of the covenant obligation to pass on the grand narrative's enduringly pertinent emancipatory message (Deut 6:4–9; Ps 78). Postponement and frustration of progress toward
the Promised Land are a result of disobedience and a neglect of holiness as
well as worship. Sin skews the itinerary, forgetfulness of the emancipatory
meta-narrative leads to cul de sacs and to bondage all over again. Reiteration
of the narrative is thus a necessity, especially where there are few fixed land-
marks. Master-narrative becomes a kind of spiritual map; the "story-line"

anchors thought when thought is most prone to drift; it encourages thought
to press forward to better prospects. Mount Zion, the City of David,
Jerusalem the Golden, seem so credibly to be the goal and journey's end.
There will be a Promised Land, a place of sabbath rest and closure: one may
say, one *must* say: "*Lashanah haba'ah bi Yerushalayim!*" ("Next year in
Jerusalem!").

In the New Testament, *Yeru-shalem* remains the vision—the *visio pacis* as
Augustine would later call it. Yet the literal historical Jerusalem under the
Romans becomes soon enough its own kind of captivity. By the first century
not the Roman occupation only but the ossification of Jewish *halakah* and,
in some quarters, a resulting spiritual bondage to a petrified notion both of
spiritual culture and of Law, has robbed Jerusalem of its *shalom*.[21] As we can
see so readily in Jesus' interlocutions with the Pharisees and scribes, for them
the Law is no longer about liberty. And this, for our purposes here centrally,
is substantially the charge Paul brings against the diaspora Galatians. A problem with some of the Galatians, it seems, is that in their diaspora struggle to
maintain Jewish identity they have become fixated on the Jerusalem they
thought was their journey's end and whose golden era they think their eventual just reward. They too are filled with *nostos*-longing, nostalgia for
Jerusalem, and Paul's tactic in addressing their spiritual misprision is to begin
by showing them that he himself has made no fetish of return to the holy
city but has consistently, constantly journeyed out in obedience to his calling, and that even when, so to speak, business drew him back (to confirm
the gospel), he stayed only fleetingly (long enough to admonish Peter's
Judaizing tendencies) and then took to the road again (1:17–2:2).

In calling the Galatians to account Paul draws heavily upon the meta-
narrative the Judaizers most cherish to make the point that the end of the
journey through history set out in Torah (3:11ff.) is not a place but a Person,
and that Person the Seed of Abraham, the true Son to whom the Promise was
made. Torah has acted as a pedagogue or tutor to bring us not to Jerusalem
but to Christ (3:24–25), a destiny in which all who belong to Christ are now
not slaves but adopted heirs. Indeed, this new state is a condition of spiritual life; the norms of political and social distinction vanish (3:28). There is no
property or geography associated with this inheritance, no distribution of
acreage from Dan to Beersheba, no condominium waiting in Jerusalem. It is
of the essence of Paul's overall argument in Galatians that the *allêgoureumena*
passage in 4:22–31 de-legitimates the diaspora, longing for a return to
Jerusalem even as it rejects the traditional Jewish reading of Torah-
covenant—a reading in which Jerusalem certainly had been both symbolic
and political home. The Promise, on the other hand, fulfilled at last to
Abraham's seed, Christ, and all those adopted in Him, points now to quite

another destination: Christ and his kingdom are the new journey's end (3:24).[22] But they are the very condition of the journey as well. Here too, we have a moveable feast, for the liberty to which we have been called is inseparable from a New Law, the Law of Love (5:13–14); the pilgrim code for those who continue to "walk in the Spirit" (5:16) includes love of the neighbors through whose turf we make our way.

In this context the counterintuitive reversals of expected significance in the Abraham-Hagar-Sarah story make perfect sense. To the faithful Jew Paul's identification of Hagar with "that Jerusalem which now is and is in bondage with her children" (4:25) must have seemed perilously close to blasphemy. It constitutes a revision of Jewish meta-narrative and historiography as decisive as that which Vergil's *Aeneid* achieves in relation to the epics of Homer. Paul is not, I think, simply undermining what N. T. Wright, in his *The New Testament and the People of God*, describes as the old Jewish conviction that "the biblical period [. . .] runs out without a sense of an ending."[23] Rather, he is preempting worldview assumptions about historical closure that people like the Hasmoneans, as well as other Zionists before and since, were so ardently to pursue: "the full liberation and redemption of Israel."[24] Wright is surely right to think that the apologia of Josephus in his *Antiquitates Judaicae* (*Antiquity of the Jews*) is inadequate as a means of obtaining closure on any account,[25] except, perhaps, a Vergilian one. By having "Israel's god [go] over to the Romans," so that Rome may legitimately decimate Jerusalem and scatter its survivors, Josephus simply exchanges a politicized version of Old Testament meta-narrative for the Gentile meta-narrative that looks most like it. But does Paul endorse in any way what Wright describes as the first-century hope for a restoration of Jerusalem? Not, I think, in this text. He seems as far from that as he is from the secularizing justification and implied politic of Josephus.

When Paul writes that since Christ it is "the Jerusalem above" which is "free and the mother of us all" (4:26), he makes diaspora unsettledness the normative Christian condition. This is the way that Origen, Augustine, Jerome, Gregory the Great, Luther, Bunyan, and a host of interpreters since have understood him: he was speaking about temporal Christian experience.[26] To be an *alienus* in the world is normative; to be a *viator* en route between the city of this world and the celestial city, "that Jerusalem which is above," is to participate in a new grand narrative. This new grand narrative differs both from the Old Testament Jewish meta-narrative and the official Roman mythos: history's destination is no longer the Jerusalem in Palestine. Nor, on the other hand, do all roads lead to Rome. To be a stranger and a sojourner is still, as it was for pre-Christian Jews, to be a creature wandering through space and time. Now, however, the pilgrim heads toward no literal land of milk and honey, nor does she return to a capital city once thought of as home. Resist it how we will, there is a deep and abiding sense in which the African-American spiritual expresses the new grand narrative accurately: "This world is not our home, / we're just a-passing through, / Our treasures are laid up / somewhere beyond the blue . . ."[27] If centuries of hymns and, as we shall shortly remind ourselves, Christian era literary texts, have since construed the Christian meta-narrative in this way, Paul's letter to the Galatians surely bears a considerable share of the blame.[28]

The Kingdom Order—if we are to use such a phrase of this particular Pauline letter—is one in which the old itinerant relationship between law and liberty has been brought to its fulfillment in Christ in such a way as to make absolutely clear that this relationship flourishes at its redemptive best when least locked down to a fixed political agenda. In the new worldview, as we have seen, political and legal status, gender, and ethnicity are all transcended. The new order of culture is fluid, dynamic, and more than ever portable. Pentecost and missionary pilgrimage are key elements in the new master story; as Old Law/Covenant gives way to New Law/Promise, much in the definition of familiar historical objectives that has been outward and of Palestinian geography is now spoken of as inward and of the Spirit. Thus, though externally bound, one may be internally free; we lose our life to find it; grace makes paradox of much that under the Old Law had been simply contradiction—discursively imperative and performatively impossible. Thus too, not only is the old Jerusalem and its Law a locus of our captivity, there is in some deep spiritual sense transience at best, captivity at worst, in any worldly city and its culture. This world is not our home: we are now again to be like Abraham, strangers, sojourners, pilgrims.

As I turn now to Hebrews, I want to affirm my strong agreement with N. T. Wright's observation that "all worldviews, the Christian one included, are in principle public statements, . . . stories which attempt to challenge and perhaps to subvert other worldview-stories."[29] That might seem, indeed, almost precisely the point of this essay. But to any who have read him carefully, it should by now be apparent that in my view Wright has gone somewhat further than either the texts or its preponderant traditions of interpretation warrant in insisting (in the way he does) on the "irreducible publicness" as he calls it, or politically immanent dimension of the Christian worldview. Here is an example of what he says:

> It [the Christian meta-narrative] claims to be telling a story about the creator and his world. If it allows this to collapse for a moment into a story

about a god who is rescuing people *out* of the world, then it has abandoned
something extremely fundamental in the worldview.[30]

What I want to offer here is a modest caveat, or at least a *sic et non*. One cannot help but be sympathetic with Wright's preemptive parry of gnostic readings of the Gospel both of the second and the twenty-first centuries.[31] But
while it may be entirely sufficient to say, even of hellenized Jews, that "as
good creational monotheists [. . .] [they] were not hoping [. . .] to 'go to
heaven', or at least not permanently, but to be raised to new bodies when the
new kingdom came,"[32] I am less sure than he that the pilgrim journey to
which Galatians and Hebrews invites its Christian readers isn't, after all,
toward a celestial rather than a restored earthly Jerusalem.[33] There are political as well as theological consequences for each view.

There is a strong hermeneutical sense in which Hebrews is a recapitulation of Galatians. This begins with its theme, but it works itself through the
expositio of the tabernacle. The apparent shift to grand narrative at chapter
11 presumably accounts for traditional discussions of the structure of the letter. From patristic times and the Middle Ages to the eighteenth century,
most saw the epistle as having two movements; Aquinas is representative in
describing chapters 1–10 as about the *excellentiam Christi*; chapters 11–13 as
an exhortation that we should follow him in the pilgrimage of life.[34] The
writer sees himself as writing *in sequentia* with the narrative of the Old
Testament, but so as to stress its messianic portent, its signs and wonders
(2:2–4), and thus his participation in the tradition of emancipatory grand
narrative to which he is heir.

But the bondage from which one journeys out is now spiritual; even the
fear of death is bondage (2:15). The deliverer is not Moses, but Christ, true
Son rather than servant of God (3:5–15). All who were on the original pilgrimage out of captivity rebelled and so did not have of that voyage any closure (3:16–19). The promise (not the covenant) "remains of entering his
rest" (4:1). Indeed, "there remains a rest for the people of God, for He who
has entered his rest has himself also ceased from his works as God did from
his" (4:9–10). We too are to "be diligent to enter that rest" (v. 11).

The eschatological overtones here are evident; in several Jewish and
Christian apocalyptic writings, as well as in Talmudic sources, the age to
come is described as a perpetual Sabbath.[35] In Hebrews 4 the temporal
Sabbath observed by physical rest is transformed into an eschatological rest,
entered into by faith. Augustine allegorizes at this point: it is "the peace of
rest, the peace of the Sabbath, which has no evening" (*Conf.* 13.35.50) and
therefore figuratively an "eternal life" (*Conf.* 13.36.51) which is anticipated

here on earth in those "reasonable creatures" who try to orient their life's journey toward "the perfectly ordered and harmonious enjoyment of God, and of one another in God" (*Civ. Dei* 19.17; cf. *De Genesi ad litteram* 4.9). As is well known, Augustine was on this model led to see world history as divided into six ages, of which the last would be followed by the millennial reign of the faithful with Christ (cf. his commentary on Rev 20:1–7; 2 Pet 3:8; etc.). But he was also led to see the foretold descent of the tabernacle of God and the eschatological making of all things new (Rev 21:2–5) as the ultimate pilgrim's reward—which, on the warrant of Hebrews as well, he is as inclined as ordinary Christians of all centuries to call "heaven." In his *De civitate Dei* (*City of God*), to which he claims as epigraph Hebrews 11:13–16 and in which he famously expounds upon Revelation 21, Augustine declares the basic understanding of the Church as he knows it that this vision concerns not the historical "city set on a hill" but the future dwelling of the "immortality and eternity of the saints." The celestial Jerusalem he calls the *visio pacis* of the Christian pilgrim, glimpsed only from afar in this life but at last "to come down out of heaven, because the grace with which God formed it is of heaven" (*Civ. Dei* 20.19.17). Principal commentators after him (e.g., Aquinas, Nicholas Lyra, Wyclif) continued to regard the New Jerusalem as the eternal and celestial city of the faithful, and the culmination of history in which history as we know it ceases to be (Isa 34:4; Rev 6:14). Were all these commentators improperly representing in their grand narrative the meta-narrative of the New Testament?

Reading Hebrews, one would seem to find little to contradict this traditional version of the Christian grand story. According to the writer of the letter, a fundamental difference between the Old Testament meta-narrative and his own reconstruction is that now the "true tabernacle [is that] which the Lord erected, and not man" (8:2) and it is not present on earth any more than is Christ, who, in effect, is himself that tabernacle now (8:4; cf. Rev 21:3). When Christ was on earth he came as the "High Priest of the good things to come, with the greater and more perfect tabernacle not made with hands, that is, not of this creation" (9:11), "for Christ has not entered the holy places made with hands, which are copies of the true, but into heaven itself" (9:24). Whatever we make of the possible Alexandrian context of this letter, it seems to me inescapably the case that a literate first or second-century reader of this letter would be invited to contrast its implied meta-narrative, a revision of the pre-existing Jewish grand story, with the most famous Hellenic grand story and its celebrated Roman revision.

Let us come now to the second "movement" in the structure of Hebrews, divided as it is neatly from the first in the *kephalaia* of all extant

early manuscripts, and in such a way, happily for these purposes, that
11:1–40 and 12:1–11 form discrete but evidently connected pericopes.[36]
What is emphasized here above all is that the heritage of faith is a multigen-
erational, transhistorical pilgrimage *through* history, and not to "Canaan
land" but rather toward a destination undisclosed. Thus, Abraham journeyed out "not knowing where he was going" (11:8), and en route he "dwelt
in the land of promise as in a foreign country, dwelling in tents" (11:9); as he
journeyed he lived in anticipation of an unseen destination: "he waited for
the city which has foundations, whose builder and maker is God" (11:10).
That this is not the journey of a single protagonist (like Odysseus or Aeneas)
but rather of a "people of God" who make their way by stages, *dor le dor,*
through history, is in continuity with the Jewish grand story which the chapter recalls. Their journey cannot be complete or "made perfect," the writer
insists, "apart from us" (11:40). But the striking revision we saw in Galatians
now appears again directly:

> These all died in faith, not having received the promises, but having seen
> them afar off, and were persuaded of them, and embraced them, and con-
> fessed that they were strangers and pilgrims on the earth. For they that say
> such things declare plainly that they seek a country. And truly, if they had
> been mindful of that country from whence they came out, they might have
> had opportunity to have returned. But now they desire a better country,
> that is, an heavenly: wherefore God is not ashamed to be called their God:
> for he hath prepared for them a city. (Heb 11:13–16 KJV)

On earth these folk were but strangers and pilgrims. The home for which
they were seeking was not, as a Greek might have it "that country from
which they had come out" (v. 15) any more than it is the kingdom from
which they became refugees and which is now "being shaken" (12:27; cf. Gal
4:22–27). As Galatians has it from the outset, there is a normative Christian
sense (or senses) in which Christ "gave himself for our sins, that He might
deliver us from this present evil age" (Gal 1:4)—not a gnostic deliverance
but emancipation from this world surely, and there is a normative Christian
sense (or senses) in which we pilgrims are to "know that if our earthly house,
this tent, is destroyed, we have a building from God, a house not made with
hands, eternal in the heavens" (2 Cor 5:1). The apparent echo of Jesus'
words of assurance to his disciples in John's gospel may be evidence of Paul's
careful attention to the disciples' report of Jesus' teaching: "In my father's
house are many mansions. [. . .] I go to prepare a place for you. And if I go

and prepare a place for you, I will come again and receive you to Myself, that where I am, there you may be also" (John 14:2–3). As we read on in this earlier gospel passage, we see that Jesus invokes the language of the Abrahamic pilgrimage, or grand narrative, to disciples who are not sure they really do "know the way" (vv. 4–5) to make this unprecedented voyage. In the Johannine report, of course, Jesus himself is the Way (v. 6)—a presuppositional assurance also apparent in the writer to the Hebrews.

Accordingly, the writer to the Hebrews is now able to return via Moses to the distinction between sons and slaves so familiar to us from Galatians (12:6–9), and to demonstrate the continuity of the journey through history, cheered on by the "great cloud of witnesses" (12:1), always "looking unto Jesus, the author and finisher of our faith, who for the joy that was set before Him endured the cross, despising the shame and has sat down at the right hand of the throne of God" (12:2). In Hellenic terms, it is not for us but for Christ to overcome shame, acquire unsurpassable *aretê* and to return to his home. But his eternal abode is not our home yet—we simply journey toward it, in holy anticipation, by a radical *mimesis* coming to obedience through suffering as he did and as he has called us to do (Heb 5:8–9; Luke 9:23). That is, to invoke the metonym of another hymn, for the Christian pilgrim, "the way of the Cross leads home." In an extension of the pilgrim imagery we are to make "straight paths" and "strengthen the lame" (12:12–13), and to "pursue peace with all people" among whom we sojourn. Finally, in a last allusion to the mistaken impulse to return to the historical Jerusalem the writer to the Hebrews invokes the same contrast Paul uses in Galatians 4, that between Sinai (Hagar and the Law) and the celestial Jerusalem:

> You have not come to a mountain that can be touched and that is burning with fire; to darkness, gloom and storm; to a trumpet blast or to such a voice speaking words that those who heard it begged that no further word be spoken to them [. . .] But you have come to mount Zion, to the heavenly Jerusalem, the city of the living God. You have come to thousands upon thousands of angels in joyful assembly, to the church of the firstborn, whose names are written in heaven. You have come to God, the judge of all men, to the spirits of righteous men made perfect, to Jesus the mediator of a new covenant, and to the sprinkled blood that speaks a better word than the blood of Abel. (Heb 12:18–24 NIV)

And the coda to this excursus is surely, for this apostle at least, definitive: "for here we have no continuing city, but we seek the one to come" (13:14). It has been largely definitive for Christian literary tradition also, and it is to that, finally and in what I hope will be indicative brevity, that I would like to turn by way of conclusion.

Vernacular Literary Understanding as Interpretation

Augustine is, of course, both famously and infamously associated with turning the implied historiography of the New Testament as he understood it into a form of historiographical *apologia* for Christianity in his *City of God*. In this he may be said to be, formally speaking, the first Christian philosopher of history. The alternative grand narrative with which he had to deal was not the narrative cherished by Old Testament Judaism or its Hellenic revision as a myth of return. It was rather a thoroughly entrenched Vergilian two cities model—the profound historicism by which Roman citizens and much of the empire clung to a worldview in which the triumph of Rome was still the only acceptable *telos* for history. When that *telos* was threatened again and again by political forces within and military incursions from without, Romans looked for a scapegoat and found Christianity ready to hand and obviously suspect. They knew, however dimly, that Christian praxis did in some way subvert their own worldview. Nor was it lost on them that in some of the regions and cultures in which Christianity had most flourished there was evident political threat to Roman imperial supremacy. For them, the prospect of an end to "Roman rule" would be as unthinkable as would be, today for many Americans, the end of American supremacy. Even Christian Romans, we know, found this prospect unthinkable, and Augustine himself was sympathetic to them. But he saw, as did few others, the idolatry in the Romanized manifest-destiny co-opting of the New Testament worldview, and in his *City of God* did his best to set it to rights.

To do this, as is well known, he had to subvert the Roman meta-narrative, in part by an extended deconstruction both of the *Aeneid* and of Homer.[37] He begins by showing that the gods credited with establishing and maintaining Roman supremacy were unable to prevent the sack of Troy (1.3), and that the morality of the Roman gods, even in the literature which mythologizes them, is so capricious as to be risible (3.1–7). Throughout the *City of God* his purpose, announced in his preface, is to show that the Vergilian *pietas*, that high *courtoisie* and patriotism which was Rome's answer to Greek *aretê*, has given way in practice to overweening imperial pride.[38] Thus, "the earthly city [Rome] [. . .], though it be mistress of the nations, is itself ruled by the lust of rule" (1.pr). The Vergilian transformation of Greek meta-narrative is carefully built into Augustine's contextualization of his theme, largely with numerous and skillfully deployed citations from the *Aeneid*. Augustine refers to Juno (goddess of marriage) and her hostility to the exiled Trojans, for example, as a means of establishing that the Roman story is effectively about the reestablishment of losers as perpetual victors and, also, to the elevation of the more frankly sensual Venus, rather than Juno, as mother of the new civic culture. "A race I hate now ploughs the sea, / Transporting Troy to Italy, / and homegods conquered [...]" (*Civ. Dei* 1.2; qv. *Aeneid* 1.71–73),[39] he quotes Vergil's Juno as saying, subverting further the Roman claim to civic morality.[40] Similarly the Roman claim to patriotic and militaristic imperial destiny is likewise undermined:

> Why allege to me the mere names and words of "glory" and "victory?" Tear off the disguise of wild delusion, and look at the naked deeds: weigh them naked, judge them naked. Let the charge be brought against Alba, as Troy was charged with adultery. There is no such charge, none like it found: the war was kindled only in order that there
> > "might sound in languid ears the cry
> > Of Tullus and of victory."[41]
> This vice of restless ambition was the sole motive to that social and parricidal war [...] (*Civ. Dei* 3.14; qv. *Aeneid* 6.813).

Augustine does not deny the pagan virtues entirely; he concedes that in some respects the Rome Vergil celebrates began well, yet insists that its progress has bankrupted itself by investing so heavily in temporal power:

> At that time it was their greatest ambition either to die bravely or to live free; but when liberty was obtained, so great a desire of glory took possession of them, that liberty alone was not enough unless domination also should be sought, their great ambition being that which the same poet [Vergil] puts into the mouth of Jupiter (*Civ. Dei* 5.12; qv. *Aeneid* 1.279ff.).[42]

The "city" Augustine will celebrate seeks other virtues than earthly power, even as its glory will be of another order of glory.

Later Augustine moves on to describe the progress of the "two cities, the earthly and the heavenly," through history, though he will settle at last on the progress of the heavenly city alone. The earthly city—whether historical Jerusalem or Rome—is indeed a city of captivity, figuratively Babylon: "the city which was called confusion" and which he associates with Babel and the project of self-made men to ascend to heaven by their own devices (16.4–5).

By contrast, the celestial Jerusalem toward which the faithful travel through history cannot be reached or conquered by human effort. One must set out in faith, joining the vulnerable company of the blessed en route, but in the end the New Jerusalem is not so much to be attained (by works) as granted (by grace), as it descends. Citizenship in this city is nonetheless proleptic, participated in already by the faithful as they journey. In the Johannine précis (John 14:6) of St. Catherine of Siena's, "There is a heaven all the way to heaven; for He said, 'I am the Way.'" But this prolepsis is experienced now through a vale of tears; it is not an earthly political realization of the kingdom of God. The City of God, Augustine says, "lives by faith in this fleeting course of time, and sojourns as a stranger in the midst of the ungodly." One day, however, "it shall dwell in the fixed stability of its eternal seat" (1.pr.).

Augustine, it seems to me, has read the New Testament grand narrative of Galatians and Hebrews against the grand narrative of the Roman epics in a manner quite consistent with the way in which the two canonical letters themselves subvert the grand narrative of Old Testament Judaism. In so doing he has assisted rather than supplanted their projection of the idea of a heavenly home, a celestial city, and a "tabernacling journey" toward it, onto the Christian literary imagination. He has thus provided a constructive constraint upon "Constantinian" co-optings of the Vergilian master narrative, with its culture-specific and aggrandizing assertion of manifest destiny. That this constraint has been better appreciated in some contexts (notably those of political adversity) than in others (notably those of political supremacy) will be apparent to the most modest reflection on ecclesial and political history.

To put this in another way: when Christians have been in largely unchallenged political power (e.g., Rome, Holy Roman Empire, British Empire, America) there has tended to emerge a neo-Constantinian reassertion of what amounts to Vergilian rather than New Testament symbolism of the "city set on a hill." The earthly city, or, in the case of Puritan America, the "New Canaan" tends to be apostrophized as a kind of heavenly kingdom in the here and now.

That was the force also of the medieval Arthuriad, or "romances" (OF gen. *romans*, 'of the Romans'), which in their meta-narrative matrix recapitulate (as did the first Old French text in the genre, *Le roman de Troie* by Benoit de St. Maur), the basic features either of the Homeric or Vergilian epic.[43] Later, the Arthurian Round Table is symbolic of the earthly city become in itself a *visio pacis*; the Grail or Chalice, were it to be recovered, anticipates in a realized temporal eschaton the dream of restored and unbroken communion. But the countervailing Augustinian redaction of New Testament grand narrative has tended to win out, if only by virtue of the persistent apprehension, even in such narratives, that heavenly kingdoms in the here and now are not realizable by human effort, even by Galahads in a state of grace. In a final gesture toward the New Testament rather than the Roman imperial story, even the Arthurian romance must wistfully look to a Once and Future King and Kingdom.

This, I think, is why John Milton, fresh from the defeat of the Puritan Commonwealth and politically at risk, rejected his first choice for an epic, the Arthuriad, and wrote instead *Paradise Lost.* In abandoning a classical structure with evident political and nationalistic potential for the "end is not yet" New Testament structure, he in effect also reverses the *Aeneid,* otherwise his most important epic source. Adam and Eve start in communion, but end in alienation and brokenness, exiled from Eden. Even as they journey toward their hope of redemption it is "with wandering steps and slow"; in *Paradise Regained* it is Christ who wins the way for them, and the heavenly city, as in Revelation, may by God's power alone come down.

Much that is too obvious to dwell on must accordingly be passed over here in silence. But just a few examples to confirm: the fact that Dante's pilgrim persona, having wandered off track in the middle of the city of this world, should be guided only part of the way en route to *Paradiso* by a chastened Vergil is a reflection of the influence of Augustine's kind of New Testament historiography. Geoffrey Chaucer's *Canterbury Tales* is another "tale of two cities," in which the city of this world (not here Rome or Babylon but London) must be left behind in a communal penitential voyage toward Canterbury, figuratively a City of God. At the end of this great work and before his "knitting up" sermon on repentance, Chaucer's Parson makes explicit the connection between the two journeys by specifically invoking the New Testament grand narrative according to Galatians, Hebrews and, one assumes, Augustine. Immediately following a series of quotations from Paul's letters he says:

> And Jesu for his grace wit me sende
> to shewen you the way in this viage
> of thilke parfit glorious pilgrimage,
> that highte Jerusalem celestial. (*Canterbury Tales* 10.48–51)

The imperfect earthly journey is trope, a metonym; the Canterbury trail is merely indicative of a deeper pilgrimage of faith. Bunyan's Christian pilgrim will also leave an English worldly city for the Celestial City, here yet more clearly heaven; examples abound.

But the Vergilian narrative of manifest destiny and the Jewish myth of return also have their voices both in later literature and in politics: there are medieval reiterations such as Torquato Tasso's *Gerusalemme liberata* (1580), and, of course the Crusades. In our time we have Zionism, Christian Zionism, and the neo-dispensationalism now made sensational by Jenkins and LaHaye.[44] What may receive less attention than it ought is the degree to which in American political and literary culture the Vergilian meta-narrative has, since the founding fathers, appropriated to itself a largely Calvinist and hence typologized Old Testament version of the Christian grand story. When in *Magnalia Christi Americana* (1698; publ. 1702) Cotton Mather advertised himself as "Herald of the Lord's Kingdome now approaching," he set to interpreting the Bible's "Prophetical as well as [. . .] Historical Calendar" in such a way as to constitute a westward expanding New England as the New Jerusalem.[45] His was far from a singular American historicism;[46] Yale President Timothy Dwight's *Conquest of Canaan* (1775) and James Russell Lowell's Harvard "oration Ode" (1865) are only two among many such Americanized or neo-Constantinian (even neo-Zionist) versions of Christian history. Herman Melville's *White Jacket* contains a narrative passage on national destiny that captures some of the most deeply troubling aspects of the New World conflation of what, for Augustine's philosophy of history, were two antithetical meta-narratives:

> The Future [is] the Bible of the Free. [. . .] We Americans are driven to a rejection of the maxims of the Past, seeing that, ere long, the van of the nations must, of right, belong to ourselves. [. . .] Escaped from the house of bondage, Israel of old did not follow after the ways of the Egyptians. To her was given an express dispensation; to her were given new things under the sun. And we Americans are the peculiar, chosen people—the Israel of our time; we bear the ark of the liberties of the world. God has given us, for a future inheritance, the broad domains of the political pagan, that shall yet come and lie down under the shade of our ark, without bloody hands being lifted. God has predestinated, mankind expects, great things from our race; and great things we feel in our souls. The rest of the nations must soon be in our rear. We are the pioneers of the world. [. . .] [T]he political Messiah has come. But he has come in us, if we would but give utterance to his promptings.[47]

It would be hard to imagine a Vergilian perversion of the New Testament grand narrative of Galatians and Hebrews more troubling than this. Yet in countless and various ways, it has become institutionalized as the *de facto* civic religion of America.

Does it matter that Galatians and Hebrews make the New Testament grand narrative a journey *through* history, but with a celestial or heavenly rather than earthly home as the journey's end? I suspect it matters a great deal for faithfulness to the teachings of Jesus. These two New Testament letters get only slight treatment, I realize, in Wright's *The New Testament and the People of God*, and in stressing them so forcefully here I fear that I may seem merely to be evading the main arguments of his eloquent and provocative book, with much of which I find myself in fact to be in most hearty agreement. But my point here is admonition concerning canonical balance: that Galatians, the most authenticated letter of Paul, and Hebrews, in many ways more influential than Romans in the *literary* history of Christendom, are very important constraints upon any disposition to make too much of history in the way the Enlightenment did.

All that matters to us as Christians is certainly of history; God's providence in history, the *historia humanae salvationis*, the resurrection of Christ on the third day—*all* these are indispensable as historical event in the plain sense, and without them, as indeed the Apostle warns, we are of all creatures most to be pitied (1 Cor 15:19).[48] In my view, both as a student of literary interpretations of biblical narrative and as a common Christian in the world, we nevertheless must pay attention also to the degree to which the New Testament grand narrative is about a journey through history to the fulfillment of a Promise that transcends history. Ours, in the end, is not a view of history that can comfortably integrate with that of the Enlightenment.[49] Georg W. F. Hegel's contention that "the God of the Jewish people is the God only of Abraham and of his seed," and that "national individuality and a special local worship are involved in such a conception of deity" is only true insofar as we do not push it to the point at which Hegel's *Philosophy of History* sets the terms for our own conception of the Christian hope.[50] Germinal as it is for the Marxist historicism which in its own drab way also for a time subverted or secularized the New Testament meta-narrative, Hegel's view can occlude for us the profound respect in which Christian history becomes, by lived faith in a living Church, history *sub specie aeternitas*. To say this is to say firmly that ours is not a history that "marches on" to a historical destiny or utopia, but that, like the pages of a book written by Another, it is a narrative of time which unfolds meaningfully until the book is complete, when the heavens shall be "rolled up like a scroll" (Isa 34:4; Rev 6:14). It is to say that the community of faith, generation upon generation, moves through history to a destination which is finally beyond history. History, or *Weltgeschichte*, is not the protagonist here; nor is *Heilsgeschichte*. The protagonist is Christ, in whom the community of faith lives and moves and has its being.

History *sub specie aeternitas*, not in Aristotle's or Matthew Arnold's sense but in the sense of St. John the Divine, is history as poetry conceives of it, a trope. Or, as Paul puts it in Galatians 4, an *allêgoria*. Nothing in this Pauline view denies the factuality of history. It does invite us to remember that some historical events have become grand narrative for us, upon whom these latter ages have come, that we might be instructed concerning what in our faith is of bondage and what of the freedom wherewith Christ has made us free.

(2002)

Chapter Three

Self-Examination and the Examination of Texts: Augustine's *Confessions* and *On Christian Doctrine*

Hoc primum intelligentes, quod omnis prophetia Scripturae propria interpretatione non fit.

2 Peter 1:20, Vulgate

It is a curiosity worth noting that Augustine's originary treatise on textual study, his *De doctrina christiana* (*On Christian Doctrine*), was an *opus interruptus*: in its first draft the author broke off after book 3.35.[1] More precisely, and this has occasioned less notice, it seems to have terminated without resolution in the midst of the problem he had intended to confront directly in the very next paragraph: unresolvable ambiguity in the biblical text: "instances in which the signification is uncertain" (*Doctr. chr.* 3.25.36).

Augustine had been discussing figurative language, trying to establish characteristics by which, in the biblical text, figurative rather than ordinary literal speech might be properly identified. He was attempting also to articulate a certain scheme by which equivocal signs such as "bread," "leaven," and "serpent" might be referred with certainty to their appropriate and contextually univocal spiritual meanings. He stumbled. For it was becoming clear to him, even as he wrote, that the evident potential of each of these terms in Scripture for either an *in bono* or an *in malo* significance was constrained not merely by textual context, as he was in the process of asserting, but by ambiguities less easy to identify and control with anything approaching certainty. One of these circumstances, of which he was becoming more aware as he wrote, was the potential for both ignorance and arbitrariness in the expositor or teacher of the text.

It now appears that there were other factors, not all of them purely intellectual, which might have moved Augustine to arrest his pen in the middle of the page. Of these, some will probably remain in their particulars unknown to us. But as to why he should have returned to this unfinished theoretical work twenty-nine years later (precisely while working on his *Retractions*) there is textual evidence that helps us. For example, there are elements in the revised and completed *On Christian Doctrine* itself which, given the tone and assembling architecture of books 1–3, we might not have expected to appear. But we also have new and extraneous texts, in particular some recently discovered sermons, several of the most important of which were preached just at the time Augustine was breaking off from the *On Christian Doctrine* and just before and as he was writing the *Confessiones* (*Confessions*).[2] Finally, there are further suasive hints and suggestions concerning the hiatus in *On Christian Doctrine* to be found in the text of Augustine's *Confessions*, the next major work to which, after his abandonment of the former, he turned his attention.

The Unfinished Theoretical Text

The structure and purpose of *On Christian Doctrine* is transparent, but curiously hybrid. As a bishop in tumultuous pro-consular Numidia, Augustine struggled to improve the biblical literacy of Christian believers in general, but in particular that of priests and deacons. Syncretism was rampant in his diocese, fueled by strong currents of charismatic tribalism and parochial heresy. A large portion of the Punic speaking populace lacked even the most rudimentary elements of that sort of education Augustine considered necessary to read the Scriptures with minimal competence. At the same time, he believed and often asserted that knowledge of the Scripture was the indispensable foundation of orthodox faith. Clearly, he had work to do.

On Christian Doctrine is both a sophisticated and an introductory book.[3] It begins with the ABCs, so to speak, of linguistic signification. Book 1 takes the reader by gentle steps up the ladder of semiotics. Communication of all sorts, Augustine explains, depends upon tacit consensus within a theory of signs (1.2.2); though at the mechanical level signs are arbitrary, the tacit dimension of consensus means that signification is never value-free (1.3.3; 1.4.4). Signification is, by definition, an instrument, a means. This leads Augustine to make a distinction between an immature or arrested development in the study of language—a kind of "enjoyment" of its aesthetic properties without due pursuit of its substantively instrumental "use" as means to an end—and the mature and deliberately informed pursuit of meaning and its communication as the end-in-view of sensible speech. Intention and the ordering of value (1.7.7; 1.10.10) are conditioned by a desire to know the truth of things. It is the "rational soul" of mankind, "made in the image and likeness of God" that is the object of our understanding, and that because the image (*humanum*) is to be loved as itself a *means* whereby we arrive at that which is alone worthy of our full *diligere,* our full delight, God himself (1.22.20; 1.32.35). Likewise, texts, including the text of Scripture, are a means, not an end (1.35.39):

> Whoever, therefore, thinks that he understands the divine Scriptures or any part of them [but in such a way] [. . .] that it does not build the double love of God and of our neighbor does not understand them at all. (*Doctr. chr.* 1.36.40)

Here Augustine introduces the constraint and proviso from which he will not himself be able to escape in book 3:

> But anyone who understands in the Scriptures something other than that intended by them is deceived, although they do not lie. However, as I began to explain, if he is deceived in an interpretation which builds up charity, which is the end of the commandments, he is deceived in the same way as a man who leaves a road by mistake but passes through a field to the same place toward which the road itself leads. But he is to be corrected and shown that it is more useful not to leave the road, lest the habit of deviating force him on to a crossroad or a perverse way. (*Doctr. chr.* 1.36.41)

Augustine wants to believe, as he says in concluding book 1, that all knowledge and prophecy struggle for the same end: faith, hope, and charity (1.37), and that someone who is "supported by faith, hope, and charity, with an unshaken hold upon them, does not need the Scriptures except for the instruction of others" (1.39.43). In the same vein, a would-be instructor of Scripture is better fitted for the task by obedience to its perspicuous ethical commands than by any other attainment:

> When anyone knows the end of the commandment to be charity "from a pure heart and a good conscience, and faith unfeigned (1 Tim 1:5), and has related all of his understanding of the Divine Scriptures to these three, he may approach these books with security." (*Doctr. chr.* 1.40.44)

Yet even as Augustine penned those words, there were those among his neighbors who were inclined to affirm the same passage in St. Paul's letter to

Timothy as license for their own vigorously divergent and heterodox exposition. They lived a life above reproach, they thought, and yet they very often did not see a passage in the same way as the Catholic bishops. Chief among these were the Donatists.[4]

Book 2 of *On Christian Doctrine* moves from these elementary semiotic principles to rhetoric and the definition of conventions and terms, taking up the initial theme of book 1 at a higher level. This escalation requires of Augustine that he now face squarely the problem, for any referential semiotic, of apparently unyielding obscurity in the text itself. Now it will be clear even in our own context that for a skilled rhetorician the presence of semantic obscurity is often less a problem to be solved than an opportunity to exploit. Augustine the *rhetor* knew this all too well. But he had a conscience about it. He had already decried such opportunistic reflexes as unprofessional deception on the part of the interpreter.[5] He could not, however, accept that there was rhetorical deception on the part of Scripture's ultimate Author. His hypothesis was thus that obscurity in Scripture is a form of "veiling" by which truth is both protected from unseemly gaze and, at the same time, made enticing to one who loves truth. He means it: true Mediterranean aesthete that he is, he loves the tease of an incipient allegoresis and thinks that his reader will love it too. But his confidence concerning truth and its eventually pleasurable disclosure rests in part on his belief that "hardly anything may be found in these obscure places which is not plainly said elsewhere" (2.6.8). Canonical context clarifies (2.8.12–13), and what it reveals is that the tease of textual obscurity is but a legitimate pedagogical enticement, an appealing adornment for the secure rewards of fidelity to a substantially perspicuous text. As in his earlier text *De utilitate credendi* (*On the Profit of Believing*), he is confident that "the veil is taken away in Christ," and that

> In this manner all [obscurities] are dealt with, who earnestly and piously, not disorderly and shamelessly, seek the sense of those Scriptures [. . .] [until] there is left no jot that agrees not; and so great secrets of figures, that all the things that are drawn out by interpretation force them [resistant readers] to confess that they are wretched [. . .] . (*De utilitate credendi* 9; my translation)

Five years later, however, Augustine is not so confident.

Ambiguity in signs is not, he now admits, entirely removed by these referential means (*Doctr. chr.* 2.10.15) when one is working from a translation: "Against unknown literal signs," he writes, "the sovereign remedy is a knowledge of languages" (2.11.16). Augustine must have felt a certain embarrassment here.[6] He instances the necessity of Hebrew and Greek, although in the case of Greek he was wobbly, and of Hebrew he had himself little if any knowledge. Jerome, who had become at great pains a true polyglot, was to goad him in this respect. Augustine is thus sensitive about the perils of working only from translation, but in his defensiveness resourceful enough to suggest that those who acquire the languages often find yet another obstacle: their linguistic achievement makes them a little proud (2.13.20). This observation leads him to reflect further that the elite education of some expositors of classical pagan texts has prompted some of them to care more about trivialities (such as correct accent) than about truth.[7] Nevertheless, Augustine is justly famous on these grounds for not being dismissive of that pagan literary learning, from which, after all, he had profited so much: "Rather," he insists, "every good and true Christian should understand that wherever he may find truth it is his Lord's" (2.18.28). He was quoting here, of course, his ultimate teacher, Ambrose, bishop of Milan (in the latter's exposition of 1 Corinthians). But he sees that present recovery of historically or culturally veiled truths is not guaranteed even by understanding authorial intent or rhetorical strategy. One must also contend, historically, with the fading of consensual understanding concerning signs (2.35.38). There is need therefore for scholars to recover what may have historically and culturally been lost, from philological matters (such as the meaning of Hebrew names) to cultural associations of plants and animals in the ancient Jewish world.[8] All such knowledge (not merely the philosophical method or rhetorical skill of the Greeks) must be appropriated—liberated so to speak, from the cultural past—even as Egyptian Gold was carried away by the Israelites in Exodus, later to be used for vessels in the Tabernacle (2.40.60). He does not mention, though later he certainly thought about it, that a peril of all such borrowing is that a sinful imagination may more likely want to use the borrowed metal to fashion a Golden Calf (cf. Exod 32:1–35).[9]

I pause over this précis of *On Christian Doctrine* only because I hope my reader may better appreciate how Augustine's attempt to provide a sustaining and predictive hermeneutical foundation was, even as he was composing it, heading in the direction of an enormous potential "defeater." I refer, of course, to his being led to consider the arbitrariness of individual free will in the interpreter. It is no accident that in book 3 Augustine turns to the role of intention as his subject. "A man fearing God diligently seeks his will in the Holy Scriptures," he begins. Then he enumerates some of what he takes to be the good reader's prerequisites:

> And lest he should love controversy, he is made gentle in piety. He is prepared with a knowledge of languages lest he be impeded by unknown words and locutions. He is also prepared with an acquaintance with certain

necessary things lest he be unaware of their force and nature when they are used for purposes of similitudes. He is assisted by the accuracy of texts which expert diligence in emendation has procured. Thus instructed, he may turn his attention to the investigation and solution of the ambiguities of the Scriptures. That he may not be deceived by *ambiguous* signs, we shall offer some instruction. (*Doctr. chr.* 3.1.1)

As we see from his last two sentences, the persistence of ambiguity is taken by Augustine to be a serious issue. Now, additionally, he is troubled by the evidence of perversity of the will as an irrational element, even amongst those well instructed, creating further ambiguities. This nagging concern takes a diversity of forms in book 3 of the *On Christian Doctrine*, but most are anticipated in preoccupations of the first two books: some people just seem to *want* to take "signs for things," and do not see narrow literalism, as Augustine does, as "a miserable servitude of the spirit" (*Doctr. chr.* 3.5.9). Slavery to the sign (3.9.13), as he puts it, is one common result of such narrowness, and in this Augustine senses a kind of idolatry like unto, I would suggest, that which he wrestled with in its cruder manifestations in his North African culture. Idolatry projects idolatry. Pagan Numidians, he tells us in one of his sermons, observe Christian peasants venerating images on the pillars of the basilica and this looks to them like something familiar—just another version of the Phoenician religious phallic worship of the cult of Tanit (*Serm.* 198, Hill 188–93). However misguided, that is to him at least explicable. But who can fathom idolatry of the dead letter (2 Cor 3:6),[10] he complains in exasperation, that "miserable slavery of the soul which takes signs for things" (*Doctr. chr.* 3.7)?

Such confusion took many forms, but there was, perhaps, a common thread connecting them. Augustine himself had on similar grounds expressed anxiety about the syncretistic superstition of those who worshiped images of martyrs at their shrines and in other holy pictures (*De moribus ecclesiae catholicae* 1.34, 74). So here, in respect to the verbal sign, his self-consciousness about misplaced reference is grounded in a wider concern about idolatry:

> Just as it is a servile infirmity to follow the letter and to take signs for the things that they signify, in the same way it is an evil of wandering error to interpret signs in a useless way. (*Doctr. chr.* 3.9.13)

Augustine's suggested remedy for perversity of the will in a literal-minded interpreter—as for that egoism or deliberate idolatry of self that also enslaves the mind—is charity. Up to this point Augustine understands charity formally as "the motion of the soul toward the enjoyment of God for his own sake and the enjoyment of one's self and one's neighbor for the sake of God" (*Doctr. chr.* 3.10.16). What Augustine now tries to do in the balance of book 3, as far as the break-point, is to show that the rule of charity, when installed as an hermeneutic principle, has the potential to cover a multitude of interpretative sins.

But he cannot get it off his mind that there are still such things as interpretative sins, and that not all ambiguity is created by figuration in the text. "It often happens," he complains, "that a person who is, or thinks he is, in a higher grade of spiritual life thinks that those things which are taught for those in lower grades are figurative" (*Doctr. chr.* 3.17.25). We can almost feel inwardly how the irony here turns back upon our author himself. Figurative interpretation is, after all, the least veridical element in exegesis, at least in part for subjective existential reasons. At precisely this point of recognition, having written himself into something of a corner, the vexed and probably weary Augustine laid down his pen.

Augustine's Episcopal Travails

Outside, in the tumultuous world beyond his study, controversy and disorder alike continued to press relentlessly in upon his daily obligations as chief pastor and teacher. The twenty-six sermons discovered by François Dolbeau, and some of the letters recently discovered by Johannes Divjak, give us a much better picture of Augustine's preoccupations during this decisive period of his life.[11] Many in his audience were Donatists or attracted to them. Theologically rigorous and sectarian, the Donatists were also ethnocentric and nationalist. They accepted no Catholic baptism, and saw Augustine as a traitor to his own African culture, even a "toady" to that imperious Roman conformism that seemed to threaten their parochial identity.

Debate between Augustine and the Donatists over the interpretation of Scripture was already by 396 in full swing in his sermons.[12] In this controversy the Donatists appear as whining and apocalyptic quasi-literalists, Augustine as the proponent of a vigorous spiritual or allegorical interpretation. In the many texts he wrote against them from the months just after completing the *Confessions,* and for the next decade, it becomes clear that they attacked him for arbitrariness in his exegesis of figurative passages.[13] That these and similar attacks may have prompted Augustine to bring his discussion of the exegesis of ambiguous tropes in *On Christian Doctrine* book 3 under self-scrutiny seems likely to me, both in the light of what happened in his preaching immediately following the break in the writing of this work and in the course of his almost immediate exploration of the role of self in interpretation in the *Confessions*. On the textual evidence I want to argue that Augustine's eventual and firm recognition of subjectivity in the interpreter—that anybody's theory of just about anything will be at least partly autobiographical—owes to an intensive self-examination begun after his impasse in *On Christian Doctrine* book 3, that it is expressed initially in several sermons preached through the summer of 397, and brought to completion in the *Confessions*.

The Sermons of Summer

During the summer of 397, as the unfinished manuscript of the *On Christian Doctrine* was growing cold in a corner and the *Confessions* was most likely taking shape rapidly in his mind, Augustine preached at least four sermons on texts he thought ambiguous, but not because of figurative language in the usual sense. Rather, the ambiguities had been created because of apparent contradiction in interpretation or even, possibly, by an appearance of authorial mendacity in the biblical text itself being represented uncritically. Two of these sermons are in the Mainz collection of sermons newly discovered by Dolbeau; the others (*Serm.* 133 and *Serm.* 89) are well known and must remain undiscussed here. All four, however, were preached between May 24 and June 24 of that year, that is, between Pentecost and the Feast Day of John the Baptist.[14]

In what may be the first sermon preached of the four, Augustine's central text was Psalm 116:11, which in the old Latin version reads: "I said to myself in panic, Every man [is] a liar." What attracts and even preoccupies Augustine in this text is the Psalmist's "panic"(Vulg. *in excessu meo*), which evidently to some degree he shares. The way he seems to apply this verse is that any acknowledgment that subjective misrepresentation is normative to the human condition can quickly pass from distress to cynicism and passive acceptance, then in turn become a tacit license for self-serving mendacity. In fact, Augustine wishes the statement of the Psalmist was a kind of misreading, or hyperbole, but its confirmation by St. Paul rules that out: "God alone is truthful, but every man is a liar, as it is written" (Rom 3:4). Now this is quite a bit more serious as a proposition than the old and paradoxical canard that "Cretans are always liars, as they themselves say" (Titus 1:12). Augustine is emphatic:

> So this is what scripture wished to demonstrate, that *every* human being—absolutely every single one—as regards being merely human, is a liar. It is precisely, you see, *from what is our own* that every one of us is a liar. Nor are we able, from what is our own, to be anything but liars—not that we can-

not ever be truthful, but that we will *never* be truthful from what is our own. (*Serm.* 28A; Dolbeau 9; Hill 49)

The only possible remedy for this universal human trait, he goes on to say, even for a person who most earnestly desires to speak truthfully, is the intervention of the Holy Spirit:

> Yes—you see, truthful man, when you say, "I am truthful from what is my own," you are in those very words being a liar. So if it happens that you really are truthful, it is because you have been *filled*, because you have begun to participate in truth. (*Serm.* 28A; Hill 49)

If we take Augustine at face value here, he who was beginning to set down on paper a fairly extensive record concerning "what was his own" (i.e., in the *Confessions*) was now beginning to see just how problematic was his task both for ethical and epistemological reasons. With him, we begin to see how necessary, both spiritually and hermeneutically, his invocation is at the outset of the *Confessions*, as well as the repeated intercessory prayer in this text. One simply cannot trust oneself to get it right, even concerning—or we might say, especially concerning—what is "one's own," one's own story, one's own memory, the interpretation of one's own life.

The problem only intensifies when dissonance or debate with another viewpoint is involved. In another of the four sermons from this same brief period, preached perhaps almost contiguously, Augustine addresses the text in Galatians 2 in which Paul reveals that he and Peter had taken sharply disagreeing stances on Jewish cultic proprieties and Christian obedience. Augustine's point? If Peter was at fault in his insistence upon the continuance of Judaizing observances, then bishops nowadays must not claim to be beyond criticism: "Peter was to blame, and shall I brazenly have the nerve to claim that I am wholly beyond reproach?" (*Serm.* 162C; Hill 168). To put this more sharply: it appears to Augustine as possible, even for a bishop, to err in biblical interpretation. The solution to such error is that which Peter showed: "He did not, like Christ, exemplify absolute perfection, but he did give an example of utter humility. He quietly accepted a rebuke from a man who did not precede him in the apostolate, but who came after him. I hope the apostle Paul will excuse me," Augustine adds, "but what *he* did was easy. What Peter did was difficult." "We live," he adds thoughtfully, "surrounded by daily experience of this [kind of challenge] in our human relationships" (*Serm.* 162C; Hill 168).

That Augustine's Numidian controversies, especially (but not only) with the Donatists, were bringing him to a keener recognition of his own liability

to misprision, to the need for correction or supplement, seems to me evident
in these lines of the Dolbeau sermon. It is already, as exegesis, a tacit confession of inevitable fallibility in the exegete, and its self-correcting candor is
transparent when Augustine says, "I am not sure it is ever more appropriate
to notice someone else's fault than freely to admit one's own" (*Serm.* 162C;
Hill 168). Augustine concludes this sermon with an appeal to his hearers to
keep carefully in mind a crucial distinction, that between the text of
Scripture and *any* act of its exegesis:

> Everything written in the holy canonical books is [authoritative]. Well, we
> who engage in public debates and write books write in a very different
> fashion; we make progress as we write, we are learning every day, engaged
> in research as we dictate, still knocking at the door as we speak. [. . .] I
> solemnly admonish your graces, don't even think of regarding as canonical
> scripture any debate, or written account of a debate by anyone. In the holy
> writings we learn how to judge, in our own writings we are quite ready to
> be judged. [. . .] But since this is difficult to achieve, that's why there is
> this other firmament of the canon, like the heaven in which are set the
> luminous bodies of the scriptures, a firmament as it were between waters
> and waters, between the peoples of angels and the peoples of men; those
> above, these below. Let us treat scripture like Scripture, like God speaking;
> don't let's look there for man going wrong. It is not for nothing, you see,
> that the canon has been established for the Church. This is the function of
> the Holy Spirit. So if anybody reads my book, let him pass judgment on
> *me*. (*Serm.* 162C; Hill 176)

Augustine concludes this remarkable sermon by saying emphatically that he
becomes far angrier "with that kind of fan of mine who takes my book as
being canonical, than with the man who finds fault in my book with things
that are not in fact at fault." Then, with uncharacteristic abruptness, he ter-
minates his remarks:

> I implore you; although I can see that you are as keenly attentive as if you
> had only this moment arrived, as if you were only now beginning to hear
> the sermon, still I don't want to say any more, so that you may hold all the
> more firmly onto this last thing that I have said. (*Serm.* 162C; Hill 177)

It is a meek and self-examining teacher who preached those confessional
words and who, as a master rhetorician, ended his sermon with an emphatic
relegation of his own exegetical authority to the status "correctable," forego-
ing the usual moving *peroratio*. For these and other reasons, I agree with

Peter Brown, in the extensive addenda to his reissued biography of Augustine, when he says that he is quite sure that these sermons preceded the writing of the *Confessions*.[15] The "progress" that Augustine had been making "as he wrote" was in fact to set him firmly on the course to his *Retractiones* (*Retractions*): the scruple that brought *On Christian Doctrine* to a halt was, by the mediation of the Scriptures upon which he had to preach, raised in the *Confessions* to a high principle of systematic examination of conscience.

Self-Examination in the *Confessions*

So much has been written on self-examination in the *Confessions* that I forbear to add much more here. What I would do is to note, simply, the way in which, in this originary spiritual autobiography, self-examination is book-marked, so to speak, by its author—referenced to the examination of texts. We have seen how Cicero's *Hortensius* sparked in Augustine an intellectual conversion (to borrow a term from Lonergan[16]) which changed the course of his life in ways which foreshadowed his spiritual conversion as he responded to another book in another garden (*Confessions*, book 8). In his early life when, he admits freely, he worked as much for applause as for understanding, he had written a work on aesthetics called *Beauty and Proportion*, now lost and, as he remembers it, not worth going back to because, it seems, it too may have conduced to a certain egoistic idolatry (4.13). It was about form and style, not truth and substance. Even at the point of his conversion he finds his intellectual motives are mixed—he is tempted to resign his teaching post before term-end as a kind of statement, then refrains, realizing that his action might well be seen as self-serving (9.2). His persistent sensual appetites he finds distracting and disorienting (10.30–31). A natural Mediterranean *bon vivant*, he has had to learn the impossibility of self-control, "for no man can be master of himself, except of God's bounty" (*Conf.* 10.31).[17] Even in the pleasures of art and music, both legitimate, he finds himself to be capable of self-serving abuse (10.33–34).

The most dangerous kind of temptation, however, "more dangerous because it is more complicated," is a life-long idealizing of the intellectual life itself. And this is because, Augustine says, a certain kind of intellectuality for its own sake also enslaves:

> For in addition to our bodily appetites, which make us long to gratify all our senses and our pleasures and lead to our ruin if we stay away from you by becoming their slaves, the mind is also subject to a certain propensity to use the sense of the body, not for self-indulgence of a physical kind, but for the satisfaction of its own inquisitiveness. This futile curiosity masquerades

under the name of science and learning, and since it derives from our thirst
for knowledge and seeing is the principal sense by which knowledge
is acquired, in the Scriptures it is called "gratification of the eye."
(*Conf.* 10.35)

That this fault is systemic is the principal burden of book 10 as a self-
examination: "Who can tell," he asks rhetorically, "how many times each day
our [vain] curiosity is tempted by the most trivial and insignificant matters?"
Thus, his "life is full of such faults," of "trivial thoughts," of "desire for
praise" which he knows is often forthcoming on false grounds from false
motives and thus encouraging of false intentions. Probing his own subjective
complexity, Augustine puts himself to the question again and again: "If it is
[really] the good of my neighbor which touches my heart when I hear my
own praises, why am I less aggrieved when blame is unjustly laid at another's
door than when it is laid at mine? Or is the truth of the matter that I deceive
myself and that in heart and tongue alike I am guilty of falsehood in your
presence?" (10.37).

Book 10 of the *Confessions* concludes one of the most ruthless of principled self-examinations, I think, in the history of literature. Its central recognition is that in attempting to possess the Truth, even the truth of Scripture
as the very counsel of God, the interpreter is capable of badly mixed and self-
deceiving motives and hence unreliable interpretation. "You are the Truth,"
he addresses the author of Scripture,

> which presides over all things. In my selfish longing I did not wish to lose
> you. [Yet] together with you I wanted to possess a lie. [. . .] And in this
> way I lost you [anyway], because you do not deign to be possessed togeth-
> er with a lie. (*Conf.* 10.41)

Changing the truth of God into a lie, as Augustine well knew St. Paul to say,
was the surest way to forsake the Wisdom of God for the worship of mere
creatures—an utter folly, no matter how apparently gifted the interpreter of
the text (cf. Rom 1:20–25). However subtly, we might say, the characteristic
form of this kind of folly is to try to play God with the text.

What Augustine seems to have acquired from his experience is a deeper
level of humility before the page from which he reads. His interpretations are
less and less apodictic; his counsel concerning interpretation is more and
more constrained. In a later sermon than those I have considered, he writes:

> Above all, however, take care not to let yourself be tempted if you do not
> yet understand the sacred scriptures, or to grow proud if you do under-

stand them. If there is something you do not understand, respectfully set it aside for another occasion, and cling with love to what you do understand. (*Serm.* 51.35; Hill 3)

In yet another, for Ascension Sunday in 412, he become open to a *diversity* of interpretations in a fashion that contrasts brightly with some of his earlier polemical compositions:

> Many exegetes have given a variety of interpretations and have sought ways of approaching their listeners. They have said things not opposed to faith: one man this, another that, without departing from the rule of truth. [. . .] I am still searching and longing to achieve greater certainty. May the Lord help me through your prayers [. . .]. I do not know the answer, therefore, but I can conjecture (*existimem*) without yet knowing, without yet having an answer that is certain [. . .] nor will I hide my lack of knowledge as long as I am still conjecturing. If the answer I suggest is true, may the Lord confirm it; if another answer appears truer, may the Lord give it. (*Serm.* 265.9; Hill 10)

This, then, is the Augustine who returns in A.D. 426, while writing his self-examining *Retractions,* to completing *On Christian Doctine,* and who now commences to address the problem of ambiguities in figurative speech or writing by providing a firm set of hermeneutical rules. They are not his own rules: they are borrowed, with full acknowledgment, from Tyconius the moderate Donatist, the most formidable of his opponents, a mere layman, almost certainly married. Because of Augustine's borrowing, Tyconius the Donatist Christian would make a contribution absolutely foundational to Western Christian literary theory for more than a millennium. Augustine both summarizes and quotes the *Liber regularum* (*Book of Rules*) of Tyconius. He is not without his critical reservations—he thinks with respect to clarifying some ambiguous texts that Tyconius promises much more than he can deliver (*Doctr. chr.* 3.30.42). But he defers to Tyconius's system for the advantage of its simple explanatory power—particularly for the ambiguities of figurative discourse.

Book 4 of *On Christian Doctrine* offers thus a very different conclusion, I think, from that which we might have expected from the original books 1 and 2. The subject of book 4 is the "Goals of Reading." There is a shift of focus from the Critic to the Reader in Augustine's clear emphasis on the way in which scriptural eloquence serves a larger Wisdom. Now it is less the explication of texts that matters than the Text itself; the authentic reader is one in whom that text has entered to become a living Presence: "For a man speaks more or less wisely to the extent that he has become more or less proficient in the Holy Scriptures" (*Doctr. chr.* 4.5.7–8). There are those who interpret well with this sanctioned and safer eloquence found in Scripture itself, "fitting for men most worthy of the highest authority and clearly inspired by God. Our authors speak with eloquence of *this* kind, nor does any other kind become them" (*Doctr. chr.* 4.6.9). We should notice how Augustine's focus has here fallen completely away from his own critical effort. Light shines now first on the Text, secondarily on the interpretative work of those whose language is not, after all, redactive of, but expressive of that Text. "Reading charitably" has come to mean not simply referring figurative discourse to a spiritual interpretation which teaches *caritas,* but means also a reading or interpretation which involves self-effacement on the part of the interpreter.

From this point Augustine is concerned to recommend analogous strategies for teaching, since "instruction should come before persuasion" (4.12.28). The polemicist gives way to the man of prayer; indeed, since silent prayer for one's hearers is more efficacious than public oratory, he becomes a petitioner before he becomes a speaker (4.15.32). Eloquence and wisdom are still the goal of textual learning, but the lesson one learns from intellectual temptation and its redemption is that "the life of the speaker has greater weight in determining whether he is obediently heard than any grandness of eloquence" (*Doctr. chr.* 4.27.59).

This is a very different voice than the one which we heard in book 1 of *On Christian Doctrine,* with its sharp, insistent rhetorical aggressiveness: e.g., "No one is so impudently stupid as to say, How do you know that an immutable wise life is preferable to a mutable one?" (*Doctr. chr.* 1.9.9). It would have been tempting to reply to Augustine at this early point with the witticism like unto that attributed by a colleague of mine to one of his philosophy students: "After this course I am not so sure the examined life is worth living either." The Augustine of those A.D. 397 summer sermons, of the *Confessions,* and of the latter part of *On Christian Doctrine,* comes to the reader now as a man among men, mastered by the text he reads and with no pretense to be master of it. Preaching from the text, we now know, he would refuse the pulpit, and instead sit on a chair before his congregation with the open Bible on his knees, a reader among readers.[18] The body-language, as we say, speaks volumes. He had become an interpreter who could, on these grounds, begin to separate the motives of the ordinary reader from the authority of an extraordinary text.

> I [. . .] give thanks to God that in these four books I have discussed with
> whatever slight ability I could muster, not the kind of man I am, for I have

many defects, but the kind of man he ought to be who seeks to labor in sound doctrine, which is Christian doctrine, not only for himself, but also for others. (*Doctr. chr.* 4.31)

It is a fine, long way for a masterful interpreter to have come; it took self-examination and his *Confessions* to get him there.

(2001)

Chapter Four

Charity and Cupidity
in Biblical Tradition

---

*Super omnia autem haec, charitatem habete, quod est viniculum perfectionis,
et pax Christi exultet in cordibus vestries, in qua et vocati estis in uno
corpore. . . .*

Colossians 3:14, Vulgate

It has occasionally been the case that problems in translation have been a
major factor in biblical interpretation and hence in theological formulation
in Western Christianity. The process by which these occasions of potentially
significant confusion tend to work themselves out in time is both interesting
in itself and highly instructive about the self-correcting character of the
Church as a community of interpretation. Moreover, as we shall see in more
detail in Part 2, this historic community of interpretation is not adequately
measured if only its ecclesiastical dimensions are considered; many of the
most important contributions are found to have come from the interaction
with Scripture of the arts, where engagement of Scripture and the formation
of its teaching is often far deeper than any mere matter of adornment or pre-
text. Nowhere is the interaction of lay and clerical understanding of
Scripture on better display than in circumstances where a central doctrine of
the faith is at issue, or where a central biblical virtue is to be expounded in
the biblical fashion—that is, by contrast with the vice or disorder which
opposes it. The historic and ongoing debate about the character and expression of Christian love affords a representative example.

The traditional opposition *caritas/cupiditas,* while reflecting a basic
moral distinction in the Bible, owes something of its particularly strong

55

formulation in Western tradition to difficulties encountered by St. Jerome in rendering several biblical words for love accurately in the Latin equivalents available to him. The Old Testament Hebrew word *'ahab,* while generally referring to spontaneous desire, applies to a range of both human and divine expressions of affection. Another Hebrew word, *hesed,* is used to connote deliberately willed or chosen affection, "loyalty," and "kindness," and is typically translated by the King James Version as "mercy," by some other translations as "compassion" (cf. *raham,* "to have compassion" [Deut 30:3]). Any of these terms may be involved in connection with sexual love, fraternal love, or God's love for his people.

In Greek literature before the New Testament, *erôs* had been the most common word for love; it suggests spontaneity (like *'ahab*) and yet is almost always sexual in connotation, even when, as in the erotic narratives of classical mythology (e.g., Leda and the swan), it refers to the love of the gods for human persons. In Platonic discourse, "noble *erôs*" can refer to the human quest for "God" (cf. Plato, *Symposium*) or for one's city, a kind of civic *erôs.* When the Septuagint translators tried to find Greek equivalents for the familiar Hebrew words for love they nonetheless rejected *erôs* because of its overwhelming cultural associations with libidinous activity, choosing instead the obscure *agapê* to translate *'ahab; erôs* appears only once in the Septuagint, in a cult prostitute's invitation to sexual promiscuity (Prov 7:18).

The New Testament eschews *erôs* altogether. It makes limited use of *philia* ("love," "affection, as for a spouse") to describe parental love (Matt 10:37), the disciples' love for Jesus (John 21:15–17; 1 Cor 16:22), and Jesus' love for Lazarus (John 11:3, 36), as well as God's love for Jesus (John 5:50) and for his people (John 16:27; Rev 3:19). It is never used, however, to describe human love for God. The principal New Testament word is *agapê, agapaô* (in English Bibles usually translated "love," though twenty-nine times in the KJV as "charity"). In St. Paul's First Epistle to the Corinthians (13:4–8), *agapê* (Vulg. *caritas;* KJV "charity") is succinctly described in terms of its contraries as well as in positive terms. Charity is not jealousy, conceit, ostentation, arrogance, self-centeredness, and resentment (various expressions of self-love); it is rather expressed in patience, kindness, truth, righteousness, hope, benevolence, and endurance (self-transcending love). It is in this register of "*caritas*" that love (along with faith and hope) becomes one of the "three theological virtues"— indeed, for St. Paul, it is the greatest of them all (1 Cor 13:13).

The King James translation "charity" derives from the Latin *caritas* (and its thirteenth-century French equivalent *charité*). St. Jerome chose *caritas* ("love," "esteem," "affection") and *dilectio* ("delight," "love," "high esteem") to translate Greek *agapê,* knowing that they were imprecise Latin equivalents, themselves overlapping in Roman usage. He then chose *cupiditas* ("lust," "desire," "passion," "ambition") to translate *agapaô* in cases where the object of the affection or desire was of a carnal order (e.g., "Demas, in love with this present world" [2 Tim 4:10]). In 1 Timothy 6:10 ("the love of money is the root of all evil," KJV) Jerome's Latin renders Gk. *philargyria* in the same way: *radix malorum cupiditas est*. *Caritas* and *cupiditas* thus become, in the Vulgate New Testament and early commentary upon it, divergent, even polar, words for love, the neutral Latin word for which was usually *amor* (cf. *erôs*, "desire"). What determines whether the *amor* tends towards *caritas* or *cupiditas* is not simply its object, but, in St. Augustine's more precise formulation, the intention the "lover" bears toward the object of his or her affection. The Vulgate translator's attempt to characterize the "sense," as Jerome was wont to say, rather than the semantic "letter" in translating the Bible, is basic to subsequent Western efforts both to translate and to interpret biblical usage concerning love. Developing the distinction in a passage of enormous influence, Augustine writes:

> I call "charity" the motion of the soul toward the enjoyment of God for His own sake, and the enjoyment of one's self and of one's neighbor for the sake of God; but "cupidity" is a motion of the soul toward the enjoyment of one's self, one's neighbor, or any corporal thing for the sake of something other than God. (*Doctr. chr.* 3.10.16)

In other words, desire (*amor*) never remains neutral, but is sharply defined by intention and object. Moreover, the intentions and objects of *caritas* and *cupiditas* are not compatible, so that "the more the reign of cupidity is destroyed, the more charity is increased" (ibid.). For Augustine this is the fundamental spiritual conflict figured in every ethical choice, whether explicitly or merely tacitly. Vice and virtue, depredation and beneficence, wounding and healing—all manner of opposites which have ethical portent—offer an occasion of choice between cupiditous and charitable promptings of the will. Augustine, on this account, is able to reduce the pedagogical strategy of the Bible to a single governing precept: "Scripture teaches nothing but charity, nor condemns anything except cupidity, and in this way shapes the minds of men" (*Doctr. chr.* 3.10.15). If this scriptural pedagogy is not immediately apparent at the literal level of a specific biblical text, one ought to seek it "beneath the veil" of the letter. The literary theory of *On Christian Doctrine* is founded upon this principle: searching for the charitable spirit beneath the letter of the text will, Augustine argues, prove both spiritually and aesthetically rewarding (2.8.6).

Elaborations in medieval iconography follow directly from this principle of the "two loves." The destination of the pilgrim (*viator*) prompted by charity is the peace and communion of celestial Jerusalem; the destination of the wanderer drawn on by cupidity is the chaos and alienation of that Babylon spoken of in Revelation as the quintessence of spiritual captivity (Rev 16:19; 17:5; 18:10, 21). For Augustine, the two cities spring from the two loves (*Civ. Dei* 24.28). For later commentators, elaborating analogies, Babylon and the celestial Jerusalem are the dwelling place of the spiritual "lineage" of Cain and Abel respectively (cf. Peter Lombard, sup. Ps 97 [PL 191.581]). These and similar analogies tend in Western theological tradition afterward to suggest that cupidity is the source of all sin and strife, making "a Babylon of the individual mind, a Babylon of society, and leads to an ultimate Babylon in eternal damnation."[1] Charity is, however, the occasion of love and peace—in the individual mind, in society, and finally in the celestial Jerusalem forever. While cupidity is haunted by the fear of misfortune, charity is conditioned by that fear of God which leads to wisdom (Prov 9:10), by which in turn the human spirit is enabled to rise above the happenstance of fortune and its temporal effects (Jas 1:2–12; cf. Peter Lombard, *Sententiarum, Libri IV* [PL 191.766]).

Numerous positive studies of the "virtues" of *caritas* in the twelfth century, notably including two by the Cistercians St. Bernard of Clairvaux (*De diligendo Deo* [*On Loving God*]) and Aelred of Riveaulx (*Speculum caritatis* [*The Mirror of Charity*]), are effectively what we should today style "psychological" treatments of their subject. Bernard related both to inward promptings, saying: "Only Charity can convert the soul, freeing it from unworthy motives" (*Dilig. Deo* 12).[2] Theologically, Aelred's *The Mirror of Chastity* anticipates St. Thomas Aquinas; psychologically it recapitulates Augustine. One of its major themes is the inner peace that derives from charity, and the role charitable affection can play in overcoming the disordering psychic effects of cupidity. The condition of charity is "Sabbath rest," enjoyed in this life as a prefiguration of the life to come. He argues further that practical charity is illuminated by the order of priorities established in the Great Commandment (Deut 6:5; Matt 22:37–40): love of God ought to be uppermost, followed by love of one's neighbor, with self occupying the humblest rung in one's ladder of affection. If this hierarchy of the "law of love" is inverted, cupidity reigns, and with it inevitably idolatry (3.2–6). "Choice," Aelred says, "is the beginning of love, whether it be good [*caritas*] or bad love [*cupiditas*]" (3.8).[3] In practice, then:

> Charity means that in the first place we have chosen something we are permitted to have; that we have gone about attaining it in the right way, and that having attained it we enjoy it in the way that God meant it to be enjoyed. Charity implies a wise choice and an enjoyment that will benefit

us. It begins as a choice, it develops as the pursuit of something good, and comes to its term in enjoyment. But if we choose unwisely, and seek what we have chosen in a wrongful manner, and end by abusing what we have acquired, this is greed, and the root of all evil. But charity is the root of all that is good. (*Spec. car.* 3.8)

Although cupidity usually signifies in the Middle Ages the entire range of self-directed desires, it was typically figured (as the connection with "Cupid" suggests) in carnal passion. In St. Bonaventure's prologue to his commentary on Ecclesiastes, perhaps because he is thinking of its author as Solomon (the Wise Man destroyed by his lust), he uses the word *libido* in place of cupidity to describe the passions that enmesh the soul, typologically, in Babylon.[4] The ambiguous possibilities of Latin *amor* also opened up a range of wordplay for medieval writers (e.g., Andreas Capallanus, *De Amore,* or *Art of Courtly Love;* Jean de Meun's Amant in *Le Roman de la Rose;* Chaucer, in his *General Prologue* description of the Prioress's brooch, inscribed "Amor vincit omnia"). Some were inclined to extended witty discourse on the principle that, as Aquinas puts it, echoing Aelred, if "Charity is love, not all love is charity" (*Sum. theol.* 1a–2ae.62.2–3; *Spec. car.* 3.7).

For Aquinas, "Charity is driven out, not because sin is strong, but because the human will subjects itself to sin." Conversely, "Charity brings to life again those who are spiritually dead" (*De caritate* 1.24). It is capable of overcoming cupidity's sorry effects, if chosen in repentance by the errant soul (*Sum. theol.* 2a–2ae.23.2). In its requirement of responsibility, charity is ennobling (cf. Richard of St. Victor, *De Trinitate* 3.2), it has the character of human friendship with God (Aquinas, *De potentia* 9; *De caritate* 1.3), and it is the basis of perfection in all the other virtues (*Sum. theol.* 1a–2ae.114.4; *De virtutibus cardinalibus* 2). Accordingly, Aquinas concludes, "we must look for the perfection of the Christian life in charity" (*Sum. theol.* 2a–2ae.184.1–2; *De perfectione vitae spiritualis* 5). For mystical writers like pseudo-Dionysius, Richard of St. Victor, or the author of *The Cloud of Unknowing,* the ultimate perfection of *caritas* is achieved in the mystical union of the soul with God.

Just as *cupiditas* was frequently associated with carnal lust, so *caritas* was often identified by Aquinas and others with *castitas* ("chaste affection"). Aquinas observes that "chastity" has both a literal and a metaphorical sense:

By a figure of speech, accordingly, spiritual chastity is engaged when our spirit enjoys God, with whom it should be joined, and refrains from enjoying things God does not mean us to mingle with: *I have espoused you to one husband, that I may present you a chaste virgin to Christ.* So also may we speak of spiritual fornication, when our spirit delights in embracing things against God's fair order: *thou hast played the harlot with many lovers.* Chastity in this sense is a characteristic of every virtue, each of which holds us back from contracting illicit unions. Yet charity is at the centre of every virtue, and so also are the other theological virtues, which unite us immediately with God. (*Sum. theol.* 2a–2ae.151.2)[5]

The persistence of this association means that in medieval and Renaissance literature especially, a cupiditous abuse of chastity can serve as an exemplum prompting to charity. This appears to be the case in Chaucer's *Merchant's Tale,* where the distinctly selfish and hence uncharitable motivation of old Januarie in acquiring his young bride May (significantly, by ogling voyeuristically with the help of a mirror in the marketplace) is debated in terms of its consequences for wider social "peace" or "discord" by Justinus and Placebo. When Januarie chooses, for reasons expressly cupiditous, to eschew "chastitee" (4.1455) and acquire a convenient and powerless sexual partner, he makes a private enclosed garden to consummate his amours. The garden is associated by the narrator with Priapus and the *Romance of the Rose*—i.e., with notoriously unchaste love. Yet when Januarie wishes to call May to a liaison "in his gardyn, and no wight but they tweye," he does so in words which derive from the Songs of Songs:

> Rys up, my wyf, my love, my lady free;
> The turtles voys is herd, my dowve sweete;
> The wynter is goon with alle his reynes weete.
> Com forth now, with thyne eyen columbyn.
> How fairer been thy brestes than is wyn!
> The gardyn is enclosed al aboute;
> Com forth, my white spouse! Out of doute
> Thou hast me wounded in myn hearte, O wyf.
> No spot of thee ne knew I al my lyf.
> Com forth and lat us taken oure disport;
> I chees thee for my wyf and my confort.
>
> (*Canterbury Tales* 4.2138–48)

Here the biblical garden of chaste love (read allegorically in connection with *caritas*; e.g., St. Bernard, *Super Canticum*) is strikingly parodied. But by juxtaposing the unchaste discord of Januarie's garden with the call of the eternal Bridegroom to his Bride, Chaucer highlights the profound contrast between self-deceiving cupidity and divine charity.

As an astute interpreter of biblical tradition in the Pauline/Augustinian hermeneutic vein, Chaucer typically stresses a hierarchical aspect to the relation of *cupiditas* and *caritas*. The lower or carnal order of love, he suggests, either through bitter experience of its imperfections in fact or through the virtues of vicariously apprehended sorrow, can be instrumental in a lover's progress to higher love. The same point undergirds his friend John Gower's poem, *Confessio Amantis*. In Dante's *Vita Nuova* (*New Life*), likewise, the narrator pictures himself as loving Beatrice first in an erotic, carnal way (Sonnets 1–7), then gradually for the character in her which the "God of love himself" admires (7), and finally (16.1) for the sake of Love himself to whom her virtues, he sees at last, are properly to be referred. Chaucer's *Knight's Tale* likewise juxtaposes the concord of a chaste married love (Theseus and Hippolyta) with unchaste, discordant passions (Palamon's and Arcite's feelings for Emilye), yet only so as to show how charitable judgment and chaste marriage can in the end restore what Theseus calls "the fair cheyne of love," that order of Divine Providence by which God established the creation (1.2987–3074).[6]

Connection of charity with the Law of Love is the subject of a treatise by the fourteenth-century spiritual writer Richard Rolle (*The Law of Love*), in which sin, especially mortal sin, is made the "enemy of love" at each level: self, neighbor, and God. A similar theme runs through William Langland's *Piers Plowman,* where the Tree of Charity has roots of Mercy and Pity for its trunk (16.3–5 [*B* text]). By the same token, *Caritas* in *The Castle of Perseverance* tells Humanum Genus that she informs other virtues and is the enemy of vice, particularly *invidia*:

> To Charite, Man, have an eye,
> In al thinge, Man, I rede.
> Al thy doinge as dros is drye,
> But in charite thou dyth thy dede.
> I distroye alwey Envye. [. . .][7] (1602–6)

The communion into which Humanum Genus is invited is the Eucharistic "Love Feast," in which sacrament, as fifteenth-century preacher John Mirk puts it, the Christian should understand charity to be "enfleshed" each time it is offered at the altar (*De Solemnitate Corporis Christi*).[8] A Wycliffite treatise of the same period, *Of Servants and Lords,* advises its hearers that "whoever is most in charity will be most readily heard by God, whether he be a shepherd or a common laborer, whether he be in the church or out in the field."[9] To summarize: medieval texts typically emphasize the crucial nature of choice (intention or *animus* of heart); an ordinate hierarchy of affections (the Law of Love, or Great Commandment); and the foundational relationship of *caritas* and *cupiditas* to all the other vices and virtues respectively. For the Augustinian canon Walter Hilton, perhaps one of the finest spiritual writers of the late Middle Ages, these all follow only upon simple gospel obedience: no one can say that they "have charity [. . .] except one who is perfectly and unfeignedly meek. Others may believe themselves to be so, or hope that they are in charity by exhibiting signs of charity. But he that is perfectly meek experiences it, and is therefore alone able to say it truthfully."[10] For Hilton, meekness, or self-effacement, is the singular attitude of heart that makes charitable love possible. Failure to "be in charity" effectively renders spiritually null and void overt acts of "charity"; this is why "many people do deeds of charity and have no actual love."

Renaissance texts of the sixteenth century innovate materially upon the medieval paradigm, but in such a way as to construe it as if in a legal context. John Calvin, for example, discusses charity as pertaining to the Ten Commandments in detail (rather than the summarizing Law of Love [Matt 22:37–40]). The two tables of the Decalogue, he assumes, are divided into injunctions concerning the "cultivation of piety" and "how we are to conduct ourselves toward our fellow men." Worship is what we owe to God, "charity" Calvin says, is what God "enjoins us to have toward our fellow men" (*Instit.* 2.8.11–12). The parable of the Good Samaritan (Luke 10:36) illustrates the principle in its widest sense for Calvin (*Instit.* 2.8.55), which is to say that charity for him is less to be understood as a matter of intentions of the heart, or their object, than in terms of external social "works"—a point which characterizes his later argument against Sadoleto that faith rather than charity is the first cause of salvation (since charity is a matter of works [*Instit.* 3.18.8]). Though St. Paul actually contrasts benevolence, or "bestowing one's goods to feed the poor" (1 Cor 13:3), with *agapê*, Calvin's own emphasis is basic to a general shift in English usage after the Reformation, in which "charity" becomes an outward action in relief of one's neighbor, or even a matter of political toleration, while "love" denotes the inward feeling or prompting of the heart. "Cupidity" largely retains its established meaning—self-love in its cruder forms—though, disconnected from the earlier sense of "charity," it ceases to be prominent. "Hate" begins to emerge as the usual opposite to "love," while when "charity" is used in its new social sense, its opposites include "greed" and "selfishness."

Already in the seventeenth century this semantic shift can be observed in even a moderate Calvinist like George Herbert, in whose poetry "charitie" appears but three times—twice with but a residue of the medieval sense

("Lovejoy"; "Trinitie Sunday"). In the third instance ("The Church-floore") it is paired with "love" in such a way as to suggest that he uses one word for the inward, the other for a complementary outward action: "But the sweet cement, which in one sure band / Ties the whole frame, is *Love* / And *Charitie*" (10–12).[11] Confirmation comes in his prose, where Herbert uses "charity" thirty times to signify the parson's duty: "a debt of Charity to the poor" (*Priest to the Temple* 11.6); "any present good deed of charity" (10.6) is proper to the faithful parson, "exposing the obligation of Charity, and Neighbour-hood" (19.34), "so is his charity in effect a Sermon" (12.17). The entire second book of Sir Thomas Browne's *Religio medici* is devoted to charity in Herbert's sense of the word—sensitivity and response to the need and miseries of others, and, above all, toleration of their various differences of religious and political opinion. Indeed, after this period, "charity" becomes synonymous with toleration for many writers (e.g., Norris, Locke, Tillotson), commencing a development in which, by the late twentieth century, toleration rather than love would become for many the singular civic virtue.

For Puritan writers this was not so, yet the emphasis upon love as a duty was, if anything, stronger. In John Winthrop's famous mid-Atlantic lay sermon aboard the *Arabella* ("A Model of Christian Charity") he tied charity to the "double law," the "law of nature and the law of grace, or the moral law and the law of the Gospel." Charity is above all an exemplary witness of Christian obedience to these laws:

> Whatsoever we did or ought to have done when we lived in England, the same must we do, and more also where we go. That which the most in their churches maintain as a troth in profession only, we must bring into familiar and constant practice: as in this duty of love we must love brotherly without dissimulation, we must love one another with a pure heart fervently, we must bear one another's burdens, we must not look only on our own things but also on the things of our brethren.[12]

Charity is here a covenant obligation; the Lord has "ratified his covenant and sealed our Commission, [and] will expect a strict performance of the articles contained in it" (ibid.).

The old usage of *caritas* did, however, continue side by side with the new usage for a time, even self-consciously. One element which continued to attract Renaissance poets was the old connection of *caritas* and *castitas*, charity and chastity, though in Protestant poets especially this likely owes as much to the Neoplatonic notion that to move toward God was to renounce the flesh as it does to the formulations of Aquinas or Aelred.[13] In Edmund

Spenser's *Faerie Queene,* Charity (Charissa) is a daughter of Dame Coelia of
the House of Holiness. Her characterization as a paragon of chastity may
seem at first glance at odds with her description:

> She was a woman in her freshest age,
> Of wondrous beauty, and of bountie rare,
> With goodly grace and comely personage,
> That was on earth not easie to compare;
> Full of great love; but Cupids wanton snare
> As hell she hated; chast in worke and will;
> Her necke and breasts were ever open bare,
> That ay thereof her babes might sucke their fill;
> The rest was all in yellow robes arayed still. (1.10.30)

In this verbal emblem Charity is allied to "married Chastity" rather than to
virginity. Later in the poem Britomart becomes the representative heroine of
the Book of Chastity. Her "chaste charity" is an active virtue: she subdues the
forces of lust, then marries Artegall in an alliance of Justice and Mercy to
reproduce Spenser's model for married chastity. Britomart's opposite in this
connection is Malecasta ("corrupted chastity"), the wanton and lustful lady
of the night who entertains in Castle Joyous, and who corresponds exactly to
medieval figurations of *cupiditas* as *luxuria* (e.g., *Roman de la Rose;* cf. *Sir
Gawain and the Green Knight*).

William Shakespeare reflects these associations in his *The Tempest,* where
Miranda, who represents the "wonder" of *caritas,* is strongly identified with
chastity. In *King Lear* Cordelia, whose love is "nothing," or no-thing, and
which knows "no cause," functions also as a representation of charity and
married chastity to counter the *cupiditas* and *luxuria* of her sisters. Milton's
Comus cannot be well understood apart from the tradition that would read
the Lady's chastity as a prima facie manifestation of Christian charity.[14]
Chastity in this light still figures in the valiant struggle of the *miles Christi* to
overcome sin in the world—a figuration particularly transparent in Bunyan's
Pilgrim's Progress, where Charity is one of the virgins who (with Discretion,
Prudence, and Piety) arm Christian with the sword and shield of faith.

Other lineaments of biblical and medieval tradition are apparent
throughout Renaissance literature. In Henry More's "Charity and Humility,"
the linkage clearly pertains to self-effacing love for God and then others, a
love which for More may never be self-generated because of pride's inevitable
complicity. Catholic convert Richard Crashaw's "*Caritas nimia,* Or the Dear
Bargain" is a poem about *agapê,* God's unparalleled and almost incompre-

hensible love expressed at Calvary. The poet can scarcely reckon with "the bargain":

> If my base lust
> Bargain'd with death and well-beseeming dust,
> Why should the white
> Lamb's bosom write
> The purple name
> Of my sin's shame? (55–60)

Crashaw's "On a Treatise of Charity" provides an interesting counter-Reformation reprise of the Reformers' derogation of active charity (construed as "works" or "merit") in contrast with "justifying faith." What can happen in such a scorning, says Crashaw, is that all sense of *caritas* love for God as a "sacrifice of the heart" in worship gets lost and love grows cold. He yearns for a spiritual renewal in which the hypocrite will no longer be regarded as "upright [. . .] / Because he's stiff, and will confess no knee," but rather the altar and its representative sacrifice will once more, even as in biblical times, be central. Then,

> [. . .] for two turtle-doves, it shall suffice
> To bring a pair of meek and humble eyes;
> This shall from henceforth be the masculine theme
> Pulpits and pens shall sweat in; to redeem
> Virtue to action; that life-feeding flame
> That keeps religion warm; not swell a name
> Of faith, a mountain-word, made up of air,
> With those dear spoils that want to dress the fair
> And fruitful charity's full breasts, of old,
> Turning her out to tremble in the cold.
> What can the poor hope from us? when we be
> Uncharitable even to Charity. (47–58)

Restoration and eighteenth-century literature tends either to codify the Calvinist and Puritan emphasis, or to define charity against such codifications by appeal to classical and rationalist authors. The latter choice produces some interestingly eisegetical results. Matthew Prior's poem "Charity" is a verse paraphrase of 1 Corinthians 13, a dialogue in Hudibrastic couplets written, he says, with ideally rational readers like Socrates or Montaigne in mind (*Poems* 252). In his view, Paul's "charity" is simply the practice of a temperate balance and mean enjoined by the knowledge that in this world all things are equivocal. Jonathan Swift's "Letter to a Young Gentleman," advising him on his desire to enter the ministry, adduces Socrates as authoritative on the greatest of the theological virtues, "charity" (his own definition proves indeed to be a blending of Socratic and Pauline wisdom). In his *Sermon on the Trinity* charity is a "duty," he says, that Socrates teaches (*Sermons,* ed. Landa 159). In his sermon on "Brotherly Love" charity is prudential temperance, standing firm in the Anglican middle of the road between two perceived enemies, "the Papists and Fanaticks" (Landa 172). Even John Wesley, whose Methodist "Love Feasts," system-disturbing works of mercy and emotional spirituality, identified him for many of his broad-church contemporaries with Swift's "fanaticks," could stress the priority of Love substantially in terms of the Christian's duty. Advising a correspondent to steer clear of mystics like Jacob Boehme, he counsels him to "keep in the plain, open Bible way. Aim at nothing higher, nothing deeper, than the religion described in our Lord's Sermon upon the Mount, and briefly summed up by St. Paul in the thirteenth chapter to the Corinthians" (*Letters* 5.342).[15]

For all this apparently unarguable similarity with the broad mainstream emphasis on charity as disinterested works of benevolence, and the Methodists' intensive involvement in ministries of relief to prisons, mental hospitals, orphanages, and the like, they were keenly disliked by latitudinarian churchmen and their sympathizers both for an apparent Spartan severity and their insistence that faith, not accrued "charity," was the redemptive agent in human salvation. For example, in his sermon "The Nature and Necessity of Self-Denial," the "Calvinist-Methodist" George Whitefield opposes what a medieval preacher would have called *cupiditas, luxuria,* and *superbia* to "denying our self-will," denying "the pleasurable indulgence and self-enjoyment of riches," and denying "pride of the understanding." What he calls "the medicine of self-denial" is based upon imitation of the self-sacrificing love of Christ, the apostles, and martyrs—their *agapê* or *caritas.* In his homiletic description of "The Almost Christian" he says of such a person that even his apparently charitable actions proceed "not from any love to God or regard to man, but only out of a principle of self-love—because he knows dishonesty will spoil his reputation and consequently hinder his prosperity in the world."[16] In a style reminiscent of William Law (a major influence upon Whitefield) he adds that the nominal Christian "is no enemy to charitable contributions, if not too frequently requested. But then he is quite unacquainted with the kind offices of 'visiting the sick and inprison'd, clothing the naked, and relieving the hungry.' "[17] One can see here how evangelical voices in the eighteenth century set out to distance their own sense of charity in relation to love (cf. Jas 1:27) from that of their latitudinarian and other contemporaries, who, they felt, increasingly understood *caritas* primarily as a social obligation.

In turn, latitudinarian preachers such as Isaac Barrow, Archbishop John Tillotson, Bishop Benjamin Hoadley, and Samuel Clark countered such preaching with their own more relaxed doctrines. On their modified Pelagian view, human nature is essentially, not accidentally, benevolent. Salvation—in effect, social as well as divine approval—is dependent upon active charity, which is "natural to mankind" (although, in a world corrupted and confused by bad custom and miseducation, an inducement of future rewards and punishments seems to be required). Comprehensive and energetic charity is a specific manifestation of "good nature"; such charity is not mere almsgiving but rather "universal love of all mankind, embracing friend and enemy, and it is limited only by the opportunity, position, or political power of the individual." In this fashion, the latitudinarians set off their view also from the proto-positivistic "politic charity" of Thomas Hobbes and Bernard Mandeville. Like George Whitefield they censured self-love (forms of cupidity such as avarice, ambition, vanity, and hypocrisy), but they stressed more strongly than he a narrow priority of one verse in particular from the Epistle of James ("Faith, if it hath not works, is dead" [Jas 2:17]) over other biblical texts, such as Paul's Epistle to the Ephesians in relation to duty or "works" ("For by grace are ye saved through faith; and that not of yourselves: it is the gift of God: Not of works, lest any man should boast" [Eph 2:8–9]). Good works, in this latter text, is not a function of natural human benevolence but of an individual person being created anew in Christ and hence discovering, as they could not have otherwise, that God has "previously prepared" works for them to do in a loving imitation of Christ (Eph 2:10). Because the agency of "grace through faith" is for Whitefield the key, grace and faith remain his focus.

In a latitudinarian divine like Barrow by contrast, the "hero of faith" becomes substantially a "hero of works." But there are some important connections back to medieval and Reformation analyses of virtue in these writings. The truly heroic individual is not necessarily the powerful, wealthy, or prestigious person but the "good man," whose moral superiority is typically described in terms of benevolence.[18] Isaac Barrow's sermon "On Being Imitators of Christ" provides a pattern in terms of which one may understand novelist Henry Fielding's preface and opening chapters in *Joseph Andrews*. The historian's task, says Barrow, is to provide examples of the "good man" which emphasize his *chastity* with respect to himself (control of reason over the passions), the biblical model for which is Joseph resisting the advances of Potiphar's wife, and his *charity* with respect to society, the biblical model for which is Abraham, the epitome of faith revealed in works and hence of active charity. But the good historians will depict, says Barrow, human imperfections as well as virtues because a flawless model of righteousness would induce only despair. In Fielding's *Joseph Andrews* (1.11–13), the theme of charity is characterized by Parson Abraham Adams, whose recasting of the parable of the Good Samaritan stresses good works rather than faith. In various ways, eighteenth-century novelists were fascinated by the older idea that chastity can be integral to a higher order of love (e.g. Samuel Richardson's *Clarissa*). Most, however, in their nod-and-wink liberality were inclined to dismiss chastity in the end as a species of selfish prudery. Fielding's *Tom Jones*, a "man of good feeling," is far less plausibly a representative of chastity than Joseph Andrews. Rather, "no better than he should be," in Fielding's phrase, he progresses from wanton amours toward a kind of genteel cultural wisdom ("Sophie" Western), union with whom entails a presumably chaste marriage and a return from the decadence of worldly London to Paradise Hall. For Fielding, as for the latitudinarian divines, a little carnal mischief is infinitely to be preferred to the slightest whiff of "hypocrisy" or "affectation," which Fielding (in *Shamela* and *Tom Jones*) calls the source of the "truly ridiculous," the laughable but pitiable morality of self-love. Chastity, in short, has come to be identified as a species of cupidity.

William Cowper's long poem *Charity* is partly on the side of Whitefield (whom he admired). This is perhaps unsurprising: Cowper was a convert from the broad churchmanship of the latitudinarians of his day to the evangelical movement, influenced initially by the Methodists and subsequently nurtured by his pastor, the converted slave-trader John Newton. Like Hannah More's "Ode to Charity" of the same period, Cowper's poem predictably associates charity less with outward actions of benevolence—though these are discussed in detail—than with his personal experience of grace, an inward peace of relationship with God which overflows into loving actions toward humanity. And if More's more pragmatic view of charity is barely tacit in her poem (she was in fact energetic in founding and funding charity schools for children), in the palpably Calvinist Cowper (a virtual recluse) it becomes apostrophized. Like More, Cowper invokes Charity as a muse by whose guidance he will write her praise, lest a writer's vanities should obscure so high a subject, "whether we name thee Charity or Love." But like the latitudinarians who first formed his ideas, Cowper takes up the theme of the *socius*, or neighbor, first: "God, working ever on a social plan, / By various ties attaches man to man" (15–16). His odd "hero" of charity is the explorer Cook, who:

> [. . .] lamented, and with tears as just
> As ever mingled with heroic dust—
> Steer'd Britain's oak into a world unknown,

And in his country's glory sought his own,
Wherever he found man, to nature true,
The rights of man were sacred in his view.
He sooth'd with gifts, and greeted with a smile,
The simple native of the new-found isle. [. . .] (23–30)

Cook's antithesis, for Cowper an icon for *cupiditas*, is Cortez, "odious for a
world enslav'd." "Mammon makes the world his legatee," he continues: the
ugly slave trade is "most degrading of all ills, that wait / On man" (155–56)
and an epitome of all that defiles charity and a Christian name" (179–217).
For Cowper, clearly convicted by his pastor Newton's preaching on the matter, this sordid trade is the effect of innate depravity, which revelation (if not
reason) shows to be the true opponent of charity (337–44); Socrates therefore must be corrected by Scripture:

Philosophy, without his heave'nly guide,
May blow up self-conceit, and nourish pride;
But, while his province is the reas'ning part,
Has still a veil of midnight on his heart;
'Tis truth divine, exhibited on earth,
Gives Charity her being and her birth. (373–78)

Here he means *agapê,* charity in the older sense, which is then celebrated in
an extended paraphrase of 1 Corinthians 13 (412–34), and his point is that
such a self-effacing love is not a virtue naturally conceived as a product of
reason, but rather supernaturally conceived as a product of revelation. True
Christian charity must therefore be distinguished from the mere giving of
alms (447–68); indeed, the motivation for "subscription" from wealthy
donors is suspect (469–84), and even what sum is collected "the office clips
as it goes." For what is commonly called "charity" to be meritorious, and not
merely proud affectation, vanity, or guilty hypocrisy, it must be an overflow-
ing of *caritas:*

No works shall find acceptance, in that day
When all disguises shall be rent away,
That square not truly with the scripture plan,
Nor spring from love to God, or love to man. [. . .]
True charity, a plant divinely nurs'd,
Fed by the love from which it rose at first,
Thrives against hope; and, in the rudest scene,
Storms but enliven its unfading green;

> Exub'rant is the shadow it supplies;
> Its fruit on earth, its growth above the skies. (557–60; 573–78)

What Cowper wishes to do, evidently, is to affirm Whitefield's "charity" against that of the Anglican latitudinarians, rooting the meaning of charity in the primary relationship between the individual and God rather than between the individual and his society. In this he was consistent with the raison d'être of "charitable" social reforms among the eighteenth-century Methodists and even with the usage of closet-Catholic Christopher Smart, in whose (most charitable) poetry charity is a reflex of gratitude, the root of all virtues (cf. Aquinas):

> Thus in high heaven charity is great,
> Faith, hope, devotion hold a lower place;
>   On her the cherubs and the seraphs wait,
>   Her, every virtue courts, and every grace;
>   See! on the right, close by th' Almighty's throne,
>   In him she shines content, who came to make her
>   known.
> Deep-rooted in my heart then let her grow,
> That for the past the future may atone;
>   That I may act what thou hast giv'n to know,
>   That I may live for THEE and THEE alone,
>   And justify those sweetest words from heav'n,
> "THAT HE SHALL LOVE THEE MOST TO WHOM
> THOU'ST MOST FORGIVEN."[19]

Smart said elsewhere, in more medieval fashion than perhaps he knew: "For I have translated in the charity, which makes things / better & I shall be translated myself at the last" (*Jubilate Agno* Frg. B1 11). But desire to achieve the goals of charity as social benevolence without the encumbrance of religious characterizations of personal responsibility was growing stronger. The term itself, because of its persistent association with Christian virtue, became increasingly problematic for those who wished to pursue a secular social agenda. Jeremy Bentham, with his plan to reform the British Poor Law in 1795 and with his plans to create a modern welfare state, is one of those who found "charity" *ab initio* a distasteful and even demeaning term. For Bentham, the function of a "national charity company" is not to dispense kindness or generosity, but rather to accord basic human rights.[20]

For the most part, Romantic poetry had likewise shown little interest in charity defined as benevolence or alms. On the other hand, love is a primary subject for the Romantics, both in its divine and human modes of expression. William Wordsworth's very conception of the poet, in his preface to *Lyrical Ballads with Pastoral and Other Poems*, is "the rock of defence of human nature; an upholder and preserver, carrying everywhere with him relationship and love."[21] But the "love" of Romantic poetry is hard to identify with the *agapê* or *caritas* of Christian tradition; even when it draws upon mystical Christian writers like Jacob Boehme, Romantic "love" is rather the integrative force binding the disparities of individual and community experience together in a comprehension, however vaguely formulated, of the divine purpose in Creation. To this ideal of love, narrow *Selbheit* (Boehme) or *Ichheit* (Schelling) is still, like self-centeredness, the technical opposite to unitive love.[22] But the means by which the Romantic poet transcends his ego is not worship; it is what Percy Shelley calls "the expression of the imagination." In his *Defence of Poetry*,

> The great secret of morals is love, or a going out of our own nature and an identification of ourselves with the beautiful which exists in thought, action, or person, not our own. A man, to be greatly good, must imagine intensely and comprehensively; he must put himself in the place of another and of many others; the pains and pleasures of his species must become his own. The great instrument of moral good is the imagination. [. . .] Poetry enlarges the circumference of the imagination.[23]

In other words, the "good" and hence heroic person manifests love not in active works of benevolence or alms, but rather—in a curious but perhaps predictable sentimentalizing of the latitudinarians and Methodists both—by vicarious imagination of the plight of the less fortunate. Many people had begun to experience a sufficient glow of virtue in the wringing of hands. Meanwhile, in the usage of Romantic poets, Shelley and Byron in particular, "love" covers "a multitude of sins," often by becoming a name for many of them. If Samuel Taylor Coleridge takes *philia* ("friendship") to be the paradigm for "love," Shelley is more visceral. As he puts it:

> [. . .] that profound and complicated sentiment which we call love [. . .] is rather the universal thirst for a communion not merely of the senses but of our whole nature, intellectual, imaginative, and sensitive. [. . .] This want grows more powerful in proportion to the development which our nature receives from civilization, for man never ceases to be a social being. The sexual impulse, which is only one and often a small part of these claims, serves from its obvious and external nature as a kind of type or expression of the rest, as common basis, an acknowledged and visible link.[24]

Thus, according to M. H. Abrams:

> In the broad Romantic application of the term love [. . .] all modes of
> human attraction are conceived as one in kind, different only in object and
> degree, in a range which includes the relations of lover to beloved, children
> to parents, brother to sister, friend to friend, and individual to humanity.
> The orbit of love was often enlarged to include the relationship of man to
> nature as well.[25]

Here we have returned to the Greek *erôs*. Augustine's basic distinction *cari-
tas/cupiditas* is accordingly by this point not only badly blurred but in some
instances hierarchically reversed. Further, the laissez-faire morality of Shelley
or Byron, increasingly self-interested, comes to have its counterpart in
broader social terms, leading writers such as Thomas Carlyle (in *Past and
Present*) to lament "our present system of individual Mammonism" in which
"cash payment is [. . .] the sole nexus of man with man." None of this has
to do with love, Carlyle insists, only with the lust of meaner desires.[26] Each
of these developments complicates thought about "charity" for Victorian
Christians, without doing much to clarify cupidity or other contrastive vices.
Charity thus becomes what Matthew Arnold would call a "problem," even as
the narcissistic pleasures of vicarious identification with the unfortunate
tend to produce ethically evasive exegesis. An example is provided by John
Ruskin, who writes:

> You know how often it is difficult to be wisely charitable, to do good with-
> out multiplying the sources of evil. You know that to give alms is nothing
> unless you give thought also; and that therefore it is written, not "blessed is
> he that *feedeth* the poor," but "blessed is he that *considereth* the poor." And
> you know that a little thought and a little kindness are often worth more
> than a great deal of money. Now this charity of thought is not to be exer-
> cised toward all men. There is assuredly no action of our social life, howev-
> er unimportant, which, by kindly thought, may not be made to have a
> beneficial influence upon others; and it is impossible to spend the smallest
> sum of money, for any not absolutely necessary purpose, without a grave
> responsibility attaching to the manner of spending it. (*Lectures on
> Architecture and Painting* 43)

Ruskin goes on to talk about fiscal prudence in relation to social ethics,
about whether "the sum we are going to spend will do as much good spent in
this way as it would if spent in any other way" (*Lectures on Architecture and*

Painting 44). But Ruskin is not able to do much more than to indicate succinctly the self-serving rationalizations anticipated by Jeremy Bentham:

> We have heard only too much lately of "indiscriminate charity," with implied reproval, not of the Indiscrimination merely, but of the Charity also. We have partly succeeded in enforcing on the minds of the poor the idea that it is disgraceful to receive; and are likely, without too much difficulty, to succeed in persuading not a few of the rich that it is disgraceful to give. (*Munera Pulveris*, App. 6)

Charles Dickens, in his *A Christmas Carol*, set out to contrast cupidity and charity in terms practical enough that the dangerous ephemerality of this debate should become clear, but he had only limited success. In such an environment, "charity" was soon to give *caritas* a thoroughly bad name. George Bernard Shaw, a Fabian Socialist, was among those who later rejected the very concept as misnomer, exploring as alternative values the grand idealism of a Christian socialist clergyman in *Candida*, and a naive but well-motivated Salvation Army charity in *Major Barbara*—a play which not only satirizes the disguising of self-interest as "duty," but teaches that "poverty is the worst of crimes" and that the *lack* of money is the root of all evil. Shaw's impatience with traditional Christian notions of charity surfaces again in *The Intelligent Woman's Guide to Capitalism and Socialism.*[27]

In retrospect, we can see that the Romantics' strong desire to find in idealized love (*amor/erôs*) the unifying and integrating of all experience soon became notoriously side-tracked into erotic confusions of that purpose. Yet their idealism persists in a significant strain of religious as well as secular poetry. The erotic mysticism of Christina Rosetti, with its theme of the spectral bride or bridegroom (*The Hour and the Ghost, The Ghost's Petition*), and her sublimation of sexual desire as the pilgrim's longing for "a better country" (cf. Heb 11:13–16) in *Marvel of Marvels* and *Passing away, saith the World* lend to the traditional medieval language of *caritas* eerily erotic overtones precisely inverse in their function to the de-eroticizing allegories of the Song of Songs by earlier interpreters such as Origen and St. Bernard of Clairvaux. Coventry Patmore's post-conversion poetry (he became a Catholic in 1864) similarly blurs *agapê* and *erôs* (e.g., *The Unknown Eros* [1877]) to the point where his spiritual advisers finally asked him to destroy a long MS, his *Sponsa Dei*, in which the confusion had apparently become full identification.

The orthodox Christian English poet of the modern period has thus had at least two misprisions to answer. These are the Enlightenment tendency to split charity as benevolence to the neighbor off from its roots in *caritas* as love directed toward God above all things, and the Romantic and post-Romantic tendency to dissolve the distinction in a notion of cosmic love so ambiguous that *erôs* or *cupiditas* can be construed as a kind of divine worship (cf. D. H. Lawrence's *Apocalypse*). Among more orthodox poets one dominant strategy has emerged: to try to re-establish the vertical or hierarchical relation of the precepts of the Great Commandment so that, in typical Augustinian fashion, *caritas* in the community of men and women becomes comprehensible only in terms of its governance by each person's prior love for God. Thus John Keble's "Charity the Life of Faith" (in *The Christian Year* [1827]) takes as its epigraph 1 John 3:13–14: "We know that we have passed from death unto life, because we love the brethren." The test of regeneration, the presence of supreme love for God and not self, is characterized axiomatically by love for those who love him, as also for those God loves (John 3:16). To love in this way is, in effect, to love Christ himself both in his divine and human nature (Matt 25: 31–46):

> Wouldst thou the life of souls discern?
> Nor human wisdom nor divine
> Helps thee by aught beside to learn:
> Love is life's only sign.
> The spring of the regenerate heart,
> The pulse, the glow of every part,
> Is the true love of Christ our Lord,
> As man embrac'd, as God ador'd.[28]

But this is what T. S. Eliot also says in *The Four Quartets*. The "liberation" from cupiditous "attachment to self and to things and to persons," he writes, lies in a type of love which is "not less of love but expanding / Of love beyond desire, and so liberation / From the future as well as the past" ("Little Gidding" 3). When this love is shared abroad Eliot suggests, then, all people, even Englishmen like those who fought bloody (religious) civil wars, will be "folded in a single party," and "All manner of thing shall be well / By the purification of our motive / In the ground of our beseeching" ("Little Gidding" 3). In other words, on that day when self-effacing love at last holds sway, desire itself shall be redeemed.

(1991)

Chapter Five

The Gospel according to Isaiah

I will also give thee for a light to the Gentiles, that thou mayest be my salvation unto the end of the earth.

Isaiah 49:6, KJV

In 1941, a Philadelphia Presbyterian minister named C. E. Macartney conducted a poll to see whom his local fellow Christians thought to be "the ten greatest men in the Bible." Isaiah came eighth on this list—not, presumably, on account of any record of his life (there is none), but on the strength alone of the book that bears his name. The opinion of prewar Philadelphia Presbyterians, it turns out, was remarkably consonant with the opinion of earlier ages. Moreover, it tallies with that of the postwar generation in every Christian denomination from Catholics to the Salvation Army. But the Isaiah who loomed in the imagination of the Presbyterians, suggests John F. A. Sawyer, may bear surprisingly little relationship to the Isaiah cherished by either medieval or postmodern theologians.[1] The "fifth Gospel," it appears, has been an unusually protean text, warm wax in the hands of many a maker of images.

Though Sawyer does not stress it, there is nonetheless a strong thread that binds most of the diversity together: messianism. Divergence among interpreters through the centuries is usually about what messianic deliverance might mean.

A quick overview helps establish the point. For Saint Jerome, Isaiah "should be called an evangelist rather than a prophet because he describes all the mysteries of Christ and the Church so clearly that you would think he is composing a history of what has already happened rather than prophesying about what is to come."[2] Saint Ambrose and his star pupil, Saint Augustine,

75

echo this view, emphasizing additionally Isaiah's role in "the calling of the Gentiles." The Wycliffe Bible Prologue follows suit ("not only a profete but more, a Gospellere"), and so, with varying emphasis, do the Reformation writers Martin Luther and John Calvin, for whom, above all, "the word of God abides forever."

Jewish traditions also feature Isaiah centrally, not only in lectionaries— in which, at least, since the Middle Ages, about half of all *haftaroth* (weekly readings from the prophets) come from this book—but particularly in Zionist writings since the nineteenth century and visibly on Holocaust memorials such as the magnificently somber Yad v'shem in Jerusalem (cf. Isa 56:5), where the emphasis is on the restoration of Israel. And for quite other purposes Isaiah is a staple of Catholic liberation theologians and "swords into plowshares" revolutionaries such as Daniel and Philip Berrigan, as well as of feminist theologians like Susanne Heine, Phyllis Trible, Rosemary Radford Reuther, and Dorothee Soelle.

Of the two works reviewed here, Sawyer's is the book most useful for reflection on these hermeneutical questions, simply because it is a history of the interpretation of Isaiah in Christianity. Sawyer believes that the myriad formal commentaries on Isaiah in our own time are often barren with respect to the affective power of this richly poetic part of Scripture; obsession with "the original meaning of the original text" has blinded the commentators to the value of a rich interpretative tradition found not only in earlier formal commentaries, but in preaching down the centuries, in hymns and other music, and in art and literature. What Sawyer offers as antidote is a lively and cross-disciplinary *Rezeptionsgeschichte*, a review of how Isaiah has been understood and, especially, *used* by its Christian readers. As a variant on reader-response criticism, the primary source material for a contextualizing of Isaiah's text is these past readings "in preference to archaeology and ancient near-eastern parallels."[3] The result is an impressive scholarly resource, sobering in its implications for exegetes, and at the same time an entertaining and culturally enriching *survoler* of the development of certain aspects of Christian theology.

Sawyer is less interested in theory than in what he calls the "empirical dimension" of textual interpretation. Consistently, he has attempted a descriptive (if selective) rather than evaluative study. While it is clear that he himself has been involved in feminist and interfaith appropriations of Isaiah, for the most part he steers commendably close to his stated attempt of an "objective" reporting. Sawyer's guiding conviction, however—that we ought to be free to select from the full range of interpretation history a "meaning" for the text "more effective in its context, or more beautiful, or more histori-cally significant, or indeed more ethically acceptable than the original" (here he cites Elizabeth Schüssler Fiorenza)—need not be shared in order for the reader to appreciate the value of his comparatist approach.

To wit: the early church, patristic writers, medieval church, and Reformation writers saw each, in their turn, elements in Isaiah's prophetic witness that to some degree were not noticed as forcefully by Christian readers in other times and places. We, in our turn, now have available to us a compendium of insight—a fuller, richer, and more complete appreciation of a text too polysemous to yield itself completely to any singular reading.

The earliest Christian interpreters used Isaiah primarily to authorize their mission to the Gentiles. This is already evident in Romans 14–15, where Saint Paul cites the "root of Jesse" image from Isaiah 11:10 (rather than Isa 11:1), presumably because in the context he is less concerned with the human ancestry of Jesus than he is with pointing to him "who rises to rule the Gentiles; in him shall the Gentiles hope" (Rom 15:13). And such promises persist: Paul's evangelical emphasis returns in a refractory fashion in the nineteenth century, when a reference to the "land of Sinim" (Isa 49:12) provided missionaries to China with a motto, and mission hymnody could refer to the overcoming of pagan bondage with Isaiah 45:2, 14, 23, "Lift up your heads, ye gates of brass," and "To Christ shall every nation bow."

Patristic writers emphasize (as later, for other reasons, did Northrop Frye) the counterintuitive literary unity of Isaiah, a unity grounded less in overt design than in an astonishingly accurate spiritual prefigurement of salvation history. Sawyer himself gives three pages of running excerpts from Isaiah that so perfectly outline the gospel narrative as to arrest the most jaded reader.[4] He does not take up a related issue—the manner of the book's division into chapters in the thirteenth century. I have myself often wondered whether the chapter divisions introduced by Archbishop of Canterbury Stephen Langton were not calculated in such a fashion as to express this unity. Do Isaiah's 66 chapters, in a synecdoche of the 66 canonical books of the Bible, prefigure, in their central division, the two testaments—the first part ending on a dour note at the end of chapter 39 (with Hezekiah's witless invitation to Israel's destruction) and chapter 40 commencing the 27-chapter announcement of the Good News of consolation, restoration, and reconciliation? For a book that comprises so many genres and layers, Isaiah has, on many counts, an astonishing capacity to project the unity of the larger biblical anthology.

The fathers, however, had no chapter divisions. Typology was their preoccupation. Exegetes such as Augustine and Jerome emphasized reference to the Virgin Birth (Isa 7:14), the Sanctus (6:3), the Suffering Servant (52:13, ch. 53) or "Man of Sorrows" of later medieval art, certain elements of medieval angelology, such as the six-winged seraph (Isa 6), and the messianic prophecies for which they found echoes in Vergil's *Eclogue* 4. These readers of the early Church and later antiquity were the first to regard the ox and the ass at the manger (Isa 1:3) as prophetic of Jesus' birth—and thus to instaurate an iconographic tradition familiar to every Christian through painting and Christmas cards: "The ox knows its owner and the ass its master's crib; but Israel does not know, my people do not understand."

Later on, Isaiah also played a key role in the establishment and development of the cult of Mary. In late medieval and Renaissance Annunciation paintings, Mary is typically found reading Isaiah 7:14 (in Latin) at the moment Gabriel arrives to announce the Messiah's conception; it is not unusual, as in the Isenheim altarpiece of Matthias Grünewald, to show Isaiah hovering in the background (here he holds his text in the "original Hebrew" for comparison), and Isaiah often appears alongside Mary in early Christian art. In the *Bible moralisée* of the thirteenth century, Isaiah points to the Virgin Mary in a rocky wilderness holding a lamb in her arms (Isa 51:1); the motif may have been adapted by Leonardo da Vinci in his *Madonna of the Rocks* in the Louvre. Much later, Isaiah 61:10 was prescribed as the introitus to the mass for the Feast of the Immaculate Conception, instituted by Pope Pius IX in 1854. More problematically, alas, Isaiah has even been employed in the promotion of anti-Semitism.

Sawyer is properly concerned with the history of anti-Semitic Isaiah interpretation not only in the Middle Ages (e.g., Isidore of Seville's seventh-century *De Fide Catholica ex Veteri et Novo Testamento contra Judaeos*) but in the eighteenth and nineteenth centuries as well. While the "ox knows his owner, the ass his master's crib" invites a charming Christmas typology, the prophet's next line has been wielded in such a way as to undo the charm: "Israel, my people, knows nothing" (Isa 1:3). Suddenly the image, like the veiled Synagoga that appears opposite Ecclesia in medieval church portals, can seem to have become dangerously polemical.

Martin Luther best illustrates the special interest of the Reformation in Isaiah, not in any abandonment of anti-Semitism, but in his choosing three new emphases. These are: (1) "the Word of God abides forever" (Isa 40:6–8), which for Luther (though not Calvin) means narrowly the text of Scripture *ipsum*; (2) a declamation against idolatry (Isa 41:7; 44:9–10), here focusing especially on biblical art, especially art representing the Virgin Mary; and (3) the importance of education: "all thy children will be taught of the LORD" (Isa 54:13).[5] The Reformer thus, like Jerome, sees Isaiah as privileged among the prophets, but for quite different reasons. Isaiah is no longer primarily the prophet of the nativity or of the Virgin Mary or of the Suffering Messiah, but preeminently the champion of truth in an unjust society. The principal text is 40:8; Luther encouraged his followers to embroider it upon their sleeves (cf. Deut 6:8). Sawyer sees a clear link between Luther's emphasis and that of the Second Vatican Council's *Dogmatic Constitution on Divine Revelation* (*Dei Verbum*, Nov. 18, 1965), though he notes that verses 6–8 are still omitted from the prescribed Catholic readings for the second Sunday in Advent, as well as from related Catholic hymns (not to mention all other modern lectionaries).

Evangelicals should find it a matter for careful reflection that Luther is inspirational for the kind of unranked interpretative pluralism Sawyer champions. The starting place is Scripture, but the platform is really one's own interpretation:

> When one considers that for Luther 'the word of God stands forever,' [. . .] one cannot help comparing this constant recourse to Isaiah 40:8 with his most famous axiom 'Here I stand [. . .]' 40:8 expresses his passionate belief that God has revealed to him the true meaning of the Bible.[6]

Accordingly, Sawyer suggests, evangelicals have been idiosyncratic in their more individualistic use of Isaiah. John Wesley uses it hardly at all, while the great Baptist preacher Charles Spurgeon makes a wide and imaginative use of Isaiah throughout his sermons. On the other hand, there are predictable hallmark affections: Isaiah figures as prominently in *The Song Book of the Salvation Army* as in the rhetoric of the liberation theologians.

Perhaps the most interesting cultural appropriation of Isaiah occurs in art and literature, which get rather skimpy treatment here, despite Sawyer's proper insistence on their importance. Part of the value of this perspective, it seems to me, is revealed in the way art and literature in the modern period tend to highlight popular *abuse* of Scripture. One thinks, for example, of Herman Melville's *White Jacket*, where mid-nineteenth-century Americans might too readily confirm a triumphalist (and secularizing) prejudice that Isaiah himself would most obviously have deplored:

> [W]e Americans are the peculiar, chosen people—the Israel of our time; we bear the ark of the liberties of the world [. . .] The political Messiah has come. But he had come in us [. . .]. [Our] national selfishness is unbounded philanthropy; for we cannot do a good to America but we give alms to the world.[7]

Yet on such points Sawyer is less steady than he might be. He thinks, for example, that Isaiah might have scrupled to find distorting the Quaker poet

John Greenleaf Whittier's removal of "justice" from Isaiah 45:8, substituting for it "quietness":

> Drop thy still dews of quietness,
> Till all our strivings cease;
> Take from our souls the strain and stress,
> And let our ordered lives confess
> The beauty of thy peace. ("The Brewing of Soma," 76–80)

In fact, prophet and poet are both misrepresented in this instance. Neither the Hebrew text (*tsedeq*) nor the KJV translation used by Whittier ("righteousness") uses the word *justice* at all (nor do RSV, JPS, etc.). More pertinently, there is no plausible evocation of Isaiah anywhere in Whittier's lovely hymn: Whittier's work is a prayer for God's peace such as settled in the hearts of those who heard Jesus teach "beside the Syrian sea"; his line "Drop thy still dews of quietness" (not, as in Isaiah, "Drop down, ye heavens") invokes, in fact, a host of Old Testament references to the salubrious teaching of God (Deut 32:2; 33:28), by whose knowledge "the clouds drop down the dew" (Prov 3:20) and whose very presence with his people shall in the time of their return to him descend upon them in blessing "as the dew" (Hos 14:5).

Such a double misrepresentation is not a good way for Sawyer to make his point about the value of literary interpretation of Isaiah, or to raise the query, valid in itself, that follows immediately upon this unfortunate example. What he wants to ask is: are we entitled to pray for peace while we evade the question of justice? Undeniably this *is* a question with which the book of Isaiah is directly concerned from the very beginning (e.g., 1:1–20).

This is also the question that prompts Daniel Berrigan in *Isaiah: Spirit of Courage, Gift of Tears*,[8] and to it his answer is uncompromisingly negative. Berrigan's book is not in the least an academic. It is rather an extended sermon, and inasmuch as Isaiah provides his text, it is by way of highly idiosyncratic selection, editing, and imaginative translating (excerpts from the New Jerusalem Bible with alterations heavily subtended by Phyllis Trible). Berrigan chooses from amongst the prophet's concerns one above all to feature. He got his own "prophetic" start as a Jesuit antiwar protester. Unlike many activists from the Vietnam War era, he has stayed the course; his "Plowshares community" in the inner city of New York is characterized by social action against the "military industrial complex" in matters both of practical compassion and public disturbance. (No quietist he.) Berrigan's key text is that which also captivates liberation theologians of the ilk of José

Porfirio Miranda, Gustavo Gutierrez, and Norbert Lohfink: "They will beat their swords into plowshares, their spears into pruning knives. Nevermore war—never again!" (cf. Isa 2:4).

Berrigan's Isaiah ranks much more highly than eighth among great personalities of the Bible. He is a kind of superhero—almost himself messianic—a visionary who "refused to separate public responsibility from the voice of God within."[9] No more *nâvî'*, simply a mouthpiece for the word of the Lord, he "becomes the measure of our own possibility of seeing, hearing, understanding with the heart, of being healed."[10] For Berrigan, "the 'holy' lives in Isaiah and in those who, like him, take the word of God seriously."

In Berrigan's case, taking the word of God seriously means taking your own appropriation of it seriously enough to attack military hardware with hammers and, further, rejecting the Catholic church's ecclesiastical authority in the constraint of such actions. His troubled reflections on the theological and ethical complexity of such appropriations of authority may, however, seem eerily familiar to students of Reformation history (cf. Roland Bainton's biography of Luther). Berrigan muses about the consequences of going perhaps too far: "[A]n anathema is inevitable. You presume for yourself the word of God, immemorially entrusted to priesthood and temple. Dare you thus blaspheme?"[11]

Well for better or for worse, he dares. "Do not imagine that some magic or other will beat the world's swords into plowshares,"[12] he writes. "You yourselves must act." He reviles the "just-war nonsense" of past and present moral theologians, and the dispiriting evasions of "preachers of an American pseudo-gospel and the tempests of secular culture, by turns enticing and brutal, [which] all but swamp us."[13] In Berrigan's United States,

> Sometime shortly after the Civil War, the strange gods of empire entered the land with a rush. It was the beginning of an apocalypse of power and dominion—and ruin. We have never succeeded in casting off that foreign spirit that holds us in tight bondage.[14]

In consequence, America is for him no new Israel but "a Babylon become our native land," a society governed by "megamachinery of untruth":

> In an election year the airwaves and video waves heat up. Promises, promises pollute the air; glib henchmen utter their foolishness, the media echo like a cave of bats—mewings, strokings, choler, anger, vituperation, verbal abuse and scufflings, much dust flung about, no clarity. Bread and

circuses are expended broadside, money seduces and unsettles and buys and sells opinions and promises that are of absolutely no sense or worth.[15]

Berrigan writes well, and much of his eloquent diatribe (more reminiscent of Amos or Jeremiah) is close enough on the mark to make an honest reader squirm. Surely our culture is indeed naked before the just judgment of God, and surely, as he says, "the nations will one day see [. . .] that God is not the God of the big achievers and half-believers, but of the helpless, the needy, the victimized, the distressed"[16] (cf. Isa 24:4–5). Berrigan's experience in San Salvador lends pith to his passion. For him America is a land in which "Christians consider themselves justified by keeping the law"—the law, which exists, he believes, primarily to advantage the holding of property and the amassing of wealth: "Sanctity, righteousness [. . .] are spurious. 'Under God,' as they say. Under God, and unjust."[17]

It is easy to imagine how many will have taken offense at Berrigan's accusations. He is no patriot, either, and that to some will be his least forgivable offense. On other grounds, his reflexive embrace of Trible's "Herself" renditions of the Servant Songs of Isaiah seems a defiance of orthodoxy more for the sake of defiance itself than out of concern for any kind of accountability to his text. Moreover, the targets of his own prophetic invective may seem a good deal more selective than the Book of Isaiah warrants. I for one do not see how any principled critique of violence in American culture can withhold criticism of television, cinema, and the pornographic Internet. And if one is to prophesy credibly against "the American culture of death" and be consistent with Isaiah, then abortion and euthanasia call for more than a phrase *en passant*. But all these reservations aside, I think contemporary Christians still need to reckon with Berrigan's criticism of the "faithful," in some of which, it seems to me, he is most faithful to Isaiah:

> There flourishes at large a hyper-spiritualized version of salvation. It is intensely concerned with self, with "rapture" (and the devil take the hindmost). Such salvation ferments, to all appearances, in the head only, a kind of pseudo-ecstasy, without cost or empathy or a sense of the suffering of the innocent. It is little concerned with our culture of death, or a critique of same, and much concerned with something known as the "afterlife."
>
> So understood, salvation also welcomes, without critique or second thought, assimilation into mainstream America (a polluted stream, if ever one flowed), into cultural attitudes toward women, money, success, ego, and, perhaps above all, violence. [. . .]
>
> Implied in this view is a quite clear conviction, a cultural one to be sure, that there is nothing seriously wrong with America. Quite the contrary, America is God's finest triumph.[18]

Sawyer's book lacks the passion of Berrigan's, even as it has over it a decisive advantage as scholarship. For all that, these books sit fairly comfortably side by side on the shelf. Both teach us important things about the witness of Scripture within and without the church; each is limited by a curiously common failure to see that, for all of the partiality in interpretation in every place and time, the common threads that run through the fabric of our historic understanding are not only many, but most are persistently visible and anchoring.

I think of the converted slave trader John Newton, for example, author of the now universal hymn "Amazing Grace." In a series of thirty-eight sermons Newton took up, Sunday by Sunday, the texts featured in the libretto to Handel's *Messiah* (then enjoying a successful rerun at Westminster). Many of Handel's texts, of course, are from Isaiah, and in his treatment of them, Newton hits on almost all of the emphases that Sawyer places, reasonably, along a historical line of development. It is true that Newton does not anticipate the "immanentizing of God" so prominent among some of the liberation theologians (he would have regarded this as a hideous, blasphemous self-arrogation), but long before contemporary feminists, he corrects a mistranslation of Isaiah 40:9 to note that "the publisher of these good tidings is written with a feminine construction," and that it was customary in Israel "for the woman to publish and celebrate good news with songs and instrument." Appropriately, he instances Miriam's song, the women announcing David's victory, and Deborah's song of victory. "In my text," Newton writes, the prophet speaks proleptically the "Good News, glad tidings indeed! [. . .] The women are, therefore, called upon to proclaim his approach, on the tops of the hills and mountains, from whence they may be seen and heard to the greatest advantage, for the spreading of the tidings throughout the whole country."[19]

I do not mean to suggest, of course, that Newton qualifies in Trible's sense (or Sawyer's or Berrigan's) as a feminist. He has a very different order of relationship to the authority of Scripture as revelation, for one thing. But his application of the text makes use of a legitimate textual meaning, even if inferential, to extend the good news without distorting it, and his sense of the social meaning of Isaiah for us all will bear firm company with Berrigan's. All of which suggests that there is more consistency in the church's interpretation of Isaiah through the ages than has met the eye of either of our contemporary commentators. Just for the sake of perspective, let me give the old evangelical the last word—from the conclusion to one of his sermons on Isaiah:

> We call ourselves the followers and servant of him who was despised of men, and encompassed with sorrows. And shall we then "seek great things for ourselves," as if we belonged to the present world, and expected no

portion beyond it? Or shall we be tremblingly [sensitive] to the opinion of
our fellow-creatures and think it a great hardship if it be our lot to suffer
shame for his sake, who endured the cross, and despised the same for us?[20]

Well, these are after all the questions any honest reading of the gospel—
including Isaiah's "gospel"—will have to conjure with, and to answer. They
persist as Scripture persists, from age to age, our own preoccupations
notwithstanding.

(2000)

PART II

Scripture in the Houses of Art

Chapter Six

Authority and Interpretation in the *House of Fame*

Certe vides, fili hominis, quae seniores domus Israel faciunt in tenebris, unusquisque in abscondito cubiculi sui. . . ?

Ezekiel 8:12, Vulgate

I

In the work of England's greatest poet of the Middle Ages, allusion and textual interplay between the text of the Bible and Chaucer's own text is important not only at the levels of characterization, allusion, and literary humor, but at the level of structure as well. In this essay I want to turn to an earlier and not much studied poem in which some of the presuppositional issues of intertextuality and interpretation are interrogated by Chaucer himself, and in which the issue of categorical authority, so basic to medieval assumptions about Scripture, is openly essayed by the poet in respect of two obvious alternatives, personal experience and diversionary fiction. It is of more than passing interest to the scriptural aspect of our study that this relatively early poem is Chaucer's most "eschatological" and visionary, and that, like the *Canterbury Tales,* it gives a deliberate appearance of being incomplete.

The year 1378 in which *House of Fame* was written seemed to many to be full of apocalyptic portent. The papacy, symbol of divinely sanctioned authority par excellence, had two claimants—one in Rome, the other in Avignon. The Great Schism, as it was called, the exceedingly bloody contestation between Pope Urban VI in Rome and Anti-pope Clement VII in Avignon, shook the faith of many in the authority of the Church. There were ugly wars of pillage and vengeful conquest, such as Bishop Spencer of Norwich's campaign of rapine in the lowlands, and even after Urban's excommunication of Clement in November of that year and assertion of supremacy, it was possible for pillars of support for papal authority such as Phillippe de Mezieres to refer to Urban as "more cruel than a serpent, Herod or Antiochus" and for the remark to be received widely as a just appraisal. When John Wyclif began his series of lectures at Oxford on the truth and authority of Scripture in that same turbulent year, uncertainty about the authority of the current papacy was part of the context for the extraordinary interest his lectures occasioned. In such a context, merely to give a major course of lectures on the authority of Scripture was to make implicit commentary on the evident lack of authority in the Church.

Like Wyclif, Chaucer was a protégé of John of Gaunt, regent protector of the boy-king Richard II, and thus well aware that public confidence concerning authority in the state was rendered even more precarious in the light of the catastrophic erosions of authority in the Church. His poetry was written for the Court effectively presided over by Gaunt, an audience literarily sophisticated, politically wary and used to indirect discourse as a means of conducting debate. It was a time of rising nationalistic independence, and not the least element in the courtly audience's understanding of Chaucer's work pertains to it having been composed in English rather than French—a possibility which had existed for less than a decade since the death of the monolingual francophone King Edward III.

The plot of the *House of Fame* is at one level simple: the poet persona, troubled in his spirit, falls asleep and dreams a dream in which he is in a glass temple in the deserts of North Africa, gazing at fresco paintings of the legendary Fall of Troy and exile-pilgrimage of Rome's founders. He has trouble, however, identifying his own history with that pictured—the usual typological connections do not suffice to lend meaning to his own experience. So he exits the temple into the surrounding desert, only to be snatched aloft by a talkative eagle who carries him up into the very heavens. There he encounters the celestial House of Fame, a kind of recording library of history, with its outer Court of Rumor. He is distressed to learn that even at this altitude there is no guarantee concerning what is retained in the annals of history, either that the meaning of history is intelligible or that the judgments of history are reliable. After three books the poem breaks off, just as Chaucer's dream-self Geoffrey begins to notice the only human beings he has encountered in his entire vision; in the midst of a great clamour for attention there suddenly arises a commanding presence, "a man of great authority [. . .]."

The structure of the *House of Fame* has always seemed to be both familiar and enigmatic. The familiar elements are its ordered construction, three parts, and a progressive education of the dreamer such as is characteristic of the dream vision genre. Enigma arises initially from the fact that although the poem is ordered, it is formally incomplete, apparently frustrated of any satisfying answer to its persona's last questions. The typical modern reader is thus puzzled in attempting to interpret Chaucer's text. The poem follows a traditional pattern of design—a three-stage ascent toward understanding. It invites careful reading according to that traditional framework, and in almost every respect encourages the reader to anticipate such an intellectual journey as he or she might find in Augustine, Bonaventure, Dante, or Chaucer's own *Book of the Duchess*. But by the time one reaches what is merely the "end" of this poem (rather than, formally, its conclusion), something has gone awry with the expected itinerary, and the reader (or "hearer") is left on an aesthetic precipice. Along with a fair number of sympathetic critics over the years, one might perhaps take the apparently fragmented work to be a bit of a blight upon Chaucer's reputation, perhaps isolate and catalogue some of its typology, locate it "ortho-culturally," and then forget about its apparent structural incoherence. But there is reason to be more careful: Chaucer assaults us at the outset with a very stern warning against misjudgment of this poem. Calling down a fullsome blessing on those who "take hit wel and skorne hyt noght,"[1] he further invokes a comprehensive curse on those who "misdemen" it:

> And whoso thorgh presumpcion,
> Or hate, or skorn, or thorgh envye,
> Dispit, or jape or vilanye,
> Mysdeme hyt, pray I Jesus God
> That dreme he barefot, dreme he shod,
> That every harm that any man
> Hath had, syth the world began,
> Befalle hym therof, or he sterve,
> And graunte he mote hit ful deserve,
> Lo, with such a conclusion
> As had of his avision
> Cresus, that was kyng of Lyde,
> That high upon a gebet dyde! (94–106)

This harsh warning against misreading of his poem is unique in Chaucer, and, focused as it is on the "conclusion" of a famously obtuse exegete, King Croesus (see *Monk's Tale*, 2740ff.), it is surely intended to focus our attention more thoughtfully on the structure and interpretation of his crafted "avision."

It might seem incongruous in this context that Chaucer's persona, "Geffrey," should begin his dream in an encounter with the venerable story of Troy. Troy was the stuff of cliché, and could seem almost to invite the insufficient reflection against which we are warned. The history of Aeneas had become fundamental to secular story in Western literature, from Vergil himself, and Ovid, but principally through the numerous and varied adaptations, translations, and commentaries on the matter of Troy which so dominated secular literature from the twelfth to the fourteenth centuries. Chaucer himself recurs to this material for plot or story in a number of his other poems, including, of course, *Troilus and Criseyde* and the *Knight's Tale.*

In these narratives, the protagonists are ostensibly characters in a Trojan/Roman drama; the significances of their pseudo-historical actions for meaning contemporary with Chaucer's audience are inferred, if consciously "read out" at all, as axioms of conventional systems of cultural reference— usually political allegory. When we read such poems, it is usually clear that the "secular scripture" of classical Rome is being heavily invested with an intermediary text—underwritten, so to speak, by the sacred Scripture of Roman Christianity.[2] Dante's *Commedia* is perhaps the most famous instance of this conventional literary heterodoxy.

In the *House of Fame* the reader is not so easily permitted to enter into the conventional interpretation of the story, as though the poem were simply another adaptation or translation of the "matter" of Troy. The persona (closely identified with the author, rather than, as is usual in dream-vision, with the reader) intervenes in his narration with a self-consciousness calculated to purchase distance from the convention, and he makes the *artifice* of historical narrative (more than the "content" of the history) explicit to reader consciousness. For Geffrey is self-consciously a critical reader: he encounters the familiar Troy "history" as *art* external to his own life, just as, to Chaucer's own readers, Troy remains external to the narrative in which Geffrey himself is a character. In short, Chaucer presents his protagonist-persona as a fictive reader critically engaged in reflective exegesis of a text held to be foundational by his "actual" readers, allowing them, in turn, to "over-hear" the fictive reader struggle toward interpretation and meaning. As the actual readers (among whom we are numbered) begin to realize that the "temple of images" in which we reencounter the Troy story is situated in a desert, as "in the desert of Lybye," and remember that what Aeneas saw in the temple of Dido, before encountering her, is almost the same thing that Geffrey sees in his dream, story and interpretation (i.e., in this instance *Aeneid* and the *House of Fame*) are forcibly juxtaposed.

At the first level, what Geffrey sees is (apparently) what Aeneas saw: history as art, or artifice. The art describes a history with which both he and his author's audience are familiar: Geffrey can speed over a number of well-known details. Because of the fused horizons of narrative and interpretation

on which Chaucer has placed him, Geoffrey may especially omit the visit to
Dido's temple in his retelling. The parallel is more than obvious: Geffrey
appears initially as another Aeneas.

At another level, the forced juxtaposition of book 1 accomplishes two
additional functions, separate, yet integrally related in their establishment of
Chaucer's argument. First, the poet has made his readers acutely aware of
their actual separation from the original substance of any story they might
read—even a story familiar enough to have been welded into their sense of
present cultural identity, as unquestioned as cliché. For the story, like historical Troy itself, is other. It is then and there; the reader is here and now.
Secondly, the poet has invited his readers to measure against that real distance the apparent close congruence of his own and Vergil's purpose, especially as directed toward questions about art, interpretation, and history. By
pitting the device of an unpredictable persona-exegete against his readers'
comfortable possession of the Troy story in its traditional modes of interpretation, Chaucer *requires* us to be continuously aware that our present retelling is merely a version according to Geffrey. This deliberate
diminishment of his "own" authorial authority prepares us, accordingly, for
exploration of the main Vergilian point about meaning and justification in
the representative life of Aeneas. Instead of affirming the conventional conclusion of the story—in which Aeneas is brought on, despite distractions, to
his proper achievement as a "Rome-bearer"—Geffrey himself becomes dis-
tracted toward a different and contrasting center of meaning. What he sees,
at least when he reads Ovid's account of the matter, is unanswered questions
and unjustified action—the issue of betrayal and false-seeming as manifest in
Aeneas's notorious rejection of Dido.[3] At this complication, with the appeal
to another text, or another version (another way of reading the story), the
central intellectual tensions in Chaucer's poem begin to develop.

It seems possible, then, that the choice of the famous and familiar story
of Aeneas as a *status quaestionis* for his poem does not constitute a failure of
imagination on Chaucer's part, but that its very status as cliché makes it all
the more appropriate as a vehicle for the poem's *real* subject, which is, in fact,
innovatively contextualized in the title: *House of Fame*. The word "*fame*"
means for us (as it did for Vergil), chiefly "reputation." Up to the eighteenth
century, as for example in Dr. Johnson's *Dictionary*, the English word still
held its ancient meaning, "rumor," as well. Both these meanings are highly
visible in Chaucer's poem, and have received a good deal of comment.[4] But
in Chaucer's own time, *fame* had another meaning, one which, though now
obsolete, gets in fact a primary listing in the *Oxford English Dictionary*. It is
"public report," "story" received, or "true report." Thus Trevisa, in translating Ranulf Higden's *Polychronicon,* describes his submission to earlier

histories: "Me schall trowe old fame, þat is nought wipseide" (1.71). As a verb the word meant to "record for posterity" (cf. Lat. *famare*), and in medieval Latin *famen*, as in its early Greek counterpart, preserved the sense of historical utterance, record, or simply *word*. None of these meanings— reputation, rumor, received history—is singular, nor to be separated from the others in an attempt to understand the title of Chaucer's poem, especially in view of the occasion, or initial matter Chaucer sets before us in book 1.

For one thing, the "fame of Aeneas" had had, to Chaucer's time, an enormous role in the development of Christian historiography. As B. G. Koonce has shown, in the earliest development of the *romans* as a genre, from the translation and adaptations of Roman story represented by *Aeneas,* the *Thebiad* and the *Roman de Troie* in the mid-twelfth century to the characterization of the good *christes milites* in Chrétien de Troyes or other Arthurian romances, there had been a strong component in these adaptations of Vergilian *pietas* and concern for *fama*. Among the signal themes in Christian "histories" of Britain such as Geoffrey of Monmouth's *Historia,* or Layamon's *Brut,* these values continued to be observed as "ideals" in Chaucer's lifetime, as, for example, in *Sir Gawain and the Green Knight,* and after him, even in the collections of Sir Thomas Malory. Every student of medieval literature is aware that the story of Troy and Christian "readings" of medieval history are so intertwined, both in structure and motif, that they remain nearly inseparable from the time of Augustine until the "rewritings" of history which took place during the Reformation, when men such as the appropriately named expatriate Polydore Vergil took pains to explicitate a separation.[5]

It was for quite different reasons that John Wyclif and others in Chaucer's time were beginning to question certain implications of the traditional connection. Especially they were questioning whether Christian thought could be regarded as peculiarly given to such an explicit Vergilian historicism in and of itself. Rather, as Wyclif was to ask: could it only sometimes seem to be that way because Christian thought was often refracted through the historicist lenses afforded by Roman culture?[6] Notably expressed in the *Aeneid,* Roman cultural historicism had argued strongly for a transcendent meaning in secular history, a grand design which in early Christian times still proclaimed the victory of Rome (now allegorically, now literally taken) as the right end to all history. "The judgment of history," men said, was that Rome should triumph. All history led up to and found its significance in Rome's glory (*fama*), and thus could all be retrospectively interpreted in terms of stages in the ascent or progress toward that consummation. Expressed in the conjoint vocabulary of the two "scriptures," this historiographical model exerted an almost irresistible pressure on Christian writers to articulate a parallel vision: Augustine's *City of God,* Orosius's

History, and Dante's *De Monarchia*, all medieval Christian classics, are evidently historicist in the manner of the *Aeneid*, arguing biblically a spiritual gloria (*fama*) in the New Jerusalem as the ultimate adequation of human history. Subsequently we see this structured representation of the meaning of history taking on blended literary shapes, visible not only in the surface details of a storic plot or narrative, but in such allied conventions as the generic three-stage ascent from the senses through *scientia* to *sapientia* (in Augustine's *De Trinitate* or Scotus's *De divisione natura*), and the associated provision Hell/Purgatorio/Paradiso (of Dante's *Commedia*). One of the most widely influential views of the *House of Fame* is that it too, in fact, is structured according to this same basic synthesis, following Dante particularly, with perhaps a few ironic touches.[7]

Traces of the fusion of Roman myth and Christian allegory are, after all, to be found elsewhere in Chaucer from the *Book of the Duchess* and the *Canterbury Tales*. But his use of the Troy story in the *House of Fame* is such as to raise serious questions about traditional assumptions in the use of that "matter," and even about the traditional three-stage ascent to wisdom which the surface structure of the poem might seem to imply.

II

To return to our text: if Chaucer seems to invoke the expectations generated by the identification of secular and sacred scripture which usually accompanied elaborate references to Troy, he certainly complicates his signals to the reader by undermining the authority of the author and principal traditions of interpretation which allowed for the identification in the first place. For Chaucer is less impressed by the traditional justification of Aeneas's "moving on" (e.g., as given by Vergil himself, or by a medieval allegorist of the *Aeneid* such as Bernard Silvestris) than persuaded by the focus of other authors (such as Ovid and *Ovide moralisé*) respecting the plight of abandoned Dido. Or at least his persona takes this position, and with some energy. In Chaucer's telling, it is the perfidy and truth-breaking of Aeneas which dominates interest: *contra auctorem*, we are led to see in Aeneas's departure from Carthage less a noble self-denial than a dimly rationalized divorce. When Geffrey comes to the Vergilian justification by way of Ovid, he finds in it less reason than *excuse* (427). The bidding of Mercury (the sycophant of intellect) that Aeneas should go on to fulfill his destiny might portray well enough a conventional expectation; the problem for Geffrey as reader is that it leaves something unsaid, something which embodies a potential contradiction to the usual way of justifying Aeneas's action and the conception of civic morality embodied in the story's ending.

I am aware that at this point my argument could be misunderstood. I do not at all mean to suggest here that Chaucer is trying to ennoble, as passionate, romantic love, the tryst between Dido and Aeneas, or that he really wishes us to see her as she would wish to see herself, almost as guiltless. What I think he does want us to reckon with is that there may be two sides, or many, to a story, rather than one, and that the conventional interpretation of the *Aeneid* story leaves completely unresolved the question of betrayal, and of *untrouthe.* In a sense, medieval allegorizations and hermeneutical baptisms of the *Aeneid,* such as are found not only in Silvestris or Fulgentius[8] but in all manner of secular literature (cf. the *Knight's Tale*), mostly read well enough in terms of their typology alone—what Chaucer calls "alle the mervelous signals of the goddys celestials" (459–60). But important *value questions* are left very much unresolved by mere mastery of this typology. Whose text is "right" in its focus? Vergil's or Ovid's? To paraphrase C. S. Lewis: what is the standard of judgment by which we accept that the success of the tyrant is more important—or more excusable—than the patience or despair of some one among his victims?[9] Let us speak of Aeneas, Chaucer says, "how he betrayed hir [. . .]" (293ff.)—that is part of the story too, and the long list of analogues to this betrayal (from Demophon and Phyllis through Jason and Medea to Theseus and Ariadne) circumvent our dismissal of his protest as a mere deferential gesture in the direction of the ladies in the court. There is clearly a plausible historical perspective in which Aeneas is a fink, a truth-breaker. What has to be determined now is: which version, Vergil's or Ovid's, really describes the *truth* of the story? What determines the reliability of history? Has it really any *unity* of truth that encompasses each perspective, each experience—including our own experience too? What would be the significance for the authority of history, if, as each of these stories suggest, the problem of sinful or mischievous narration were a significant factor in the history of human affairs? Whom would we trust? Faced with a plurality of authorities, how should we judge?

At the conclusion of his "reading" Geffrey acknowledges that yes, he is impressed with the "noblesse of ymages" (471), but also that he is still beset by two questions. One appears to be minor and tangential: who was the intermediary artist who provided a visual interpretation of the *Aeneid*? ("not wot I whoo did hem wirche," 474); the other question immediately appears as both crucial and personal: "Well enough," he seems to be saying, "I see the old familiar historiography . . . ; But where am I? Or in what country?" (475). In short, he asks: "is this *my patria,* or that of someone else?" It seems to be the lack of a sense of his own place in the scheme that causes him anxiety. Unlike Aeneas (who saw himself in the art of Dido's temple, and thus

secure in the great scheme of things), Geffrey is left without *personal* reference by the history he "reads," and he runs outside looking for someone, as
he says, "that may me telle where I am" (479). With respect to narrative
development then, the key question is existential, and not purely formal.
Nor is Geffrey's flight to another book or tableau of history. Rather, he runs
out to see if he can find "any stiryng man" (478). Yet he sees no living person, and his alienation is made graphic by the desert landscape which confronts him. Ironically, though Geffrey as persona is not aware of it, it is just
this landscape, the desert of Libya, which turns us, as readers, back again to
the old book, the *Aeneid,* for reference,[10] for we see that Geffrey is still tacitly compared to Aeneas—not as the Roman hero stepping out of Dido's temple, but as we find him later in the *Aeneid,* when he leaves Dido to
recommence his pilgrimage. For now, instead of Mercury, but in the very
same role, Jove is said to send down an eagle to draw the contemporary pilgrim Geffrey another stage forward on his predestined itinerary.

From this point, the classical story which occasioned the poet's questions
seems to fade away. Despite the clear parallel with Mercury, the eagle has often
been seen as a biblical, rather than classical, commentary on the story.[11] As
with the eagle image in Isaiah (40:31), the eagle of St. John's apocalypse (or
the golden eagle of the *Paradiso*), the bird has been associated with contemplation, "translation," the perspective of intellect, and even the Word—one
thinks of the eagle bearing up on his wings the *Word* (the carved lecterns
for reading the Gospels).[12] We should be cautious: Geffrey's eagle does not
act like a bearer of "The Word."[13] When it comes to snatch Geffrey out of
his sluggish malaise and befuddlement in the realm of Venus, it may seem to
function well within the conventions of the medieval dream vision. Yet the key
is to a somewhat wider genre. The eagle is a kind of parody, first perhaps of
Lady Philosophy in her advent to Boethius, imprisoned in his slothful and
concupiscent wilderness. It might pretend kinship to Knowledge in the
play *Everyman*—"I am thy frend," he says to Chaucer (582). As a symbol for
the powers of intellect, as these sometimes grow more keen following the dis-
appointments of concupiscence, the eagle could prepare us to anticipate,
accordingly, a Boethian or Dantesque hermeneutic and an appropriate conclusion—perhaps the sort of final revelation we get in *Pearl.* But we do not,
despite this intuited expectation and teasing, arrive at such a conclusion.
Why?

We might begin to essay an answer, I think, by attempting to get inside
the conventional structure of the poem in such a way as to examine further
the problem of contradiction in perspective and attribution. We discover this
in the narrative voice, particularly that part of it which belongs to the

persona. A curious circumstance attends upon Chaucer's invocation, following the proem to book 1, to Morpheus:

> [. . .] the god of slep anoon,
> That duelleth in a cave of stoon
> Upon a strem that cometh fro Lete,
> That is a flood of helle unswete. (69–72)

By convention the reader anticipates that an invocation to Morpheus will be
a prolegomenon to whatever condition of sluggishness and torpor is sufficient to occasion the necessary dream (cf. *Book of the Duchess*), since
Morpheus is notably personification of *forgetfulness,* whose dwelling is beside
Lethe and whose floral icon is the poppy.[14] Yet Chaucer has just promised us:

> as I kan now *remembre*
> I wol you tellen everydel. (64–65) (italics mine)

He has carefully labored to tell us that he wants to reconstruct his dream for
us with all clarity, and needs memory to help him out. But he invokes
Morpheus. Here is a patent contradiction, and it is not in book 1 resolved by
introducing the problematical variety of ways in which one might remember
the Troy story, but in fact only exacerbated by this reminder. The desire the
narrator expresses is for memory, but his invocation is curiously contrary, to
the influence of oblivious Morpheus.

　　A similar problem persists in the next section of the poem. Though the
invocation in book 2 is to Venus, the appeal is to Thought, the processes of
intellect that "wrot" (wrought, wrote) all that the poet has encountered, and
subsequently transmitted to memory:

> O Thought, that wrot al that I mette
> And in the tresorye hyt shette
> Of my brayn, now shall me se
> Yf any vertu in the be
> To tellen al my drem aryght. (523–27)

With this probable allusion to the beginning of the *Inferno* (2.7–9), we move
from memory to its sponsor, intellect, and thereby encounter a progression
of interpretation at least as familiar as concupiscence-knowledge-wisdom, or
hell-purgatorio-paradiso, but not, however, necessarily to be identified with
them. To be sure, the eagle clearly recognizes Geffrey's concupiscent state

("You are a noxious little load to carry," he says), and, in tones all too much like one Chaucer could tell about ("Geffrey —wake up!") he invites Geffrey, but in words also reminiscent of Scripture (Eph 5:14)[15] and the liturgy ("*Exsurge anima mea*") to leave off his heaviness of heart.

> Awak!
> And be not agast so, for shame! (556)

The eagle, like Mercury, moves the protagonist forward physically—pilots him through the plot. Yet whether Geffrey moves spiritually is a matter not of force, or plot, but of his own will and perspective. The apparent contradictions in the prayers of invocation are thus an important continuing reflection of Geffrey's *lack* of solution (cf. Jas 1:5–8). Even while the appeal to Thought (the warden of memory) strives to move him forward, his initial invocation to Venus reminds us of the temple in which Geffrey has been sojourning. Venus is his tie to earth—but also, as in the "temple of Venus," his tie to story, and to story with all of its ambivalent possibilities, historiographical and personal.

The eagle, whether we see him as intellect, contemplation or reason, has ostensibly been sent by Jove to provide Geffrey with a bit of perspective.[16] The poet's problem has been that he spends all of his time up to the *hals* in books, out of contact with experience as such (654–60), and the implication is that he has become one who cannot see the forest for the trees, the structure of things for particulars, because he is so narrowly engrossed with the pursuit of particular textual authorities. But because he has been a diligent student, has sat up nights and persevered (despite his dullness and intellectual limitations), Jove's will is that he should get some higher perspective, even on the authorities he has been reading. The intellectual journey thus sets in relationship to the vagaries of human history something of the larger structure of the universe during which a number of authorities, on points of cosmology, philosophy, and mythography, are confirmed (e.g. 712; 759–60; 985–89).

The context for this dialectic between scriptures and author, we remember, is a very Boethian discussion (cf. *Boece* 1–3) of the doctrine of natural place, in which the *House of Fame* is reported to be the "natural place" of ingathering for every kind of tiding, news, or human history. Recalling (as does Dido, by the way) the alarming Mediterranean notion that every human word spoken is preserved perpetually (*vide* Matt 12:34–37) and thus an *ultimate* subject available for recollection, the eagle concludes his "philosophy" and asks Geffrey to make a judgment—"How thinketh the my conclusyon?" (871)—i.e., what does Geffrey think of the idea that *every* human story, every utterance, every viewpoint is all recorded, in the entirety, somewhere up in the air as a kind of master library of history? Geffrey's answer is testily skeptical: "A good persuasion" (i.e., opinion), he says—not entirely swept away either by the rhetoric or the presumed "confirmation" of authorities on points cosmographical. Miffed, the eagle then retorts:

> "Be God," quod he, "and as I leve,
> Thou shalt have yet, or hit be eve,
> Of every word of thys sentence
> A preve by experience,
>   [. . .] What wilt thou more?" (875–79, 883)

Swearing by St. James, he urges Chaucer then to confirm, if he can, by personal experience, the "trouth" of his physical and present place, hovering over the terrestrial landscape. What the eagle asks, in short, is a more explicitly empiricist version of Geffrey's own urgent question of himself: *Where are you?* Can you tell? The answer is that Geffrey sees recognizable but only *general* features—cities, fields, seas, ships—and soon he is so high he sees only the whole globe as a tiny point, defying particular discernment (909). When the eagle asks, "Seest thou any token (sign) or aught that in the world of is spoken?" (911–12 [Fisher]),[17] Geffrey's answer has to be "Nay." Clearly, there is a perspective which is "true," yet defeats practical validation because accurate confirmation is simply beyond it. The story of Phaethon's difficulty in holding the mean between earthly and terrestrial (corporeal and spiritual) inclinations, repeating a motif from the first two proems, follows as a warning to the reader of the persona's instability, of Geffrey's own need to keep these points of reference in balance.

The persona's own (partial) recognition here of the validity of the eagle's instruction embraces both an acknowledgment of God's ultimate authorship and the continuing pertinence of the philosophy of Boethius (970ff.). But Geffrey is still lost between the poles of two inclinations, clearly uncertain of the integrating point of his own experience (980–82). So, to proceed, he refers his insight, habitually, as a reader, to a textual confirmation of typography (e.g. Martianus and Alanus), seeking experiential support for them as conventional authorities. When admonished by the eagle to "let be" his "fantasye" and take a short scientific course (on location) in astrology, Geffrey finds the wit to demur. When the eagle protests, "How are you going to read poetry without astrology?" Geffrey can say wisely enough, "hyt is no nede"—he can believe for this sort of thing in the authority of books as easily as his present interplanetary experience.

This statement (especially given Chaucer's scientific interest in astronomy) would seem to suggest a measure of the persona's growing discrimination. It contains two recognitions. First, in view of the fact that one has not time to learn everything, summistically ("For I am now too old," Geffrey says), it suggests that there are some kinds of truth for which authority provides as helpful an adequation as experience. Second, the persona rejects the notion that it is the function of poetry, or its use of typology, to point merely to the "empirical" validation of received typology in this sense. Typology is one means—at the first level—of systematizing understanding. It serves to identify a group of ideas approximately by situating them within a familiar set. It is absolutely necessary as the first ground of figurative language. But "true" historical or intellectual understanding, seeking to grasp the way in which a story develops, its central intuition or its organic intellectual structure, begins precisely at the point where these rudimentary identifications end. The mere citation of authority on such points of identification does not really speak to the main issues of the dream (or poem). As Geffrey prepares to examine the *House of Fame,* his concerns, like those he had at the end of book 1, are still with the larger issues, and are (in the philosophical sense), personal rather than typological. In book 1 the problem had not been merely the abstraction which is history, but establishing a personal relationship to it: "Where am I?" Here in book 2 the problem is not merely the availability of information, but "What is the *point* of the information?"

> "Now," quod I, "while we han space
> To speke, or that I goo fro the,
> For the love of God, telle me
> In sooth, that wil I of the lere-" (1054–57)

"What am I going to *learn* in all of this?" he asks. "Give me some unified meaning, the *sentence* of it all." Suddenly it is the eagle's turn to demur:

> "Noo," quod he, "by Seynte Clare,
> And also wis God rede me!" (1066–67)

"Nothing doing," he says, swearing by a saint of silence: the perspective of intellect will not of itself yield up that kind of knowing. The eagle is not necessarily discourteous—merely constrained: it wishes him God's grace, as assistance for the quest "*some* good to lernen in this place." But the limiting quantifier is a confirmation to us that this scene is more to be distinguished from than paralleled with that moment at the end of the *Purgatorio,* when Vergil hands Dante on to Beatrice for ultimate revelation. In suggesting partial knowledge in its plurality rather than truth in its unity, the eagle's viaticum confirms a growing apprehension that the curriculum in book 3 may provide Geffrey anything *but* a glimpse of The Reader's New Jerusalem.

III

The departure of the eagle should not be taken to mean that Chaucer, as a poet, has abandoned or forgotten his appropriate concerns for the schema, or structure, of his poem by the beginning of book 3. In fact, in his request for Apollo's blessing of "science and light," Chaucer as narrator emerges again from behind his persona to tell us that he is far less concerned that his own book illustrate a mastery of "art poetical" (whereby *he* might have "fame") than that it reveal "o sentence" ("only meaning," or, "unified meaning"); his present object is not to "shewe craft" in skillful effects, but rather to reveal design:

> O God of science and of lyght,
> [. . .] entre in my brest anoon! (1091–1109)

This proem, though less obviously ambivalent than the others, proceeds to a redoubled invocation in which each aspect of the invocation is more clearly a mirror to the other. The "divyne vertu" to which he prays in the second part of the proem is personally addressed; he now seeks a divine *inspiration* such as can help him to find a shape for what memory and thought have already "ymarked" in his head. Thus, while Apollo's typology of ordered exposition looks backward to the intellectual analysis of book 2, his "virtue," divine inspiration, looks forward to a dimension of revelation for which the structure of the poem still entices us to hope. As in many dream visions, the advantage to the dream's perspective of divine inspiration is for transformation of the will.[18] For all that, many readers have felt that in book 3 the moment of revelation never comes—there appears to be no unified meaning discerned, no key to all mythographies proclaimed. Fame's palace and the bird cage are complete and deliberate inversions of imagery from Ezekiel and St. John's Apocalypse, and instead of unifying truth which answers the dreamer's questions, Geffrey is bombarded with a veritable frenzy of contradictory, patently false, partially true, but all unsortable data without judgment or ordering of any kind. What he gets is simply *more* and *more* histories, not any integration for their reconciliation and understanding. Far more than book 1, it is book 3 which parallels Dante's *Inferno*. Certainly here is no *Paradiso*. So for the "o sentence" and design, the persistent reader will still have unanswered queries concerning the architecture of the *House of Fame*.

Let us reflect and reconsider Chaucer's structure as if it really were rather like that of Dante's *Commedia*. There, as in Dante's own *De Monarchia*, Augustine's *City of God* or the *Antiquities* of Josephus, what we really have is Vergil's historicism "baptized." The three stages of a history whose meaning is unified, whose means are all satisfactorily subsumed to the end, are basically ex patria/via/patria. Since the end of the story had been reached, for Vergil, it was quite possible to reconstruct the details of narrative so that they all achieved their significance in terms of the happy political conclusion. Predestined to glory, this time the Trojans win. Moreover, as Romans, they are predestined to remain victorious. For Augustine, who experimented with these ideas in his *Confessions* and *City of God,* Christian historiography was less well equipped to proceed with such temporal assertiveness: the Christian goal in history, though foreshadowed in biblical prophecy and dream vision (e.g. St. John's Apocalypse) had not been fully realized. Dante, on the other hand, more explicitly images the Vergilian promise: his pilgrim reaches the New City. In his work we see that the external hermeneutical model (the "grand narrative") was presently available in allegorical readings of civic history, or their articulation, for history still "unfolding," of a larger, more politically oriented historiography.[19]

Such an historiography is not, of course, history in the chronicler's sense, but a model, a metaphor. Dante knew this. Others at the time and up to Chaucer were even more literalist, however, in their temporalizing. From well-known historicists like Joachim da Fiore and Otto von Freising to numerous minor apocalyptic writers in Chaucer's own day, thousands of pages had been devoted (against all the explicit warnings of Scripture) to fixing the literal details of European history to biblical metaphor as though it were a kind of future calendar. The most extravagant reaches of this habit, from certain wild interpretations of the days of Frederick II to incessantly repeated predictions of the year of Christ's second coming (1233, 1260, 1300, 1366, 1400), are far too numerous to mention here, but one can read about them at leisure, as well as see their influence upon other English poets of Chaucer's age, such as William Langland.[20] The effort of such prognostications was to try to provide a unified meaning for history that would allow for the interpretation and justification of mediate events. Their effect was to place the possibility of a unity of truth *in* history under incalculable strain, to drive some Christians to despair of meaning in history and authority alike. Supposing one had been told, really believing in Christ's prophesied return, that the demonstrable date of that coming again was last year and it did not happen? Supposing one had

been told that the infinitely more significant destiny of the state or the political Church rendered the accidents of personal or national destiny insignificant, and one had lived long enough to wonder?

It is the biblical language, allusion, and direct critical quotation which
really point to these questions in the *House of Fame,* not the story of Troy or
its panoply of typologies. The secular scripture, Troy, is the initial *matière,*
the occasion of his essay. But Chaucer's critical angle comes from the other
text. Whereas Dante had used his national poet, Vergil, as an irrefragably
"authoritative" interlocutor, Chaucer uses the "intellectual" but more
ambiguous eagle. For Dante, the point is that poetic history and its historicist schema becomes a confirmation, a guide to the truth of the theological,
or of revelation. For Chaucer it is just the other way around, that a revelation—far beyond the sight of intellect—would be needed as a guide to the
truth value of history or the historical "authorities" one reads.

The actual text of Scripture itself does not read according to an historicist model at all, except in the largest sense of expectation, of an openness to
the ending known to be coming, but not yet known. Chaucer's contemporary, Wyclif, is sensitive to this point, quoting Christ: "No man knows the
day or the hour, not even the angels of heaven, but my Father only" (Matt
24:36).[21] The reason we can't "read" the story of history in that definitively
literal way is, just as literally, that we do not have the whole text. It may be
that the significance of the biblical December tenth date, cited twice at the
beginning of the *House of Fame,* is not simply for announcement of apocalyptic insight or revelation.[22] Rather, as the date (tenth day of tenth month)
in which Ezekiel "saw" in his vision the destruction of Jerusalem, it may signify to Chaucer much what it did to Ezekiel—the end of the illusion of historical security, the death of history, a separation, an ending of the past order.
Wyclif in his lectures points out that the vision, as indeed the destruction of
Jerusalem itself, is an irrefragable corrective to Israel's tendency to create its
own literalist historicism, to expect a heavenly kingdom on its own terms, in
the here and now.[23] The destruction of Jerusalem, the prophets argue, cuts
off that "progressive" history and blows the theory away like chaff from the
threshing floor. From such a point of understanding the text of Scripture is
read not according to an external and historicist schema, but according to an
internal hermeneutical model, well known to commentators from Nicholas
of Lyra to John Wyclif as a kind of *forma tractatus* for Scripture's consolatory
dialogue with its readers. It is relevant to the whole canon of Scripture, but
particularly the books we call "prophecy," the visionary literature of Isaiah,
Jeremiah, and Ezekiel.[24]

Several factors invite a recapitulation of the form of Ezekiel's dialogic for
comparison with the *House of Fame.* First, there is Chaucer's repeated refer-

ence to the visionary date from Ezekiel (40:1–2), the tenth day of the tenth month. Further, there are many echoes of the imagery of that book throughout Chaucer's poem, some elements of which have already been noted by Koonce and others.[25] But there are specific structural relationships between Ezekiel and the *House of Fame* which merit critical consideration. For form, the chapter from Ezekiel which first occasions comparison is not in fact the fortieth chapter, but the eighth, which recounts a much earlier vision. Here Ezekiel is confronted by Yahweh in his desert exile and "lifted up between earth and heaven" (v. 3) to be shown a vision of the historical temple of his day. Corrupted by the unseemly presence of a statue of Ashtoreth, or Venus ("The image of jealousy" [v. 5] because Yahweh's "jealousy" is thereby aroused),[26] and defiled by distorted vision ("every man in the chambers of his imagery" [v. 12])[27] the temple proves less the prophet's "true country" than did even the desert wasteland. Whereas Ezekiel's vision was concerned with the parody by which a temple devoted to concupiscence contradicted the ideal Temple of the New Jerusalem revealed at the end of his book, Chaucer's vision begins in such a temple of Venus, also a "chamber of imagery," only to reveal to us a Geffrey who is "actually" like the historical Ezekiel, in a desert, alienated and unsure of his own country. Then, in a fashion which bears further structural comparison with the continuation of Ezekiel's book, Chaucer's vision proceeds to the description of another temple, comprised of two "courts," the Houses of Rumor and Fame. That the described structure of that "temple" may invert the "Outer Court" and "Inner Court" of Ezekiel's description is a possibility which merits more detailed study, especially perhaps in light of the fourteenth-century commentary on Ezekiel's temple by Nicholas of Lyra and, subsequently, by Wyclif.[28]

In the present comparison we may concern ourselves primarily with the form of Ezekiel's total narrative, the structure of his book. Despite the conveyance of some aspects of historical sequence, this book is typical of visionary literature in manifesting narrative design as rhetorical and psychological, rather than as "historical." Its three-part organization may be capitulated in this way:

Proem: announcing the genre: vision, or prophecy (ch. 1)

I. *The Confusions of History* (chs. 2–24)
    a. Israel (the reader) exemplifies a sinful history, and goes astray from true understanding being forgetful of its "Author."
    b. The result of this forgetfulness is confused and distorted perspective, alienation in the wilderness, diseased interpretation. The parable of the eagle (ch. 17) is a parable of captivity. Israel is shown to need this extreme therapy because she is apparently

incompetent to remember without reinforcement the true lessons of history.

II. *Analysis* (chs. 25–32)

    a.   Human judgment and interpretation, especially of alien authorities (here exemplified by Egypt and her neighbors) are shown to be presumptuous and inadequate.

    b.   Yahweh's judgment is that truth comes from another source.

III. *Options* (chs. 33–48)

    a.   A conversation with the Author by which our mediate author (Ezekiel) is also tacitly admonished concerning the pitfalls of a visionary vocation by negative examples of his art (the lying prophets [chs. 33–36]) then shown that by itself history is dead—a valley of dry bones (ch. 37).

    b.   An answering of questions by action, by event. What can vivify these bones, bringing them to life in coherent fidelity to the meaning in their history? Only that divine inspiration which the visionary poet (prophet) is commanded by Yahweh to invoke (17:9–10).

It is revealed that the true temple can only be situated in the "true country" which actually transcends history, where the Author's final authority is to be revealed to the reader in person. The name of that place is simply *Yahweh Shammah* (*Dominos ibidem,* "the Lord is there").[29] This outline of argument for Ezekiel is admittedly cryptic.[30] Its essential features are, unsurprisingly, all anticipated in fourteenth-century commentaries, notably in Nicholas of Lyra and John Wyclif.[31]

Narratively, a notable feature of apocalyptic such as Ezekiel (cf. Daniel 7–12, or Revelation) is its self-conscious address to the reader, one consequence of which is insistence on a conclusion taking place effectually only *outside* the historical text of the story. Implicitly, this is to reject the possibility of definitive interpretation by the reader. With respect to Chaucer, what we might try to estimate is the probable influence of such an analysis in a poetic critique of *historicism* and its kind of justification for interpretative closure.

Here is a hypothesis: let us suppose that, superimposed on our readers' expectation of the historicist and progressive hermeneutic (signaled by the Vergilian desert, engendered by the temple of Venus, and encompassed by the progression of Morpheus, Venus, Apollo), Chaucer may have skillfully introduced a second textual framework of reference—another historiographical design (underwritten by the desert and temple of Ezekiel 8). Let us imagine that this design might be cued by the biblical rhetoric found in

Ezekiel (problem/analysis/option), and that, as applied to the problem of history and a possible unity of truth, its development might progress not only through temporal *states* of mind (e.g. concupiscence/science/sapience) in which the possibility of formal closure is inherent, but by an appeal to *faculties* of mind (e.g. to memory/intellect/will) in which it is not. In such a case, the structure of the *House of Fame* might plot in something like this three-stage, binary fashion:

I.   Problem:
  a.   The reader has a fragmented, fallen perspective; he is "forgetful" of Authority.

                                        Morpheus is invoked; (67–69)

  b.   What the reader sees is a fallen history; his experience is that of everyman, sickness in body, spirit, head, the alienation of a desert;

                                        Memory is appealed to; (64–65)

II.   Analysis:
  a.   What the reader offers: venal sacrifices, wrong "readings";
                                        Venus is invoked; (518–19)

  b.   What Jove wants: "learn to do well, seek judgment";
                                        Intellect is appealed to (the Eagle); (523–28)

III.   Option:
  a.   The poem is engaged as a "conversation," dialogically to order perspective on authorship, etc. "Come let us *reason* together [. . .]";

                                        Apollo is invoked; (1091–93)

  b.   The poem becomes an invitation to an *act* of acknowledgment (beyond the poem), recognizing the necessity of silence before an ultimate authority irreducible to human utterance.

                                Divine inspiration is sought, for a transformation
                                        of the Will. (1101–9)

   The dialectic which the biblical model affords would seem to suggest that if the view of the poem as an incomplete fideistic celebration seems finally less than adequate, then so too is the view that the poem is a classicist-humanist attack on faith.[32] Chaucer's skepticism, reflected in the narrative structure of the *House of Fame,* is not in fact directed toward Christian revelation or the notion of ultimate and unified truth, but toward the problem of a reader's human perspective, his overwhelming difficulties in recovering truth from history. *In what sense can anything of the past be a true authority for us today?* That is the question Chaucer poses of his standard models and authorities, and what his intellect gives him back is the answer that trust in them involves as much (or more) an act of will, a leap of faith, as any other he could imagine.

The plurality of authorities, a series of parallel histories and points of view contradicting each other, naturally leads us in the direction of skepticism. The ambiguous histories that we live with, unfortunately, are what equip our state of asking. We are, in measure, what we remember. Like Aeneas bearing Anchises on his shoulders we carry our history with us. (But not all of the way). Or, as Chaucer puts it in this poem, the burden of history is unevenly distributed: Fame bears upon her shoulders not only the history of the great (1410–13), of nations (1432–36), or universal history (1460–1500ff.), but also that of the mundane good, of unjudged villains, and of a veritable host of liars and their lies. Laboring along under a share in this burden, it is unsurprising that a thoughtful reader should sometimes stagger, and to long for a truth which is independent and demonstrable.

Most readers at one time or another expect history to have a certain objectivity—what, in the words of one philosopher, "thought has worked out, put into order, understood, and what it can thus *make* understood."[33] The historicist, or revelationist (Joachim, Dante, Hegel, Marx) is one who asks that this objectivity be extended systematically to a universal, and yet literal, history. Chaucer, on the other hand, is one who asks of history a different type of question, one which candidly discloses his *subjective* concern.[34] He is concerned above all with the emergence of values, of the truth of attitudes and states of mind, with knowing, personal action, the mutual encumbrances of life and death—values which, in fact, emerge through the temporal span of human societies but whose point of asking is always (in the Augustinian sense) existential, the arena of the personal question. For Chaucer in the *House of Fame* one's search for truth is thus characterized by being stretched between two poles: our personal situation, and a certain objective intention with respect to being. Our contemporary, Paul Ricoeur, puts the epistemological problem in this way:

> The latent parodox is this: we say history, *history in the singular*, because we expect this unique history of mankind to be unified and made reasonable by a human meaning. [. . .] But we also say men, *men in the plural*, and we define history as the science of past men because we find persons who emerge as radically manifold centres of mankind.[35]

It is well recognized that Chaucer, in most of his poetry, suggests that however much we try to pursue the truth of history objectively, we cannot escape the personal, the subjective—and that almost certainly we do not entirely wish to do so.[36] Even the Wife of Bath suggests (however whimsically) that the study of past men is motivated not just by a desire for *explanation,* but by a will for *encounter.* Of course, as Chaucer also shows us with Geffrey in the *House of Fame,* that means there will always be frustration. We are unavoidably, as readers, limited, for the encounter we have with history is never in fact a dialogue. Texts do not answer, not even when we cast them in the fire. We have communication, yes, but without reciprocity. (As Ricoeur says, "like unrequited love.") It is the personal in our own questions which reminds us that though we speak of history as singular, we are always dealing with persons in the plural. And we find that we must acknowledge that the appearance of a great (indeed *any*) human personality is not simply more data, but an *event* which is irreducible to the surmise of reason as that could be transmitted by words alone.

The frustrated conclusion of the *House of Fame* draws attention to itself, and thus, at its first meaning, to an unavoidable limit. Of history, the writer does not have the complete text. The experience of books—the "academy" of Fame's household—only makes this reality more evident. Its "bookish" authority, like the temporal authority of the Court, or House or Rumor, is a mixture of information and frustration. The very sense we have of incompleteness drives us to search for a unity of truth, for a oneness which we intuit, yet, like the persona, don't know yet nor can we know—unless there be revealed, face to face, "one" who could compose such a convincing unity of perspective, containing and transcending our diverse particularity of vision, our divergent readings—in short, a genuine auctoritee, "author and finisher" of the whole story. Yet that is clearly not the only point of Chaucer's arrested conclusion. In the midst of all the compounded and all too courtlike confusion of Rumor's whirling jumbo ("mischief upon mischief," "rumor upon rumor," as the prophet Ezekiel puts it), there has been little so far to suggest any such possible unity of truth. Geffrey has in fact come hither, he plainly says, neither to seek fame himself (1872–82), nor to add to the confusion merely one more tale (1906–09), but to get something categorically different—"newe tydynges for to lere" (1886) and though he cannot, of course, yet specify what that would be, by definition these must be differentiated in *quality,* not merely an addition to the astonishing quantity of contradictory proclamations which make up Fame and Rumor's confusion. In short, having dispensed with the pursuit of *fame* as either reputation or rumor, he is now focused intently on its other meaning, and would like to bring his search to a conclusion. Or, we could say, to a point of judgment.

Tidings, we are reminded, had a primary meaning in Chaucer's time (*Old English Dictionary*), not of "report" or "news" but of "event," or "happening"—the *occasion of fame,* not just its happenstance reporting. The request for "newe tidings for to lere" (to be taught) is thus a request for something transformational to happen—in a sense, for history to be *made* rather than simply reported. The *tidings* should be fresh from some different "countre," he says, of which he need not speak, since there are others who can sing its praises better than he (2134–38). There is more to fix our sense of that far country, for in a further allusion he says that there will one day come a sorting out of the wheat from the tares, the true from the false, "alle the sheves in the lathe" (2140; cf. Ps 125:6).

It may be that this penultimate allusion to a final Judgment, authoritative beyond dispute, actually opens up, rather than closes down, the horizons of Chaucer's poem. It seems that plurality is not for Chaucer the final reality, nor is misunderstanding the ultimate end of attempts at communication. The last element of the vision is not to be another flood of reports, or even one report, but a concrete event. With everyone scrambling to try to see, Geffrey turns for his frustrated attempts at concluding his search for truth to see what is happening. And what he sees is the first emergence of another human, personal entity in the poem—at last an answer to his initial search—running out of the temple, weighted with the authorities of history, to see if he could find "any styring man" to tell him where and who he was:

> Atte laste y saugh a man,
> Which that y [nevene] nat ne kan,
> But he semed for to be
> A man of gret auctorite [. . .] (2155–59)

The reference is, I think, to that mysterious One before whom all things are to be uncovered, and from whom nothing is hid—to the ultimate Judge, or interpreter.[37]

If the allusion suggests also that One who "taught them as one having authority, and not as the scribes" (Matt 7:29), it may be because Chaucer took these to be one and the same *auctor*. If it recollects "the woman of imperious authority" from the *Consolation of Philosophy*, who drives away the shamefaced strumpet muses surrounding the bewildered Boethius (1 pr. 3), that too fits the penultimate disclosure in the *House of Fame*: a teacher of authority is about to take the stage. But why should Chaucer deny his reader the benefit of Wisdom's teaching? In the face of the difficulty of determining authority as exposed by the poem, it is in fact only such an open (or, eschatological) ending, however fearful that openness, which could provide the reader with any hope. That is, Chaucer puts before his reader the intractable problem of determining truth in a history in which confusion reigns, but as a problem which is at least illuminated by an optional framework for understanding, an eschaton, a "fullness of time" which can hold out hope for a unified and eternal "reading" for history without presuming to be in any facile sense literalistically coordinated with the fragmented history of our own recollection.

Giuseppe Mazzotta, writing of Dante, asks a question pertinent also for Chaucer in the *House of Fame*:

> If the journey of writing has not an end where all its promises are fulfilled, how does the poem come to an end? What is the exile with which poetry seems to be synonymous? We must provisionally single out as having a special, revelatory function the ending of the poem, the point which is conventionally given special importance, because it is there that the sense of the poem lies.[38]

Dante's more historicist framework develops a markedly different form for conclusion than that which emerges from the biblical model by which Chaucer contravenes it in his *House of Fame*. Yet in Chaucer's poem the two models do speak to each other; many of the same questions are put with intensity, and in Chaucer we ought certainly, as Mazzotta suggests for Dante, to "single out as having a special, revelatory function the ending of the poem."[39] Yet it is their divergence concerning the relationship between revelation and history, truth and poetry, which so distinguishes the form of argument in the two poems by which these two writers are most often compared.

Let me summarize: What I have tried to suggest is: (1) that in his *House of Fame* Chaucer abandons hope for a univocal truth based on "history"; (2) that accordingly he limits the ambition of the writerly project to characterize truth to strategies of hypothesis and trope; (3) that for Chaucer the function of the biblical (as opposed to the classical) component in this poem is not simply a fideistic *oblige,* or merely another descriptive typology, but a means of introducing, amidst the skepticism engendered by a plurality of authorities, a category of hope for deferred understanding. The result is a new hermeneutic horizon, opening the way to an authoritative conclusion not yet grasped by individual readings, but possibly to be anticipated by them. In this perspective, "readings," such as the seriously playful reading of a poet, can be truly helpful, if only because the questions, less presumptuous than pseudo-answers, are really proposals concerning a story—a "hidden scripture"—that is still unfolding.[40] (4) The structure which the poem appears to have—and by which it invites its reader into a conventional set of temporal interpretation—Chaucer portrays as the inevitably historicized property of all temporal interpretation, including his own. But by exposing an ambivalence of reader motivation toward this structure, and then by leaving it (temporarily) open, Chaucer underscores the role of will and inspiration in the reader's response. Thus, he opens up a logic for closure in which the formal logic of conventional poetic structure may be traced, but in which that formal logic is also transcended by the silent space of his reader's choosing. (5) Finally, an inference: the problem of (sinful) subjectivity in the reader is for Chaucer the most limiting problem in interpretation—(one which he will explore more fully in the *Canterbury Tales*). For it, an ultimate *judgment* separating the true from the false is needed. The ending of the present poem is thus not "apocalyptic" in the usual catastrophic sense, but *hopeful* or "eschatalogical" in the sense that such an eschaton is not the limitation of a "historical" conclusion, but rather an *openness* to the final perspective of a full text and authorial reading.

The "conclusion" to Chaucer's *House of Fame* can be, in this openness, itself a kind of eschaton. As a poem, it concludes neither in a pluralistic quandary—skepticism—nor in a dogmatic assertion. Rather, it rests in a simple suspension of the story: "the end is not yet." In what is *not* said there is, perhaps, an invitation to the reader to offer something of her own. Yet in the perspective of the poem's last rejections this invitation is not merely for more information. Rather, almost as it would be in the liturgical context suggested by Ezekiel, the invitation is, in silence, *to* silence before the unutterable Word.[41]

(1984)

Chapter Seven

Chaucer's Friar's (Unpaid) Rent

So plesaunt was his "In principio,"
Yet wolde he have a ferthyng, er he wente.
His purchas was wel bettre than his rente.

Chaucer, Canterbury Tales, 254–56[1]

No man can serve two masters . . .

Matthew 6:24, KJV

The professional ethics of Geoffrey Chaucer's wandering and dyspeptic religious figures are sufficiently inconsistent that we anticipate little of his characterization of them will be without irony or point. Yet, with respect to the lines just quoted from his description of the Friar in the General Prologue, the edge of Chaucer's irony typically has been blunted by a literal, or at least prosaic, glossing of the key word *rente*. Arnold Williams, for example, in a notable article on medieval friars, has interpreted the lines to mean that "the friar must get all by his purchase, his daily winnings at beggary, and nothing from his rent, or permanent investment from income or land."[2] But *rente* is a much more expansively used term in Middle English literature, particularly in Chaucer, and this traditional interpretation underestimates his semantic drift.

Rente is used by Chaucer in several instances with an understanding clearly different from the legal sense of "permanent income from investment or land." For example, another of his clerics, the friar in the *Summoner's Tale*, self-righteously raises himself above the presumed negligence of local curates:

> I walke, and fisshe Cristen mennes soules,
> To yelden Jhesu Crist his propre rente;
> To sprede his word is set al myn entente. (1820–22)

Here the *rente* is clearly not material, but rather the service a good cleric owes to the Lord whom he loves and serves. One point of the Summoner's story is surely to suggest that the friar is not doing a very good job of yielding up his proper rent.

Chaucer also uses *rente* in explicit connection with love-service. Antigone, on behalf of Criseyde, prays to the god of love:

> O Love, to whom I have and shal
> Ben humble subgit, trewe in myn entente,
> As I best kan, to yow, lord, yeve ich al,
> For everemo, myn hertes lust to rente. (*Troilus and Criseyde* 827–30)

This, too, is a nonmaterial understanding of the term, and one which is more closely related to the example in the *Summoner's Tale* than may at first be apparent. The connection between the two is based upon the concept of *rente* as homage service. It becomes explicit in the following speech of the Black Knight from the *Book of the Duchess*:

> Dredeles, I have ever yit
> Be tributarye and yiven rente
> To Love, hooly with good entente,
> And throgh plesaunce become his thral
> With good wille, body, hert, and al.
> Al this I putte in his servage,
> As to my lord, and dide homage;
> And ful devoutly I prayed hym to. (764–71)

This last passage is intended to be specifically reminiscent of medieval oaths of homage, as the terms "thral," "servage," "lord," "homage," and "rente" indicate. The *rente* usually owed to a lord by his thral was, until Chaucer's time, mostly labor or service rather than money or substance.[3] Moreover, the relationship which bound the lord to his vassal was considered to be a "love" relationship; a very common early synonym for vassal was drû, or lover.[4] The nature of this tenure and the ceremonies associated with it—the pledge, the symbolic enfolding of the hands, the covenantal oath—are well known, and need not be rehearsed here.[5] What should be remembered is that the conventions of the feudal relationship and obligation were typically associated with all kinds of love relationships, including those of marriage, the relationship between monks and their abbot, the King and his God, and, significantly, the priest or cleric and God.[6] The good priest was considered to be a servant in his Lord's vineyard, "rooster" of his flock, "married" and subject to his lord and bishop through whom he owed spiritual homage to God, the Lord in whose service he was an husbandman.[7] On the other hand, since the attitude of spiritual commitment was one of homage, to give oneself over to the Devil was to become his vassal.[8] The use of *rente* in connection with both love pledges and clerical service in the passages quoted from Chaucer is thus essentially the same. It is clearly meant to indicate the love-service owing to one or another God of Love. Chaucer uses the word in several other places with the same intention, and this understanding, in fact, is commonplace.[9]

The scriptural source for this idea is the parable of Christ concerning the Lord of the vineyard (Matt 21:33–41, Luke 20:9–16, Mark 12:1–9). After establishing the vineyard, the lord withdraws to a "far country," sending servants to obtain the fruit of it. The wicked husbandmen unto whom the vineyard is entrusted refuse their proper *reditas* (*reddere*: the process of rendering rent in both Vulgate and legal texts) and beat servant after servant, finally killing the vineyard owner's son. The parable was directed against the Pharisees and Sadducees, false clerics and "husbandmen" of their day, and to medieval audiences its significance was to be derived from an allegorical interpretation. According to the reading of various commentators, the vineyard should be seen as Israel, the church, or the individual soul, and the husbandman as the individual charged with serving God in this life. St. Augustine and St. Bernard relate the parable to John 15:1–5, where Christ, extending the vineyard image, says "I am the vine, ye are the branches, my Father is the husbandman." Augustine explains that the husbandman God expects fruit, or else prunes the useless fruit-bearers, here the branches, just as those wicked husbandmen in the Matthew parable who *fructum reddere contempserunt*.[10] The vineyard parable thus becomes a useful figure for describing the homage relationship to God of both the individual lay Christian and the cleric.

The fruits of love to be rendered by the ordinary Christian are the good works of love, joy, and peace (Gal 5:22), the greatest of these having its motion defined in the Great Commandment. So we read in *Charta Redemptionis Humanae*, purportedly in the words of Christ:

> I have ʒyve and made a graunt
> To alle that askyn hyt repentaunt,
> Heven blysse wyth outen endynge,
> As I am here hyest kynge.
> Kere I no more for all my smerte,
> But the love man of thyn herte,
> And that thu be in charyte,
> And love thy neyghborn as I do the.
> Thys ys the rente thu schalt ʒyve me,
> As to the chef lorde of the fee.[11]

The relationship is to be reciprocal. As God has given to us, so we ought to render to him the fruits of his gift which have matured in our use of them. This is an understanding of spiritual rent that extends itself into dictionaries of the period, it lies behind "the fourthe point that oughte maken a man to have contrition" in Chaucer's Parson's sermon (231–48), and it outlines an essential hierarchy of *rente* obligations.[12]

But the vineyard parable also shows how the *rente* which the ordinary Christian owes to God is likened to the *rente* owed by the cleric. A vineyard exposition in *The Orchard of Syon*, focusing on the need for contrition, moves away from a warning that "he þat bryngeþ not forþ fruyt of gode werkis schal be kilt awey fro þe vyne" to a condemnation of those who "laborid not ne tilied not her vyneʒeerd, but raþir distried her owne vyneʒerd, and oþire mennys also," concluding "My seruauntis doon not so."[13] The language here is reminiscent of the charges against friars and other mendicants in Chaucer's day as recounted in Williams's article, and in the explicit usage by Chaucer in regard to his Friar it gathers irony from the fact that English Franciscan friars spoke of their province as a vineyard, and had used the vineyard parable themselves to warn against the very sins of which Chaucer shows Huberd to be guilty.[14]

On the other hand, the *rente* of the good fourteenth-century cleric is described succinctly in terms of pastoral duties, in the *Cursor mundi* where we read:

> It fell saint petre als for rent,
> To call men till amendement,
> Sua au all preistes, bath mare and less,
> In als mekil als in þaim es. (19593–96)[15]

For the cleric, *rente* is properly the love-service owed in the vineyard of the world or Church; his responsibility is to extend the grace given him to others, to "call men till amendement," and when a man takes the part of St. Peter this is what everyone expects of him, and what he is supposed to believe God expects of him.[16]

Thus, when *rente* imagery is associated with the Friar and the Summoner, its reference almost certainly involves clerical responsibility. When we read that the Friar's "Nekke whit was as the flour-de-lys" (Prologue, 238), we recognize that he has not been toiling under the hot sun in the vineyard, and suspect that he might be identified with the high priests, Pharisees, and Sadducees pointed to in the New Testament parable, who did not fulfill their duties as husbandmen.[17] The same might be said of the summoner in the *Friar's Tale*. In line 1347 we learn that Huberd's summoner held the prospect of eternal damnation over people's heads to fill his own purse; he was a thief, his "maister" had "but half his duetee" (1390), that is, the rent of St. Peter was not being yielded up. In line 1373 we read that the "fruyt of al his rente" was evil doing and personal gain or purchase. The devil also rides[18] to raise up a rent that "longeth" to his lord's "duetee" (1390), and he says he has the same "entente" as the summoner (1446). The force of this lends justice to the conclusion of the story: since the summoner has the same attitude toward God as the devil, and so like him raises rent to the devil's "duetee," he has become the devil's vassal. Therefore his "purchas is th' effect of al his rente," and his reward is appropriate. Significantly, the earning of that reward provides yet another insight into the dichotomous spiritual state of the Friar, who with the same "entente" is accordingly in a very dark spiritual condition. It is amusing, thus, that when the Friar's summoner meets the devil (1443), his first oath is "by Seint James"—the patron saint of good Christian works, without which faith is said to be dead.

In the *Summoner's Tale*, the same pattern exists for the friar there. He gives only lip service to his proper obligation, which he understands but does not perform: "I walke, and fisshe Cristen mennes soules, / To yelden Jhesu Christ his propre rente; / To sprede his word is set al myn entente" (1820–22). The fact that the friar does not render proper service to Christ imparts bitter irony to line 1956, where we read that he considers himself a *parfit leche*—a fitting pun indeed.[19]

Now, as we reconsider the lines from the Prologue description of the Friar quoted at the outset, we see two concepts opposed—*purchase* and *rente*. As Walter W. Skeat and David Williams have already noted, *purchase* in this fourteenth-century context means begging, accruing to oneself gain or profit in an irregular way, or "shifting for oneself."[20] It therefore functions here to distinguish the nature of *rente*, and thus provides part of the irony of the phrase, viz. English law characterizes rent as that which is yielded, i.e., "in render" (*reddere*), as opposed to something which is taken, like profits, *in prendre*.[21] The feudal concept of *rente* is demonstrably personal and spiritual as well as material, and contains a distinction which is apparently inverted for the Friar and Summoner, who are altogether *pour prendre*. We are reminded of that archetypal priest of the Old Law, Cayphas in the Wakefield *Coliphizacio*, who, preparing to torture and condemn Christ (the Vineyard Owner's Son), supposes:

> Whoso Kepis the law, I gess,
> He gettys more by purches
> Then bi his fre rent. (160–62)[22]

In the description of the Friar, then, the opposition of *purchase* and *rente* is polar. Huberd's proper *rente* was spiritual, the *rente* he owed to God as husbandman in the vineyard: if he had any rent owing to himself in the sense Williams explains it, it would clearly come under what was meant by his *purchase*. In this context, Huberd's *rente* was the homage he presumably intended to render to one Master, his *purchase* something he did not realize bound him to another. He had forgotten that "no man can serve two masters" and, as the summoner in his *Tale* proves, that to suppose otherwise is self-delusion or presumption.[23] To say that the Friar's *purchase* is better than his *rente* is to say in no uncertain terms that he has reneged on his spiritual and prelatical homage, and that in his fixation on worldly purchase he is in a state of spiritual idolatry and disobedience with all the consequences attendant on that state. To say in addition of any cleric that his *purchase* was "the fruyt of al his rente" on which he had "sette al his entente," is to say that his disobedience is moreover self-conscious, which paints him in the blackest spiritual colors possible. And that, it seems, is exactly what Chaucer was doing with Huberd and the Summoner.

(1965; 1971)

Chapter Eight

Conversion in the English Saints' Plays

And when the Gentiles heard this, they were glad, and glorified the word of the Lord.

Acts 13:48, KJV

I

Thomas Carlyle's suggestion that religion and human history have for their basic measure the biographies of great men was probably never better appreciated than by our medieval forefathers. Yet their own sense of history, less linear and with a much more comprehensive scope of "present" than Carlyle's, found its most attractive margin in spiritual biography—the lives of the saints. It is difficult for us to imagine how large and important a body of medieval literature was devoted to this subject. Stories of martyrs such as Katherine, Laurence, or Thomas à Becket were as popular in their own day as tales of Sigfried, Roland, or Arthur, and whether as conventionalized portrayals of a high romantic ideal or as a recurrent token of God's power in the world of men, they were much prized and faithfully preserved until the time of Henry VIII. The dramatic form of the saint's life, no less than its now more familiar versified counterpart of the legendary, very much participated in this general popularity. Between the mid-thirteenth-century play of St. Nicholas and the last play of Thomas the Apostle at York in 1535, extant records attest to the performance of English plays on a veritable host of saints: Christiana, Clara, Feliciana, Margaret, Sabina, Susanna, Andrew, James, John, George, Placidus, Swithin, Sylvester, Martin, Eustace, Dionysius, Robert King of Sicily and others.[1] The dramatic quality of some of these plays, many of whose protagonists we now scarcely recognize, must have been superior; for their performance span of three centuries is much longer than that generally reported for cycles and moralities. It is

117

unfortunate, then, that (aside from the Cornish *St. Meriasek*) we are now left with but two late fifteenth-century texts from a once-great repertoire of English saints' drama.

The Conversion of St. Paul and *Mary Magdalene* both occur in the same manuscript, MS Digby 133. Happily, they are not only in good condition, but are complete, well-wrought plays, capable of offering a splendid theatrical experience to the student of English drama. *Mary Magdalene* particularly has an enormous potential for modern production. And while it would be unfair to expect either play to be fully typical of its genre, with certain allowances they can stand very well as representatives of the tradition to which some criticism has made them seem but dusky shadows.[2]

Our most important allowance must be that suggested by the textual history of the saints' plays. They have not always been universally popular. Following Henry VIII's break with Rome, even references to saints' plays very rapidly disappear, and, as with the representation of saints in sculpture and stained glass, it is more than likely that at this or in Oliver Cromwell's time their texts suffered a similar fate.[3] It is not difficult to imagine why this should have happened. As with other dramatic literature, audience engagement of the saints' life is in identification and, as in all good drama, its proper experience a kind of participation. That at least some of the English saints' plays were powerful in this way is made more than clear by Henry's damning bans and proclamations, which unwittingly commend the plays' effectiveness in so insistently regarding them as seditious. (The last York play of Thomas the Apostle, for example, was held to be directly responsible for a general uprising against the new order.)[4] But Henry was not the first opponent of the plays, even particularly of the saints' plays, and many of his theologically orientated anti-thespians were simply following a prejudice already established among their philosophical predecessors of the fourteenth century. These men must have been aware that the roots of their opposition struck at a deeper level than mere political tactic or expediency.

Some of the earliest objections to the plays give us a fair apprehension of what was to become their insurmountable opposition. As we have seen in the previous essay, one Wycliffite, after viewing some performances by the Franciscans, wrote a critical review in verse. Following his description of one sequence, he says:

> A cart was made al of fyre as it shuld be,
> A Gray frere I saw ther inne that best lyked me.[5]

What this rather uncharitable fellow seems to have observed is a lost play on the life of St. Francis, involving the stigmatization and the saint's vision at

Rivo Torto, besides other visionary material from the early spiritual biographies. Clearly he did not like what he saw, partly for personal reasons perhaps (apparently he was an ex-Franciscan), but ostensibly because he objected to the untruthfulness of what he considered to be blasphemous representation. This becomes even clearer in his critique of the crucifixion staging, probably part of the same objectionable play about St. Francis. Let us take up his objection more closely:

> With an O and an I, thai praysen not Seynt Poule,
> Thai lyen on seyn Fraunceys by my fader Soule;
> First thai gabben on God that alle men may se
> When thai hangen him on hegh on a grene tre,
> With leues and wit blossemes that bright are of ble,
> That was neuer Goddes Son by my leute. (5–10)

Our critic has a fundamentally historical bias: what he sees is, he thinks, an unfaithful representation. Having read the text he knows that Christ wasn't really crucified that way. Later Protestant criticism even of the bare fact of representation seems to be anticipated in his virulence: since the figure on the Cross could not be God's son, surely the "crucifixion" cannot avoid being blasphemous pretence. The attack accords with others which survive: as, for example, one by another Wycliffite, which finds the plays composed of "lies," "distortions of Scripture" and "abominations,"[6] and this general sort of criticism seems to have gradually built up the position from which the saints' plays in general came under insurmountable fire in the early sixteenth century.

Together, these criticisms help to illustrate a point of major importance in the study of drama at the end of the medieval period. The change in theology following Henry's break with Rome entailed (as do all philosophies of revolution) a changed view of history as well. The old view of history as an artificial frame for the recurrence of divine pattern had been common to several centuries of European culture, and had been codified in interpretations of Scripture as diverse as Augustine's *City of God*, the *Meditations of the Life of Christ*, the *Biblia Pauperum*, the program of sculpture at Chartres, and all traditions of Christian hagiography. This view saw men of every generation participating in one great *historia*—in the *speculum humanae salvationis*. In this view nothing happens for the first time. What "happened" in the Old Testament recurs to fulfillment again in the New and again in the lives of the saints. The theme is recurrence. Christ lives and dies and is born again daily in the sacrament and in the hearts of men. There is no "pretense" as such even in a crucifixion play, for the actor, like his audience, is participating in a divine pattern. Like Paul, Peter, or Francis, they try to come to grips in a powerful way with what it means to be "crucified with Christ." Nor is there false pretense in what may seem to be the extravagant common stock miracles of the typical saint's life, for while these may be as conventional and artificial as any similar device in romance, their function is not more demanding, but simply by being a *signum* of the one Christian Spirit in which all may participate, they invite that participation. This is why the medieval hagiographers saw nothing incongruous in attributing to the life of a saint who lived in the tenth century precisely the same miracles as were reported for one from the fourth century—as Reginald of Canterbury put it, "all things are common in the communion of saints."[7] In fact, it is better to talk about the life of the saints than the lives of the saints, according to Gregory of Tours, "because though there may be some difference in their merits and virtues, yet the life of one body nourished them all in the world."[8] Here is a view of history, but history *sub specie aeternitas*—or history as poetry. It was not a view shared by English reformists of the sixteenth century.

For the late medieval dramatist, the essence of the reformists' position is their rejection of catholicity in its widest sense, in their assertion that time and space and the community of men were not, *in conspectu Dei,* continuous. To refuse the doctrine of the "real presence" is to reject a view of history as much as a view of theology, as the awkward reconstructions of later seventeenth-century typologists make clear. By participating in its recurrent signs, the medieval dramatist re-presented the Atonement; the new theologians wished to remember it.

The medieval saint's play is a kind of history play as much as a romance. Its reformist objectors saw that, and in their secularized theological perspective rejected the plays as a falsification of history. Both perspectives, medieval and reformist, now prove necessary to an appreciation of the tension between tradition and circumstance which shapes the early English saints' history plays, *St. Paul* and *Mary Magdalene.*

II

The first speech of *St. Paul* is a kind of prologue or *apologia* by the "poeta," reminiscent of Shakespeare's choric "Gower" in *Pericles.* After an invocation of God's blessing, the poeta turns to the audience:

> Honorable frendes, besechyng yow of lycens,
> to procede owr processe, we may, vnder your correccion,
> the conuersyon of seynt paule, as the byble gyf experyens,
> whoo lyst to rede the booke • Actum Appostolorum,
> ther shall he haue the very notycyon;

> but as we can, we shall vs redres,
> Brefly with yowr fauour begynyng owr proces. (8–14)[9]

His extra sensitivity to potential criticism, his humble leave-seeking, and careful assertion that his "processe" truly follows the biblical account, are peculiar, and in returning to this posture repeatedly the "poeta" of St. Paul suggests that there is some circumstantial need to claim before his audience the biblical authenticity of the play. Accompanied by some unspecified choreography (simply a "Daunce"), he then concludes the first "station" by appealing to the audience to check with his source, "the holy bybull for the better spede" (159). At the outset of the second "pagent" he again asks "lycens" to "redress" "another part of the story" (164ff.) and concludes this station "as holy scripture tellyd" (352) with a repeated submission of his play to the "correccyon of them that letteryd be":

> How be yt vnable as I dare speke or say
> The compyler here of shuld translat veray
> so holy a story—but with fauorable correccyon
> of my fauorable masters of ther benygne supplexion (356–59)

Still, at the end of the play he finds it necessary to reassert yet again the accuracy of his translations, the proximity of his dramatic text to the historical record of the Acts, "as the bybull sayeth" (652). Why should the author be so careful to frame his text with these protestations? The compilers of the cycle plays, for whose larger enterprise we might perhaps have expected some initial pose of this kind, did not think any apology necessary, and they took many more extreme "liberties" with the biblical text, if we wish to judge them by that standard, than did the dramatist of *St. Paul*. The answer presumably lies in a rising opposition by the time of these texts (1490–1530) to the open-ended exemplarist view of biblical history that they typically contained. This criticism would come particularly from those new churchmen whose use of the Scriptures was based upon a reverence for literal historical accuracy. I doubt whether it is accidental that our only saints' plays to survive the Reformation celebrate biblical saints.

Even before the bans, it seems that the reformists would have looked more kindly on a reasonably biblical text like *St. Paul*, or the first part of *Mary Magdalene*, than on one which (like the second part of *Magdalene* and many other plays now lost) elaborated on the original story with spectacular miracles not found in the New Testament. Though the *St. Paul* dramatist adds a marvelously humorous debate between two turd-toting stableboys (85ff.), the spurious episode is kept short and virtually incidental to the main plot. The entrance of high priests Caypha and Anna involves the artifice of

invented dialogue, but the priests were familiar figures from another portion
of the biblical text, and their role was at least consistent with the Acts story.
Even the frustrated council of Belyal after Saul's conversion could be considered in the contextual spirit of the source. For the rest the author follows the
biblical text closely at all significant points, utilizing direct translation where
he can. Paul's sermon on the Seven Deadly Sins, for example, is largely
shaped by scriptural paraphrase, not only of the Pauline epistles but of words
of Christ from the Gospels (e.g. Matt 11:28–30):

> Lern at my-self, for I am meke in hart:
> owr lorde to hys seruantes thus he sayth:
> ffor meknes I sufferyd a spere at my hart;
> meknes all vyces annullyth and delayeth;
> rest to soulys yt shall fynd in fayth:
> *Discite a me, quia mitis sum, et corde humilis,*
> *Et invenietis requiem animabus vestris.* (538–44)

The passage that follows, about fleeing sensuality and youthful lusts, comes
from Paul's injunctions to Timothy (2 Tim 2–3). No conventional saints'
miracles are added to the Paul story, and while there is typical dramatic
expansion in the speeches of Ananais, Anna, Caypha, the knights and hostel-
ers, and typical imaginative exegesis and restructuring of the story to have
Paul's conversion bewailed in Hell, all of this is self-consciously held in careful tension with an apparent need for fidelity to exact biblical history.
Presumably, a critic would find it difficult to complain of this play, "With an
O and an I, thai praysen not Seynt Poule!"

III

Mary Magdalene, on the other hand, is a biblical saint about whom much
less is given in the Scriptures, and in traditional hagiography even some of the
biblical source material for her life is conjecturally employed. The sister of
Martha and Lazarus, she sits at the feet of Jesus (Luke 10:38–42), is attendant
upon the resurrection of her brother (John 11:1–46) and anoints the feet of
Jesus with costly oils and ointments, wiping them with her hair (John
11:1–8). The anger of Judas at this extravagance immediately precedes his
betrayal of Jesus, and since it is Magdalene to whom Christ first appears in the
garden after his resurrection (John 20:11–18) her role in the Gospels almost
exactly outlines the chief symbolic events of his ministry, death, and resurrection. To these events she becomes a kind of representative of mankind in the
story, a compelling reference for personal identification.

That valuable narrative function, assisted by her own emotional character (and the general impression of her social role suggested by John 11:45) probably contributed to the early attribution to her life of an incident recorded by Luke (7:36–50). Here Jesus has been invited to dinner by a Pharisee named Simon, and while the dinner is in progress a whore of the city comes to him weeping in remorse. She washes his feet with her tears and the hair of her head, and anoints them with ointment. While this last story is clearly a separate one, coming early in Christ's ministry, its similarity to the others together with a highly dramatic potential caused it to be associated with them. As a result, Mary Magdalene became an even more attractive and enigmatic figure, in prospect a moving example of the fallen sinner, the harlot who repents in sorrow and comes to her reward. Anyone who has seen Donatello's magnificent wooden sculpture of her in the Florence Baptistry, her ragged and decaying prostitute's body rapt in an upward gaze of transcendent adoration, would expect the story to have become popular. Indeed, it was so good that the medieval hagiographers could not leave it go without a much fuller fictive supplement. This expanded to include, even in the most modest versions, her conversion of the Saracen Emir of Marseilles, a miraculous restoration of life and preservation on a desert island of the prince's wife and newborn child, numerous miracles of her aging years in the wilderness, and up to the time of her remarkable death at Marseilles, daily ascensions into heaven assisted by ministering angels.[10] Much more than a simple saint's biography, her life acquires the stuff of legend and romance, coming to stand close beside the life of the Virgin in familiarity and popular appeal.

The first part of the saint's play follows the basic biblical stories from which Magdalene's character is derived. But the author divides his play into two sections, giving us in the last and longer part the creative expansion of her life and miracles common to his legendary sources. The result is a play which, when both parts are taken together, is undoubtedly much more broadly representative of the saints' plays we have lost than is *St. Paul*. It offers us, for one thing, that remarkably effective dramatic balance of allegorical and naturalistic technique which came to fullest flower in the saint's play, and which was theatrically realizable largely because of the old exemplarist premises about truth and history, to which both the political science and the theology of Henry's new England stood resolutely opposed.

We usually think of romance and realism as natural contrasts, realism as "a truthful depiction of nature, especially human nature," and romanticism as "an elevation beyond the range of the familiar into aspiration." Indeed, as C. W. Jones has shown, words like aspiration, elevation, exaltation, and edification, all used to describe the purpose of romance, are the purpose of saints' lives as well.[11] But while it would be right to see the saint's life of the

legendary as thus closely related to medieval romance, the saints' plays could
be much shortchanged by too sweeping an extension of the comparison. For,
if *Mary Magdalene* is any example, the English saint's play makes superb dramatic use of its view of history, combining the conventions of romance and
realism at a level of achievement not surpassed in English theater before
Shakespeare.[12] Although his play makes much use of the allegorical and faculty psychology conventions of the morality play, with bevies of vices,
virtues, devils and angels roaming about his stage, his "real" people are more
plausibly "real" than the protagonists of his predecessors, and in sensitivity
and sophistication of character revelation no medieval dramatist is closer to
the psychological verisimilitude and subtlety of the best Elizabethan drama.
Both "modes" exist quite happily together.

     To begin with, the author has provided a much larger and more complete
social frame for the biblical actions of Mary's life. Exploiting the tensions he
knew to exist between Roman and puppet Jewish power in the occupied
Palestine of Christ's day, he builds up a dramatically convincing foil of temporal power for what he will ultimately portray as the more powerful meekness of the Gospel. We are presented with three civil authorities, each a
potentate in his own right. Tyberyus Sesar's ranting claims to "Magnifycens,"
chief rulership of heaven and hell, and veritable deity (4–16) stamp him as a
stock-in-trade, if colorful, anti-Christ type. But he stumbles on to a richer
stage characterization in his craving for fresh confidence from his courtiers:

> Lord and lad, to my law doth lowte;
> is it nat so? say yow all with on showte.
> [Here answerryt all þe pepul at ons, *3a,* my lord, *3a.*] (43–45)

Like many "imperators," in constant need of reassurance, when he finally
gets enough of it for the moment his response becomes comfortably egocen-
tric: "Now have I told you my hart, I am well plesyd" (47).

     The second *tyrannus,* Herowdes, figures in his uncontrollable temper
and foul abuse a kind of barbarian egocentricity less self-conscious than
Sesar's as it is less refined than Pylatt's. But, more confident than either, he
needs no support beyond his own *braggadocio* (140–64). That marvellous
paradox of the anti-intellectual who at once despises and is awed by his
philosophers, he proves yet barely sensitive to their most obvious advice.
After half listening to the "phylyssovery's" prophetic answer to his rhetorical
question, "Am I nat þe greatest governower?" (165), Herowdes slumbers
through their rehearsal until, at a quotation in Latin from the Vulgate ("et
ambulabunt gentes in lumine, et reges / In splendore ortus tui," 175–76) he

is jolted to irritable attention: "and what seyst thow?" On hearing the rest of the prophecy he then explodes in rage, only at last to be calmed by his knights, whose welcome comfort is a denigration of the philosopher's word and a panegyric to temporal power.

Pylatt's task is to proclaim his power as judge of Jerusalem, and so he does, though with full consciousness that he is "ondyr the emperower tiberius cesar." Like many under the duress of middle administration, he is a prey to insecurity. Pylatt's great need is for acceptance; here, acceptance of his judgment:

> my ser-jauntes semle, quat sye ye?
> of þis rehersyd, I wyll natt spare.
> plesauntly, serrys, avnswer to me,
> for in my herte I xall haue þe lesse care. (240–43)

So the Digby playwright puts before us three imperious characters, all of whom are genuinely threatening, and yet who are all in one way or another insecure. To be set in context with these three men is Syrus, lord of the "castell of maudleyn," father of Mary, Martha, and Lazarus. Syrus, too, struts with temporal splendor, and though his claim to dominion is less extravagant than Sesar's (merely Castle Magdalene, Jerusalem, Bethany and "Berdes in my bouer"), and though his manner is more confident than Pylatt's, his dominant pose also involves an attitude towards security. Presenting us with a man worthy to be father of such notable children, even if necessarily a pagan, the Digby dramatist apparently also wants us to see him as bespeaking the impermanent virtues of temporal power. Cleverly he gives Syrus much more self-assurance than the Sesar whom he follows, but makes it a comfort built upon recognizably false foundations. Reciting his wealth, Syrus reflects on the security it gives him, naming his children as that good fortune's beneficiaries:

> I am sett in solas from al syyng sore,
> and so xall all my posteryte,
> thus for to leuen in rest and ryalte (63–65)

and further of his children,

> þey haue fulfyllyd my hart with consolacyon.
> Here is a coleccyon of cyrcumstance,
> to my cognysshon never swych a-nothyr [. . .]. (74–76)

Here is a kind of pseudo-Boethian ploy, a consolation of fortune rather than of philosophy which makes Syrus, like Sesar, think himself protected by temporal goods from a bad end. By the time old Syrus begins, Lear-like, to divide up his "lordshep" amongst Mary, Martha, and Lazarus (while "in good mynd"), we sense how fragile is the promise of security in their father's wealth. Shortly Lazarus himself will be dead and Mary a tattered courtesan.

The Digby dramatist has added considerably to the stock characterization of villain tyrants from the medieval cycle play. In their manifestation of temporal power his characters not only form a foil for the triumph of spiritual power in Christ's resurrection and the mission of Magdalene, but also become an integral part of the framing for Mary's early role. For from a psychological point of view Mary's own greatest problem is a kind of insecurity. As her character slowly emerges in the first part of the play, the dramatist adds to our sense of his heroine's vulnerability by carefully "framing" her position in the family. From Syrus's introduction in his opening speech, Mary is curiously placed in the middle between Lazarus and Martha—an unusual rhetorical arrangement. Similarly, in their first speeches, a response to their father's gifts, Mary, "ful fayr and ful of femynyte," has the middle rather than the first or final speech. Like Lazarus and unlike Martha, she appreciates in her father's gifts their power over fortune and worldly labors, and welcomes her protective Castle Magdalene, a "place of pleasans." Her next speech on her father's death is still a "middle" speech, and only as she realizes that she is now by her father's fortune mistress of the castle do her speeches begin to assume rhetorical and dramatic prominence (303–4). As she moves away from the protective bracketing of her siblings, however, we see that she too counts too much on the security provided by things temporal, in this case her fortune.

It is this turn of circumstance which sets the stage for the council of the traditional "foes of man." The Kyng of the World ("for þe while of fortune with me hath sett his sentur," 312), the Kyng of the Flesch, and the Dylfe (on a separate "stage and Helle ondyrneth þat stage") enter, together with their retinue of Seven Deadly Sins, a Bad Angel, and a Good Angel. World, Flesh, and the Devil, in contrast to Caesar, Herod, and Pilate, seem much more sure of themselves, and get on well together. The culmination of their dark plotting (apparently in the garden of Castle Magdalene, under the stars [313–25, 334ff.]) is a decision to have Lechery tempt Mary by flattery, and, in a contrivance reminiscent of the intrigues of Oberon and his fairies in *A Midsummer Night's Dream*, the Puck-like Bad Angel is stirred from his impish games to begin arousing her, apparently close by in her "castell," yet unaware of their presence. At length Lechery and the Bad Angel gain entrance, and though there is no speaking part or direction for the Good Angel, one can only assume that he flits fretfully about in vain defensive action while the "siege"—so reminiscent of the dramatic strategy of the *Castle of Perseverance*—is taking place. In the company of Lechery, Mary inevitably agrees to leave her castle for a tavern. There she meets the "gallant" Curiosity. Flattery proves handy, liquor makes it quicker, and in one of the play's most sure-footed "scenes" the gallant is soon able to dance an inebriated Mary Magdalene offstage. The Bad Angel, still the unnoticed attendant of Magdalene—Titivillus to this feminine Mankind—can now run off in glee to report his good news.

The prominent role in *Mary Magdalene* of abstract powers, vices, and good and bad angels, may seem at first glance to make it a kind of bastardized relative of the morality plays. Actually, its combination of psychological verisimilitude with these most "unrealistic" of faculty psychology conventions is entirely appropriate to the saint's play. According to the rules of his genre, the romantic hagiographer distinguished between factual and ethical truth, "but not in the Baconian manner."[13] Sesar, Herowdes, and Pylatt are different from, but no more real than, their psychogenic counterparts. The perception afforded by the council of World, Flesh, and Devil, and the assault of Castle Magdalene with entrance by Bad Angel and Lechery, is as valid and important as the insights yielded up in the carefully developed characterizations of insecurity, and they reinforce each other. The standard by which both perspectives are judged is the end in view, discovery of the surety of God's goodness, "that unchangeable life which is not at one time foolish, another time wise, but on the contrary is wisdom itself."[14] From his resurrection of Lazarus, the life, death, and resurrection of Christ is artfully interwoven into the second half of the play and into the legendary events at Marseilles to provide the standard to which Mary will finally conform. On the level of moral virtue, the contrition for which she was usually heralded by her biographers (686ff.) is made by the Digby dramatist to transform the vices of pride, anxiety, and lechery into humility, patience, and charity (682ff.). As the medieval synonym has it: *miraculum = virtutes*. The wildly traumatic departure from her body of seven devils into Hell with a roll of "thondyr" may be a spectacular feat of theatrical engineering in the allegorical style, but when the audience has recovered they see in quite another way that Mary's insecurity and anxiety have been miraculously transformed into confidence and unshakeable faith. The spiritual metamorphosis by which she becomes the unwavering saint of Marseilles and fearless hermit in the wilderness is more subtly characterized as the psychological redressment of her former personality problems:

> O þou gloryus Lord! þis rehersyd for my sped,
> sowle helth attes tyme for-to recure.

> Lord, for þat I was In whanhope, now stond I In dred,
> But þat þi gret mercy with me may endure;
> now may I trost þe techeyng of Izaye in scryptur,
> Wos report of þi nobyllnesse rennyt fer abowt. (692–98)

There is not so much a disparity of styles here as a deliberate counterpoint of generic conventions. In the range of speeches that occupies Mary from her encounter with Curiosity in the tavern to her encounter with Christ at Symond's dinner party, there is no more or no less *sublimitas* of style than in the range of speeches from Lechery in the tavern to the final commendation of the Good Angel. The conventions involved, nevertheless, are quite opposite. While both techniques serve the play's romantic purpose, and both are true to the "end in view," their combination in this way amply demonstrates how irrelevant would be a concern for literal time and place, biblical or otherwise.[15] As hagiographical literature, the play is a romantic enactment of man's fall and restoration, dramatically adding an opportunity for participation in a *signum* (the Middle English word is usually "tokene") of the power of God's goodness at any time to make exemplary a human life. The presumably apocryphal miracles and conversion of the king of Marseilles are in this context no less "true," theologically or dramatically, than the "historical" events recorded in the play. Yet as the saints were considered to be historical persons, their plays were still a kind of history play. They were plays, however, whose view of history—characterized by expectations of presence and recurrence rather than change and development—seemed more intrinsically dramatic than the modern perspective of their detractors could afford.

IV

The proper analysis of the saint's play ought to be in performance, of course, and while that always proves impossible to realize artificially on paper, the directions in *St. Paul* and *Mary Magdalene* are full enough to aid us in better appreciating the uniquely successful fusion of techniques which is the heritage of their development. For *The Conversion of St. Paul* it may prove helpful to remember that the medieval saint's play probably had at one time a close connection with sermon literature. One suggestion of this comes in a thirteenth-century collection of poems and sermons, where a St. Nicholas legend, written as a verse sermon, is apparently addressed to a general audience out-of-doors:

> Ye ou rede ye sitten stille
> & herknet wel wid gode wille

of godes wordes ant is werkes
beþe þis lewede ant þis clerkes (1–4)

Consisting of a running series of translations and paraphrases of biblical passages directed against worldly riches, it includes in the section that refers to
St. Nicholas an explicit mention of a "pleye" which is to follow:

yf ye wellet stille ben
in þis pleye ye mowen isen
þis mon hauede lond & lede [. . .][16] (39–41)

So direct a connection between the sermon and play to follow is reminiscent of certain medieval Italian manuscripts which include both sermons
and plays together, suggesting that in England as in Italy the early saint's
drama may have been more directly connected with preaching occasions
than has been generally supposed.[17] *The Conversion of St. Paul* is little
enough direct evidence to go on, but both in its arrangement by the "poeta"
and in Paul's internal sermon to the audience on the Seven Deadly Sins the
play resembles the tradition of Italian saints' plays sometimes referred to
under the heading "sermo semi-drammatico." While not reserved exclusively for saints' plays, this kind of dramatized sermon or homiletic narrative,
with parts either pantomimed or supplemented with short speeches, proved
entirely compatible to the genre in Italy.[18] If, as it seems likely, there was a
comparable tradition of saints' plays in England, then we can probably
assume *St. Paul* to be its descendant. With *Mary Magdalene* as the representative of the more elaborate and more typical large-scale saint's play, we
would thus seem by good fortune to have had spared for us examples of the
two most important varieties of saint's play performance.[19]

Either play offers the modern producer an ingenious exercise in staging,
although if one wished to recreate a medieval production, *St. Paul* probably
offers the least difficulty. The text seems to call for three acting areas, either
as three stations within an expansive playing-area (a town square in
Wickham's persuasive view, overlooked by a coaching inn), or perhaps, an
alternative possibility, as a mobile stage (pageant-wagon) moving from one
point to another so as to gather a larger crowd en route. At the end of the
first section or "station," for example, the "poeta," whilst a dance is taking
place, addresses the audience:

ffynally of this stacon thus we mak a conclusyon,
besechyng thys audyens to felow and succede
with all your delygens this generall processyon, (155–57)

where he will offer a similar choric framing speech at the outset of the second part. Moving the audience between station one and two allows for an ingenious engagement of audience participation. No sooner has the audience reached the site (near "Damascus") than rapidly following their walk between the stations "commyth saule ryding in with hys servants" (stage-directions, 168). Here horses can be used effectively, and members of the audience join the action as fellow travelers on the road to Damascus. If the mechanics for the thunder and lightning which the directions require to enhance Paul's violent apparition are provided in the same way as the thunder and fireworks for the council of devils in Hell, then with horses rearing and plunging, crowd scattering and a booming voice of God from the heavens we may assume that the conversion scene could provide some marvelous spectacle.

Mary Magdalene, as the complexity of plot and length of text will suggest (2,144 lines with more than 65 parts), requires a very different type of staging. For one thing, the producer would have had to provide for scenes in palaces and castles, taverns and graveyards, hell, shipboard and the desert. Moreover, many of the changes of place are in rapid succession, which adds to the problem. The text itself is not absolutely clear about the staging, but the general picture can be constructed with reasonable accuracy. The appearance of Sesar, Herowde, and Pylatt would seem to be in three scaffolds surrounding a central *platea* where most of the main action will occur. It is here, presumably, that Syrus first appears with Lazarus, Mary, and Martha; and here that the resurrection of Lazarus, temptation of Magdalene, and the voyages to and from Marseilles will probably have to take place. Whether as theater in the round or according to the more usual simultaneous mansions convention—the two are not necessarily mutually exclusive—the performance requires a large area:

> Here xal satan go hom to his stage, and mari xal
> entyr In to þe place alone, save þe bad angyl and
> r1 þe seuen dedly synnes xal be conveyyd in to þe
> howse of symont leprovs, þey xal be a ray-yd like
> vij dylf: þus kept closse, mari xal be in an erbyr [. . .] (at 563)

The scaffoldings are undoubtedly the same upon which appeared "þe Kyng of þe World, Flesch and þe Devile," adding thus to the symmetry, and if one of the scaffolds or "stages" is destroyed when the disgruntled chief devil herds his outcast assistants into the "howse" (741) to be set on fire, one of the others, probably the central one, might well have served as a backframe for the double-tiered action of Mary's ascensions from the wilderness (2004–39). The directions require no small technical competence:

> Here xall to angylles desend In to wyldyrnesse;
> and other to xall bryng an oble, opynly aperyng *wafer*
> a loft In þe clowddes; þe to be-nethyn xall bryng
> mary, and she xall receyve þe bred, and þan go
> a-ȝen In to wyldyrnesse (at 2019)
> Her xall she be halsyd with angelles *saluted? houseled?*
> with reverent song.
> Asumpta est maria in nubibus; celi gavdent,
> Angeli lavdantes felium Dei; et dicit mari [. . .] (at 2031)

No less demanding is the appearance and movement about the "place" of the ship, which, unless the outdoor stage can somehow make use of a small pond with an island, must have been constructed, like some Noah's arks and a host of spectacular pageant-ships from the popular *entremets* and court entertainments, upon wheels or round a pageant-wagon.[20] (This might earlier have been the third scaffold.) The ship, sufficient for six actors, is clearly able to enter and leave the principal playing area, e.g., *et tunc navis venit ad circa placeam* (1839); "Here goth the shep owt ofe the place" (1923).

But the playwright does not depend upon extravagant machinery alone to gain the engagement of his audience. Ranging from farcical comedy, in an Uncle Screwtape-like dispute between the pagan priest and his boy, to simple but emotionally powerful dialogue at Lazarus' death and subtle verbal games in the house of Symond the Leper, the Digby dramatist provides for a marvelous variety and orchestration of both tone and pace. The "Midsummer Night's Dream" sequence, with devils and vices plotting around the unseeing Magdalene, is as engaging a dramatic effect as its parallel, the potentially beautiful but awesome dream-vision appearance of white-robed Magdalene and her candle-bearing angels to the King of Marseilles, troubled, in his sleep (158ff.). Yet one "dream" sequence is congested, boisterous, and comic, the other awesome, tranquil, and mysterious.

V

The subject of the saints' plays is conversion. More obviously evangelical than the morality or even perhaps the cycle play in this respect, they present us with a wayward life undergoing spiritual revolution, and then show forth the rewards and various consequences of that revolution. Though St. Paul's conversion is a classic illustration, Mary Magdalene provides perhaps the more appealing example of a contrite and repentant sinner who, turning from her ways, is freed from evil to become a saint. In a marvelous evocation of her salvation's history, and in the paradoxical language of Paul and St. Augustine, she cries,

> I was drynchyn In synne deversarye
> tyll þat lord relevyd me be his domynacy-n,
> grace to me he wold never de-nye;
> thowe I were nevyr so synful, he seyd 'revertere' ! (754–57)

The familiar Augustinian play on *verterel reverterel convertere* (from the *Confessions*) is emblematic in her description of what has taken place (cf. 768–75), helping to express how from a medieval Christian perspective conversion can be a "dramatic" event in all senses. By his paralleling of Mary's story with the action of Christ in divine redemption, and the repetition of the pattern in the story of the converted King of Marseilles and his resurrected wife and child, the playwright gives lively dramatic form to the traditional Augustinian idea of conversion as a repetition of the Incarnation in personal guise. To participate in the one transformation produces others: from prostitute to saint, or from tyrant to pilgrim, because the Word becomes flesh. The enacting itself becomes theological statement. Both Paul and Mary Magdalene symbolize the moment by putting on new costume (*St. Paul,* 502; *Mary Magdalene,* 683; cf. 1618).

A chief strategy of the saint's play is itself biblical: prolepsis and recurrence. In *Mary Magdalene,* the story of the resurrection of Lazarus is used by Christ in his speeches to signify his own death and resurrection, and the playwright then utilizes the *signum* to imply without performance the events of Calvary and the open tomb. Space is similarly symbolic. For example, we might consider the "erbyr" in which the drunken Mary falls asleep, waiting for her lovers, only to awaken sobered with remorse and longing to seek out Jesus. From the point of view of staging, it takes little imagination to discern that the place will be the same in which Mary's fall was plotted by the council of vices, and the flowers in which the Kyng of Flesch took such delight (334–51) still available to frame the Magdalene's last attendance "tyll som lover wol apere" (570). But the "erbyr" will also provide the garden in which Mary is first to discover the risen Christ, whom she has

> [...] porposyd in eche degre
> to have hym with me werely,

the wyche my specyall lord hath be,
and I his lover and cause wyll phy [*trust*]. (1065–68)

She takes him, of course, to be a gardener. It is hard to imagine a more effective synthesis of the naturalistic and symbolic action of the play than Christ's response:

So I am, for sothe, Mary:
mannys hartt is my gardyn here;
þer In I sow sedys of vertu all þe ȝere;
þe fowle wedes and wycys, I reynd vp be þe rote. *vices*
whan þat gardyn is watteryd with terys clere,
than spryng vertuus, and smelle full sote *sweet* (1080–85)

One love becomes another. A complex psychological realization of such parallel and recurrence is not the sort of thing to which the classical unities (or their view of history) are much assistance. There are too many occasions in the performance of a medieval play like *Mary Magdalene* or *St. Paul* where one is not, in the classical sense, wholly a "spectator," and as theatrical folk well recognize, there is a profound connection between the stage as a proscenium-arched set-piece and the expectation of classical unities for which the medieval playwright does not provide.

The objective of the saints' plays is participation. Whether by playing out part of the dramatic action amongst the crowd, or by appealing to shared and deeply felt ideas, the achievement and the effect of such participation is bound to be psychological and emotional. *Mary Magdalene* seems likely to have generated a great deal of emotion in performance. Following the miracle of Lazarus's resurrection, a direction for general participation suggests that the play might induce a charismatic spiritual fervor:

Here all þe pepull, and þe Iewys, mari, and martha with one woys sey þes
wordes: we be-leve in yow savyowr, Iesus, Iesus, Iesus! (920)

Ecstatic response, familiar also in medieval Italian saint's plays, expresses the internal characterization of biblical history as personal present to which the whole play points.

St. Bonaventure, first and most important medieval philosopher to address himself to the aesthetics of drama, wrote in his *De reductione artium ad theologiam* that the illumination of the arts can be precisely that of Scripture. They both show us "the eternal generation and Incarnation of the

Word, the pattern of human life, and the union of the soul with God." But of all the arts, he continued, "it is dramatic art, or the art of putting on plays, which embraces every form of entertainment, whether song, music, fiction or pantomime," which best fulfills, according to Horace, the goals of art.[21] Had he been there to see, one feels sure that he would have heartily approved *The Conversion of St. Paul* and *Mary Magdalene,* and found in their orchestration of song, dance, pantomime, and spectacle some justification for his most concise appreciation of their medium: *theatrica, autem, est unica.*[22]

(1973)

Chapter Nine

Parody and Piety in Bosch's *Haywain*

The great day of the LORD is near . . . a day of wrath . . . I will bring distress upon men, and they shall walk like blind men, because they have sinned against the LORD . . .

Zephaniah 1:14–17

What is the chaff to the wheat? says the LORD. Is not my word like a fire?

Jeremiah 23:28–29

I

Criticism of institutions, especially when it comes from within and must necessarily make an approach to those authoritative texts common to the institution, is often both learned and complex. This is particularly noticeable in the late medieval Christian Church in Europe, where real and fervent piety often produced the most stinging assaults upon the practice of professing visible representatives of the church. It is typical of these critiques on the eve of the Reformation that they were grounded in the foundational authorities acknowledged by all Christians, the Scriptures and the liturgy, and also that they were accordingly deeply hermeneutic in their character and purpose. Rhetorically, a familiar tactic of the most successful critics of institutional hypocrisy and abuse was verbal or visual parody. The paintings of Hieronymus Bosch offer many excellent examples of such complex and learned parody: one panel painting must here suffice to illustrate the genre.

Three great triptych panels by Bosch survive; the one on whose interpretation there seems to be the least consensus is also the one that seems least well suited to be an altarpiece.[1] Like the others, it has eschatological portent. The *Hooiwagen Panel*, or *Haywain*, frames with perspectives on Paradise Lost and Apocalyptic retribution a central scene that appears to be neither scriptural (as in *Sicut erat in diebus Noe*) nor hagiographical (as in *Temptations of Saint Anthony*), but contemporary and perhaps proverbial. Surrounded by greed-driven burghers and corrupted clergy, followed by a procession of civil and ecclesiastical powers, and drawn by a throng of Hell's grotesques, a heavily mounded haywagon moves slowly through an apparently contemporary landscape (fig. 1). Burghers and clergy alike, involved in all kinds of community misdemeanor and personal inconsistencies, simultaneously devote themselves to grasping at the hay on the wagon. This dominant activity in the painting traditionally has been related to Dutch and Flemish proverbs ("*al hooi*," ["all is vain"] "*niet een hoo*," and so on) which associate hay with the vanity of the world, and so the *Haywain* has been interpreted both as a satirical treatment of cupidity and as a Solomonic denunciation of the promise of the world: *al hooi*.[2] But if the Flemish proverbs connecting hay with worldly vanity do not seem inconsistent with the central image in the panel, they do very little to involve satisfactorily the two wings of the triptych with the centerpiece in any overall reading of the painting, and do not as yet enlighten us concerning the place of such a work in church or chapel. Most important, the hay proverbs do not themselves inform us as to the relationship of interior sections of the actual haywagon panel; for example, there seems to be no direct connection between *al hooi* and either the apparent anticlericalism of the panel, or certain important groups of figures in the painting, such as the musical symposium at the top of the haymound itself.

It is in fact with the grouping at the top of the haymound, at the high center of the whole painting (fig. 2), that we get our first distinct notions of a thematic focus in the *Haywain* which transcends the merely proverbial. There are eight persons in this grouping, and they cluster about a musical manuscript that one of the two couples in the group is employing in order to learn to sing a song. The rather intent but suspiciously air-borne young man in white plays a lute, and the seated girl attends carefully to her vocal part, the notation of which is being outlined by a tutor in red headgear. The tutor may be teaching the couple to sing together harmoniously, since the young man appears to enunciate a different portion of the lyrics than his counterpart. These gracefully proportioned figures are comparatively relaxed and composed, unlike most others in the panel. The initial effect of this expression of tranquil *concordia* in the midst of a world raging with *discordia* is one of striking incongruity, and is, I think, what Bosch must have expected this element to produce. And, in his utilization of music to provide a foil for the discord he paints, Bosch, perhaps "the most medieval painter of the fifteenth century,"[3] has ample and commonplace precedent.

In the fifteenth century, music, musical theory, and hence the iconography of music involved (as it has fairly consistently since the time of the Pythagoreans) much more than the sound of music.[4] In this tradition, for example in such a standard work on the subject as Saint Augustine's *De musica*, beauty itself is related to the principle of harmony. Here whether in the order of Creation or the beauty of dancing, what is loved is the "proportionate intervals" presented to us; from the proportions of metrical feet to the ultimate Equality, each of these to be considered as traces of the mind of the Creator (1.6). Music was considered to be the natural voice of ordinate love, so that in truly harmonious love the body is loved but the spirit still more;[5] and it was considered that the same love that governed the harmony of nature could best provide in extension that happy concord in human nature.[6] From the time of Saint Augustine the octave itself, with its ratio of 1:2, was often taken to be figurative for the love-concord made possible by Christ between himself and the inferior nature of humankind.

The musical scene of the *Haywain* then (in its inner circle one of apparent concord), when carefully superimposed on a particularly chaotic outer world, seems to compose some sort of commentary on that chaos. Further, if it proposes such a commentary, the scenario in its larger context speaks then not merely in terms of "music that soothes the troubled breast," but more probably of the whole subject of human relationships in the "world" that the artist is portraying: it speaks of the role and purpose of community, of Love. Pursuing this line of reflection the viewer is enabled, in turn, to consider the second pair of lovers in the setting, and to relate their activity to that of the first pair. There are models for this comparison.

One of the chief commonplaces concerning love in the Renaissance is that it was understood to take two forms, one chaste and one sensual. Since the Pythagoreans had divided the deities and identified one celestial and one terrestrial Venus, Western tradition had been able to look upon Venus as "mother of the twin loves" (or capable of two moods),[7] and this commonplace idea is elaborated upon at length by the compendium for artists composed by Albericus, the Third Vatican Mythographer.[8] Some have seen this idea at work in a well-known painting by Titian, for example, his *Sacred and Profane Love.*[9] The celestial Venus was regarded as "mundana musica," and associated with the harmonious Divine Love that orders Creation, but the sensual Venus, as Bernard Sylvester put it, "we call concupiscence of the flesh, which is the mother of all fornication."[10] This binary opposition, familiar in late medieval and Renaissance writing, sees concupiscence as a congenital problem in postlapsarian creatures, and in fact John the Scot in his famous commentary on the Gospel according to Mark had already associated the profane Venus with the primal Edenic malady.[11] As for the love symbolized by her celestial sister, it was frequently associated with music in late medieval art, so that it became possible to distinguish two very different symbolic melodies of love in late medieval and Renaissance iconography, one the music of the spirit and the flesh in the harmony of created nature, and the other the music of the flesh impulsively seeking to encompass its own ends.[12] Each is a melody of love; but while one is a "rational" love of harmony and concord, the other is, of course, a discordant appetite for essentially carnal gratifications. In theological terms the melodies can be represented as the "New Song" of Saint Paul's "New Man," and the "Old Song" of the "Old Man," fallen and as yet unregenerate (cf. Eph 4:22ff.).[13]

Certain obvious possibilities in the relationship of music to carnal love could, in this period, receive "explicit" artistic representation, even in religious contexts. For example, in illustrating the course of the "Old Song," the artist who illustrated Guido Faba's *Summa de viciis* invites us through duplication of the same face to see a musician with his instrument and a lover with his "instrument" as the same person.[14] In this illustration, both activities illustrate indulgence in inferior and ultimately discordant appetites. This is the kind of music that we see being practiced by the second pair of lovers in Bosch's *Haywain.* They too have their whispering tutor (or perhaps voyeur) who, like his counterpart in the Garden of Eden panel at the left, hides in the bushes and does not fully expose himself to the light. Moreover, this tutor watches nervously out of the corner of his eye an angel who, looking heavenward toward the resurrected Christ, prays fervently—presumably on behalf of Celestial Love—in the apparent conflict between the two loves which rages on the little "stage" atop the hay. And if the two pairs of lovers are representatively engaged in a conflict of one "music" with another, the good angel is engaged in prayer, presumably invoking the triumph of marriage over adultery, or, to put it in musical terms, of divine harmony over the prancing solo performance of an even more obvious ally of *discordia.* The devilish bad angel, tinted blue and energetically blowing his instrument against the harmony of the New Song, thus completes a symmetrical débat: on one side the *concordia* of the Divine Love prayed for by the good angel is by the rather spiritual-looking lovers; on the other, the raucous piping of the blue devil offsets the ordered measures of the lutanist, presumably with an urgency of cadence more suitable to the amorous action of the lover in the bushes. These juxtaposed images remind us of the perpetual struggle between *caritas* and *cupiditas* (concord and discord), which is the heart of each medieval drama. In fact, with good angel and bad, false counselor and true, moral action and conflict, and even the stage qualities of the setting itself, we may begin to see in the grouping atop the haywagon a kind of pageant or play. But despite the sweep of this triptych from Creation and Fall to Judgment and Retribution, the painting does not make immediate connection to the biblical cycle plays we might expect to be in the painter's mind.

II

Foremost among the entertainment that charmed the citizens of Bosch's own s'Hertogenbosch, and indeed the people of all the Netherlandish regions, were mystery and morality plays.[15] Unfortunately, not many of the early texts survive, and nothing in the way of a regular cycle-play text from this region is left to us, though fragments, records, and a few extant Creation-to-Doomsday texts give us a fair idea of what the early drama was like.[16]

We know, for example, that in the Netherlands, as in England and in Italy, Franciscans were foremost among instigators of vernacular religious drama.[17] Through guilds and confraternities, in the formation of which the Franciscans and other fraternal orders played a large part, the plays received elaboration and further development,[18] so that down through the mid-sixteenth century dramatic activity flourished under the guidance of such confraternities as the Brotherhood of Our Lady at Roosebeke ("van Onser Vrauwen van Roosebeke") and its equivalents in Alveringham, Isenberghe, Nieuport, Audenarde, Ghent, Ypres, Grammont, and elsewhere.[19] It is noteworthy that these plays were very frequently associated with processions, and in the Netherlands confraternities in particular were heavily involved in the production of *haegspel* (processional plays), which moved from one village to another. One of these, that of the *Pilgrim*, performed in Grammont in 1545 at Pentecost, required as much as three days to produce.[20]

Now it is commonly recognized by historians of the drama that important to the connection between procession and religious drama in the late Middle Ages, and indeed perhaps fundamentally to be associated with cycle drama in particular, is the liturgical feast of Corpus Christi.[21] This feast has its origins in the Lowland countries. Inspired by a particular devotion to the Holy Sacrament on the part of Saint Juliana of Liège and eventually adopted by Pope Urban IV, it was firmly established by action of the council of Vienne in 1311 under Clement V. Coming into approbation with it was a theophoric procession, already being practiced as part of the rites of that day in some Netherlandish areas.[22] In such a procession the Host was ceremonially paraded through the city—probably on a special vehicle—followed by a hierarchically ordered procession of both civil and ecclesiastical personages.[23] Celebrated the Thursday after Trinity Sunday, the feast became a prime

occasion for the performance of religious plays, the actors of which in some
cases may have followed with pageant-wagons (modified haywagons)
through the city the route taken by the Host on the previous day.[24] At
Alveringham, Isenburg, and Nieuport, often twice a year and as late as 1554,
the guilds assembled such plays "pour y contribuer à l'embellissement de la
procession de la localité et notamment à celle du Saint-Sacrament,"[25] and
the *Comptes de la uitle de Nieuport* (*The Book of Vices*) show a procession play
connected with the honoring of Holy Communion as early as 1488, twenty-
two years before the probable date of the *Haywain*.[26]

It was just about this time that the young Bosch undertook what was likely a significant step in his own spiritual and artistic life. He became a member
of the Illustre Lieve-Vrouwe Broederschap of s'Hertogenbosch.[27] Shortly he
was tonsured, and in 1488 sworn in as a *frère juré*. The particular duties of
members of the Brotherhood of Our Lady of s'Hertogenbosch are of interest
here: besides training members for the cathedral orchestra, the Brotherhood,
like so many others of its type, had "a theatrical company which specialized in
staging dramatic performances of various kinds, Mystery plays, devil dances,
ballets of ghosts and skeletons, farces and *diabeleries*, all of which called for a
formidable array of stage properties." Robert Delevoy, in his study of Bosch's
life in his confraternity, observes that "for months in advance the members of
the brotherhood made ready for the parts they were to play in the annual procession, in which they sometimes acted scenes from the Gospels."[28] Working
from records of the Brotherhood,[29] Delevoy was able to determine that Bosch
himself played an active part in stage performances as well as religious ceremonies, that he was involved in designing costumes and stagecraft, including
a "copper crown and model for a Crucifixion," that he acted in the plays and
sang in the church choir. Moreover, it seems that at least one of his other two
great triptychs may relate to his theatrical experience: the records inform us
that of all the floats in the procession of s'Hertogenbosch the one that most
continually met with applause represented "The Temptations of the
Hermit."[30] Nor is this the only connection that has been suggested between
Bosch's paintings and the procession and drama of their time, for as early as
Philip II of Spain a comparison had been drawn between Bosch's paintings
and the characters in a Corpus Christi procession.[31] Accordingly, we should
anticipate possible influences from the theater on his paintings, and not
excluding that greatest annual occasion for religious drama, the feast and procession of Corpus Christi.

Aside from the strong suggestion inherent in the structuring of the
group on top of the haywagon which we have just begun to consider, it is
obvious even at first glance that the haywagon of the central panel is itself

integral to a special *processus*, one that dominates the flow of motion in the picture as it moves away from the barred portal of Eden at the left toward what appears to be apocalyptic judgment on the right.[32] The procession is moving toward the right panel and Hell, with the motive power of the wagon provided by recognizably demonic grotesques. Arrayed in orderly fashion behind the wagon are the ecclesiastical and civil powers of the World, riding in stately ignorance both of their imminent destination and of what is descending in the clouds above them. Further, we see that they are made blind by the wagon load to what they are really following. The *processus* that we see is designed to remind us, I believe, not only of the *haegspel* that would have been familiar to Bosch's contemporaries as it processed from village to village—and to which the pageant group atop the wagon-load relates—but of that *processus* firmly connected with the drama that played its part in the celebration of the feast of Corpus Christi. It is evident that the haywagon procession embraces the hierarchical parade-order of both civil and ecclesiastical officials prescribed for Corpus Christi processions. Connection with the drama of that feast, in the light of Bosch's own theatrical activities (particularly if we view the musical grouping on top of the wagon as a pageant), seems unavoidable. If the solemn columns of civil and ecclesiastical powers suggest the feast's theophoric procession almost as much as its pageants, what is missing is merely the usual object of the Corpus Christi parade. Here powers of the world are *not* following the Host. But that, I think, is precisely what Bosch intended to say.

To grasp the profundity of the irony in Bosch's image we need to recollect one of the most commonplace distinctions in late medieval aesthetics, that made between the wheat, or essential germ of meaning in a text or statement, and the chaff, the superficial dross to be laid aside in search for the wheat.[33] In Scripture the distinction between the wheat and the chaff pertains to the just and the unjust in God's judgment (cf. Zeph 2:1–2; Matt 3:12), but in the traditional exegesis available to Bosch (from Augustine to the Ordinary Gloss of the Bible) the wheat or fruit was typically likened to an understanding of the Spirit, the chaff to the mere letter, or external nature of things.[34] For example, in Isaiah 11:7, "the lion shall eat straw (*paleus*) like the ox," the marginal *Glossa* for this verse interprets that "the princes of this world and other simple persons are content with the surface of history, for they do not understand the wheat and the pith, or the inner sense."[35] However surprising in itself, this commentary is not at all inconsistent with the center panel of our painting. It leads us to wonder if the people on parade in the haywagon panel are intended by Bosch to betray an unwise contentment with the "surface of history" (after all their hellish destination is developing historically). If so, what for them might be the "wheat" or "inner sense" of history that they have instead? What we have here is the visual equivalent of a rhetorical question. In the Christian culture of Bosch and his audience the overt theological answer to that question comes from the fourteenth verse of the Gospel according to John: "And the Word was made flesh, and dwelt amongst us." Christ the Incarnate Redeemer enters into and provides the "inner sense" of Christian history. He becomes "flesh" for all men who truly participate in Holy Communion,[36] and it is this central Christian doctrine, that is the "wheat germ" of the Corpus Christi feast and its drama, the heart of their meaning. The very first words of the entrance hymn for the Mass of Corpus Christi, chief among celebrations of the Holy Eucharist, were: "He fed them with the fat of the wheat, alleluia!"[37] But as we gaze at the central commodity of the *Haywain* we are forced to observe that it is not, of course, such true wheat that the princes and other simple persons are following. Nor is it the Corpus Christi processional Host. Rather, we see in the color and texture of the cargo they snatch and sack that they blindly pursue a wagon load of *hooi, brin d'herbe*, chaff.[38] That is, on closer observation, the wagon proves actually to be loaded with straw rather than hay, gathered as it would have been after threshing the grain to be brought in for animal bedding. In this scene, however it will not be loaded into any farmer's barn, but rather into a cave entrance (behind the wagon) which looks suspiciously like "Hell Mouth" from a medieval morality play—fuel for the "unquenchable fire" (Matt 3:12; Luke 3:17; cf. Isa 5:24). This is the scene upon which the atoning Christ, man of sorrows, looks down as he descends through the clouds.

III

As symbol, the value of the wheat (or the Host) and the destiny of those who partake of it (and so become one with it as part of the Body of Christ) is in biblical perspective opposed to that of the straw or chaff. This opposition, it seems to me, links Bosch's implicit statement about human concord to Holy Communion, as well as to the apparent anticlericalism and obvious eschatological nature of the painting.

Anticlerical statements were a common enough feature of the literature and drama of Bosch's time, particularly where lay confraternities of the sort to which he belonged were involved, since their own spirituality was often sincere and intense. By the first decade of the sixteenth century, such sentiments had been growing in Northern Europe for more than a century. Often the focus of this dissent fell on the mendicant orders most heavily, since they were associated with abuses such as the sale of indulgences and other forms of extortion. It is worth noting, for example, that prominent at the very center of the panel and just below the theatrical grouping, a Franciscan friar struggles with a woman who is beating his companion, fallen on a snatch of straw. That the Franciscans, who had much to do with early developments in the drama and confraternities, should be specifically foremost in the anti-clerical criticism of the painting is not surprising; since by this time they were thought to have fallen badly from a distinctly Christ-like ideal they were frequently attacked, especially by those who, like Bosch, belonged to confraternities that still retained their memory of early fraternal spiritu-ality.[39] This detail reminds us of another Bosch painting, *Ship of Fools*, where the primary fools in the ship are Franciscan and where the nature of their folly is chiefly expressed in their song. (Indeed, it is a scene well worth com-paring to that in the *Haywain*.) There are other contemporary statements of a general anticlerical nature which also bear a remarkable similarity to Bosch's painting. One passage from the remnant annals of medieval Flemish drama is trenchant:

> In the streets it's hard to tell a priest from a layman, such is his costume [. . .] shame! a well sharpened dagger hangs from his side [. . .] The high prelates—ah—it is not fitting even to speak of their habitual folly. They imagine that foolishness is a "constitutional" privilege of their estate. Consequently they throw snares at the feet of the simple and so upset them [. . .]. They are ignorant, and they charge with error those who do know anything. They urge us to sobriety, but daily drink themselves silly. They preach peace and themselves wreak discord. They say also: flee adultery! and they run around with women in full view of everybody. They wish us to help the poor, and they themselves give not so much as a mite.[40]

Our attention might be drawn here to the nun, below and to the left of the wagon, her dagger drawn, and to the generally self-indulgent, glut-tonous, lecherous misdemeanor of clerics at the right bottom side of the panel that seems so aptly to illustrate this dramatic complaint. But there were other forms for such criticism. In a ritual anticlerical condemnation of those who are so "bound to the love of the things of this present life," that is, who love only the chaff, Juan de Valdes says:

> Satan directly sets before such persons certain marked passages, which he gives them to understand are the right paths and they, blind with the love of themselves, willingly yield themselves to be deceived and injured by sup-posing that God carries them whilst all along it is the devil who is leading them. Hence are born superfluous ceremonies; hence arise pernicious superstitions; hence come false worships.[41]

Here, too, the language describes well enough the center panel of Bosch's painting. Who could appear more hopelessly sure of themselves than those civil and ecclesiastical personages who follow the haywagon? Or who, more blinded by self-love and "superfluous ceremonies," could be less aware that theirs is a path of the devil's leading, and not God's?

The liturgy for Corpus Christi itself continues to be of relevance to our closer reading. The first psalm of the first nocturn is Psalm 1: "Blessed is the man who has not walked in the counsel of the ungodly, nor stood in the way of sinners, nor sat in the chair of pestilence, but his will is in the law of the Lord." Such a one, it says, shall "be like a tree, which is planted near the running waters, which shall bring forth its fruit," the very opposite of the wicked, whose "leaf" falls off (v. 3), who are like the "chaff, which the wind drives away" (v. 4), and of whom the psalmist concludes, "the way of the wicked shall perish" (v. 6). Over and against such familiar scriptures are scripture passages frequently cited in anti-fraternal literature of the time, some of which apply just as directly to the images of the *Haywain*, particularly in terms of the chaff, or straw, which is its principal image. A popular scriptural passage that might be invoked in this connection is Jeremiah 23: "Woe be unto the pastors that destroy and scatter the sheep of my pasture saith the Lord." What the prophets are charged with is mistaking the true substance of spiritual nourishment: "What is the chaff to the wheat?" (v. 28). The *Ordinary Gloss* of the Bible, commonest marginal commentary in the Bible of Bosch's day, sees this chapter as a warning to the "princes of the Church," and says that "the pleasing doctrine of heretics compares with the chaff, for it has no pith, nor does it offer refreshment."[42] But the whole passage from Jeremiah is pertinent, with or without exegetical commentary: "Woe be unto the shepherds that destroy and scatter the sheep of my pasture!" (v. 1 KJV); "Both prophet and priest are profane" (v. 11); "wherefore their ways shall be unto them as slippery ways in the darkness: they shall be driven on and fall therein: for I will bring evil upon them, even in the year of their visitation, saith the Lord" (v. 12); "they commit adultery and walk in lies: they strengthen also the hand of evildoers, that none doth return from his wickedness: they are all of them unto me as Sodom and Gomorrah" (v. 14); "he that hath my word let him speak my word faithfully. What is the chaff to the wheat? saith the Lord. Is not my word like as a fire?" (vv. 28–29).

The force of such anti-clerical criticism was to contend that clerics of this profane kind were not fit to represent and administer the Blessed Sacrament, for, as the *Ordinary Gloss* puts it, they are sterile of virtue and grace (*virtutum et gratiarum sterilitas consequitur*).[43] Along with the Corpus Christi liturgy, a scripture like the Jeremiah passage could well have been in

Bosch's mind when he composed the *Haywain*. (It had already received extended pictorial elaboration at least once, and in a source certainly available to him, the *Bible moralisée*.)[44]

In this light the apparent anticlericalism of the *Haywain* would seem to relate rather well to a main subject for the painting, and in such a way as to make possible our imagining it as an altarpiece. If we allow into our perception of the work associations borrowed from liturgical and dramatic processions of Corpus Christi (and it would seem to me that the painting's first audience could hardly avoid that), then the *Haywain* can involve a proper and yet most serious charge to clergy and layman alike as they actually come before the altar: to examine their hearts before participation in Holy Communion. For it is at this point, according to Christian theology, that any Christian, layman or priest, through an improper attitude of his heart can engage in false worship of most serious consequence; self-examination is necessary, "for he that eateth and drinketh unworthily, eateth and drinketh damnation unto himself, not discerning the Lord's body" (1 Cor 11:28–29). As for the clergy, the offertory hymn for the liturgy of Corpus Christi reminds that "the priests of the Lord offer incense and loaves to God; for that they shall be sacred to their God and shall not profane His name."[45] Even in the ecclesiastical warning there is continued the metaphor of the wheat and the chaff; here it is extended to the whole body of Christ and the world in Judgment, when the victorious Christ "will [. . .] gather his wheat into the garner, but he will burn up the chaff with unquenchable fire" (Matt 3:12). The *Ordinary Gloss* explains that here the chaff represents "those who have been imbued with the faith of the sacraments, but are not firm in it."[46] The connection of mistreatment of Holy Communion and final judgment are thus as theologically clear as they would appear to be in the painting: the Christ who comes to renew his Sacrifice in the Eucharist is also the Christ who will descend again finally victorious, judging men according to whether they truly have become one with his body in the Sacrament. Bosch paints his Christ as the mysterious Sacrifice, the "suffered" Christ, but significantly also as the Christ of the Second Coming, who descends through the clouds in the same manner as we see him in *The Last Judgment*.[47]

In the Hell of the *Haywain* we see at least one indication that final judgment is to be appropriate to the judged: the helmeted but naked soul seated on the ox carries numerous receptacles about in a fruitless search, but there is no Water of Life in that place; indeed, the dry cistern is being bricked up, tower-of-Babel fashion, by several industrious grotesques. And in his hand the helmeted soul carries what is clearly an empty chalice. His is the opposite fate, surely, to those blessed described in the psalm of the second nocturn for

Corpus Christi, whose "chalice overflows" (*poculum* [. . .] *exuberans*, cf. Ps 22).[48] I submit that this desolate figure, among the damned, represents those clerics who have profaned the true Host. The ox (it is not a cow) on which he rides is a traditional symbol for the priesthood,[49] and I think that the robes on its back are probably priestly vestments. One attribute of his iconography is particularly ironic: his helmet, traditional accoutrement of the *Christi milites*, has in his case hardly proved to be the helmet of Salvation (Eph 6:17).

IV

It is appropriate now that we return to the musical morality play at the top of the haywagon, in the central panel whence we began. We have concluded that the procession in Bosch's painting most likely relates, as did the processional plays themselves, to the feast of Corpus Christi, that the chaff or load of hay so blindly pursued intends a warning against carelessness with the chief mystery and worship of Christian faith, and that this in turn has a natural apocalyptic portent. What then is the relationship of the theme of music to Holy Communion?

The music of harmony and of concord, we remember, is the music of "true communion." This is the love of Christ for men, which when shared by a man entunes his body and his spirit so that he loves in proper *ratio*, and enjoys thus the restored communion of the New Man in his New Song. (In fact, the New Song had become in Augustinian exegesis actually a celebration of the successful separation of the wheat from the chaff).[50] That "good" music could be regarded as a tool of Aesculapius for restoring "the madman to his former health by a concord of sounds"[51] may suggest why a man of medicine is pictured among the reprobate clerics next to the discordant bagpiper (bottom center). Like the fortune-telling gypsies (bottom left)[52] who see into the future no more clearly than the *hooi*-blind clerics and powers of the world, his also is a false remedy. And his pockets are likewise full of straw. For the discordant chaos of human vices, it was appropriately the true Sacrament that was regarded as effective *remedium*. As Thomas à Kempis, Bosch's contemporary, near neighbor, and member of the Brethren of the Common Life of s'Hertogenbosch said:

> For this most high and worthy Sacrament is the health both of soul and
> body, the medicine for all spiritual langour; hereby my vices are cured, my
> passions bridled, my temptations overcome or diminished; greater grace is
> infused, virtue begun is increased, faith is confirmed, hope strengthened,
> and love set on fire and spread abroad.[53]

And when the passions are bridled and vices cured, then the proper ratios of love can operate to fill the soul with that harmony that produces true virtue. Hugh of Saint Victor, writing about "human music," has it that "music in the spirit exists in virtues like justice, piety, and temperance"—the qualities of the concord in which the little community of the tutor and two singers attempt to harmonize, but hardly the brawling crowd below them.[54] Yet harmony and concord in the Body of Christ (in his community) is precisely what Communion with his Divine Love is supposed to achieve. We see that the tutor of the harmonious lovers has his natural correspondent in Paradise too—it is the red-crowned Sovereign God who there conjoins Adam and Eve in the primal harmony of pre-fallen nature, the perfect community of the human and the divine subsequently to be forsaken.

In several of his paintings, Bosch is concerned to show that the biblical doctrine of the Fall has very much to do with community. The separation of man from God involves also a certain separation of man from other men, man from woman, even division within the self. And the effect of Fall in the world, as the central panel makes very clear, is one of further separation, strife, and discord. But salvation has equally to do with community. The Great Commandment is that we should love the Lord with all our heart, soul and mind—and our neighbor as ourself (Matt 22:37–39). When we truly become one with his Body (in Holy Communion), for a medieval Catholic part of the mystery is that we may become one with his body (his Community). It is in this aspect of communion with his love that we may learn to sing together the harmony of the New Song, which is, if you like, the *ratio* of love (*caritas*) expressed in the Great Commandment.[55] It is this that true Christian community is all about.

Finally, the Corpus Christi mass itself is of all the masses of the calendar year the one that most explicitly invokes the role of music in joyous response to the Blessed Sacrament, calling in Pope Urban IV's bull concerning the Feast, for "songs of praise" and "hymns of joy."[56] It would seem that the apparently incongruous harmony of the peaceful couple atop the haywagon is not inappropriate. Yet the harmonious lovers are not themselves unthreatened by their environment. Love is always capable of ambiguity. After all, there is more than one "music" being made atop the hay. The bad angel plays his discordant melody too, in which the other couple "joins," and indeed their song is the very cacophony of the chaos and cupidity below them. In fact, directly beneath the bad angel at the bottom of the picture a suspicious character, dressed likewise in blue, pipes with a typical instrument of carnal love—a bagpipe[57]—the discordant melody to which the carnal monks and nuns collect and sack their hay. We begin to suspect, alas, that this is the tune to which the whole procession moves, not in a pilgrimage towards the celestial city, but in precisely the opposite direction. The central lovers would seem to point to a possibility, hardly to a certainty.

There are a few major details of the grouping on the hay which remain to be considered. They are the presence of the jug or vessel on a stick, and the owl. There is in the Corpus Christi liturgy a comparable constellation of symbolic objects, which, in the treatment given them by Bosch, would be consistent with the moral reversal represented by the Wain itself. The grouping responds to an established relationship between the *plaustrum* ("wagon") that bears the Host with its archetype, the *plaustrum* of the Exodus which bore the Ark of the Covenant. The ark, symbol of the Covenant and thus, in later typology, of sacramental communion between God and man,[58] contained the Law, Aaron's rod, and a pot (or vessel) of manna (Exod 37:1, Heb 9:4). These elements received traditional and predictable spiritual interpretations, the law as "witness" of God's word, the manna as prefiguration of Christ's body (the Host) and Aaron's "florent yerde" as a symbol of Christ's incarnation and virgin birth, the rod that blossoms forth into the fruit of God's love for man, and brings into focus the "line" of our redemption. These ideas are common, of course, in the liturgy, and find graphic representation in the typology of popular picture Bibles such as the *Biblia pauperum*.[59] What seems to be offered here once again is a visual parody. The rod protruding barren and the presumably empty jug may seem more readily commensurate with the scriptural and liturgical model than the defecating owl. Yet the association of the owl with the witness of the Law was an old one by Bosch's time, most memorably in medieval pulpit carving, where the owl was turned away from in uttering the "new law," the witness to whose light the eyes of the old law could not fully adjust.[60] Together then, these three details satirically invoke the futility of the procession, and add strength to the image of spiritual fruitlessness which the Wain itself makes central to the painting.

A further and more immediately accessible aspect of the iconography of the vessel may be that which is invoked as well in Bosch's *Ship of Fools*. As is typical of much of the iconography Bosch employs, it has a biblical source: 1 Thessalonians chapter 4 considers the Christian's "walk" or progress in the world toward the time when "the Lord himself shall descend from heaven with a shout" (v. 16 KJV). Speaking to the nature of "brotherly love" (*de charitate autem fraternitatis,* v. 9) the writer notes that it is in the nature of God's will for one who would "walk and [. . .] please God [. . .] that every one of you should know how to possess his vessel in sanctification and honor, not in the lust of concupiscence" (vv. 4–5 KJV). While the *Ordinary Gloss* relates this passage specifically to sexual continence in the time of sacred celebration,

Figure 1: The Haywain (triptych) by Hieronymus Bosch (c. 1450–1516)
Prado, Madrid, Spain

Figure 2: The Haywain: central panel of the triptych, c. 1500 (oil on panel)
by Hieronymus Bosch (c. 1450–1516)
Monasterio de El Escorial, Spain

The Haywain, with panels closed showing Everyman walking the Path of Life
(oil on panel)
by Hieronymus Bosch (c. 1450–1516)
Prado, Madrid, Spain

The Vagabond/Prodigal Son by
Hieronymus Bosch
(c. 1450–1516) Museum
Boymans van Beuningen,
Rotterdam, The Netherlands

not irrelevant in the instance of the *Haywain*, we may conclude that "vessel" has also here its wider theological value of the spiritual person.[61] Another correlative feature of the iconography of the vessel is expressed in its connection in the opening lines of an exceedingly popular Latin poem with worldly vanity:

> cur mundus militat sub vana gloria,
> cuius prosperitas est transitoria:
> tam cito labitur eius potentia,
> quam vasa figuli, quae sunt fragilia.

> [Why does the world labor under vain glory,
> whose prosperity is transitory:
> its power disintegrates as quickly,
> as the fragile potter's vessel.][62]

The vessel, it will be observed, hangs over the head of the carnal lovers' tutor, and thus may connect here on several counts with the sterility or vanity of worldly, chaffy pursuits. It is in such an amplified connection that we may also view the owl. There existed a Flemish expression "voer eenen huijbeen ane sien" ("to take someone for an owl"—that is, a fool). It occurs on a copper plate, in fact, of the *Ship of Fools*.[63] The owl, not noted for much beauty in his song either, sits above the malevolent angel.

In the moral theology of Bosch's time, worldly vanity is foolishness. It is significant for the *Haywain* that there are as many Dutch proverbs connecting *hooi* with foolishness (for example, "*Al hooi*") as with vanity. "Om tlange hoy plucken" ("to grab at the long hay"), "met hoy croonen" ("to crown with hay"), and "iemand de kaper vol hoi stoppen" ("to stuff someone's cap with hay") all have the force of "to make a fool of someone."[64] The opening chapter of Thomas à Kempis's *Imitation of Christ*, composed within a short distance of Bosch's studio, urges contempt of all the vanities of the world and scores just those sorts of worldly wise foolishness in which particularly a cleric might easily indulge. Some of what follows is worthy of quotation in full:

> *Vanity of vanities, and all is vanity*, except to love God, and to serve Him only. This is the highest wisdom, by contempt of the world to press forward towards heavenly kingdoms.
>
> Vanity, therefore it is, to seek after perishing riches, and to trust in them. Vanity also it is to hunt after honors, and to climb to high degree. Vanity it is to follow the desires of the flesh, and to long after that for which thou must afterwards suffer grievous punishment. Vanity it is, to

wish to live long, and to be careless to live well. Vanity it is to mind only
this present life, and not to foresee those things which are to come. Vanity
it is to set thy love on that which speedily passeth away, and not to hasten
thither where everlasting joy abideth.[65]

This first chapter of a work that builds carefully toward its lengthy "devout
exhortation to the Holy Communion" (book 4) had begun: "*He that fol-
loweth me, walketh not in darkness* [. . .] and he that hath the Spirit will find
therein *the hidden manna.*" Beyond its parodic ironies, Bosch's *Haywain,*
very much like the *Imitation of Christ,* would seem to be concerned with
proper preparation for Holy Communion.

The initial effect of this painting on its first viewers may have been one of
shock. There is a sense in which Bosch seems to paint scandalously in order
to expose scandal. At first we are disturbed by the whole scene of chaos in
which laymen and clerics alike virtually exemplify the vices and make fools
of themselves. Then, on closer examination, we are startled by the incongruity of the little scene of musical concord on top of the "hay." But as we
study that scene, discern the role of *musica humana* within it, then recognize
its affinities with the *haegspel* drama of its time, we are led to consider the
whole procession of which it is a part. Hence a third disturbance, that what
appears to be a Corpus Christi procession is not following the Host, but a load
of *hooi* with all of its proverbial and theological significance. That leads us to
recognize that what is ultimately portrayed by Bosch is the spiritual condition
of the whole of nominally Christian society—indeed ourselves, as we relate to
the question of our actual direction of worship. We need no longer doubt that
the *Haywain* was conformable to use in a chapel: it may even have served as
an altarpiece in the chapel of one of the confraternities of s'Hertogenbosch;
perhaps for the Illustre Lieve-Vrouwe Broederschap, or the nearby Brethren of
the Common Life.

The *Haywain* provides a sweeping insight into all three times zones of our
historia salvationis. The left panel, with its story of Creation, Fall, Exile, and
the beginning of human pilgrimage, tells the tragedy of time past. The right
panel, with its scene of God's final judgment and retribution, is at least one
perspective on time future. And the large middle panel, where the people are
dressed as contemporaries, is time present. Only God with his eternal eye may
see all moments of life at once, as does the crucified Christ who descends in a
cloud. But in Bosch's triptych, as in the time scheme of medieval drama,[66] our
point of view becomes by means of a painter's perspective analogous to that of
God with respect to human history: we are enabled to see metonymically the
whole spiritual autobiography of our race. And as we observe in the *Haywain*
the futility of one notion of progress, we may derive from the overall scheme

of this great triptych identifications that will ensure a more redemptive pilgrimage, even if often it seems that we are harried through a sin-burdened
world, much like the troubled Pilgrim on the exterior of the folded *Haywain*
triptych.[67] For the essential message of Holy Communion (and of the Gospel
itself) is that however lonely we might feel on our pilgrimage, if we are tread-
ing our way toward the New Jerusalem we need not walk alone. As we look at
the unfolded triptych, in the context of the Eucharist we may reflect that it is
in time present that Christ also comes, to atone, to provide a remedy for alienation, and to open the way to the harmony and concord of real community.
That the Christ who comes in the sacrament is also the Christ who comes in
apocalypse may be a warning to those who pursue the chaff, but to those who
experience the "real substance," the fruit of Holy Communion, this is a
blessed hope. Bosch wishes to turn us toward this hope by showing us the true
character of its alternative.

(1973; 2002)

Chapter Ten

Sir Orfeo's Harp:
Music for the End of Time

---

*In convertendo Dominus captivitatem Sion, facti sumus sicut consolati. Tunc
repletum est gaudio os nostrum, et lingua nostra exultatione.*
Psalm 125:1–2, Vulgate [Ps 126:1–2, Eng.]

Despite its native grace and lyric simplicity, *Sir Orfeo* remains one of the
most perplexing of early English poems. Probably the greatest curiosity it
raises for a modern reader is that, in a move unique among retellings of the
Orpheus legend,[1] the unknown Orfeo poet has eliminated from his romance
the climactic second death of Eurydice. Why, among all versions of the story,
should the "skillful narrator" of this fourteenth-century tale of faërie so
deliberately distort the obvious psychological high point of his story?[2] What
can we say for a writer who, in his twisting of a traditional tale, ignores its
classic expression of the deepest of human fears—that despite all our longing
after unbroken communion and wholeness death comes anyway? There is
universally compelling recognition in the irresistible backward glance, the
haunt of memory, harbinger and prophet of each lover's looming loss. That
death cannot be cheated—this, surely, is the natural end of Orpheus and
Eurydice which eclipses all other sensibility in the story, and has appeared as
true to Vergil and Ovid as to Anouilh or Cocteau.[3] For most readers the original myth has primordial power, and *Sir Orfeo* can thus hardly evade comparisons to some extent invidious.

Even the best studies of the medieval poem have offered dubious detours
around this problem. Should we accept, with one critic, that a particularly
sensitive narrator would emasculate the powerful classical legend in favor of

155

a "happy ending" . . . in order somehow to domesticate the Orpheus myth as "a wonderful human story?" Such a diffuse justification of the poem's apparent perversity as a dedication to "human interest" seems to me irreconcilable with any claim for the poet's skill and sensitivity.[4] When a poet fashions his poem from a famous story reasonably well known to his audience in its traditional form, and when he gives his leading characters their old names, even beginning his narrative with the established outline of the old story, we may strongly suspect that a violent wrenching away of the traditional conclusion of a tale so deliberately recalled will have real narrative consequence for his own version.

In a more promising interpretation of the Orfeo poet's radical version, James F. Knapp has offered us a Boethian perspective on its unique literary strategy. Knapp sees Orfeo, like Boethius, suffering a reversal of fortune, first calling for "the peace of death," knowing despair, and ultimately raising the question: "What are the conditions of the world in which man must live?" The answer, "joy after sorrow," becomes evident, Knapp says, in the narrative structure of the poem.[5] This reading is much more appealing, and I shall return to it. Yet without wishing to discount the pertinence of a Boethian sensibility to *Sir Orfeo* (it is certainly at the heart of medieval Latin interpretations of the original story),[6] the reader may remain unsatisfied that in this application it provides a sufficient explanation for the Middle English artist's refashioning of the Orpheus myth. If there is a Boethian mode of discourse in *Sir Orfeo*, it might seem to be paralleled by the kind of relationship which has been argued for the *Consolation of Philosophy* and the elegiac structure of Chaucer's *Book of the Duchess*, where, for example, we are invited to see the Boethian structure in the poem as offering a kind of artistic therapy, a poetic treatise on the restoration of spiritual and mental health.[7] While still insufficient to account for elimination of the second loss of Eurydice, such an association at least places the emphasis of the poem where it is consonant with the ethos of the original story, on the profound sense of loss and heart sickness which attends a personal confrontation with the problem of Death. It is at the point of expressing this inevitability that the Orpheus story has always seemed one of the strongest, most comprehensive myths dealing with the human predicament. No embrace is forever.

The original story, like much of Arthurian romance in the Middle Ages, speaks eloquently in the manner of several Western myths of the fall. These tales, whether in Nordic, Greek, or Hebrew, lament a universal erôs-longing. Unhappily, as Plato recounted of his fractured, once-spherical, "man," the great irony of obvious human "solutions" to the split between death and desire is that it is just at that moment when *erôs*-longing seems surely fulfilled one is liable to be made most acutely conscious of the gulf, the separation that still remains.[8] Rather than being granted the satisfaction of present closure we yearn for, we suffer intermittance and postponement; the best for which we can hope is to be found in the (perhaps inadvertent) commencement of other stories, narratives whose protagonists will, in their time, likewise be driven by desire toward a closure perpetually out of reach. The theme is a recurring one in Western literature, and not least in medieval romance. It is the old story of Humpty Dumpty again, which from childhood we have come to recognize and find believable. All the king's horses and all the king's men do not seem to put Humpty together again, or Round Tables either; the problem of erôs continues to be the problem of Death. It has always seemed fitting that the traditional story of Orpheus should have begun in love's union and ended in both separations.

The original separations of *Sir Orfeo* are, like those in the *Book of the Duchess*, separations from love by death. But if one is not far wrong in seeing for Chaucer's poem a kind of elegiac structure which resolves the structural dilemma and fragmentation in a fundamentally Boethian way—by simple but dramatic acceptance of historical reality: "She ys ded!"[9] "Oh!" the dreamer can exclaim, "Now I understand"—the problem of death and separation are not so resolved in *Sir Orfeo*, and it is here that an extended Boethian analogy would seem to fall short. The parallel recognition of the inevitability of death and its use as a "consolation" is indeed to be found in *Sir Orfeo*, yet not as the resolution to its narrative structure. After Orfeo has returned and the harp has been recognized by his steward, Orfeo, it will be remembered, feigns that he found it beside a man who had been torn to death by wild beasts. Concluding his master's death, the steward swoons for sorrow. He has to be raised by his courtiers, who offer him a summary Boethian admonition and consolation:

> His barouns him tok vp in þat stounde
> & telleþ him how it geþ
> —'It nis no bot of mannes deþ!' (550–52)

Yet as he recovers to Orfeo's skillful and beautiful revelation, "if ich ware Orfeo þe kyng," we are aware that this poem, of course, does not, like Boethius's or Chaucer's, end here. It goes on to refute the courtier's wisdom.

If there exists an acceptable rationale for the Orfeo poet's drastic reconstruction of a good story, perhaps it can be approached through a closer examination of the principal symbolic objects of his poem. These I take to be the harp of Orfeo, and to a lesser degree, the recurrent *ympe-tre* under which his bride Heurodis was first rapt into the power of faërie. Let us begin with the tree.

The *ympe-tre*, as Alan Bliss recounts in the introduction to his edition, is a "grafted" orchard tree of the variety found in many Celtic stories and romances, being cognate with the *ente* of a similar story in the *Tydorel* for example, and is to be associated with the "apple tree" of Ablach-Avallach-Avallonis familiar from the Arthurian cycle.[10] Trying to pursue a contemporary sense of the poem, we can readily imagine that when in a paradise garden in May a fair woman falls prey to the king of faëries, resulting in her husband's wending forth from his former glorious condition to "hard heþe" (243), "grete malaise" (240) and to "al day digge & wrote/Er he finde his fille of rote" (255–56), that it would be possible for a medieval reader to see in the story some sort of suggestion of the Fall and the beginning of human erôs-longing in Judaeo-Christian terms.[11] Indeed, without belaboring the point, the equation of Eurydice with Eve was not an unusual one in medieval readings of the original Orpheus story. As John Friedman has shown, Pierre Bursuire made this connection, as did the illustrators of the *Ovide Moralisé*, and in recollecting that Ovid, Vergil, and Boethius in their versions have her bitten by a snake, they saw Eurydice's plight as suggestive of the Genesis story of temptation and Fall.[12] These medieval readings of the old story are initially attractive for several reasons. The "temptation" of Eurydice is perhaps reminiscent of the traditional Satanic method (from the faërie king's palace she is shown "castles and tours," riches and worldly domain, and finds the king and his company not at all ugly, but "so fair"). Further, the biblical association adds a level of meaning to Orfeo's root-grubbing exile, and offers a deep spiritual plangency to the reader's sense of what Adam lost in the garden. But, however medieval readers stretched it to fit the classical story, such an allegory does not make much sense of our fifteenth-century poet's perversion of the tale's conclusion. Does a man descend into the realm of death to claim a victory over it, and by his own skill win back his wholeness and paradise? In medieval moral and theological terms, this would seem very nearly blasphemous.

If we were to press another theological analogy to the story, Orfeo's descent into the realm of death might suggest the example of Christ. An association familiar to early Christian art, it was also read into the Orpheus legend in the Middle Ages, and curiously enough, into the story in its traditional classical form. In the twelfth century, Arnulph of Orléans comments on the Ovidian version that Orpheus is a type of Christ, who, out of his own goodness provided a wife for himself, but lost her under a tree "through the teeth of the serpent, that is to say, by the counsel of Satan."[13] One cannot help but feel, however, that Ovid's story is bent still farther out of shape by this sort of "medieval" reading than the former one, for here the end of the classical story must assert an eternal defeat for Christ—a consistency which we can doubt would have been approved by Arnulph of Orléans, the writer of the *Ovide Moralisé*, or anyone else with Christian theological convictions.

This problem, however, does not occur at the ending of *Sir Orfeo*. With the harpist's victorious descent into the underworld to free his bride and a homecoming to the full splendor of paradise regained, we might well anticipate that medieval readers could be tempted into following Arnulph's lead much more plausibly into *Sir Orfeo*—perhaps even to seeing the fourteenth-century poet's change in the story as a deliberate accommodation to Christian allegory. Once again, however, there remain significant cautions to such a view. Why, if Orfeo were Christ (or God), should the leaving of his throne be carefully described in terms of abdication and abandoned self-exile (206–26), or why, if the allegory were reasonably consistent, would he attempt to defend Eurydice with all of his horses and men—and vainly? (175–94). If the events of the last portion of the story were meant to be considered by us as reasonably parallel, then we are offered very awkward analogies in the first half. But more than this; if medieval readers were expected to see the story from the outset as an allegory of the Christian plan of redemption, presumably there would have been little or no suspense in this casting of the story—merely the expectation of a customary resolution. While there is nothing wrong with that—it is after all effective in the art of the medieval drama—I cannot quite conceive that a poet of such rightly acknowledged abilities would have used a story whose genius is tension (unresolved tension) as a vehicle for Christian allegory in this way. For the Orfeo poet to have done so would have been to ignore in himself what most critics have praised him for, his narrative sense. Moreover, the most telling point must be our recognition that many in his medieval audience would have known some version of the original story (Ovid, *Ovide Moralisé*, Vergil, Boethius), and would thus have been in confident expectation of the second loss of Eurydice as the psychological climax of the poem. Even in the only medieval version which suggests the possibility of a return of Eurydice, her return is represented only as the reopened chords of the poet's song:

> ingemit Euridicen
> atque semel *fidicen*
> retulit Euridicen.

[He sighs for Eurydice and at once the lutanist brought back Eurydice.]

—the poet's *unica verba* is his perpetual lamentation.[14] It is with these reservations in mind that I would like to turn to the most important symbolic object in our English poem, Orfeo's harp.

The harp evokes well-worn traditional associations. Constructed of eight to eighteen strings, with a "holwe tree," or sound chamber at its base, in the Middle Ages it is first of all the kingly instruments, the instrument of

David and Apollo.[15] An instrument of ratio and harmony, it has a significant range of employments: it is sounded to glorify God, to make merry, even to signify a penitential mood.[16] As it is used more often and in a wider variety of ways in *Sir Orfeo* than in classical versions of the story, it assumes in the medieval version a more critical importance.[17] To begin with, the "gle" of Orfeo's harping has created a kind of "Paradis" (37), one whose harmony is shattered by the abduction of Eurydice. The harp then falls more or less silent. For ten years it is hidden in the "holwe" of a tree. Only "when þe weder was clere and bright" (269) would the lonely and self-exiled Orfeo come to take it out again, to quiet the wild beasts around him, to harmonize nature. But after the dramatic encounter with Heurodis, her vanishing so reminiscent of the original ending, and Orfeo's perilous descent, we see in the dark and terrible realm beneath the rock Orfeo committing himself to his instrument in a new way (382), retempering his harp (437), and unlocking its melody to charm away the malevolent power of the faërie king, to win back his Eurydice from the kingdom of the dead. From this point the role of the harp becomes increasingly central, becoming the means of Orfeo's entry back into his own kingdom, the instrument whereby he is revealed to his court and reassumes his identity. Finally it is the harp which sounds the introit to "al maner mynstralcie" in celebration of Orfeo's return with his bride to a new coronation.

In the context of these symbolic associations we may remember that in the Middle Ages the music of the harp was considered above all to be spiritual music, and although music in general was thought to be capable of curing the soul,[18] to the harp particularly was given the power to overcome evil, to heal the mind. The most ready analogy was the story of David and Saul, where it was

> þe harp of Dauid, which mooste might avayle
> Whane þat þe feonde Kyng Saule did assayle[19]

and the "evil spirit" (*spiritus malus*) of the Vulgate was hardly less "spiritually" translated in the Middle English (*feonde*) than in the exegesis of the *Ordinary Gloss* to the Bible (*daemonium*).[20] It hardly seems necessary to invoke patristic commentary to suggest the relationship of David to Christ in medieval typology: what may be so familiar is the role of the harp in this connection. John Lydgate, for example, in his *Interpretation and Virtues of the Mass*, prays:

> I shall (be) shyrue and confesse vnto the
> In that Harpe whyche for owre alther goode
> Was set and wrestyd on Caluary, on a tree. (1.122–24)[21]

This connection of the harp with Christ's body, or more properly, Christ's sacrifice, does not seem to be a particularly successful metaphor, but it falls into a tradition concerning the role of the harp which underwent a typically interesting development at the hands of Robert Mannyng of Brunne, in his *Handlying Synne*, where, in explaining why Robert Grosseteste loved the music of the harp, Mannying gives us Grosseteste's analogy of the harp to the Cross itself:

> þe vertue of þe harpe, þurgh skylle & ry3t,
> wyl destroye þe fendes my3t
> And to þe croys by gode skylle
> Ys þe harpe lykened weyle. (4753–56)[22]

Continuing with his image, Robert has the Bishop suggest a reason for his conflation of the "harpe" with the "tree" of Calvary:

> Anoþer poynt cumforteþ me,
> þat God haþ sent vnto a tre
> So moche ioye to here with eere;
> Moche þan more ioye ys þere
> with God hym selfe þere he wonys;
> þe harpe þerof me ofte mones;
> Of þe ioye and of þe blys
> where God hym selfe wonys and ys. (4757–63)

This type of extended symbolic association for the harp, given the elaborated role of that instrument in the structure of *Sir Orfeo,* implies support for some sort of Christian reading for the poem—perhaps even as the allegory of Christ so unpalpably suggested for the original Ovidian story by Arnulph of Orléans. Could it be that the poet meant us to see in his story ourselves lost under the *ympe-tre* to the power of death, and Orfeo ("He þat hadde had castels & tours," 245) as suggesting the Christ who leaves paradise, going to lowly estate and another tree in order to win us back ("Al his kingdom he forsoke," 227)?

   If so, might that give tongue to the language of marriage and adultery used by Orfeo and Heurodis at the crisis of their separation,[23] or later add motive to her weeping at his lowly estate (327), his descent into the realm of death through a rock (348), and the harping which harrows hell? Could the metamorphosis of the old story be occasioned by seeing this imagery extended in Orfeo's successful return, and in the testing of the faithful steward who for the sake of his Lord Orfeo has been always hospitable, so recognizes the harp, and is thus enabled to become a king with his King? These possibilities would certainly exist for a literate audience; they are available in the poem's language, and ought to be weighed, at least, against its narrative structure. Indeed, the Orfeo poet seems to have arranged his allusions so deliberately that one is left wondering if the people's salutory exclamation at Orfeo's first appearance in the city is not calculatedly ironic:

> He is y-clongen al-so a tre! (508)
>
> [He is shriveled as a tree]
> [He is stricken as to a tree][24]

By the time we reach a second crowning to joyous "menstraci" of a harper who has proved himself "lord and King" (580–82) by rescuing his bride from the King of Death, it seems implausible that the poet should not have intended at least a partial association with the Gospel story. If some of the critical flaws apparent in Arnulph of Orléans's allegory would still appear to remain, perhaps what we need to search out is any strategy of the Orfeo poet which might have led him to employ all of these leading allusions—congruently with the harp and the *ympe-tre*—to tempt us into an apparently inconsistent reading of his poem. How can we reconcile the character of an Orfeo associated by the poet with Christ (in the harp) with a predicament which as clearly evokes a kinship to Adam (the *ympe-tre*)?

If there is an answer to such a question, it may begin, I suspect, at the point of the courtier's appropriately Boethian and all too believable counsel to the grief-stricken steward:

> It nis no bot for mannnes deþ. (552)
>
> [There is no remedy for the death of Man.]

Such, indeed, was the lesson of the original story told by Vergil, Ovid, and Boethius. It is surely the inevitable conclusion that the harper's audience must have anticipated, and it is effectively forshadowed in the silent anguish of Heurodis's vanishing from Orfeo in the forest. And such an ending would seem to do justice to our appreciation of Orfeo, with his lost paradise and divided self, so much then the more archetypal of our own nature, our universal mortality, than a Christ figure. But to our consternation there has been for this Eurydice no second death, no final frustration. Why? What excuse? Here we are offered not precisely an argument, but a hypothesis. It comes when Orfeo stands up and in the unfolding of his masterful conditional clause; reveals who he is:

> ӡif ich were Orfeo þe king,
> & hadde y suffred fulӡore

> In wildernisse mich sore
> & hadde y won mi quen o wy
> Out of þe lond of fairy,
> & hadde y brou3t þe leuedi hende
> Ri3t here to þe tounes ende [. . .] (558–564)

Then what?—then, in short, at the end of the harper's song has appeared a remedy for "mannes deþ" after all. The archetypal problem of death's lovesickness, which despite first Adam's yearnings must still be labor lost, can apparently by the pilgrimage of another "Adam" be won, and in his love find Death's remedy. And if this is what the Orfeo poet means, then it would seem that he has clearly calculated the effect of his reader's natural anticipation for the old story, and split the planes of his narrative and allegory (natural man and God man) in such a way that we are invited to see how our archetypal misfortune is by a new song happily frustrated of its otherwise inexorable conclusion. In this event the reader is left not so much with the double allegory as with a merging of one story into the other, or, to remember Ovid, a metamorphosis of natural by supernatural history.

Pursuing this thought, we might look for points in the narrative at which the poet has begun to effect his metamorphosis of the story of Orfeo, and in addition to the numerous and suggestive scriptural allusions already mentioned, there seem to be two critical moments of transformation needing our attention. The first comes after line 281, where Orfeo, having once again played his harp, begins to see farther into the realm of his problem, discerning the king of faëries' now vain mid-day hunt for the souls of men.[25] The knights and ladies dancing in "queynt attire" to the "menstracie" of "tabours and trumpes" follow, and finally the falconing of the sixty ladies, where the falcons successfully achieve their "pray."[26] At the last he can "lour":

> 'Parfay!' quaþ he, 'þer is fair game;
> þider ichil, bi Godes name!
> Ich was y-won swiche werk to si!'
> He aros, & þider gan tc. (315–18)

This passage is followed by the silent amazement of his vision of Eurydice, the breaking of her tears, and then in the endless silence as she vanishes, his swift return to the grief he had first known at her loss: "Allas!" he cries (four times), "Whi nil min hert breke?" (331–38). But suddenly, without any explanation, one word effects a radical alteration in the mood of his speech, as abruptly he returns to the phrase in which spirit he "lou3":

> 'Parfay!' quaþ he, 'Tide wat bitide,
> Whider so þis leuedis ride,

þe selue way ichil streche
Of liif no deþ me no reche.' (339–42)

The rhetorical and psychological force of this startling repetition transforms
both the spirit of Orfeo's exile and our own sense of relationship to him.
Orfeo in one line has taken up his pilgrim's "sclauin," laid "harp upon his
bac," and with "wel Gode wil to gon" entered in at the rock. From this point
on his actions become decisively more than natural, and it is to this point in
the poem that we must presumably appeal for any "split" in the planes of the
narrative, for here, given the simple development of the *Sir Orfeo* story itself,
is the essential moment of metamorphosis.[27]

That Orfeo's new vision and decisive action to turn exile into pilgrimage
should come after he once again has played his harp is, of course, a striking
change in itself from the original tale, and as he carries his harp into the
court of King Pluto, there with minstrel's "gle" to charm away death's power,
our mind is drawn back to the established symbolism of the harp and its
commonplace evocation of David before Saul. If we turn to the common
medieval reading of this famous biblical story, the exegesis of the *Ordinary
Gloss*, we see that it sheds a pertinent light on the role of the harp in *Sir
Orfeo*, suggesting how both potential allegorical levels of the story can be
brought together in the reader's identification with the protagonist of the
poem. Typically identifying David with Christ, and Saul's *spiritus malus* with
the *Diabolus* whose power is permitted until the emergence of the true King,
the *Ordinary Gloss* then suggests a moral and psychological application of the
story which internalizes its understanding:

> David was skilled in song ("canticus musicae"); so, as it were, by the sweet-
> ness of the harp of speech ("citharae locutionis") our peace of mind ("tran-
> quilitate") is restored. Saul was (thereby) refreshed, (whereas), before he
> was truly tormented by the devil almost to the point of suffocation. Note
> that Boethius refers in his philosophy to the touch of the harp, which pla-
> cated the devil of corporal obsession ("corpore obsesso").[28]

The philosophy referred to is, of course, again the *Consolation of Philosophy*,
where Boethius in his stubborn *corpore obsesso* is likened by Lady Philosophy
to an ass who cannot hear the harp, and this renewed connection between
the stories thus, develops in reference to the harp and the Boethian notion
of "music." In his *De musica* Boethius had described music as the harmony
of the universe, the concert of whose strings when correctly heard is able to
cure marvelously the illness of the soul (1.1),[29] and this idea, as David
Chamberlain has recently shown, is carried forward into the "songs," or

metres, of Lady Philosophy in the *Consolation of Philosophy*.[30] In that story, love itself is essential music, becoming even another name for it, since it extends the universal concord into relationships amongst men, spouses, children, and friends. It is love's "music" that can bring about true human happiness:

> Love binds together people joined by a sacred bond; love binds sacred marriage by chaste affections; love makes the laws which join true friends. O how happy the human race would be, if that love which rules the heavens ruled also your souls. (2m8, 22–30).[31]

Yet the harp, instrument of David and Apollo, may restore universal harmony in terms even more satisfying than the fateful reconciliation of individual fortune to cosmic destiny. As we have seen, the *cithara* can be at the same time the entuner of the new song, the melody of the Cross whereby in medieval Christian theology men's spiritual sickness is totally and finally healed, where Death is made life. The figures for this are often arresting. For Bernard of Clairvaux, Christ on the cross is like the strings stretched to temper over the wood of a harp, which, if we learn to play and sing to it, will move ourselves and others to a knowledge of our redemption.[32] For St. Bruno, the harp is the humanity of Christ, but also our humanity, and in tempering our inferior tones to the sweetness which God produces, that is, by obedience, we discover how to respond to his call to our humanity, to awake (*exsurge*) from our *morte humanitas* and spiritual torpor.[33] For Alcuin too, the harp is the Passion of Christ, and in his commentary on the Apocalypse he sees in the "new song" harped by the redeemed their "imitation of the passion of Christ in themselves, as the divine members are made one in concord" through Christ's atonement.[34] Late medieval paintings which show David playing his harp at the foot of a Jesse tree containing the whole plan of Redemption, and references to "the harpe of holy scripture" are in this light compatible with paintings which show David playing his harp at the foot of Christ on the cross and equations of Orpheus with Christ and his *cithara* with the *verba singula singulis*: the references involve, typologically and dramatically, both the poet's word and the Word Incarnate.[35] It is this last suggestion which helps us to appreciate, I think, how Orfeo's harp contains Christian as well as classical values in its symbolism; how in Boethian vein it "makeþ the wit sharp"[36] and how, as in both 1 Kings 16 and in the *Consolation of Philosophy*, in overcoming *obsesso corpore* it is meant to heal the mind. For in *Sir Orfeo* it becomes the harp which transforms and renews the mind eternally, confirming a love which death cannot defeat.

According with these concordant values given to the harp by medieval art and literature are a number of intriguing and related analogies.[37] In one account in the *Gesta Romanorum* the harp is taken to be the word of "holy Scripture and [. . .] theologie," and in its treatment in the nineteenth book of Bartholomaeus Anglicus's *De proprietatibus rerum,*

> Men in olde tyme callyd the Harpe
> Fidicula and also Fidicen
> For the strynges therof accordyth as some men
> accordyth in *fey.* (19.139.945ff.)[38]

"Fey," "fay," or faith, is a convenient way for the medieval Christian of expressing all of the harp's spiritual and psychological values at once, and is a word most relevant to *Sir Orfeo.* The instrument which heals the soul, which "makes the wit sharp," which entunes man with the natural order, which brings him to know himself, the kingly instrument identified with the tree of Calvary, the sacrifice of Christ and even "holie Scripture and theologie"—all of these are contained in their association with "fey," or faith. Faith is words acknowledging the Word. On this simple level of its understanding that the harp can achieve the poem's separate "melodies" and yet, paradoxically, ultimately provide their point of concert. "Parfay!" cries Orfeo, as he sees in the double hunt of the fairy world that it is but flesh that is prey to death. This is a fair "game," after all, and he concludes as he should:

> þider ichil, bi Goddes name!
> Ich was y-won swiche werk to se. (316–17)

> [Fore Heaven, I will betake me there!
> I once was wont to see such play.][39]

It is a reasonable Boethian response, and demonstrates that the psychopharmical virtues of the music of the harp have begun to achieve their purpose. Yet here is not just one exclamation of "Parfay!," and it is the second that precipitates the more-than-Boethian conclusion to the poem. The function of the arrangement is emphatically rhetorical. As it were, in the very middle of his grief-stricken response to the realization that separation from Eurydice is more than the loss of flesh, Orfeo cries "Parfay!," happen what may, he will follow those ladies at the cost of death in order to win back his own. And of course, in one sense, he does "die"—willing to lose his life to save his wholeness, he enters in at the rock to the realm of Death, and the subsequent portion of the saga unfolds the story of his—and Heurodis's—

"rebirth."[40] But is it not perhaps intrinsic to the poem's allusory structure that his victory over Death itself exists in identification with another victory—*par fay*?

For who is Orfeo? Descended from King Pluto (god of adultery and the underworld) and Queen Juno (presumably from the queen of marriage and of heaven), he is of mixed lineage, containing opposites in himself which must be reconciled. And this alloyed heritage suggests that the parallels between Orfeo's court and that of the King of the Underworld (presumably Pluto) are not entirely fortuitous—their alternate palaces, their alternate thousand knights, the faërie king's two knights who parallel Heurodis's two ladies. Did the poet not mean us to see that in learning to temper and use his harp with good "skyll" Orfeo has really learned, "parfay," to harmonize (as it were) himself? Orfeo, it seems, in a sense which a Duns Scotus would appreciate, is indeed both an Adam and a Christ. He comprises in his experience two worlds. The key to their reconciliation is the skill of the harper. In leaving his harp in the hollow of a tree he may have entered a spiritual wilderness,[41] but when in finally tempering his harp he learns to play the *musica mundana*, to entune himself to the harmony of created nature, he regains the health of perspective which that brings, and has recourse to retemper his harp to the concordant harmonies of the love which wins over death. If the *ympe-tre* suggests man's fall, the harp suggests the means of his restoration. The spiritual levels of the poem which seem so deliberately to offer themselves in the poem's imagery—fallen man and Christ—are not vitiated by the contribution of Boethius, but are rather through the philosopher temporarily arrested so that they might be the more beautifully reconciled with one another—just beyond the philosopher's reach. Once we recognize that the "menstraci" and "grete melody" enjoined by the harp from the "tounes end" is an eternal conclusion to cosmic music, we can better appreciate the full meaning of harping. For the harper's "gle" becomes then truly the most "ferli" thing of all, the transforming melody of the soul whose fundamental love-longing after wholeness can at last be placated, and can then respond with steward and court in the epithalamion so long associated with the harp and the second crowning of a King.[42]

If *Sir Orfeo* still seems to the modern reader psychologically a weaker poem than its predecessors, perhaps we can be willing at least to absolve its author of omitting the second death of Eurydice in a failure of narrative skill. For our poet actually seems to have held that old story in suspension with another, and woven out of their separate melodies a striking polyphony of psychological and literary effects. The sudden hope of Heurodis—met in the forest and lost again to darkness in her shadow's fading—is both effective anticipation of the legend's original ending and, in retrospect, its minute portrayal. To this moment of fearful apprehension the courtier's consolation is a balanced resignation, an appropriate Boethian conclusion.

But the Orfeo poet gently urges the temporality of such a resolution. His is both a human and a more-than-human story. *In conspectu dei*, the release won for Heurodis by the harp of Orfeo is unconditional, and the reunited lovers can slip upward to the light of day in only four lines. The harper's remedy heals an incompleteness which is more than physiological; Orfeo's erôs-longing has been in the fullest sense a struggle for meaning, for community, for wholeness of mind. As in much of Arthurian romance, the reserve embedded in the first half of this poem is that in the promise of horses and men such a consummation still proves improbable, and that ultimate solace must be contingent upon a metamorphosis from one plane of reality to another—the triumphant return of the King. In short, that the Orfeo poet should attempt a mending of Humpty at once psychological and spiritual is not here so much a fault in the telling of the old and classical tale as the genius of a new, and another, myth. If the new myth has a happy ending, that ought not to make it necessarily less good or "true" for its audience than the old one, for the happy ending in this story is one snatched, entirely unexpectedly, from the very gullet of death. Here is the quintessential magic of the faërie world, a world in which *Sir Orfeo* participates in ways that the old story does not. Orfeo's consolation is the good consolation of the true fairy story, which, as Professor Tolkien has said of that genre, is, in its "otherworld setting,"

> [. . .] a sudden and miraculous grace: never to be counted on to recur. It does not deny the existence of *dyscatastrophe*, of sorrow and failure: the possibility of these is necessary to joy of deliverance; it denies (in the face of much evidence, if you will) universal final defeat, and in so far is *evangelium*, giving a fleeting glimpse of Joy, Joy beyond the walls of the world, poignant as grief.[43]

Appropriately, then, at the center of the new story, human will looms large. As Orfeo enters exile by a deliberate act of will, so at last he takes up his harp and harps "at his owhen wille" (1271), and with that to give him "gode wil to gon" (344), he travels on to harp not just for the sake of harping, *but for the gift of the will to harp.* "Parfay!" he cries for the third and last time, "Icham a minstrel, lo!" (382). And it is then that the "gle" of harping overcomes for Orfeo the greatest fear of all, turning even the power of death to "gode wille" (444). If Orfeo had lost his identity by going into exile, he now re-establishes it by putting on a higher identity.

The last analysis of a Breton lay should be in performance, and in the hesitant clerical style of the poem's opening the singer's acute consciousness of performance reveals a very special involvement with his principal motif:

> We redeþ oft & findeþ y-write
> & þis clerkes wele it wite,
> Layes þat ben in harping
> Ben y founde of ferli þing. (1–4)

> [We often read and written find,
> as learned men do us remind,
> that lays that now the harpers sing
> are wrought of many a marvellous thing.]

That is, we are aware from the outset that the poet, in signifying the "marvellous" nature of his tale, is also in his choice of genres acknowledging himself such a harper.[44] As the lay is passed on, it thus becomes in each telling more than "universal," indeed, in the best sense personal, for by singing this new lay the performer becomes, in measure, himself Sir Orfeo. His song, unchaining both the transforming "gle" of the harp and a verbal reconciliation of disparate melodies, proves again the *citharae locutionis*, the archetypal poet's instrument. At every level the harp is the Word upon which he may play, and from which flows a tissue of words harmonizing history with that which is more than history, the physical with the metaphysical. In the carefully wrought final lines of this poem all of its meanings converge to offer us not an ending but a beginning:

> Harpours in Bretaine after þan
> Herd hou þis meruaile bigan
> & made her of a lay of gode likeing,
> & nempned it after þe king.
> þat lay 'Orfeo' is y-hote:
> Gode is þe lay, swete is þe note
> þus com Sir Orfeo out of his care:
> God graunt ous alle wele to fare! Amen! (597–604)

> [Harpers in Britain in aftertime
> these marvels heard, and in their rhyme
> a lay they made of fair delight,
> and after the king it named aright,
> "Orfeo" called it, as was meet:

good is the lay, the music sweet.
Thus came Sir Orfeo out of care.
God grant that well we all may fare!]

In the Orfeo poet's narrative, the second death of Eurydice has been so artfully anticipated that it is effectively "there," as well as not there, in the structure of the poem. The restoration of Heurodis therefore comes as a shock, as a "new story," and the resolution which these final lines offer to her unexpected and marvellous release follows from a simple, yet powerful catharsis. Its intellectual synthesis develops in the growing recognition that at an important level of the poem's meaning the music which heals the soul and brings Sir Orfeo "out of his care" can be entuned upon the same harp which, "þurgh skylle & ry3t, wyl destroye þe fendes my3t." That the result-ing song should be called both "Orfeo" and "Gode" is the realizable double-ness of the marvel begun by the "gle of harpying," and the tempered paradox of the "fay," and the "lay," in which history in the end becomes poetry— music for the end of time.

(1976)

PART THREE

Scripture in a House of Mirrors

Chapter Eleven

Reading Wisely, Reading Well

[Philip] asked, 'Do you understand what you are reading?' He replied, 'How can I, unless someone guides me?'

Acts 8:30–31, NIV

Through many years of reading and teaching literature I have come to believe that to read well one needs two apparently contradictory virtues— intellectual toughness and imaginative sympathy. To put this paradox another way, the mature or faithful reader (they are the same person) is one who simultaneously employs both disciplines of the analytical mind and generosities of an open heart. That the disciplines should be as rigorous as the generosities amiable is the *sine qua non* of a fine reader. In lesser readers there is usually a notable imbalance to one side or another.

C. S. Lewis was an exemplary reader. Even before his days as a student "reading Greats" (Oxford's famous formal program devoted to the study of great foundational texts in classics and philosophy), he had been that sort of reader who, while reading a book, abandoned himself utterly to his author. As a schoolboy he would go so far as to extend the fantasy world of his favorite books into fictional creations of his own. With formal education he then added a knowledge of languages (including Latin and Greek) and of English philology, literature, and poetics such as equipped him to understand the linguistic architecture and formal achievements of the works he loved. Thus balanced and grounded in his understanding of great texts, he was enabled not only to become a revered teacher to his Oxford and Cambridge students, but a cherished tutor to millions of other readers around the world.

There is little in Lewis's writing that is not the product of superior and sustained reading. Though much of what he says is striking in its force of insight and precision of expression, Lewis would be the first to insist on the derivative and traditional character of his plots and even their intellectual and spiritual content: "No man who values originality," he once wrote, "will ever be original."[1] However, the practice of rereading great texts down through the years (beyond our undergraduate education and into maturity) will in the end produce what the world perceives as "originality." This happens in part, Lewis suggests, because it is by the putting of new and ever-changing real questions to familiar and wisdom-rich authors that fresh insight refracts and even generates intellectual and spiritual light.[2]

Most of us can remember from our student days occasions when the Socratic style of teaching, in which the professor insistently questions students about their understanding and even assumptions, made us distinctly uncomfortable. A major purpose of this interrogative method is strategic—first to reveal with diagnostic accuracy our lack of understanding, and then to prompt us to move through a refinement of questions toward more reasonable prospects upon an answer. In practice there can, of course, be procedural embarrassments, sometimes stemming from the teacher's necessary assumption that the students have all read their text carefully!

Lewis favored the Socratic method for some kinds of teaching. But he favored it still more for the practice of vigorous intellectual debate among his peers. He was the first president of the Oxford Socratic Club, a debating society which focused on the case for (and against) Christianity, and it is characteristic both of his literary criticism and his theological writing that in a Socratic fashion he attempts to ask and to wrestle with obvious (and not so obvious) questions which an informed and serious reader might put to texts—whether secular or sacred.

It is thus unsurprising that Lewis should have preferred for his own spiritual reading works of hard theological enquiry rather than devotional or inspirational Christian reading of the sort which typically preoccupied his boyhood evangelical friend Arthur Greeves. In the preface Lewis wrote for a translation of St. Athanasius's *The Incarnation of the Word of God*, he makes this preference a gentle recommendation to all serious Christian readers: "For my own part, I tend to find the doctrinal books more helpful than the devotional books, and I rather suspect that the same experience may await others."[3]

It is unlikely, I take it, that many of my readers would claim with Lewis that "the heart sings unbidden while they are working their way through a tough bit of theology with a pipe in their teeth and a pencil in their hand."[4] Yet Lewis's point is that this joyfully fortifying sort of reading (with or without the pipe) is likely to be the preferred choice of those who have in fact really learned to read. Others, of course, may flee it, precisely because in Lewis's sense they do not yet know how to read—that is, they have only a mechanical literacy.

It is important, I think, that in this sort of prescription Lewis is not thinking of the general reading habits of uneducated folk but rather of persons with some claim to a better education. It is these readers in particular he would challenge to live up to the level of their ostensible learning. Lewis believes that reading deeply in tough and intellectually demanding writers is an essential practice for thoughtful Christians, and he assumes that achievement of such careful and meditative reading will follow naturally from Christian dependence for spiritual authority upon venerable and authoritative texts—in particular, of course, on the Bible itself. Further, thinking reasonably and writing clearly are both a product of mature reading and a route back to it. Right reading renews the mind as well as the heart.

One of the questions to which we may thus be prompted by Lewis's reflection on the character of spiritually "helpful" reading is this: Have we contemporary American Christians really learned how to read in a manner and maturity consistent with our text-based faith?

Attempting to answer this prickly question, I am grateful to be able to confess, is not my task here. Prospects upon an answer, nonetheless, could hardly fail to be assisted by reflection on Lewis's account of the two balancing elements in mature reading. He regards both elements as essential. The first is that self-forgetful and submissive abandonment to the authority of the text which one sees in an intelligent child. The second comes later: that disciplined, informed, and discerning questioning of the text which is the work of an educated mind.

Lewis's *An Experiment in Criticism* is an attempt to distinguish "true" or "literary" readers from "unliterary" ones in this sense: his "true" or" literary" reader reads "every work seriously in the sense that he reads it wholeheartedly, makes himself as receptive as he can," since, as Lewis says, "the first demand any work of art makes upon us is surrender. Look. Listen. Receive. Get yourself out of the way."[5]

"Bad," or "unliterary" readers, by contrast, never get self out of the way. In practice they do not even much like reading—often for pretty much the same reason they do not like listening. They almost never read a book more than once, even a book they have thought better than most. What they prefer to the text is its information (a digest of the "main points") whether in a class or in church. "They are," says Lewis, "like those pupils who want to have everything explained to them and do not much attend to the explanation."[6] If such a person turns to the task of reading's tough intellectual disciplines it is likely to be also at second hand; criticism or exegesis done by others which gives one the illusion of having "mastered" the text, or of having been safely placed beyond its reach. "Especially poisonous," says Lewis, "is that kind of teaching which encourages [us] to approach every literary work with suspicion"[7]—that is, teaching which encourages a predisposition to aloofness so categorical as to render reading itself next to pointless.

Among other things, what we learn from Lewis about reading, then, is that it is almost inescapably an ethical as well as an analytical activity. It obliges us to choose between acceptance and denial, trust and suspicion, self-effacement and mere selfishness. In "good reading," Lewis writes, as in mature love, "we escape from our self into one another," thus "transcending our own competitive particularity."[8] The educational parallel is exact: "In coming to understand anything we are rejecting the facts *as they are for us* in favor of the *facts as they are*."[9] Part of the ethic is to acknowledge that there is an abundant reality which transcends our own ego and that reality is not, after all, merely self-referential.

One criticism of much of the popular Christian reading material of our time is that in one sphere or another it is so transparently self-preoccupied and self-referential, from self-help manuals to promotional autobiographies and "star status" devotional guides. Despite its authors' intentions, it is inherently difficult for this sort of writing, generically, to bear witness to a universal truth, or reality. Moreover, in its fashion-conscious preoccupation with contemporary idiom and issues, much popular Christian writing— including some of the devotional variety—ignores the inescapably unfashionable and historically derived character of biblical revelation itself, much of which was *never* fashionable and was even scandalously indifferent to its readers' comfort zones.

As former students of philosophy are likely to recognize, positivism is no longer the force against Christian texts and worldviews that it was during Lewis's years in Oxford (though some of our sentimental and pop-therapeutic piety could bring it back). But the claim of modernity against history, with which Lewis also debated, continues in various forms into the present. One of the ways in which this fashion asserts itself, as Lewis observed, is in a kind of "chronological snobbery" with respect to the reading of older books, no matter what their order of canonical greatness or cultural authority. This "uncritical acceptance of the intellectual climate common to our age and the assumption that whatever has gone out of date is on that account discredited,"[10] Lewis says, can have the effect of unduly paralyzing common sense. One instance of this, Lewis thinks, occurs whenever fashionable academic arrogance—usually offered as learned judgment—actively discourages rather than encourages questions about its own presuppositions.

But for a Christian reader in particular there is one presuppositional question about the reading of texts which should not be permitted to go unanswered. With my own students I sometimes put it in this way: Can *anything* of the past be a relevant authority for us today? It will be apparent immediately that if the answer to this question is "no," then Scripture itself cannot function as an authority (let alone the principal authority) for contemporary Christians. Lewis thought that the tendency among his theological contemporaries to prefer the German biblical scholar Rudolf Bultmann was in effect to answer "no" to this question about the enduring authority of the Bible.[11] But Lewis took the views of Bultmann and his adherents to be above all else examples of astonishingly naïve or willfully obtuse reading, not only of ancient but even of modern texts. The working presupposition of many twentieth-century biblical critics is, "if miraculous, not historical." This, Lewis says, is simply a prejudice that "they bring to a study of their text, not one they have learned from it. If one is speaking of authority, the united authority of all the biblical critics in the world here counts for nothing."[12]

Prejudice against great texts from the past—not only Scripture but classical texts of all cultures—Lewis came to regard as especially dangerous in times of national cultural crisis. It is precisely when men are arguing for the preeminence of present political imperatives that we need "most of all, perhaps . . . an intimate knowledge of the past." It is "not that the past has any magic about it," he writes in his essay "Learning in War-time."[13] Rather, the past is of value "because we cannot study the future, and yet need something to set against the present, to remind us that the basic assumptions have been quite different in different periods and that much which seems certain to the uneducated is merely temporary fashion."[14] Living in the past, a kind of antiquarian nostalgia, is not at all what Lewis has in mind for his faithful reader. Neither is historicism, "the belief that men can, by the use of their natural powers, discover an inner meaning in the historical process."[15] That too is the sort of system-abstraction produced by bad, unliterary readers, Lewis thinks, and notably it corresponds to no actual texts. At best, an historicist paradigm is an artificial construction, a meta-narrative superimposed upon specific texts (such as Scripture) in denial, as he says in his essay on "Historicism," of their concrete and particular, even local sense.

Lewis's ideal reader is in some radical sense a "mere" reader, much as his faithful Christian is a "mere Christian." "Mere" here means, of course, not "slight" or "simple," but "radical" and hence "willing to be instructed." It is more the mere reader than the critic that appears in Lewis's own professional literary criticism, and this reflex is apparent also in his Christian apologetics. In both cases, notably, Lewis presents himself to his own readers as a servant to the greater texts. None of this is to deny that Lewis was a literary critic of impressive learning—he was certainly that, and his life-long habit of reading great books again and again had made him so. It is rather to say that a measure of his enduring value is precisely his posture of readerly self-effacement before the text, regardless of how much sheer learning he was able to bring to it. To put this another way: to be a "mere reader" for Lewis was not to be a naïve reader, but rather a committed, disciplined, accomplished, and yet self-effacing reader.

The same dedication obviously applies to his views of what should pertain to the Christian life. Lewis was not an "evangelical" in the belated Puritan sense familiar to us in this country. Indeed, he distrusted the characteristically effusive personal style of some evangelicals, partly because he found that all too often, when actually asked, they could give "no reason for the hope that was in them" (1 Pet 3:15). Style had come to substitute for substance. In a letter to his friend Arthur Greeves, he writes as disparagingly of the actual understanding of the Bible among Greeves's evangelical community as he does of the exclusivist liturgical formalism common among his Anglican friends in Oxford. He sees both species of smug self-assurance as evidence of a bad reading of Scripture, but in the case of Bible-quoting Greeves his charge that evangelicals often fail to understand what they quote is particularly cutting: "Your relations [fellow worshipers] have been found very ill grounded in the Bible itself and as ignorant as savages of the historical and theological reading needed to make the Bible more than a superstition."[16] The modernized form of Puritanism represented by too many evangelical congregations, Lewis goes on to say, "is simply the form which the *memory* of Christianity takes before it dies away altogether in a commercial community: just as extreme emotional ritualism is the form it takes on just before it dies in a fashionable community."[17] High Church Anglicans do not necessarily fare any better on this account than do evangelicals, because for Lewis it is evidently obedience to the living gospel itself which matters; neither obsessively contemporary nor antique fashions will substitute for a primary encounter of the reader with the text of Scripture. To pursue this point is to recognize one's susceptibility to self-preoccupation. Yet while there is a faithful sense in which Scripture can become to us a mirror, revealing the actual character of our motives and intentions (Heb 4:12), it will not perform this service for us if we go to it simply to confirm that "we are the fairest of them all." In fact, the obtusely selective use of Scripture as a confirmation for our own preconceptions and prejudices is the very bane of mature Christian reading. At its narcissistic worst this practice leads at last to abandonment of the thoughtful reading of the Bible, even in preaching, an abandonment sadly visible in churches of almost all denominations.

In church circles Lewis the apologist is often still the Lewis to quote, in part because he has intellectual prestige and yet can be regarded as "one of us." Yet outside of Christian circles little attention gets paid to his intellectual defenses of Christianity. This would not, I think, have surprised Lewis, who thought of his apologetic efforts less in "evangelistic" terms than we might. His friend the theologian Austin Farrer thought that the apologist in Lewis quite sagely preached to the choir: "It is commonly said that if rational argument is so seldom the cause of conviction, philosophical apologists must largely be wasting their shot. The premise is true, but the conclusion does not follow. For though argument does not create conviction, the lack of it destroys belief. What seems to be proved may not be embraced; but what no one shows the ability to defend is quickly abandoned. Rational argument does not create belief, but it maintains a climate in which belief may flourish."[18]

On this view it might be appropriate for Baylor students, both past and present, to read more of Lewis's apologetic writing than many do—and not merely because, as Lewis says, "good philosophy must exist because bad philosophy needs to be answered."[19] There is, in Lewis's view of "giving a reason for hope that is within you" (1 Pet 3:15), more than a debater's motive; it is the teacher's and good student's motive of learning to read deeply enough that the substantive questions do not go begging in the inward and reflective mind of the ordinary believer. To achieve such readerly maturity, however, it would do us by far the most good to make a lifelong practice of reading *the sort of books Lewis read.*

Farrer's point about the value of preaching to the choir notwithstanding, Lewis has engaged his apologetic tasks in sufficiently persuasive a manner that many intellectuals have become Christians largely through reading his books. When this happens—as in the adult conversion of Francis Collins (Director of the Human Genome Project) through reading *Mere Christianity*—it tends not to be because Lewis has seemed to the reader overpoweringly clever but because he has seemed admirably clear. In my experience it is this same virtue of clarity—both about the real issues and in expression—which has enabled Lewis to become a road back to faithfulness for educated Christians who were in danger of losing their way in the murk of subjective emotionalism and foggy theology. Because he himself *read* well, Lewis *reads* well.

Consistently then, natural debater though he was, Lewis showed himself in the end to be less concerned to win a debate for its own sake than to join argument and create real intellectual dialogue on matters of abiding importance. That he chose to do this as often through the hypothetical "as if" of imaginative fiction as by means of polemical theological exchange is a measure of his disposition to balance analytical rigor with a constant renewal of the open-hearted reader in himself. Lewis seems to have understood better than most that the invitation of Jesus to come "as little children" was not by any means an invitation to superficiality or sentimentality. It was rather a warning against premature hardening of the categories.

Consequently, though he loved and excelled in the weekly thrust and parry of argument at the Oxford Socratic Club, Lewis was well aware that in debate-as-debate, those who oppose the Christian faith will quite often come out on top. It is entirely appropriate, he thought, for Christians to try with utmost diligence to be persuasive about the truth and reasonableness of Christianity but unnecessary for them always to "win" an argument. Finally, as he writes in his poem "The Apologist's Evening Prayer," it is never appropriate—even for an apologist—to trust to argument more than to the "Lord of the narrow gate and the needle's eye."[20]

Lewis's God is Lord also of the literary word, the very Master of metaphor and parable. It is thus to the heart of the faithful reader, not to the skeptic or technophile, that some of the meaning in irreducible mysteries may most likely come. Even in something like his *Chronicles of Narnia*, Lewis thinks, it is not escapism or fantasy which in itself finally compels, but a glimpse of that profundity in truth which resists reduction to a formula. But to grasp that profundity or even to glimpse it, one needs to be the sort of reader who will walk through the wardrobe door, enter the world of wonder like a child, and so have the opportunity to discover a kingdom which is not of this world. Such a reader is thus enabled to face again an "outside" world which is no child's play, but now, made more wise, to face it as one intellectually and spiritually more fit for its daily tasks.

(2002)

Chapter Twelve

Reading the Bible with C. S. Lewis

. . . how the mystery was made known to me by revelation . . . I wrote above in a few words, a reading of which will enable you to perceive my understanding of the mystery of Christ.

Ephesians 3:3–4, NIV

In one of the most useful literary essays of this generation, George Steiner distinguishes two more or less distinctive modes of textual engagement, that of the "critic" and that of the "reader." Briefly, the critic is more than just a professional reader; his intentional approach to the text favors a distanced, analytic exegesis aimed at epistemology and an authoritative judgment. To précis Steiner, "The critical act is a function of the ego in a condition of will," so that in the end the critic is "*judge* and *master* of the text."[1] On this view the critic's agenda is only apparently epistemological: *epi-stemme*—he stands upon the center of what is to be known. Actually, the critic wants to make each text "his own."

By contrast, the "reader" exhibits an opposite desire. His stance is one of yielding acceptance; he favors personal encounter with the "living presence" projected by the text: "The reader is servant to the text [. . .] called to a clerisy of service."[2] Considered philologically, the reader is one who finally "*under*stands" (*sub stantia*). Thus he "stands under" an *auctoritas*, most often regarded as a "who." The reader wants to know this "who," and for him it is this person whose art the work remains.

Steiner is speaking critically of the practice of secular professors of literature, and he is at pains to allow that in such practice the two modes will to some extent overlap. Yet his distinction is actually a very old one, and bears upon what can also be seen as two discrete pedagogical activities in the same person. St. Augustine of Hippo, for example, made skillful use of his very considerable critical powers in much the same register Steiner suggests, most notably in the way he "read" Scripture in his philosophical and general theological writings (e.g., *City of God, Freedom of the Will, On Christian Doctrine*). His approach to Scripture in his work as a preacher was quite different. There, precisely to repress the inevitably egotistical character of a critic's powers and the rhetorical mastery of which he of all people was so capable, he labored to read through the text patiently, expositionally, referentially, reading "with" rather than "teaching down" to his congregation. To emphasize this intention he refused the pulpit, instead sitting in front of his hearers with the text of Scripture open upon his knees, as a reader among readers, or we might say, simply as a reader with an audience.[3]

C. S. Lewis, I want to say in what follows, though incontestably a literary "critic" (and a formidable one), was, as much for the Bible as for literary "greats," much more a "reader" in Augustine the preacher's or in Steiner's sense.

Since Lewis's death, especially in the last two decades, books about the Bible have become surprisingly fashionable. Among the most prominent of the authors of these books are Northrop Frye, Frank Kermode, Robert Alter, Gabriel Josopovici, Stephen Prickett, Naomi Rosenblatt, Avivah Zornberg, Burton Visotzsky, Harold Fisch, Meir Sternberg, Patrick Grant, Amos Wilder, Regina Schwartz, Wesley Kort, David Norton, Meike Bal, John Gottcent, David Jaspers, Michael Fishbane, not to mention Leland Ryken, Bill Moyers, and Walter Wangerin, Jr.

It is noteworthy that many of these books bear no commitment to the *religious* claims of the Bible; their focus is strictly on its influence as literature or its merits as a therapeutic text. In fact, some among these writers, like Northrop Frye, are explicitly in the tradition of Matthew Arnold's determination to wrest the Bible *away* from religion, and to create a kind of replacement for religion in the sphere of a purely secular aesthetic enterprise. Frye is not alone in believing that one reason for doing this is the abandonment of the Bible as Revelation by the theologians themselves: "the single most important revision of theology in modern times," Frye writes, "has been a re-imagining of God as immanent rather than transcendent"—that is, a re-imagining of the modern self as all the god there is.[4] The Bible having been abandoned by modish theologians, why should the tabloids, talk-shows, therapists, and teachers of literature not have at least as good a go at it as the televangelists?

One wonders what Lewis might have made of all this—a momentous academic commercialization of Bible-reading, even a kind of popularized psychoanalysis of the Bible for fun and profit. For Lewis, both transparently a Christian and a distinguished literary critic, wrote very little on the text of Scripture itself. Only his *Reflections on the Psalms* is a primary engagement of the biblical text. If he had lived into the 1990s, would he have felt obliged to add to his many tomes a definitive "statement" on the Bible in the manner of Frye, Alter, or Kermode? And if he had done so, would the evangelical Christians to whom he has been so important have welcomed what he wrote?

One of several odd things about the welter of recent neo-Bultmanesque or otherwise secularizing literary books on the Bible is that evangelicals *have* for the most part liked them—or perhaps we should say, liked the fact of their prominence—rather indiscriminately. That major literary scholars should have judged the Bible worth talking about flatters us, I suppose, despite their general deprecation of its claim to any status whatsoever as divinely inspired truth. Perhaps this is just our version of the Dolly Parton principle.[5] Yet I have the impression that if Lewis *had* written more on the text of Scripture directly, or lived to write a book to answer the neo-Arnoldians, many who think of themselves as evangelicals might not have found his experiment unambiguously good publicity.

Let me explain, beginning with the issue most recent literary studies of the Bible consider beneath respectable consideration—the claims of Scripture to be divine revelation. Lewis did not avoid this issue. Yet he was in no way amenable to the notion of a verbally inspired and textually inerrant Scripture. This has already proved disconcerting to some evangelicals, and early scholarship on Lewis and the Bible focused on this fact as a major problem to be solved. Michael J. Christensen's *C. S. Lewis on Scripture* and Gary Lee Friesen's MA thesis, "Scripture in the Writings of C. S. Lewis" agree in their wistful regret that "though he alluded in his writings to biblical inspiration," Lewis "never addressed himself to the question of inerrancy."[6]

This way of putting it strikes me as not quite accurate. Lewis was aware of the concern for inerrancy among his American readers especially, and in a letter of 1959 to Clyde Kilby of Wheaton College he offered several reasons for thinking the preoccupation with verbal inspiration (soon to become a crisis under the guidance of Francis Schaeffer and Harold Lindsell) to be something of a theological red herring. Of these, the most advertant reason was his own reading experience:

> To me the curious thing is that neither in my own Bible-reading nor in my religious life as whole does the question *in fact* ever assume that importance which it always gets in theological controversy. The difference between reading the story of Ruth and that of Antigone—both first class as literature—is to me unmistakable and even overwhelming. But the question "Is

Ruth historical?" (I've no reason to suppose it is *not*) doesn't really seem to arise till afterwards. It can still act on me as the Word of God if it weren't, so far as I can see. All Holy Scripture is written for our learning. But learning *of what?* I should have thought the value of some things (e.g. the Resurrection) depended on whether they really happened, but the value of others (e.g. the fate of Lot's wife) hardly at all. And the ones whose historicity matters are [. . .] those where it is plain.[7]

Lewis included some further notes with his letter to Kilby, and though the general content of these is well known among devotees of the Inklings, it will probably be helpful to others to have them recalled in particular here:

Whatever view we hold on the divine authority of Scripture must make room for the following facts: 1. The distinction which St. Paul makes in I Corinthians 7, verses 10 and 12. ["not I but the Lord. . . ." "I and not the Lord."]   2. The apparent inconsistencies between the genealogies in Matthew 1 and Luke 3; between the accounts of the death of Judas in Matthew 27:5 and Acts 1:18-19.   3. St. Luke's own account of how he obtained his matter (1:1–4).   4. The universally admitted unhistoricity (I do not say, of course, falsity) of at least some narratives in Scripture (the parables), which may well extend also to Jonah and Job.   5. If every good and perfect gift comes from the Father of Lights then *all* true and edifying writings, whether in Scripture or not, must be *in some sense* inspired.   6. John 11:49–52. Inspiration may operate in a wicked man without his knowing it. [. . .] It seems to me that 2 and 4 rule out the view that every statement in Scripture must be *historical* truth. And 1, 3, 5, and 6 rule out the view that inspiration is a single thing in the sense that, if present at all, it is always present in the same mode and the same degree; therefore, I think, [it] rules out the view that any one passage taken in isolation can be assumed to be inerrant in exactly the same sense as any other. [. . .] That the over-all operation of Scripture is to convey God's Word to the reader ([who] also needs His inspiration) [and] who reads it in the right spirit, I fully believe. That it *also* gives answers to all the questions (often religiously irrelevant) which he might ask, I don't. The very *kind* of truth we are often demanding was, in my opinion, never even envisaged by the ancients.[8]

These objections are, in fact, mostly to be found elsewhere in Lewis: his deep sense of offense at the "immorality," as he has it, of some of the "cursing Psalms,"[9] lyrics which include in Psalm 109 "as unabashed a hymn of hate as was ever written"; his conviction that the cynicism of Ecclesiastes is eccentric

to biblical morality, his belief in the fictionality of Jonah, Esther, and probably Job.[10]

So then, Lewis stands aslant of two positions: while a preponderance of
recent books by literary scholars on the Bible consider questions about
divine inspiration and inerrancy to be beneath notice, Lewis, though he took
the issue itself to be important enough to consider thoughtfully, certainly
disagreed with many evangelicals about how to conclude on the matter.

We should remember that Lewis came to the Bible first as a philologist,
theorist of translation, and literary critic. And, in the first instance, as a non-
believer. The issues that occupied his critical attention were, in respect of the
Bible, not substantially different from the issues which preoccupied him as a
reader of literary texts. However unfashionably for most postmodernists,
Lewis was deeply concerned to recover the author's intention: "it is not
enough to make sense" when we interpret, he writes in his introduction to
Studies in Words, "we want to find the sense the author intended."[11] This
means that a precise and scholarly knowledge of the language in question is
indispensable for serious study. It was entirely typical of Lewis's intellectual
habits and academic training that shortly after his conversion he commenced
upon reading John's Gospel in Greek, and that he read some portion of the
Bible in Greek every day.[12] In a similar vein, when he wants to understand a
biblical term such as the "Day of Judgment," he pursues the lexical history of
mishpat, and then the actual work of the judges of Israel until he ferrets out
the notion not merely of "sentence" or "decree" but of avenging and the
righting of wrongs.[13]

For Lewis there is no such thing as a special "religious language," as there
is possibly a "scientific" language: "the language of religion," he writes, seems
"to be, on the whole, either the same sort we use in ordinary conversation or
the same sort we use in poetry."[14] On this point he has much in common
with his recent fellow literary critics, and little in common with many theologians, who themselves, he says, use in fact a kind of scientific or pseudo-
scientific language which cuts them off from the literature upon which they
depend.[15] This fault he regards as in fact crippling for their understanding of
Scripture, and so he wants to "correct theology," as he puts it, by sending the
theologians back to the Bible itself[16] so they can learn to speak of it *in its
own language.*

Francis Petrarch, the fourteenth-century poet, once described theology
as "poetry about God." Petrarch meant, evidently, that sound theological
language was also *necessarily* figurative (*Familiar Letters* 10.4). Lewis, who
almost certainly would have known this passage in Petrarch, had a less than
sanguine view of the reductively prosaic language used by his own theological contemporaries. "If [our] theology is poetry," he said, "it is not very *good*

poetry."[17] The Bible, on the other hand, he found to be replete with a poetic language that *works*. His advice to interpreters of the Bible is to leave the figurative speech of the Bible stand, and not to try to reduce it to theological formulae or literalization:

> I suggest two rules for exegetics. (1) Never take the images literally. (2) When the *purport* of the images—what they say to our fear, and hope, and will, and affections—seems to conflict with the theological abstractions, *trust the purport of the images every time*. For our abstract thinking is itself a tissue of analogies: a continual modeling of spiritual reality in legal, or chemical, or mechanical terms. Are these likely to be more adequate than the sensuous, organic, and personal images of Scripture—light and darkness, river and well, seed and harvest, master and servant, hen and chickens, father and child? The footprints of the Divine are more visible in that rich soil than across rocks or slag heaps. Hence what they now call "demythologizing" Christianity can easily be "remythologizing" it—and substituting a poorer mythology for a richer.[18]

Here is a warning which cuts two ways, and which has in fact been appropriated better by the secular literary critics of Scripture than by theologians of *either* evangelical or liberal persuasion. As Kermode and Alter put it in their introduction to *The Literary Guide to the Bible*, it is not that form-critical questions do not have their narrow interest, but rather that they do little or nothing to account for the cultural and religious power, or the literary unity, of the text as we have it.[19] With this conclusion, at least, I think, Lewis would have heartily agreed.

But Lewis went much further. His few contacts with professional theologians at Oxford show him to have had a pronounced disdain for their general competence as readers of any kind of text: "whatever these men may be as biblical critics," he told an audience at Cambridge, "I distrust them as critics."[20] They cannot even recognize the properties of genre, wanting to apply terms such as "spiritual romance" to the Fourth Gospel, not in the least being able to judge from experience of such texts how foolish such a judgment must appear from any kind of mature reader's point of view. He attacks even Bultmann for obtuseness as a reader, and the kind of wrongheadedness that could lead him to proclaim that "The personality of Jesus has no importance for the Kerygma of either Paul or John. . . ." As far as Lewis can tell, the personality of Jesus is precisely the phenomenon upon which the whole New Testament turns. The reason the apocryphal Gospels are not to be trusted as authentic eyewitness accounts, he insists, is that we know from the four canonical Gospels how Jesus talked, and any kind of literarily sensitive reader will know immediately that he is confronted by literary forgery, just as much as he would if confronted by "pseudo-Johnsonianna"—forged conversations attributed to Dr. Samuel Johnson.[21] But the typical biblical critic, he suggests, has a tin ear; he cannot even recognize a dominant textual "voice."

Another more general kind of literary forgery is the liberal theologian's attempt to transform the protagonist of the Gospels into a "mere moral teacher"—an attempt entirely contradictory to the text of the Bible.[22] "He did not produce that effect on any of the people who met him," observes Lewis. Rather, Jesus "produced mainly three effects—Hatred—Terror—Adoration. There was no trace of people expressing mild approval."[23]

The firm presuppositions of twentieth-century liberal biblical criticism, e.g. "if miraculous, then unhistorical" is, Lewis says, similarly a prejudice "they bring to the study of their texts, not one they have learned from it. If one is speaking of authority, the united authority of all the Biblical critics in the world counts here for nothing."[24] To the attempt to degrade the power of the Gospels by calling them, effectively, legends—also a strategy of the most flamboyant New Testament scholars—Lewis has this to say:

> Now, as a literary historian, I am perfectly convinced that whatever else the Gospels are, they are not legends. I have read a great deal of legend and I am quite clear that they are not the same sort of thing. They are not artistic enough to be legends. From an imaginative point of view they are clumsy, they don't work up to things properly. Most of the life of Jesus is totally unknown to us, as is the life of anyone else who lived at that time, and no people building up a legend would allow that to be so. Apart from bits of the Platonic dialogues, there are no conversations that I know of in ancient literature like the Fourth Gospel. There is nothing, even in modern literature, until about a hundred years ago when the realistic novel came into existence. In the story of the woman taken in adultery we are told Christ bent down and scribbled in the dust with His finger. Nothing comes of this. No one has ever based any doctrine on it. And the art of *inventing* little irrelevant details to make an imaginary scene more convincing is a purely modern art. Surely the only explanation of this passage is that the thing really happened? The author put it in simply because he had seen it.[25]

It is relatively easy to see why evangelicals have welcomed *this* aspect of Lewis's criticism and also why we might wish for a comparably authoritative reader of texts today when the so-called "Jesus Seminar" is obtaining widespread popular notice for pseudo-textual judgments which, on a literary level, are often more ludicrous than anything Lewis could have imagined.

Nevertheless, Lewis presents, at least for those who want to maintain even a proximate notion of verbal inspiration, many real difficulties and challenges. A key question tacit or explicit in earlier evangelical examinations of Lewis's approach to the Bible (e.g., Christensen and Friesen) is: "How, if he is not an inerrantist, does Lewis hold such a high view of Scripture?" I suspect that something like that must have been asked of Lewis by Clyde Kilby in order for him to have elicited the famous letter of May 7, 1959. To this question, I roundly suspect, Lewis's first response might well have been a wan and painful smile. It continues to illuminate my own reflection on the great tact and charity of Lewis, as well as the matter of his view of the authority of the Bible, that four days after he wrote his letter to Kilby disassociating himself from the historicist/inerrantist position, he gave a superb paper at Cambridge denouncing the follies of *liberal* biblical criticism (May 11, 1959).[26] He must have been preparing to answer the curiosities of what he regarded as *two* species of ill-formed criticism at the same time.

What most undergirds Lewis's convictions concerning the authority of the Bible, aside from his mature literary sense of the text, is his strong belief in the continuous operation of the Holy Spirit in transmitting the intention of the Divine Author to the consciousness of all who well attend to it. He does not imagine that there is no relation between worldwide Creation myths and the early chapters of Genesis, nor, on the other hand, does he accept that Genesis is simply one among many such nebulous accounts. Rather, he sees that the Genesis account bears about it a sense of God's transcendence as Creator more clearly than any other, and takes it that the clarity itself is a sign of the distinctive operation of the Holy Spirit:

> When a series of such retellings turns a creation story which at first had almost no religious or metaphysical significance into a story which achieves the idea of true Creation and of a transcendent Creator (as Genesis does), then nothing will make me believe that some of the retellers, or some one of them, has not been guided by God.[27]

This operation of the Holy Spirit, he believes, was present in the Councils and in the establishment of the biblical canon.[28] But in order for the Bible to be read accountably as revelation, this same Spirit must be present in the reader reading the text too. In a sense, this spiritual principle in Lewis is very close to a literary principle, even as it was in St. Augustine (*On Christian Doctrine*) and St. Anselm (*Monologion; Proslogion*), and it suggests this: that in faithful reading, *lack* of critical distance may be the almost indispensable condition of getting things spiritually right. In his copy of Samuel Taylor Coleridge's *Aids to Reflection and Confessions of an Enquiring Spirit*, Lewis heavily underlines Aphorism IV: "There is a small chance of Truth at the goal where there is not child-like Humility at the starting point."[29] On the next page he underlines Coleridge's affirmations of Augustine and Anselm's "unless ye believe ye cannot understand."[30] Like Coleridge, Lewis deeply suspected the habit of devising, in Coleridge's words, "a scheme of picking and choosing Scripture texts for the support of doctrines that had been learned beforehand from the higher oracle of Common Sense." [. . .] "What you find therein coincident with your preestablished convictions, you will of course realize as the Revealed Word. [. . .],"[31] says Coleridge with a perceptible smirk. Lewis underlined these passages both the first time he read them (likely in the 1920s) and again in ink, "25/9/62,"[32] at which time he also cross-referenced the two. But his agreement with Coleridge is here manifestly an agreement against some of the more *evangelical* theologians; it is, instructively, echoed in a passage on the strengths and limits of poetic language in his essay on "The Language of Religion":

> Such information as Poetic Language has to give can be received only if you are ready to meet it half-way. It is no good holding a dialectical pistol to the poet's head and demanding how the deuce a river could have hair, or thought be green, or a woman a red nose. You may win, in the sense of putting him to a *non-plus*. But if he had anything to tell you, you will never get it by behaving in that way. You must begin by trusting him. Only by so doing will you find out whether he is trustworthy or not. *Credo ut intelligam* (it is time some theological expression came in) is here the only attitude.[33]

That is, as he says elsewhere,[34] it is an act of intellectual impertinence to ask a text to deliver assurances in the propositional language of theologians when it is written in the evocative language of poetry. And contrary to what the theologians typically think, it is the language of poetry which requires of the reader the most mature attainment—self-transcendence. However paradoxically, according to Lewis, this self-oblation of the good reader is the best means of self-discovery: "Here, as in worship, in love, in moral action, and in knowing, I transcend myself; and am never more myself than when I do."[35] Here we see that Steiner's distinction between the ambition of the critic and the desire of the reader has been fully anticipated.

In the end, what Lewis seems most to have wanted to affirm is a confidence in what Christians *get* from reading the Bible. What he itemizes, however, is not what one might expect. For one thing, Lewis suggests, it gives us a strong sense of filiation with Jews: "no Christian," he writes, "can read the Bible without discovering that [the] ancient Hebrews, generally so remote, may at any moment turn out to be our brothers in a sense which no Greek or Roman ever was."[36] And there are other surprises, such as finding injunctions that we should show charity to our enemies already in the Psalms, even though nearby are "expressions of a cruelty more vindictive and a self-righteousness more complete than anything in the classics."[37] The latter sensibility he finds highly confirming of the biblical contention that God chooses the "unlikely" to fulfill his purposes. But most especially, reading the Gospels also disabuses us of our cherished fantasies about God, contradicting them with the reality of Jesus. Jesus proves not to be the sweet anemic of nineteenth-century sermons and pre-Raphaelite painting, who is, after all, says Lewis, just the product of "19th-century skepticism."[38] The authenticity of the Gospels, Lewis says, lies in its repeated confirmations that "reality, in fact, is always something you couldn't have guessed."[39] Moreover, reality is far better than our own inventions: "We've got to take reality as it comes to us: there's no good jabbering about what it ought to be like or what we'd have expected it to be like."[40] Above all, the Bible is a book which offers us reality. And the essence of that reality is that the reader's response to the Bible is a matter of the utmost consequence, and not in any merely academic sense.

This sense of divine authorial intention in the Bible is what puts Lewis most at odds with modern literary expositors of the Bible with whom he is in other ways so much in agreement. One result of this is that, unlike many secular litterateurs, present company included, he has little or no veneration for the ageless standard in its literary translation, the Authorized Version (KJV). Whereas Alter, Rosenbeg, Rosenblatt, and others hold the KJV to be the best ever translation of the Hebrew Scriptures into English, and Prickett thinks Robert Lowth perfectly insightful when he announced in 1753 that the KJV had got Hebrew parallelism right and made it poetically English, and while Matthew Arnold and Northrop Frye revere the KJV for its metrical tact and poetic sublimity, Lewis thinks that stylistic elegance of the KJV and the veneration it occasions combine to obscure many an essential theological truth. As he puts it:

> The New Testament in the original Greek is not a work of literary art: it is not written in a solemn, ecclesiastical language, it is written in the sort of Greek which was spoken over the Eastern Mediterranean after Greek had become an international language and therefore lost its real beauty and subtlety. In it we see Greek used by people who have no real feeling for Greek words because Greek words are not the words they spoke when they were children. It is a sort of "basic" Greek; a ministrative language. Does this shock us? It ought not to, except as the Incarnation itself ought to shock us. The same divine humility which decreed that God should become a baby at

a peasant-woman's breast, and later an arrested field-preacher in the hands of the Roman police, decreed also that He should be preached in a vulgar, prosaic and unliterary language. If you can stomach the one, you can stomach the other. The Incarnation is in that sense an irreverent doctrine: Christianity, in that sense, an incurably irreverent religion. When we expect that it should have come before the World in all the beauty that we now feel in the Authorized Version we are as wide of the mark as the Jews were in expecting that the Messiah would come as a great earthly King. The real sanctity, the real beauty and sublimity of the New Testament (as of Christ's life) are of a different sort: miles deeper or *further in.*[41]

Lewis resisted even the claim by both English writers and literary critics that the Authorized Version has been, especially stylistically, a prime model or foundation for English prose. While he agreed that the Authorized Version was a literary source of profound importance, he denied that this had much to do with any special literary properties of the translation, even in such an AV-associated writer as Bunyan ("The Literary Impact of the Authorized Version," in *They Asked for a Paper*). Finally, he resisted the notion that the Bible could even be considered as literature apart from its role as religious authority:[42]

Unless the *religious* claims of the Bible are again acknowledged, its literary claims will, I think, be given only "mouth honour," and that decreasingly. For it is, through and through, a sacred book [. . .] so remorselessly and continuously sacred that it does not invite, it excludes and repels the merely aesthetic approach. You can read it as literature only by a *tour de force.* [. . .] It demands incessantly to be taken on its own terms: it will not continue to give literary delight very long except to those who go to it for something quite different. I predict that it will in the future continue to be read as it always has been read, almost exclusively by Christians.[43]

On this point he had the weighty concurrence of T. S. Eliot, who insisted that "the Bible has had a literary influence *not* because it has been considered [critically] as literature, but because it has been considered as the report of the Word of God."[44]

Lewis went so far as to counsel readers who retain "childish associations" with ecclesiastical usage of the Authorized Version to read the New Testament in "some other language" or in a version like Moffatt's.[45] As he says elsewhere, "though it may seem a sour paradox, we must sometimes get away from the Authorized Version, if for no other reason, simply *because* it is so beautiful and so solemn. Beauty exalts, but beauty also lulls."[46] His

preference for the "what" that is said rather than the "how" comes out crisply
in his negative response to Arthur Quiller-Couch's Arnoldian defense of the
Authorized Version against the Basic English Version; for Lewis, accuracy of
translation ought always to trump the less essential aspect of style.[47] Lewis
refused, however, to offer counsel to American translators of the Bible, saying he was incompetent to do so, since American vernacular would be different, if only in small ways, from his own colloquial expressions. He felt that
understanding such subtle differences was so important that both American
and English ordination exams should contain a passage from a theological
work which requires translation into the vernacular of the particular country.
If the candidate failed in this respect, Lewis added sagely, then he should fail
the entire examination, since genuine belief and understanding of one's faith
requires the ability to express it in the vernacular, and not simply in
"learned" jargon or, as he would have it, "scientific" language.[48]

As for Scripture translation in general, he felt it to be a perpetual under-
taking: "The truth is that if we are to have translation at all we must have
periodical re-translation."[49] His own modern favorites were Moffatt and
Knox—neither of which, as far as I know, has interested any other literary
commentators. One can only guess at how he would have reacted to the
plethora of narrowly interested modern translations—Bibles for men, Bibles
for women, Bibles for singles, Bibles for couples, Bibles for teenagers, Bibles
for men in mid-life crisis. (I would not be surprised to find any day now a
Bible for pipe-fitters.)

In summary, it seems as though in this as in many other respects Lewis
maintained his own ground, not fully satisfying his interlocutors on either
the right or the left, the sacred or the secular sides. What would he have
thought of our contemporary academic industry, so many English literature
and psychology professors writing books on the Bible? Of course, we shall
never know. In the light of what we do know of his prejudices, however, my
guess is that he would have thoroughly disliked the work of some of the neo-
Arnoldians, such as Kermode and Frye, but rather enjoyed the acute and
earthy literary interpretation of some of the linguistically competent Jewish
critics such as Robert Alter and Avivah Zornberg. Would he have felt com-
pelled to write such a book himself? Here I am at still greater risk, but my
guess is that he would not. More modest than most, and a master of the critical essay and small, well-crafted book, he would, I think, have let this fad of
our own generation pass him by.

It strikes me that his view of the Bible, broadly taken, is quite in the
mainstream of pre-Reformation tradition, which is to say that it is not, in the
modern sense, a "critical" view. Scripture is important to him because it
communicates the person and work of Jesus and thus the content, the *credo*

of faith. But the function of Scripture is purely instrumental. The status of the Bible, or the dependence of its authority on a precise, unitary and once-in-time verbal inspiration is not a matter which can strike upon either his literary or his spiritual sense except obliquely. As with Augustine, or Anselm of Canterbury, Lewis thinks that real faith must in any case precede any approach to the text that would lead to understanding, and as with them, he arrived at his *credo ut intelligam* not as a rejection of reason but in consequence of an application of reason and also a grasp of reason's limits.[50]

What he did not believe the Christian could live without was the mediation of the living Gospel in the life of the Church. "There are three things," he says, "that spread the Christ life to us: baptism, belief, and that mysterious action which different Christians call by different names—Holy Communion, the Mass, the Lord's Supper." He does not include the Bible in his list, except indirectly, perhaps, as nourishment to belief. In his view Jesus "taught his followers that the new life was communicated in this way," and that he, and we, should be willing to accept this on authority.[51] Then he launches into an excursus on the necessity of our accepting authority—which returns us to where we began, with Lewis insisting that in matters of Revelation, at least, the critic's ambitions ought always to be subordinated to the reader's desire for faithfulness, communion, and celebration of the Author.

(2000)

Chapter Thirteen

Scripture, Gender and Our Language of Worship

. . . ut omnes unum sint, sicut tu, Pater, in me, et ego in te, ut et ipsi in nobis unum. . . .

John 17:21, Vulgate

The quest for inclusive language in theological discussion and worship continues to unsettle many worship communities. In many of the liberal congregations of our major denominations, "gender neutral" translations of the RSV as pulpit Bibles and the *Inclusive Language Lectionary* are becoming widely used. As these and comparable "revisions" have been adopted successively by Presbyterians, Episcopalians (Anglicans), the United Church of Christ, and the United Church of Canada, among others, the effect has been often to create controversy and to put pressure to conform on those of more conservative theological persuasions. Discussions—often heated—have spread across a broad spectrum of denominations, from the Roman Catholic to the Reformed and, more recently, Baptist churches. Thus, innovations that have ostensibly been offered to advocate greater unity in the community of faith have in fact tended toward precisely the opposite effect. The emergence of the renewal movement in the American Episcopal Church (Episcopalians United for Revelation, Renewal, and Reformation) and the United Church Renewal Fellowship in Canada, to take two examples, have been occasioned by a complex of issues among which inclusive language has tended to be seen by both advocates and opponents as indicative.

Theologically speaking, the cutting edge of this issue now has relatively little to do with the language we use to speak to and about each other in

195

community; it has everything to do, however, with how we speak to or about God. This is the point that has most exercised theological conservatives, yet often they have not been able with much more clarity than their opponents to disentangle it from the case for inclusive language in community, and so have found themselves cast in an unattractive, apparently uncharitable, or even antifeminist role as they have tried to defend what they take to be a scripturally sanctioned language of worship. Is the case in our day for speaking not merely of the "sons" but also, considerately, of the "daughters" of the covenant inseparable from learning also to speak of the "motherhood" as well as of the "fatherhood" of God? How do we handle these things?

It was concerns of this sort that some years ago brought a letter to my desk from a theological discussion group in the United Church of Canada. Could I, as a philologist and a Christian, offer some reflections on the use of inclusive and feminine language in worship, especially in reference to God? Though not a member of their denomination (I am a sometime evangelical Anglican who was raised Baptist and am now again a member of a Baptist church), I undertook to do what I could, conscious that the issue was one that cut across denominational lines. And the motto on their church stationery—*ut omnes unum sint* ("that they all may be one" from John 17:21)—struck me forcibly as most relevant to the issues of unity and inclusiveness in the body of Christ generally. The chapter from which the phrase comes, in fact, speaking as it does to the character and purpose of those who would follow Christ, proves a fruitful preparation for consideration of these matters. It is, of course, the great intercessory prayer of our Lord Jesus Christ for his people, and I encourage my readers to renew their memory of it, as a context for similar discussions in which they may find themselves.

In this prayer, the stress our Lord puts on unity (or we might say "inclusivity") is clear and explicit in the language he uses. Moreover, the prayer itself emphasizes the central role of language in "defining" those who will follow Jesus, who, as we see from the previous chapter, are literally and figuratively the ones who take up his cross. For the content of relationship with God he expresses and the apostolic continuity he prays for (vv. 15–20) are unavoidably a matter of language, both words (v. 8) and the Word (v. 14), the incorporation of which is, ultimately, a bearing of the name of God (vv. 11–12). That is, our Lord has given us the words given him by the Father (v. 8), which, when we receive them, are the basis of our recognition of God in Christ, even if they are also the occasion of our being despised by a world that rejects godliness (v. 14). But that "all may be one," a phrase repeated three times in this prayer (vv. 11, 21–22), the prayer of our Lord is that we be kept through the name of the Father, through his eternal authority: "Holy Father, keep through thy own name those whom thou hast given me, that they may be one, as we are" (v. 11). Biblically speaking, then, the unity in which Christ desires we be included is that of the "family" of God, an inclusion obtained for us by Jesus and maintained through the Father's authority. Consideration of Christian language, we may assume, ought to reflect and not undermine that purpose.

Language Change

A crisis of language is always a crisis of meaning—that is to say, a crisis of authority. Linguistic history, intellectual history, and social history converge to reveal that it is at turning points or crises in the history of civilization that the concept of "linguistic validity" is most keenly attacked and defended.[1] And this happens, of course, because every cherished and remembered speech-act has occurred at some place in time past. When we use such "historic" or "authoritative" words we wake into resonance their entire previous history. When people begin to find that resonance "oppressive," it is the history, and the relevance of its authority, that they are usually calling into question.

In this context, we recognize an obvious feature of language, which is that none of us, strictly speaking, invents it. The language we speak, like the air we breathe, is a creational inheritance used (or abused) by us as we in our turn make further contributions to that history. Now, as in the case of the air we breathe, it is notoriously easier to degrade than upgrade the linguistic environment: persistent reports of more than one-quarter of our population grown illiterate offer discomforting evidence of this.

Concerns to improve language, on the other hand, focus of necessity on its superficial features: speech pattern and vocabulary (*parole*). The desire to improve language can thus mean either to bring idiom into a more precise relationship to contemporary usage (a matter of what language specialists call intersubjective agreement) or, more narrowly, to revise phrasing to meet certain given criteria (called, naturally enough, presuppositions).

The first of these motives reflects the fact that understood meaning changes with time; sometimes within a few centuries near reversals of original understanding can arise. When the King James Version has the psalmist reflect on the God who "prevents" him with blessings (Ps 21:3), it is necessary for even a moderately literate reader to look up in his modern version a translation such as "meets him with blessings" (Jerusalem and New English Bibles) or "welcomes" him (New English Bible) if he is not to be misled by the now archaic use of this English verb in the King James text.

There are a number of words like this, and by and large Bible translators and liturgists have done a good job of handling them. But a much larger number of terms are changing meanings in our own time than in any previous period of English language development, and this creates an enormous burden of difficulty for those whose task it is to bring forward words from the past into contemporary understanding. For the most part, these are not function words (like my previous examples) but *value* words, and their transformed standing is recent enough that many of you will have already reflected on the ambiguous status of my examples:

> *Conservative, Hierarchy* (in the political arena)
> *Fundamental, Evangelical, Fear of God, Doctrine* (in the religious realm)
> *Wholesome, Traditional, Obedient, Chaste* (in the sociological realm)

All these words have tended to become obscured, or even lost, to positive value association: indeed, in some contexts of general usage, such as in the mass media, each of these is typically used in a negative or pejorative way. In some quarters, the word *religious* is heading in the same direction. In educational circles at least, this has to some degree happened already to the word *value* itself. Once, while I was questioning a curriculum directive to allow high school students to make collages of magazine cutouts and write a haiku poem instead of taking examinations and learning to write essays coherently, my doubting opinion was attacked by the representative of the local teachers' federation as "meaningless—a mere value judgment." By this my opponent meant, of course, that my opinion was of no value at all. (Most of us are aware that what passes for "values education" in our schools is often similarly dismissive of the exercise of judgment, of any discrimination between right and wrong, as "meaningless.")

A final example, more blatant, must suffice to conclude my illustration of this point. The word freedom in our own society (perhaps especially since my own sixties generation) tends to be identified with *autonomy, independence,* and *personal liberty from restraint.* In the fourteenth century, the time of Wyclif and Chaucer, its primary meaning was none of these, but rather generosity. (Thus Chaucer's Knight, who "loved truth, honour, freedom and courtesy. . . .") This is to say, the older understanding is really polar from our own, implying entirely an outward-flowing response to others; our modern reflex tends to make freedom, by contrast, almost anarchic, an insular or private value. The old concept now needs to be translated by charity, or possibly community spirit; also contained in it is the idea of openness, or of liberality. Without these components, something is lost to us in the words of Jesus, "You shall know the truth, and the truth shall make you free" (John 8:32). Free does not mean here simply independent, or self-assertive. It means that because we know the truth—the revealed truth of Jesus' word (v. 31)—we are able to be secure in that and experience a freedom from the bugaboos that haunt our contemporaries, be they legalisms or self-preoccupations of any kind. The truth sustains our own identity in the midst of these things, overcoming bondage to our own sinfulness (v. 34), simply because it is God's truth and therefore not open to variableness or change.

A third value or meaning for freedom, at odds with both so far given, is found in *Izvestiia* for August 27, 1968, which describes the invasion of Czechoslovakia on that day as "a spontaneous, ardently welcomed defence of popular freedom." This shocking twist to expectations of usage in our culture is not, of course, at all shocking in the Soviet Union, and the example illustrates well a self-conscious revision of meaning of the type that arises out of a revolution in basic presuppositions. In our own press we are familiar with the imposed redefinition involved in propaganda terms such as "freedom fighters" or "wars of liberation." Historical changes in words of the categories I have been discussing, whether slow and a matter of evolving shared perspectives or sudden and the result of a political redefinition, are *never* value free.

The Evolution of Self-Consciousness

In trying to think about these things, it is worthwhile to bear in mind that, since about the latter part of the seventeenth century, there has been a general shift of Western consciousness well documented in many fields. This shift is amply reflected in theological controversies of both Protestant and Catholic churches and, because it is less a matter of vocabulary or phrasing than of what linguists refer to as grammar—the deep structure of language itself (*langue*)—it is both harder to detect and far more influential than any of the merely lexical changes that usually capture our attention.

Let me illustrate this briefly. There is a whole category of relational verbs that have undergone a revolution since the early eighteenth century in their relationship to the grammatical subject and object of the constructions in which they occur.

If, for example, I say of a woman that she is "charming," what part of speech is "charming"? Typically, of course, we recognize in this modern context an adjectival function: "charming" modifies the name of the woman in question: "charming Katherine." If, however, I create another sentence with these words: "Katherine is charming your minister," suddenly we are aware of a value shift of striking proportions; Katherine's "charming" is now pejorative, and the second sentence is as uncomplimentary as the first was intended to be complimentary to the woman to whom it was applied as an adjective. For of course, strictly speaking, the word is not an adjective at all. It is a form of the verb "to charm," its present participle. As such, it requires an object. In modern parlance, when an object is provided, and the quality of "charming" is actually attributed to the subject of the sentence, Katherine, the effect can be social criticism. When, however, I use it without an explicit object and thus *adjectivally*—which is almost exclusively the way we do use it in modern parlance—what has actually happened is that I have provided, silently, a hidden object. This "hidden object" in my sentence is actually myself. My sentence, "Katherine is charming," does not necessarily describe anything that Katherine is *doing*; she may not even know I exist, or be completely preoccupied with other matters. My phrase simply describes the effect she is having on me. I have made myself the imposed object of her "charming," regardless of any willed participation on her part. Strictly speaking, I am not referencing the verb "charm" to her at all.

Increasingly, we use the word *understanding* in the same way. If I say about your minister that he is "an understanding person," I do not mean that he is understanding anything at all. "Alan is an understanding fellow" means nothing more than "it appears to me that Alan likes me," or "Alan and I are getting along." That is all. The power to understand as a virtue has, in this popular usage, been stripped away from Alan and focused instead on my own imagination, my own ego. What I am really saying is that "Alan knows what I am like," or perhaps even more simply, "what I like."

There is a large category of such verbs that are so redefined adjectivally during that period of general secularization of values in our culture that we call, somewhat ironically it seems to me, the Enlightenment. For the English language, you can clearly trace this general shift in the full *Oxford English Dictionary*; there are almost no "adjectival" cases cited for some terms before 1725—and almost no "verbal" uses cited after 1775.

The effect of this major grammatical shift is a *radical ego-centering of discourse about persons*. Now, such statements are disguised expressions of a consumerist view of reality, in which object-values are replaced by subject-values. Conditioned by such language, we are inclined not to ask whether a rumor is true or false, or a book good or bad, but simply whether or not it is "interesting" (to us). In much the same way, this shift of centering has tended to affect the language we use about God, and that long before the rise of the particular concerns of today's gender-feminists.

Our language about God, or the Bible, reveals quite clearly how we regard God and the Bible, and not merely at the level of vocabulary. We make this clear also in the very structure of our grammar. Do we, as the name *Christian* directly implies, see ourselves as ones who are "followers" or "disciples" of Christ or, as in the popular evangelical idiom, as ones who have "accepted" Christ? As a matter of fact, the Scriptures are unequivocal about who it is that does the accepting (Jer 14:10, 12; Amos 5:22; Ezek 20:40; 43:27). Some of us who are evangelicals may—glibly, I fear—merely have reflected the secular reversal of order in our "grammar of assent," talking for a generation or more of Christ as if he were a commodity. While the New

Testament encourages us to "receive" Christ, it is in the sense of opening our doors (i.e., in hospitality) to allow him to occupy us. In the hospitality code of the New Testament, this makes us his servants; to "receive" him is automatically to relegate ego to a lower place, to give him preeminence. Because of the association of "acceptance" in contemporary idiom with the values of the marketplace (e.g., "consumer acceptance"), where ego reigns, "accepting Christ" can become a formulation that does violence to the grammatical hierarchy of both Scripture and traditional English translations, making the crucial biblical business of self-denial, servanthood, and taking up the cross disappear like the magician's rabbit in the process. In so doing, it paves the way for the "I Found It" bumper sticker mentality and some of the obvious distortions of the television evangelists.

My point about grammatical shift as a measure of the evolution of (self) consciousness is more substantial than I can develop here; I will return to this subject briefly, however, in my concluding remarks.[2] What I want to stress now is simply the fact that grammar—the hidden structure of language to which words are but as flesh on the bones—is much slower to reflect a real change in values, but not at all invulnerable to change, and that changes at this level are far more devastating, by means of their foundational nature and their hiddenness, than change at the level of the words we see on a page. It is often unrecognized assent to "grammatical transformation" which makes an issue like that of inclusive language difficult both to understand and to evaluate.

Translation and Interpretation

The usual motive for modern English translation has been a sense of fading currency of idiom, a feeling, for example, that the King James Version, especially, has grown not only archaic but possibly unintelligibly so. The Revised Standard Version, the (further) revised RSV, the American Standard Version, the New International and New English versions, and many of the less admirable paraphrases, have ostensibly grown up in response to these feelings. Committees engaged in liturgical revision commonly speak of the same imperative.

A difficulty with any type of translation, however, is that every translation is unavoidably an interpretation.[3] Thus, it is abundantly clear to those who compare translations of the Bible that at various times and places the process of rendering the Hebrew and Greek of certain biblical texts has been filtered through a diversity of understandings of the text as a whole, and further shaded by the cultural biases of the translators. Some of this is merely colorful rendition: one of my favorites is Tyndale's almost mercantile English rendering of Psalm 19:2 ("Day unto day uttereth speech, and night unto night sheweth knowledge" in the Douai and King James) as "One day telleth another: and one night *certifieth* another" (*Book of Common Prayer*, 1564). But not all of the "interpretation" in translation is so incidental to the principal meaning of the text. The distinguished British philologist, Professor Ian Robinson, in deploring the Good News Bible translation, finds that the character of its mistranslation is often to deny to God his transcendence and to humanity its soul. In fact, the word "soul" is conspicuously deleted in many modern translations of the Bible, including much of the Good News Bible. "For what shall it profit a man if he gain the whole world, and lose his own soul?" (Mark 8:36 in the KJV) becomes in the New English Bible, for example, a question about losing one's "true self"; in the Good News Bible (perhaps worst of all), the verse asks "Does a person gain anything if he wins the whole world but loses his life?" Robinson comments: "But if we could gain the whole world without losing life? It was the Devil who offered Jesus that option. He would have lost his soul in accepting it."[4]

The problem of obtrusive interpretation in translation is this: How do translators establish the precise meaning of a word, verse, or passage in the Bible? A translator *must* begin by establishing as closely as possible what the original text says, and only then take up the question of how most faithfully to express that idea in English. That is, we are not at liberty to act as though the world of the ancient Near East was not radically different from our own, or to pretend that the original text is not saying something different from what we might choose to say on the subject, if we are to translate responsibly. Application of a text, and study of it, is open to cultural accommodation and discussion; translation is not. I make this basic point because I take it to be central that Christianity is a revealed religion, that the Scriptures themselves have authority over any translator or interpreter, and also because some of what passes now for "translation" is so often riddled with subversive intention in these respects that what we end up with is effectively a perversion rather than translation of the biblical text.

In the case of the *Inclusive Language Lectionary*, a companion work under the National Council of Churches to the RSV revision, we have, I am afraid, such a perversion rather than "translation" of the text. Much of its revision, of course, falls into the area of gender revisions, especially pertaining to the name of God. In propounding a view of God as "bisexual" and as "the motherly father of the child who comes forth," the committee replaces "God the Father" with "God the Mother and Father" and removes references to God as "Lord" or to Jesus as "Lord" and "Master," arguing that these are male sexist terms.[5] In the New Testament, "Lord" is normally replaced by "Sovereign," an archaic and near obsolete word (which suggests a remote figurehead rather than an immediate and acknowledged authority). Male pronouns are never used to refer to God, or to the risen Christ: "For God so loved the world that he gave his only Son" (John 3:16) becomes "For God so loved the world that God gave God's only child."

The first problem here is not a feminizing of God, but rather a kind of neutering and abstraction, by means of which the central character of all biblical language about God—that it is personal and intends to reveal divine personality—is blunted or entirely effaced. And most critical of all, de-emphasis of the lordship of Christ, of the biblical insistence that he is master of the universe and king of kings, entirely opposes the character of the relationship between ourselves and God through Christ that is inherent in the original New Testament language. When the *Lectionary* consistently replaces "the kingdom of God" with the "commonwealth," what it is doing is rewriting the Bible so as to "democratize" and "socialize" it. In so doing, it robs the concept of "the kingdom" of its power of reflecting the covenant and promise, its eternal and transcendent character. In short, what is being written *out* of the text—by means of addressing the ostensible problem of "male" vocabulary for God (whom Scripture says—in Exodus 20:3–7, for example—is above human anthropomorphism, sexual or otherwise)—is that all-pervasive biblical idea of God's absolute *authority*, and the hierarchy of values to which we are called to be obedient.

By now you will begin to see the point I am getting at. I am not so concerned about the gender revisions for themselves as for what they signify.[6] I deeply regret most of what the *Inclusive Lectionary* does in this respect, because even in passages not referring to God, by its insistence on neutering male persons in the text (the man born blind becomes "the one who had been born blind," etc.), truth to the text even in small things is everywhere violated. The real issue is not gender, but authority.

Though there is not time to explore the matter adequately here, a similar process of distortion is observable in the modernizing of liturgies. As one who worshiped for many years in an Anglican context, my reflection on this matter is to some considerable extent autobiographical. In a compelling chapter on the *New Prayer Book* (Anglican), Margaret Doody (University of Notre Dame) describes a systematic deletion of the language of repentance, by means of which the offer of forgiveness and reconciliation effectively loses its sense of profound grace and deliverance. Except in Asia and Africa, Anglicans are, with rare exceptions, no longer allowed to say of their sins in confession that the burden of them is "intolerable," too great for us to bear alone, or that "there is no health in us"; one simply admits that "aw, shucks" we probably haven't done our best. As Doody puts it, in these new versions, "being loved by God means never having to say you're sorry—almost."[7]

Consistent with this emphasis, perhaps, was a Good Friday service my wife and I attended in an Anglican church some years ago. In it the young curate who gave the homily argued that the significance of the cross for us was simply that Jesus had to learn there what it was really like to be one of us, and to suffer like a human person. She went on to say that this is what "authenticates" Jesus for us—makes him "relevant." That her sermon did radical violence to the explicit order of fact and value in the Scriptures was not apparently a matter of concern; that the atonement of Jesus was the explicit witness of God the Father in him, of him, and of the Holy Spirit in the Scriptures, and entirely sufficient whether we agree with that host of witnesses or not, was readily deleted from her discussion of the meaning of Good Friday as uninteresting or inconvenient—evidently because of her concern to make our humanity rather than Christ's atoning sacrifice the central object of value.

Among such changes of perspective, or focus, some of the liturgical changes with respect to inclusive language have had perhaps unforeseen but nonetheless disturbing results. Let me instance but one example. In the old *Book of Common Prayer* Communion service, after corporate confession of sins and a biblical reminder of the forgiveness of God in Christ for those sins, the congregation was invited to "lift up our hearts unto the Lord" in thanksgiving. We answered, "It is meet and right so to do." The 1962 revised order had, acceptably, "It is right to give Him thanks and praise." The 1985 *Book of Alternative Services*, in the interest of inclusive language, has "It is right to give our thanks and praise." The effect of the change here, of course, is not simply to "un-sex God," if that is what is imagined, but to take emphasis off the One to whom we owe our gratitude and place emphasis instead upon *us who do the thanking*. It is another reversal of grammatical order, which is to say, essentially a shifting of authority. The *Book of Alternative Services* was advertised and hailed in a proximate issue of *The Churchman* as "a book with a view."[8] The phrase was apt, though many Anglicans remain disturbed that the "view" it provides is so much more largely of the self, and correspondingly includes less of Christ in the picture.

The Character of Theological Metaphor

That the issue of authority—divine authority—should be central to discussion of the language of worship is not, according to the Scriptures, avoidable. For any translator the text being translated has authority over the translation. That is the first principle of translation. But in the Bible, and biblical religion, the authority of God is of absolute preeminence. This applies most of all, logically and linguistically, to things he says about himself.

"God the Father" is, of course, in *linguistic* terms, a metaphor, the power of which—as for all metaphor—is inherent in its revealing—or "truth telling"—juxtaposition of two radically dissimilar things. This is particularly evident in metaphors of personification: when an American sings "My country, 'tis of thee," or a Russian speaks fondly of "Mother Russia," the power of these metaphors lies in their providing to things too vast and awesome to relate to in themselves—huge, whole countries—a personal referent that allows Americans and Russians to imagine their national allegiance in filial, family terms.

In *theological* terms, however, "God the Father" is not really a metaphor at all—at least not in the minds of the writers of Scripture or early interpreters in Christian tradition. For them, it is the logos of the universe made flesh in Christ Jesus who is the agent of creation "out of nothing" (*ex nihilo*), and all creatures of this world derive their being from him, having no existence at all except by participation in him (Col 1:12–29; John 1:3). As Jaroslav Pelikan puts it:

> In the fullest sense, therefore, only the Creator could be said "to be." For the same reason, using the name Father for God was *not* a figure of speech. It was only because God was the Father of the Logos-Son that the term father could also be applied to human parents, and when it was used of them it was a figure of speech. As the Father of the Logos, God was, according to the New Testament, "the Father, from whom every family in heaven and on earth is named," and in human families both the parents and the children were an "imitation" of divine prototypes. That was also why the Logos could not be a creature, not even the primary creature; for all creatures had been brought out of nonbeing, and as the agent who had brought them out of nonbeing the Creator-Logos must "have being" in the full and nonmetaphorical sense of the word.[9]

It is in line with this reasoning that before the eighteenth century, English usage of the word *being* is, on a scriptural basis, cognizant that the term is grammatically verbal—the present participle of the verb "to be"— and, as such, it occurs in a nominative way only in references to God, who is of course "Being" in the absolute verbal sense (Hebrew "I am that I am" or "I am that I will be" as in Exodus 3:14). Only in this later, secularizing period does *being* become a general noun, as in the term *human being.* But it remains a reflection of the older order of meaning and hierarchy of values that *human being* is a derivation from "Divine Being" (*Old English Dictionary*). Any sense that divine being is merely an anthropomorphism, or "metaphoric" term for God based on our "being," is thus an unwitting reversal of historical meaning, a projection or attribution of metaphor to Scripture and Christian tradition in which divine names are not metaphor at all, but the "given" upon which metaphors for our own existence are drawn.

In the Scriptures, among the Hebrew people to whom the name "God the Father" was first given (Isa 9:6; Micah 2:10, etc.) the power of this name lay in an astonishing conferral of relationship—family relationship—upon the awesome and distant magnitude of God. It brings the divine being into imaginable focus, and elevates the value of human life in relationship to God. This sense of relationship is intensified in the words of Jesus in the New Testament, a striking example of which is his prayer from John 17, with which we began, and also, of course, the more familiar Lord's Prayer. The name Father in all of these passages conveys three essential biblical ideas about God: his personal nature, his authority, and his provident love and care for his people.

People who use such language—and this includes the writers of Scripture—realize even as they do so, of course, that God is not a father in any literal human sense (any more than Russia is a literal mother or America is a sweetheart). He is a spirit, neither seen nor fully grasped by us at any time; and although he is personal, he is certainly not, as we are, "human" (*humus*, "of the earth"). On the other hand, Scripture presents God as Father in his person in a way that no state can even be like a "mother." Now from a strictly linguistic or philological perspective, this is an important point, and relates forcefully to the matter at hand. From a theological perspective, as Pelikan indicates, it entirely determines what we are able to say on the subject.

Some feminist writers have told us that the Scriptures contain, among a range of metaphors for God, some that attribute to him qualities that we might well identify as feminine or maternal rather than paternal.[10] I think we need to be cautious here. Those most frequently cited often simply arise from linguistic gender in the Hebrew language; the words for spirit (*ruah*) or wisdom (*chokma*) are two such words that take the feminine article, much as *la table* does in French. Strictly speaking, their doing so does not make them metaphorically feminine. This is particularly evident in the case of the Spirit, who is never referred to as feminine in the Bible.

In the case of *chokma*, that divine wisdom that those who would be wise are encouraged to seek and honor in the book of Proverbs, feminine metaphor *is* central to the biblical presentation. She is "Dame Wisdom," and her ultimate celebration, as the wisdom of a whole life, is personified as the *mulier fortis*, ("strong woman") of chapter 31, who is at the same time both a superb idealization of wisdom in action and a model for a rich and effective womanhood. Opposed to her, of course, is "Dame Folly," the woman who entices the simple-minded and unwary from the alleyways, luring them away from obedience to God's law and virtuous pursuit of Wisdom into alternative adulterous liaisons and, as Hebrew scholars have pointed out, into the idolatry of cultic prostitution associated with the fertility "goddess" religion of the Canaanite neighbors of Israel.

That *chokma* is an attribute taking its value from God himself is made explicit in Proverbs 8 (especially vv. 22–31). Wisdom describes her eternal qualities, and her presence at the creation itself, delighting daily both in God himself (v. 30) and also, through creation's history, in his people (v. 31). This chapter concludes the metaphor with Wisdom still speaking:

> Blessed is the man that heareth me, watching daily at my gates, waiting at the posts of my doors. For whoso findeth me findeth life, and shall obtain favour of the Lord. But he that sinneth against me wrongeth his own soul: all they that hate me love death. (vv. 34–36 KJV)

That is, Dame Chokma is a powerful personification metaphor for that same wisdom that the Scriptures say begins in the fear of the Lord (Prov 2–3) and that, finally, is to be identified with it: "the fear of the Lord, that is wisdom" (Job 28:28). The point here? That spiritual wisdom is a quality not derived from ourselves, especially in our carnality, but revealed in God (his wisdom is above our wisdom, his ways not our ways). It is held out to us, therefore, as a quality or attitude we ought to bear toward God. That quality is "fear of God," reverence if you like, absolute respect not only for his authority but for a love so profound that we would do almost anything to avoid offending it. Hence we obey, in freedom. We "freely obey," and it is Wisdom that teaches us to do so.

The fact remains that language about God is overwhelmingly male in its orientation (some radical feminist authors have said "hopelessly" so). As Elizabeth Achtemeier (of Union Theological Seminary) has observed: "God is never addressed as 'Mother,' never invoked as 'Mother' in the Bible."[11]

Anthropologically, we can "explain" this for the Hebrew Scriptures partly in terms of the consistent opposition of Yahweh to the cultic earth-goddess religion of the Canaanites—their panentheism in which the deity is indistinguishable from the earth (not merely, as in pantheism, coexistensive with the earth). The Hebrew God is saying, in unequivocal terms, a contrary: that he is to be understood as Wholly Other than the earth, which is, after all, his creation. He stands in relationship to it as an artist to his art (or, to use a specifically biblical metaphor, as a potter to the clay). The art is to be identified with him, but it is certainly not the same thing as he. But while an anthropological perspective is helpful here, it does not provide an "explanation" or "justification" for the way God has revealed himself to us in Scripture. Nor does it allow for wholesale revision of that revelation in the light of new cultural circumstances.

Is there, then, any place for feminine metaphors for God in an obedient Christian spirituality? What about, for example, Julian of Norwich, with her mystical reflections on God as Mother?

My purpose here is neither to oppose nor to defend Dame Julian. (Some of her writing, including the passages about God as Mother, I included in my anthology of spiritual writings from the fourteenth century.) I do wish to point out, however, that she has often been misrepresented by modern commentators. What she has perceived, and wants to relay to her readers, is that God's provident and loving nature has a personal character that may well be enhanced in our imagination by reflection upon his tenderness, his "nurturing" and sheltering of our spiritual immaturity. There is a particularly helpful sense, for her, in which, spiritually speaking, he can be imagined as a mother in giving us birth, a "new birth" which we cannot produce in ourselves. She does not apply her metaphor to liturgy or Scripture, and cannot, I think, be made an advocate of redefinition of biblical language.[12]

When feminine metaphors come into Christian spiritual literature, whether in this same medieval period or almost anytime down through the ages, they are drawn straightforwardly from the Scriptures and applied to personal dispositions of heart. Thus, the church is seen as the bride of Christ, and individual Christians figured as virgins who have prepared themselves for the coming of the bridegroom, as opposed to the foolish ones who have spent their spiritual capital and not replenished it, so to speak, with the wisdom of the Word. The cost of this lack of wisdom, Jesus says, is that they lose their place in the kingdom of heaven (Matt 25:13), for which the standard of admission is not, alas, either self-generated or a matter for democratic discussion and redefinition. The overwhelming metaphor for characterizing Christian fidelity in the history of Christian spirituality is that of the bride, Christ's spouse and beloved, working and preparing for that day of final union and, while doing so, writing and praying, as it were, love letters to the bridegroom.

The majority of writers in whose works such metaphors appear are, in fact, male. Yet in their spiritual works, as in Scripture itself, feminine metaphor is attached not to God but rather to themselves, and to us, to the conception of what it is to be human and a Christian; whether we happen to be male or female makes no difference. The great authors of Christian spiritual books do not reduce the beauty of this scriptural metaphor to literalistic application, which would be to ridicule and rob it of its reference and meaning. They do try to live out the meaning of the metaphor.

The words we use to describe and address Jesus Christ are similarly established in Scripture, and therefore Christians have always taken them to be sacrosanct. A distinguished cardinal puts it this way:

> Christianity is not a philosophical speculation; it is not a construction of
> our mind. Christianity is not "our" work; it is a revelation; it is a message

that has been consigned to us, and we have no right to reconstruct it as we like or choose.[13]

It is this fact, central to Christianity, of the explicit revelation of God to us in his Word that distinguishes sharply between the issue of the language we use among ourselves as members of the body of Christ with respect to each other, and the language we may use faithfully of God and Christ whose servants we are. The fact that Jesus was given to us, Emmanuel (God with us), as the Son of God and humanly male is not open to our second-guessing. If God has chosen to reveal himself in Christ in time, "once and for all time," as a Christian I am hardly in a position to argue about that. When the *Inclusive Lectionary* systematically deletes "Son," replacing it with "Child," the effect is to rewrite Scripture not only by neutering Jesus, but by denying him the categories of maturing and princely regality, his "oneness" with the Father. That is to say, the imposition of the term "child" is consistent in the *Lectionary* with its abolition of his titles "Lord" and "Master." Its effect can only be to downgrade his authority, his supreme entitlement to worship.[14] It is just this concern that prompted Eastern Orthodox icon painters to represent the Madonna and Christ with our Lord as a miniature man, rather than as a baby. It is not that they didn't know how to paint babies, or were denying him his humanity, but that they were wanting faithfully to represent his Lordship.

The desire to abolish a given authority is never, of course, an intention to do away with authority *per se*, but merely to replace one authority with another. The Marxist bias of much radical feminism is as much to be expected as the concurrent advocacy of goddess religion.[15]

Worship

Worship, after all, is what we really are talking about. What gives us our collective identity is just that: we assemble ourselves together to share in worship of one whom we, the "many," are all called to acknowledge as having "power over all flesh" (John 17:2).

As a verb, "worship" means, of course, not only or merely to "engage in worship" or to "take part in an act of worship," but to "regard with extreme respect and devotion," "to adore," "to honor or revere as a supernatural being," "to bow down to"; worship is intimately associated with submission, obedience, and consistent living under the authority of that which is worshiped.

The language of the temple, to paraphrase George Herbert, or of the church, is analogous to the language of the court. It is intrinsically, and not artificially, hierarchical; it is charged with specific value not created by individual worshipers, but by the canons of authority they acknowledge. Accordingly, it is not the language of the street or the marketplace. In the context of Christian worship it is preeminently God's terms that dictate our language of response, not the other way around. The language of worship, as distinct from the language of discussion about worship, or teaching, or sharing, is given, as the models for our prayer are given, in the revelation that is Scripture. We may "translate" this language, if we do it faithfully, but we abuse it or redefine it at the absolute peril of our unity in Christ and oneness with the Father. To their worship, and by the power of the Spirit, we are called, through the words of the Father (John 17:8, 14) given us through Christ and recorded by the apostles (e.g. Col 1:12–29). This is the whole basis of the unity Christ prays for in his great high priestly prayer; we most certainly are *not* being invited in the gospel to reject these terms of reference for some redefinition of our own. There is, we see, a sobering sense in which our "language of worship" is bound to be indicative; it will always, when scrutinized, reveal what it is we really do worship.

The language we use in speaking to and about each other seems to me a somewhat different question. The plain facts are that language does change, and terms that were once entirely inclusive, such as "man," have now, because of the process of literalization, acquired for some in our community polemical overtones. In such a circumstance, there is little scriptural reason to insist on singing, "Rise up, O men of God," when the same invitation may now better be rendered as "Rise up, servants of God." We are all that, after all, and it makes the call to service more personal and appropriately "inclusive." A key spiritual attribute leading to Christian unity in the church is humility—considering others better than ourselves (Phil 2:2–4). Saints of any age are distinguished not for their self-assertion but for their self-effacement, and such accommodation is likely, in present circumstances, to be in the best interest of Christian community. But this pertains, of course, to language about ourselves, not to language about God.

Language about God, language expressing the character of God, and language of address to God is, of necessity, as the psalmist noted long ago (Ps 19), provided for us by God, both in his Word and his Word made flesh in Jesus. And the more we discover about the inadequacies of our own language, the more we recognize this as a profound blessing. The Christian life, in fact, is represented to us as one that is created by the Word of God being enfleshed in us, and growing to fullness of expression in the experience of his grace. Our receptivity to that, our humility, is essential. Without that his gift of life eternal could not grow in us. But both logically and scripturally, primacy clearly rests with what he has given.

Perhaps we would do well to take to ourselves in these matters the example of the Blessed Virgin Mary, human mother of our Divine Lord, in whom the Word took on flesh in this primary and life-giving way. Her attitude of heart was quintessentially worship. When the angel came to her to announce God's terms of salvation for the whole human race, in words that confounded her whole sense of human limitations and role determination (Luke 1:1–29ff.), she nonetheless yielded the limits of her own framework of reference to "the power of the highest" that was to "overshadow" her. She said in response, "Behold the handmaid of the Lord; be it unto me according to thy word" (Luke 1:38 KJV). In matters of that Word, and worship, we should, I propose, take our model here, and our cue in worship from her *Magnificat*:

> My soul doth magnify the Lord, and my spirit hath rejoiced in God my Saviour. For he hath regarded the low estate of his handmaiden: for behold, from henceforth all generations shall call me blessed. For he that is mighty hath done to me great things; and holy is his name. And his mercy is on them that fear him from generation to generation. He hath shewed strength with his arm; he hath scattered the proud in the imagination of their hearts. He hath put down the mighty from their seats, and exalted them of low degree. He hath filled the hungry with good things; and the rich he hath sent empty away. He hath holpen his servant Israel, in remembrance of his mercy; as he spake to our fathers, to Abraham, and to his seed forever. (Luke 1:46–55 KJV)

When Jesus prayed in the garden that prayer of prayers for the unity of his people he was offering to us the model for inclusivity for those who would follow him: "That they may all be one" [. . .] "as we are" (v. 11), "in us" (v. 21) "even as we are one" (v. 22). He concluded that prayer by saying, "And I have declared unto them thy name, and will declare it: that the love wherewith thou hast loved me may be in them, and I in them."

If Mary offers the prototype for our worship, here is the prototype for our fellowship. As that fellowship respects the goals of inclusiveness, it reminds us that the name in which we are all included, male or female, is "the only name given under heaven whereby we may be saved" (Acts 4:12).

(1987)

Chapter Fourteen

The Teaching Authority of Jesus and the Fatherhood of God

---

*For this reason I bow my knees to the Father of our Lord Jesus Christ, from
whom the whole family in heaven and earth is named . . .*

Ephesians 3:14–15

In the novel *Midnight's Children* by Salman Rushdie, a young Catholic priest
advises one of his flock, during her time in the confessional, concerning "the
color of God":

> "Blue," the young priest said earnestly. "All available evidence, my daugh-
> ter, suggests that Our Lord Jesus Christ was the most bounteous, crystal
> shade of pale sky blue."[1]

When the penitent expresses some dubiety over this point, the somewhat
distraught cleric reflects inwardly that what he has spoken was prompted,
after all, by high theological authority, that of his Bishop:

> "Remember," thus spake the Bishop, "God is love; and the Hindu love-
> god, Krishna, is always depicted with blue skin. Tell them blue, it will be a
> sort of bridge between the faiths. [. . .]"[2]

But in the ensuing debate with his Portugese-Indian parishioner the priest's
new palette transfers its pigment poorly; in the end he has to give it up.

One is reminded, in reading Rushdie, as surely he intends, that other such attempts at "bridging"—even those with a much more wide-ranging and enduring effect—have also come at last to be rejected. The Aryan insistence that Jesus had blond hair and blue eyes, or that, on account of his insuperable antiquity, God the Father ought to be depicted as having a long and flowing white beard—these too, in the end, have had to be abandoned.

Selectively, as fashion permits, ecclesiastical culture eventually tends to let go of most such awkward projections of social consciousness, even with a kind of relief. Yet as long as they remain comfortable illusions and so institutionalized they can involve a serious problematization of the sources of religious authority—or at least confusion about that authority. The Aryan-Christ example makes this clear, and almost everyone is now willing to be warned by it. Yet this sort of problematization is likely to recur in other guises, especially when it is the very notion of an authoritative source beyond social consciousness which is being questioned. When this more radical questioning becomes highly visible, as now again it is, the fact if not the form of the questioning makes clear that it is not merely a matter of style or cultural translation which is at issue. More deeply, the issue is a quest for hermeneutic constraint of the textual sources.

And so it is with current "imaging" controversies in the nominally Christian West. As with either the Aryan or the blue Jesus, or with Blake's "Ancient of Days," the new feminist imagings of God are more popularizable than some other theological inventions, and perhaps quite precisely because of the shift in religious authority they are seen to represent, even at the vernacular level. Stories normalizing "goddess religion" appear almost daily. Venues may vary, but not the theme. A Catholic cathedral in Sacramento celebrates a Mass with diaphonously veiled dancers and a version of Psalm 23 in which the feminine pronoun is used exclusively: "she restores my soul." In the new service book of the United Church of Canada, by far Canada's largest Protestant denomination, as in some lectionaries in the United States, baptism is no longer required to be in the name of the Father, Son, and Holy Spirit. One declares now in the name of the "Creator, Liberator, and Healer" or, alternatively, in the name of "God, Source of Love; in the name of Jesus Christ, Love incarnate; and in the name of the Holy Spirit, Love's power." In the first one hundred pages of the Canadian text there is only one reference to God the Father. One prays instead to "Mother and Father God" or more simply "Mother God." Like the *Inclusive Language Lectionary* on which it is modeled, this new type of liturgy has prompted both celebration and condemnation; among the latter reactions one critic has representatively described such institutional gestures as a "systematic attempt to remove sexuality from males and to impose it on God."[3] Elizabeth Achtemeier's point retains an instructive pertinence, I believe, for both sides in the contemporary debate.

In a culture in which no subject so predominates as sex it should not be surprising that gender and sexuality are more frontally present, so to speak, in our syncretisms than the colors blond or blue, or the white-beards of antiquity either.[4] Nor are we to imagine, presumably, given the tumult of our cultural identity wars, that there can now be an identity more firm and longstanding than one based upon our own consensual habits, or more persuasive than those arising from our personal, polymorphous "bridging" efforts. A recent article by Margaret Merrill Toscano makes succinctly a general hermeneutic point of departure: its title is "If I Hate My Mother, Can I Love the Heavenly Mother? Personal Identity, Personal Relationships, and Perceptions of God." In it, Toscano shares her assumption concerning how both theology and "reading" are to be done:

> In this essay I mix personal narrative with theological analysis not only because I see this as effective methodology but also because my thesis assumes that all of our theological constructs are based on personal and cultural preference.[5]

Toscano's assumption is, of course, often expressed with greater sophistication. Elisabeth Schüssler Fiorenza, for example, has it that

> The insistence that feminist christological discourses must be rooted in Christian Scriptures is encumbered by the same theoretical problems and methodological difficulties that impeded the attempts of dominant biblical scholarship to reconstruct "New Testament" christology.[6]

But in either formulation, the point is the same.

Christology is explicit in the preoccupations of more scholarly feminist theological writing to the degree to which there is candor about what is more directly at issue in the deeper theological debate. What Schüssler Fiorenza and others wish to subvert, even dismiss altogether from our language about God, is not merely the Hebrew Scriptures but the teaching authority of Jesus in the Gospels specifically.[7] Textually, on the face of it, this has proven very hard to accomplish without engaging in nearly intolerable levels of sophistry. To their credit, Schüssler Fiorenza and her colleagues have been candid about that; Sandra M. Schneiders's contention *in fine* that Christianity is ultimately inhospitable to women—however debatable in itself, and indeed disputed by many female biblical scholars—is another such evidence of sober reflection on the central problem:

> The established fact that Jesus' preferred address for God was "Abba," the caritative form of "Father," raises two questions. Did Jesus experience God and therefore present God as exclusively masculine? Did Jesus intend to present God in patriarchal terms? If the answer to either question is affirmative, the New Testament has little to offer to women.[8]

Academically, the usual *bête noire* theologian for Schneiders and others is Joachim Jeremias.[9] The hermeneutic implications of their opposition to Jeremias and his ilk, perhaps needless to say, cuts a much wider swath. Scholarship in hermeneutics in the last two or three decades has done much to help us recognize that the sort of exegesis which attempts to get at the meaning a text had for its author is not determinative for the sort of interpretation which the "horizon" of a contemporary reader may unavoidably color: it is clear that none of us are innocent of local color in our imaginations of anything, even of texts in which, to the exegete, there is a remarkable degree of perspicuity.[10] Nor is all of this coloration without redeeming virtue. And most Christians would want to insist that the Holy Spirit still speaks to the Church, that there is thus an authority correlative with the authority of Scripture in the magisterial teaching of the historic Church. But what about situations in which all hermeneutic operations of credible reason having been vested, there still appears such contradiction to source texts as cannot, without the most radical sort of sophistry or denial, be rationalized to the text? Such, I think, is the actual situation of moment which confronts credal orthodoxy, evangelical and Catholic, concerning the Fatherhood of God.

Hermeneutic and Translation

In an earlier article on inclusive language I tried to show how the biblical doctrine of the Fatherhood of God is even more central to Christian identity than it was to faithful Jewish identity.[11] It had seemed to me then that attacks upon the naming of God as Father—including those which attempt to reduce this central plank of biblical theology to a prejudiced cultural metaphor which supposedly "excludes" women—were in principle, at least, attacks on two indispensable foundations of Christian identity: Scripture and the traditional teaching of the universal Church. I want to develop this commonsensical point further, and along a line of hermeneutic reflection to which I had not then given sufficient scope.

Let me begin by drawing attention to the obvious. The assignation of "Mother God" or goddess vocabulary to previously trinitarian liturgies helps to make it apparent to all concerned that what is at stake is not, as is often argued, a matter of translation. Something much deeper, and more violent in respect of biblical text and tradition, is involved. In modernist biblical scholarship there is nonetheless an historical analogue for this sort of revolutionary propaedeutic, and it also manifested itself initially as merely disagreement about translation.

During the tense but outwardly civil years of the Weimar Republic in Germany (1918–1933) two distinguished scholars were working on a new German translation of the Bible. They were Martin Buber and Franz Rosenzweig. Among the most respected members of the European Jewish intellectual community, Buber and Rosenzweig were nonetheless acutely aware of their vulnerability to a growing hostility to Jews and their religion. It was becoming harder and harder for religious Jews especially even to get their work published by mainstream publishers and journals.[12] In a scattering of articles announcing their new translation they made many favorable comparisons and complimentary references to the German standard version of Martin Luther, at least partly in a sincere effort to be diplomatically positive toward their Christian fellow-Germans.

In the most remarkable of these essays, Franz Rosenzweig, in an evident tip of the hat to Jesus, wrote this provocative first sentence: "Translating means serving two masters. It follows that it cannot be done."[13] He then promptly admitted the obvious dilemma: translation nevertheless *must* be done if Scripture is to be served. But (as he went on to suggest) it ought not to be done in such a way as to transfer authority from the text to the reader, to reduce the text merely to a mirror for the reader's own subjective or ego-determined prejudices. For then what we would have would not be, in any responsible sense of the word, a "translation." Instead it would be a new and different book.

Rosenzweig's point applies to contemporary attempts to present biblical and liturgical revision as "new translations." In many cases such revision is rather a matter of creating new textual authority, rewriting Scripture and the creeds so as to give some of those uncomfortable with these texts new means to assert and establish institutional control or, to put it in the more familiar way, to "develop doctrine." The actual question at issue here, as Humpty Dumpty famously said to Alice, is about "which is to be master—that's all."

As Buber and Rosenzweig were working on their translation, German Lutherans were likewise occupied. In this instance the most visible bugaboo was not gender but race. A notable reluctance to use the words "Jew" and

"Israel" had begun to be evident in the German church in the early years of the Nazi era; it expressed itself in the de-Judaizing of biblical language in the liturgy and hymns, in changing of worship references from "Jews" to "People of God," and in eschewing of readings which made the Jewish identity of the "chosen" people too transparent to disguise by "re-translation" alone. This felonious and often fraudulent strategy had, predictably enough, voluminous academic defense. The ploy, as Wolfhart Pannenberg has observed, was already an old one—insistence that religious language was in any case simply a projection of prevalent social experience onto images of divinity. On this view, whether or not anything accountable to the plausible meaning in the original text was to be retained, change in social conditions required a change in religious language.[14]

What we are now experiencing is essentially the same phenomenon. In Pannenberg's terse summary, "As the Nazi Germans were bothered by Jesus' Jewishness, so are our contemporary feminists bothered by the contingency of language about God as father."[15] In both cases, and for similar reasons, response to the irritation which takes the form of erasure of the offensive "name" is an act of propaedeutic linguistic violence. It portends further degradation, perhaps institutionalized opprobrium, and exposes the potential for other kinds of attack.

Of course I do not mean to say that every German professor or pastor saw it that way from the beginning. It is entirely probable that many among those who wished the words "Jew" and "Israel" to disappear from worship and the biblical record would have insisted, in 1933, that nothing in what they were doing was preparing the public for acquiescence in the annihilation of Jews. Their claim, after all, was that the changes simply made the text "more inclusive."

Consciousness and Conscience

We need not press this analogy to the limit. Rather, I would simply ask a brief series of plausibly connected—albeit contentious—questions, the answers to which, I think, are by now both evident and constructively provocative. Why in our own tremulous time, does the idea of fatherhood—especially of a goodly, godly, and finally a divinely modeled exemplar of fatherhood—excite such hostility among would-be revisers of Christianity? Why is it that those made angry, sometimes angry enough to wish annihilation of any vestige of worthy images of fatherhood, imagine that what we need as a replacement exemplar of positive authority is a "mother goddess"— a figure whose religious tradition in every non-biblical culture is that of "fertility worship"? And which has as its typical concomitant, "fertility" sacri-fice—the sacrifice of children?

These are, of course, elaborations of one question. The answers most often given, and credibly so, point to the poor record of human fatherhood in our recent past, even among Christians. That the flight from responsi-bility and even predatory cruelty on the part of many fathers has been a direct cause of a more general rejection of the institution of fatherhood few will deny. Indeed, one may wonder if such "bad" fathers have not presaged our present crisis by being the first to reject the biblical relationship of sexu-ality to parenthood—long before they became fathers.[16] If so, that this too is a pre-textual condition with hermeneutic implications should be apparent.

Let us then approach the mine field in a somewhat more tentative way. Might it be that, on the Christian view, responsible fatherhood constitutes a framework of circumspection, perhaps particularly sexual circumspection? Is it possible that part of the reason that fatherhood is under attack is not just the actual plague of irresponsible fathers, but that fatherhood *per se* is seen as a species of authority that, in its highest exemplar, the Fatherhood of God, implies a limit, even a contrary to our culture's most cherished credo—that sexual autonomy is the highest human good? Is it not the case that what rampant sexual appetite wants and what *un*circumscribed sexuality, in attempting to legitimate itself, tries to achieve is what Freud reasonably char-acterized as "the death of the Father"? Death of the Father (Freud), death of the Author (Barthes), death of God (Nietzsche and a great chorus of semi-narians)—are they not, in spiritual terms, diverse manifestations of a com-mon impulse?[17]

But this is not a Christian impulse. In none of its manifestations, what-ever flimsy garb of institutional propinquity it wears, is it capable of bowing the knee to God the Father or to Jesus Christ his only begotten Son. If it appears to do so, it will be in pretense—at its most unwitting a self-deception, at its most informed and articulate a cynical deception of others. And nowhere, in the Church or out of it, will we be immune to confusion about what is really being worshiped—or, to put it more clearly, obeyed. For the issue here, both ecclesial and hermeneutic, is quite precisely the issue of authority and as such it is, strictly speaking, a matter neither of sex nor of gender, but rather of role.

On what authority may we dare to reflect upon the deeper motives of revisers and, as it may seem on occasion, disguisers of biblical language? After all, many of the most flagrant of such revisers have already dismissed from their counsel the teaching authority of the historic Church, and that on principles they declare to be non-negotiable. In a remarkably large number of cases, they substantially control the present institutional Church, especially in Protestantism. Perhaps, some say, anti-authoritarians though they may be, these folk represent the authority "set over us" in our time, and we must accept that.

Yet one authority remains by which we are obliged to ask questions about evident revision of biblical language. In the canonical or global sense, this is, of course, Scripture itself, especially when we ask out of a competence in and respect for the languages and the textual tradition of Scripture. This perspective has been the basis of a great deal of rational and, for those who have ears to hear, credible constraint upon hermeneutic and linguistic anti-authoritarianism. With varying degrees of scholarly precision, this is particularly apparent in respect of "naming the Father." Yet rarely in biblical textual scholarship has textual evidence proved more contentious.

It has already been shown that God is called Father more than 250 times in Scripture. We have been reminded that in Scripture God is most jealous of his name, and names Himself, forbidding this prerogative to any other.[18] It has been shown that in Scripture God is rarely given plausibly feminine characteristics, and that he is never called "Mother."[19] Masculine metaphors for God are persistent and characteristic,[20] though not in such a manner as would give them sexual content.[21] In fact, Yahweh proves to be unique among the deities of the universally patriarchal cultures of the ancient Near East (even those which had goddess worship were culturally patriarchal) in that he is not *sexually* male.[22] His fatherhood over us is, notably, by adoption—a point definitive for Paul's understanding of Christ, as well as Jesus' self-understanding as the Christ.[23] We have seen that feminist metaphors for God, by contrast, especially when used in the context of "goddess" language, can ironically replace non-sexist metaphors with overtly sexual, thus sexist, ones.[24] It has also been pointed out, and frequently, that for some the real agenda in much of this conflict over interpretation, translation, and the language of worship is a repudiation of the Bible as the authority above all authorities of Christian life as for faith and worship.[25] The critical strength of these arguments by biblical scholars and theologians is not wanting. Yet their lack of influence upon all but the "converted" so to speak—even within the Church—has been a source of frustration and discouragement to them and, one gathers, to others.

Why has this scholarship been so ineffective? In my own view, part of the frustration for many involved in the ecclesial aspect of this debate has occurred because of a tacit concession that the dispute can be engaged as a matter internal to the Church. That is, we have not been as clear-minded about this as many of our feminist interlocutors. We have tended to regard the prolonged debate, often out of politeness as well as a commitment to practical charity, as yet another example of conflict in interpretation among faithful believers. But neither hermeneutically speaking nor theologically speaking is this issue now accurately so represented. It is not finally comparable to disagreements over ecclesial practice for ordering the understanding of sacraments, for example, or to differences concerning our sense of the role of human freedom in responding to God's offer of grace in Christ. For if the teaching of Jesus is to have any authority, acceptance of the Fatherhood of God becomes a matter of definitive separation between those who may in any meaningful sense be called Christian and those who, however religious in their reasoning and practice, are not in the most crucial of matters following Christ. Unambiguous acceptance of the Fatherhood of God, I want to say here (to this extent in agreement with Schneiders and others), is not open to revision by those who would be Christian because it is, unambiguously, the central and persistent teaching of Jesus *about* God, and the transparent mode of his own relationship *to* God.

Textual Consistency

Narrative analysis of the Gospel of Matthew alone makes it impossible that we should construe resistance to biblical characterization of God as Father to be motivated by a faithfully Christian impulse. From the account of Jesus' own baptism, where the words of institution are pronounced by the Father from heaven in such a way as to confirm that Jesus is the Son in whom He is well pleased (3:17), to the Great Commission in which Jesus commands his followers to go into the world and to teach all nations, baptizing them in the name of the Father, Son, and Holy Spirit (28:19), there is evident consistency on this matter in the life and teaching of the Lord.

His teaching actually begins with Jesus identifying his faithful ones as children of the Father: those who will take up his cross so as to love their enemies and do good to those who hate them (5:44) will by this obedience be filiated to God as Father. Obedience is required so "that you may be sons of your Father in heaven" (5:45), and radical obedience is not less high in its imitative aims than filial resemblance: "Therefore you shall be perfect, even as your Father in heaven is perfect" (5:48). Our heavenly Father, Jesus assures us on the basis of his own matchless intimacy with Him, is so deeply caring that he is aware of the needs of his children before they ask (6:18); if he provides for the creatures of his world (6:26), how much more his own children (6:32)? What the children of the Heavenly Father are to seek most from him is not these natural gifts of his providence, however, but "first the kingdom of God and his righteousness." This motivation is a necessary condition of accountable hermeneutic and reading practice where Scripture is concerned.

After all, Jesus says, "not every one who says to me 'Lord, Lord' shall enter the kingdom of heaven, but he who does the will of my Father in heaven" (7:21).

Much is said in the preambles of the inclusive lectionaries and new worship books about "the movement of the Spirit." What Jesus tells his disciples about the Holy Spirit is that at moments when their own words cannot persuade those who would mislead or condemn them then it will be the "Spirit of your Father who speaks in you" (10:20). This speaking will clearly be to point to the authority of Jesus as true Son of the Father. Accordingly, "whoever confesses me before men, him will I also confess before my Father who is in heaven" (10:32). However scandalously, and by the same token, whoever denies Jesus in so many words, that person Jesus will deny (disclaim) before his "Father which is in heaven" (10:33). When we are told that the Spirit speaking "in our times" requires evident contradiction to the Spirit of the Father who Jesus assured us would speak in his faithful always, we are at a point where application of the apostolic injunction is urgently necessary: "Beloved, do not believe every spirit, but test the spirits [to see] whether they are of God" (1 John 4:1).

It can be an irritation, understandably, to those who present themselves as more intelligent or, because of certain learning, more wise then others, that recognition of the truth of Scripture and authority of Jesus is not theirs alone to control. Jesus prayed, "I thank You, Father, Lord of heaven and earth, that You have hidden these things from the wise and prudent, and revealed them unto babes" (11:25). It is not only within Free Church traditions that this passage has been taken as a caution against contradicting theological *droit de seigneur*. No Christian who is thinking straight ought to be bent away from the teaching authority of Jesus or the witness of Scripture at any point merely by the educational credentials, cleverness, or institutional prominence of an evidently contradicting authority. (Nor by an autobiographical assertion of "bad associations" or personal woundedness, however these may most legitimately prompt our compassion.) Moreover, we ought to be zealous to protect children in particular from the religious abuse, however "well intended," of those who would usurp Jesus' guidance concerning the trustworthiness of their heavenly Father. Children may grasp the value of God's Fatherhood more truly than anyone. "Take heed," he says to us, "that you do not despise one of these little ones, for I say to you that in heaven their angels always see the face of my Father who is in heaven" (18:10).

If it is true that in this world no one truly knows the Father but the Son, nor truly knows the Son but the Father (11:27), it is nevertheless also the reward of those are faithful that their righteousness will one day "shine forth as the sun in the kingdom of their Father" (13:43). In the meantime, all in the Church are bound in a reciprocal covenant with the Father through Jesus, a covenant that entitles us to his care in the world but also a covenant by which we will be judged in the next (18:19, 35). It is in the Father's disposition alone to reward the faithful (20:23). When we pray, as Jesus taught us, "Our Father which art in heaven," we pray to be conformed to the will of the Father—so perfectly accommodated to that will that we accept that our own forgiveness is conditional upon our reflecting his forgiveness in our dealings with others (6:9–15; cf. 18:21–35). Jesus is serious about our loving our enemies. Recrimination against our ecclesiastical opponents is thus also a clear violation of his principle.

Textual Cues

To return then to my main point, which I have posed as a question: Do we have any hermeneutic basis, any authority, for resisting resisters of Jesus?

> Now when He came into the temple, the chief priests and the elders of the people confronted Him as He was teaching, and said, "By what authority are You doing these things? And who gave You this authority?" But Jesus answered and said to them, "I also will ask you one thing, which if you tell Me, I likewise will tell you by what authority I do these things: 'The baptism of John—where was it from? From heaven or from men?' And they reasoned among themselves, saying, "If we say, 'From heaven' He will say to us, 'Why then did you not believe him? But if we say, 'From men,' we fear the multitude, for all count John as a prophet." So they answered Jesus and said, "We do not know." And He said to them, "Neither will I tell you by what authority I do these things."(Matt 21:23–27)

We ought most diligently to study what Jesus was doing here. There is always going to be debate (human willfulness being what it is) between those who see religious belief and practice in terms of revelation and those who want to see it in terms of the projection of evolving social consciousness, particularly their own evolving consciousness. There is nothing novel, historically speaking, in the predicament of this moment in the Western Christian church. Ours is a recurrent symptom of a systemic spiritual decadence, and it affects us in many more ways than in the issue here under discussion.

The decisive point is engaged in the parable which Jesus tells, immediately following this challenge to his authority. Here is a story of two sons, one of whom is quick (and perhaps glib) to proclaim his allegiance to do the will of his father. The other son is resistant to the point of initial denial of his father's will. Nevertheless, in the end the one who readily proclaims his vocation fails to work in the vineyard of his father (we are not told what he was doing instead). The resistant son surprises us by repenting and fulfilling the call of his father. When Jesus asks, "which of the two did the will of the Father" (21:31) he is asking about actual obedience, not about the verbalization of piety. This word is a sword which cuts two ways.

Either way, the issue of obedience remains. Jesus is not ambiguous in his claim that his own authority derives from his Father, rather than from his creative imagination or from a projection of some social or political pragmatism.[26] That he is the Son of God, not just a man among men, is the essence of his rebuke to the Pharisees (22:45). We are to call no one but the Father "father" in this religious sense, "for One is your Father, who is in Heaven" (23:9). And in these matters there is a judgment coming which is not a matter of either social consciousness or human politics. On that day (which moment only the Father knows [24:36]), those who have accepted the revealed authority of Jesus concerning the Father's gift of reconciliation through him—and who persevere in obedience to the will of God—will hear the words, "Come ye blessed of my Father" (25:34).[27] Others, presumably, will not on that day have such a Father.

At the Last Supper (26:20–29), in Gethsemane (26:39–42), as in the great prayer of Jesus recorded in John 17, it is his own obedience to the Father which characterizes everything that his atoning sacrifice means. He prays specifically that, on the witness given by the Father, we shall be united to him and the Father in love and faithfulness. This same Jesus whose prerogative it was to summon from his Father legions of angels to smite his oppressors, chose in obedience rather to be faithful to the Father's will in sacrificing his life. Nowhere do we see that he made that issue, or any language concerning it, a matter for "comfort-zone" compromise.

I do not wish to suggest that there is not a great deal more that might be said on this subject. Clearly there is, and I myself would be grateful for it, especially for that which in the spirit of fraternal correction would point my own heart and mind to a more accurate obedience. What I do mean to say is that, so far as I can tell, for a Christian—one who would follow Christ in his teaching and in his example (cf. Luke 9:23)—the authority of Jesus concerning the Fatherhood of God is irrefragible authority. Opposition to it is not therefore an intramural debate, and we must learn, as graciously and yet as clear-mindedly as possible, to acknowledge that.

The perennial problem of translation—which is to say, interpretation— is inextricable from the question of authority. Franz Rosenzweig's dictum about tension in translation is helpful in that it declares not against the possibility of translation, but against any imagination that we can avoid in such work the choice of "which is to be master." Or rather, Master.

Conclusion

Let me conclude with a brief observation and summary. Striking a note of dissonance, even in the social consciousness of our time, two most improbable recordings appeared at the top of the pop music charts in Europe and Britain in 1999—the CD "Abba Pater," with Pope John Paul II chanting prayers, and Cliff Richards' phenomenally successful "Millennium Prayer," a version of "Our Father Who Art in Heaven," sung to the tune "Auld Lang Syne." At the turn of the millennium, from out of the vast unchurched proletarian ranks (especially the ranks of the young) there seems to have come, as it were unbidden, some sort of deep yearning for ultimate Fatherhood. Have the makers of the new lectionaries noticed this cultural phenomenon?

Even if they have, one may reasonably doubt that it will much alter their altar. There is now a substantial, if aging, vested interest in feminized prayers, deities, and priestly vestments. Institutionally, there has come about a de facto "development of doctrine" (*pace* Newman) for which a tradition of sorts has been established, and with it the anxious jealousies of institutional prerogative. In most North American churches committed to the inclusive lectionary, the feminizing of God and erasure of the actual language of Jesus has after all been consistently and persistently part of a larger disenfranchisement of what has come to be regarded as an inflexibility in biblical teaching. Historically, the desire for a "softening" of biblical language appeared first in the seminaries and only then in the pulpits. Avoidance of language which invokes the presence or idea of authority—whether textual, theological, or ethical—has been a principal preoccupation in biblical and theological studies, just as it has in education, politics, and ethics in the secular sphere. Discomfort with Father language in particular closely mirrors gender warfare and generational conflict in the secular culture, notably and at least initially, as voiced among intellectual elites in the West. (It is certainly not a universal phenomenon.) Yet response to "comfort zones" in the culture concerning these issues is so strongly at odds with both the language and the self-characterization of Jesus as Son of God the Father that the theological dissonance is no longer able to be harmonized either by rhetoric or by diplomacy. Visible discrepancy between the two nomenclatures confounds, creating an intellectual barrier to coherent thought about Scripture that, in my opinion, must be overcome if the project of a rich and accountable biblical hermeneutic is not itself to become incoherent.

That which rejects the overwhelming teaching of Jesus, I think we must be prepared to concede, is anti-Christ, not Christian. It may hurt us to admit it, but not to admit it would be to deceive ourselves and others. Goddess religion, for example, is certainly religion. But it is not Christian religion, nor can it be made to cohabit with it without spiritual adultery. The incorporation of mother-god language and the corresponding deletion of the Fatherhood of God from the prayer life and hymnody of any church will make of those who use that language refusers of the teaching authority of Jesus. On *his* authority, such refusal is a matter of the gravest consequences for those who so choose.

How can academic theologians and biblical scholars best help those who seem prone to be led in this path to consider the consequences? By faithfully pointing them again and again to the words of Jesus. It is his authority which is decisively the basis for our adoption by the Father, and it is on his authority that we have the means to recognize those who would (and those who would not) seek membership in his family in such terms as he has offered. "Whosoever shall do the will of my Father which is in heaven," said Jesus, "the same is my brother and sister and mother" (Matt 12:50). That makes the conditions of our inclusion, academic theologian and layperson alike, clear enough.

(2001)

Chapter Fifteen

Postmodern Theology
and Perennial Truth

Thirst was made for water; inquiry for truth.

C. S. Lewis, *The Great Divorce*

Send out thy light and thy truth, that they may lead me.

Psalm 43:3 KJV

In the next-to-last decade of the seventeenth century a certain priest of the Diocese of Ely, Robert Midgley by name, translated the celebrated *Morals* of the Greek biographer and philosopher Plutarch. The fourth and final volume bears a dedication to his Bishop, one Francis Turner, soon to be "removed." This volume has for its opening chapter one of Plutarch's most intriguing essays. It is entitled "Why the Oracles Cease to Give Answers." Briefly, the conclusion of the ancient author is, in the first instance, that it is because people stopped asking the oracle honest questions. Some grew impatient when the oracle did not respond as they wished; still others would not stay for an answer. Eventually, he suggests, people thus conflicted in their motives came to forget about the oracles altogether; their priests were neither sustained nor replaced, the sanctuary became desolate, and at last it was inhabited by a fearsome dragon. To explain the demise of the institution it was generally said simply that "the oracles had ceased to give answers." The last excuse of the last faithful worshipers for not coming was fear of the dragon. "Yet," says Plutarch, "those that have written this did not well comprehend the occasion of the oracles ceasing; for the dragon did not make the place solitary, but rather, the solitude of the place occasioned the dragon to repair hither."[1]

There are, of course, a number of possible applications for this story. Here is but one of them: Sometimes the denials we make of truth are really a product of our long absence from its oracle. Having learned to placate our consciences with a substitute for going there—a study of old reports, perhaps—then later becoming content with someone else's analysis and perhaps some reinterpretation of those old reports, we come at length to the point where it suffices for us to say that we, too, once visited the oracle in our youth. Now, of course, we have moved on to more immediate preoccupations. We put our current questions, self-serving as they are, to almost any other source. Even if the oracle should suddenly and miraculously proclaim truth loudly in our ear, or write it on the walls of our chamber, we would not recognize its proclamation as truth, but only, perhaps, as an unwelcome disturbance in the midst of our festivals. Then suddenly, one day, judgment stands at the door.

I would like to make three basic points about knowing truth in the present age. Each is biblical. First: the recognition of truth depends in part upon the authenticity of one's intention to find truth: "Ask, and it shall be given you; seek and ye shall find. Knock and it shall be opened unto you" (Matt 7:7; Luke 11:9). Second: would-be discerners of truth must anticipate that now, as ever, truth will tend to be at odds with fashion (cf. 2 Pet 2:15-18). Third: coming to know what is theologically true when we meet it depends in large measure upon our already knowing that One who is Truth (John 14:6).

Recognition of Truth Depends On a True Intent to Find It

The fashionable preoccupation we call postmodernity presents, I think, no fundamentally new problem to the Church. This, if only because attacks on truth (even the very possibility of truth), are as old as the blandishments of Eden's serpent, even though now very much in mode. Pascal, who died in 1662, could thus define both our problem and its only possible solution in terms which evoke the universal wisdom of Holy Scripture: "Truth," Pascal says, "is so obscure in these times, and falsehood so established, that unless we love the truth, we cannot know it" (*Pensées* 14.864).

On the other hand, when loving the truth is quite out of fashion, as it is at present, the very mention of the word can call up hatred. *Veritas otium parit* ("truth engenders hatred"), said the Roman poet Terence. The desire to flee truth is deep, deep in human nature, and that fact is not obscure to anyone. "How is it that to affirm the existence of truth seems to be tantamount to dogmatism and intolerance?" Jean (Cardinal) Daniélou asks this question in a fine little book called *The Scandal of Truth*.[2] Daniélou observes that when "nothing is less loved than truth," it is a certain sign that intelligence is in crisis, that people are not thinking straight. Usually there is an unself-flattering reason for this.

St. Augustine, writing sixteen centuries earlier, brings us to consider how it is that the expression of hatred for the truth that we ought to love implies plainly that there is something other than truth that we love more; and also, of course, that we see truth as an impediment to our indulgence in whatever, besides truth, we love.

> Why does truth call forth hatred? Why is Your servant treated as an enemy by those to whom he preaches the truth, if happiness is loved, which is simply joy in truth? (*Conf.* 10.23; my translation)

And then, as is often the case with Augustine, he answers his own question:

> Simply because truth is loved in such a way that those who love some other thing want it to be the truth, and precisely because they do not wish to be deceived, are unwilling to be convinced that they are indeed deceived. Thus they hate the truth for the sake of that other thing which they love, because they take it for truth. They love truth when it enlightens them, they hate it when it accuses them. (*Conf.* 10.23; my translation)

What Augustine is getting at here, of course, is a fantasy in every age— the sinful, self-centered desire that "truth" should be subjective, individualistically defined. St. Thomas Aquinas makes the same point with reference to theological truth in particular. "We sometimes hate a particular truth when [we] wish that what is true were not true," says the great Doctor, and this reflex becomes particularly apparent when we "wish not to know the truth of faith, in order that [we] may sin freely" (*Sum. Theol.* 1–2, 29.5).

Old soldiers have a saying that, in war, truth is the first casualty. But surely this is the case with every kind of conflict, including inner and spiritual conflict. In all such cases we see that hatred of the truth begins not in fact with disbelief of the truth, but rather with a powerful desire to mask or rationalize appetites with which the truth is in evident conflict. Thus, as Friedrich Nietzsche put it, "The most common lie is the lie one tells to oneself" (*Antichrist* 55).

Every school child once used to know the story of a certain ancient who was said to have searched the world in vain for an honest man. (The story of Diogenes and his lantern is no longer part of the public curriculum.) But in the same vein, there is a notable passage in the book of the prophet Jeremiah which describes how a servant of the Lord might go looking in vain even for such a seeker as Diogenes:

> Run ye to and fro through the streets of Jerusalem, and see now, and know, and seek in the broad places thereof, if ye can find a man, if there be any that executeth judgment, that seeketh the truth [. . .]. (Jer 5:1 KJV)

What most provokes him, says the Lord to his prophet, is the arrogant discrepancy between the hypocritical credal affirmations of religious men and the character of their actual belief and life: "Though they say, the LORD liveth, surely they swear falsely" (v. 2). This leads the prophet to a grief-stricken rejoinder:

> O LORD, are not thine eyes upon the truth? Thou hast stricken them, but they have not grieved; thou hast consumed them, but they have refused to receive correction: they have made their faces harder than a rock; they have refused to return. Therefore I said, Surely these are poor, they are foolish: for they know not the way of the LORD, nor the judgment of their God. I will get me unto the great men, and will speak unto them; for they have known the way of the LORD, and the judgment of their God—but these have altogether broken the yoke, and burst the bonds! (Jer 5:3–5 KJV)

The result for these "great" men—every one of whom, the text says, like an overfed horse, "neighed after his neighbor's wife" (v. 8) and whose house was "full of deceit" (v. 27)—is that they have lost the capacity for moral discernment and just judgment altogether.

Similar self-deceived repression of the truth occasions the apostles' warnings about apostate leadership in the last days of the Church, when:

> men shall be lovers of their own selves, covetous, boasters, proud, blasphemers, disobedient to parents, unthankful, unholy, without natural affection, trucebreakers, false accusers, incontinent, fierce, despisers of those who are good, traitors, heady, highminded, lovers of pleasure more than lovers of God; Having a form of godliness, but denying the power thereof: from such turn away. For of this sort are they which creep into houses, and lead captive silly women laden with sins, led away with divers lusts, ever learning, and never able to come to a knowledge of the truth. (2 Tim 3:2–7 KJV)

Even when the truth is preached, says St. Paul, in such an age people will "turn away their ears from the truth, and shall be turned to fables" (2 Tim 4:4).

A similar warning about apostate churches in 2 Peter adds another dimension to the problem. This text suggests that, when such self-protecting motives are strong enough, subversion of the truth can become remarkably clever. Making reference back to Jeremiah's days, the epistle speaks of "false teachers" who through skillful redefinition and verbal sleight of hand insert into the doctrine of the Church "damnable heresies" by means of which many will be deceived and even "the way of truth" shall be represented as an evil. By feigned words and clever rhetoric they will make the truth itself to seem a lie (2:1–3).

In our own age we can confirm that deliberate theological error seldom lacks for sophisticated articulation. Indeed, an apparent liberality of spirit and cleverness with words is often the hallmark of those who hate the truth. This can develop to the degree that, as St. Peter suggests in his letter (citing the case of Balaam the prophet [Num 22]), even a dumb ass may more likely speak the truth than the official prophets (2 Pet 2:15–21).

This does not mean that misguided prophets do not have a lot to say; it is often the case that they seem more voluble than anyone else. Søren Kierkegaard thought that "talkativeness," in fact, was a good indicator of the sterility of one's spiritual life, and that pseudo-intellectual talkativeness was a certain sign of it.[3] Such wordy would-be-revolutionaries in the Church, for Kierkegaard, are to be expected to try to effect a dissociation between truth and the intellect. Intelligent people, they are most likely to pretend, are the ones whose superior enlightenment recognizes no such thing as objective truth. Capital "T" truth, they will sneer, is fodder for donkeys. But amongst themselves they will say, "look—if we don't want the donkeys to get angry and buck us off then we must try to anesthetize them with ambiguous verbiage, as well as by employing other shrewd means of subverting their resistance." These strategies, to which whole courses are devoted in some of our seminaries, have the added advantage of providing further opportunities for cleverness. But as Oscar Wilde suggests ironically, in his essay "The Decay of Lying," when put into practice in the parish, such cleverness can nonetheless appear to the common layman as asininity:

> [. . .] In the English Church a man succeeds, not through his capacity for belief, but through his capacity for disbelief. Ours is the only Church where the sceptic stands at the altar, and where St. Thomas is regarded as the ideal apostle. Many a worthy clergyman, who passes his life in admirable works of kindly charity, lives and dies unnoticed and unknown; but it is sufficient for some shallow uneducated passman out of either University to get up in his pulpit and express his doubts about Noah's ark, or Balaam's ass, or Jonah and the whale, for half of London to flock to

hear him, and to sit open-mouthed in rapt admiration at his superb intellect [. . .][4]

That Wilde intends a rebuke to the pew as much as the pulpit is, of course,
clear, just as, with a more virtuous intent, did St. Peter in his catholic epistle.
Both say that truth would not be so often hidden from view if so many of us
were not so responsive to having our ears tickled, content to receive a
humorous placebo instead of the medicine we need.

It would be a mistake to think that truth-denying postmodernists never
themselves assert anything as true. Indeed, the determination to assert as
"truth" what cannot be supported in fact has become a poisonous epidemic
in academic and religious institutions in our time. A favorite target is, unsurprisingly, saints of the Church and distinguished Christians. Thus, the
Cambridge Encyclopedia of English Literature calls, without a shred of evidence whatsoever, two eminent Christians of the fourteenth century—both
Wycliffites, and one a Christian poet (Sir John Clanvowe)—homosexual
partners.[5] Similar claims, without foundation in evidence, are sometimes
made about biblical characters such as David and Jonathan or about major
theologians of the historic Church. The people who make these kinds of
assertions may well be prompted by vested interest—of that it is difficult to
judge—but the consequences of such fabrications are readily apparent: the
vast majority of faithful Christians who read these falsifications find them
painfully disorienting, while the enemies of the Gospel find them simply
"amusing" and, of course, conveniently self-serving. But this is merely one
amongst many spheres in which truth, in any normative veridical sense of
the word, is a casualty in postmodern discourse.

So what can we do to recover for our own language and logic a clearer
sense of the actual character of truth? Here is one suggestion: we need to do a
much better job of cultivating the Christian intelligence. To begin with, we
need to stop confusing intelligence with levels of formal "education." As innumerable current events make clear, there is no necessary connection between
intellectual capacity (or training) and moral intelligence. Indeed, with respect
to moral or spiritual realism there seems just now to be an inverse correlation
in many quarters. In his remarkable parable, *The Great Divorce*, C. S. Lewis
captures admirably the actual relationship between truth and intelligence as
we find it in the teaching of Scripture and in the persistent understanding of
the Church. In Lewis's parable, you may remember, theologians and bishops
do not come off any better than the rest of us. We find that intellectual attainment is no guarantee of access to truth whatsoever, that education (including
theological education) often serves simply to multiply the strategies for subversion and evasion. But such evasion, of course, does not change the nature

of truth any more than it models a proper use of the intellect. What Scripture, the Church, and individual Christian experience teach us, as Fr. Daniélou so nicely puts it, is that, whatever else men may pretend,

> there is an order of the real where things are ranged hierarchically accord-
> ing to their density of existence, their weight, what St. Augustine called
> *auctoritas.* Truth consists in the intelligence's conforming itself to this
> order. Being intelligent means simply that. Intelligence does not consist in
> the more or less brilliant performance of the mind. No, it consists in know-
> ing reality as it is. That is why for the Bible being intelligent means recog-
> nizing the sovereign reality of God. Who but "the fool says in his heart,
> There is no God" (Ps. 13:1)? This is the complete reverse of what modern
> man calls intelligence. For in the biblical view a great intellectual may be
> perfectly stupid, and some poor uneducated woman praying in a church
> infinitely more "intelligent" than he.[6]

Discernment of Truth Must Anticipate That Truth Will Typically Be at Odds with Fashion

Reality is one thing; the ideas and judgments by which we think about reality are another. The first is objective, the second subjective. Yet in the present age these two are increasingly conflated. This is particularly the case with impressionistic and, as we like to say, "theoretical" religious discourse.

The phenomenologists are certainly right about one aspect of this subjec-tivity. We tend to find (or invent) what we are looking for. And what we are looking for, though we hate to admit it, is seldom the truth. Why is this? Well, as Scripture, the teaching of the Church, and experience all make clear, it is often because we tend to prefer self-justification, a rationalization for some-thing for which we have an ardor more intense than we feel for truth, and which truth seems to threaten. But what Scripture tells us is that in this as in any other age what will follow from a general attempt to exchange the truth of God for a lie is a kind of ludicrous anti-realism which is spiritually and psy-chologically self-destructive, and in which a lot of other people will also get hurt. Eventually the lie makes fools of those who choose it, even if for a time the whole culture chooses it with them and they feel secure in the safety of numbers. (We should perhaps remind ourselves that a certain northern rodent also takes its bearing from where the crowd is moving, and tends not to notice until too late that the crowd has thinned out rather precipitately.)

Samuel Johnson, the great essayist and dictionary-maker of the eigh-teenth century, gets at St. Paul's point in a slightly different way: "Truth, sir," said Johnson, "is a cow; which, when skeptics have found it will give them no more milk, they have gone off to milk the bull." Milking the bull, as Johnson's audience knew, is not only futile but positively dangerous to one's health. Johnson expected skeptics of revealed truth thus to be corrected by the power of barnyard reality more quickly than did Wilde; by the 1890s, bull-wallop was for most people just a figure of speech. By the 1990s it has become, at every possible level, a kind of staple in our cultural diet. "Infotainment" is another word for it. You can get yours on the Net, on TV, or in the ubiquitous tabloids. You can also get it in some more formal and "churchy" environments. You know the headlines from your grocery shopping: "Bigfoot Got my Sweetheart," "Chocaholic Mom gives birth to Sugar-Coated Baby," "Church Organist Inseminated by UFO Aliens, spawns new Primate," etc. (Okay, I confess: I made that last one up.) A feature article in the Ottawa Citizen recently (January 4, 1998) characterized the tabloid as the exemplary postmodern phenomenon. Nietzsche's dictum that "there are no facts; the true world has in the end become a fable" may be almost perfectly realized in this popular medium. Articles which claim the preposterous as true are, according to Eddie Clontz, editor-in-chief of *The Weekly World News*, just a popular application of the same postmodern theory that more or less equally characterizes politics, preaching, and the academy: "People rewrite history all the time," he says, "and so do we." In his stable are a completely fictitious corps of doctors and scientists of obscure origins, complete with "scholarly looking headshots." On-line editor Cynthia Rigg refers to a cadre of fictitious "Bible scholars" who have been "used over and over again by the tabloid, and are now quite respected." And of course there are always a few mostly warm bodies from the Jesus Seminar or ecclesiastical offices closer to home when their creativity falters. Yet according to repeated surveys, forty percent of the millions who regularly read these rags believe their stories to be true.

What is truth? What is the truth of hypnotically induced "memories" in an environment where it is the victimization *du jour* to "discover" the most sordid sort of abuse under every gesture of parental affection or constraint? What is the truth preserved in legal judgments based on a perceived need to "correct social imbalances" or to "empower" some groups at the expense of others, abusing where necessary fact and accountability? What is the justice which ensues in legal judgments formulated on such fabrications? What is the value of scholarly findings or exegesis of texts based upon raw advocacy rather than an intention to understand what is actually there? If the truth of the matter is not what we want to hear, does it really matter so much if we get a social construct—or vivid invention—in its place? After all, as Oscar Wilde would say, the lie is often more "interesting." What makes it interesting may be that it gives temporary advantage to the will to power over the will to truth, though this is seldom admitted. But this motive is surely there, prompting hatred for the notion of an objective truth, for truth that by definition must be true for you just as it is true for me.

In this light we can begin to see why truth is seldom fashionable. The illusion so cherished by people of all ages, so apparent already in the serpent's tempting in Eden, is an illusion of anarchic self-empowerment achieved by denying the truth. We shall be as gods, we think, able to decree for ourselves what is to be evil and what is to be good. This allure, so transparent in the Genesis account of our fallen nature, is what continues to make the impulse to hubristic anti-realism so irresistible—and so dangerous. For "rejecting objective truth amounts to a subtle willingness to set my face against God." Conversely, "acknowledging what is, submitting to the real [e.g. the reality of Creation], means acknowledging something I have not decided for myself and therefore already saying yes to God."[7]

There is, therefore, much at stake in what I am here calling "fashion" and what the Bible typically calls "worldliness." It is not to the credit of Western Christianity that we have made so many ardent and repeated accommodations to fashion, courting the gods of the marketplace. Much of what is essential to the truth of the Gospel has been sacrificed to our desire not to seem too different from our contemporaries—much more than the truth can afford. What Kierkegaard said about this tension more than a century-and-a-half ago still holds:

> The true must essentially be regarded as in conflict with this world; the world has never been so good, and will never become so good, that the majority will desire the truth, or have the true conception of it in such a way that its proclamation must consequently immediately gain the support of everyone. No, he who will proclaim some truth in truth, must prepare himself in some other way than by the help of such a foolish expectation; he must be willing essentially to relinquish the immediate. (*Works of Love* 2.10)[8]

Willingness to relinquish the immediate, even if the immediate is preferment in what C. S. Lewis called the "inner ring" of popularity, or just the acceptance most of us would some days be grateful for a little more of, is indispensable to our discernment of the truth.

As Christians we are called to be a "sign of contradiction" to our age by the One who endured such "contradiction of sinners against himself" (Heb 12:3). Contradiction of fashion, so far from being bad for us, is essential to our spiritual health and thus to the integrity of any witness we might hope to have. For the Christian, "abolition of the principle of contradiction, expressed in terms of existence, means to live in contradiction with oneself," as Kierkegaard says.[9] So much is this so that "knowing truth in the present age" is pretty much impossible if we are unwilling to be known as a sign of contradiction to the age, or unwilling to learn to let our yea be Yea and our nay, Nay. As St. Basil (in his *On The Holy Spirit*) once said, "Yea and nay are but two syllables, yet there is often involved in these little words at once the best of all good things: Truth, and that beyond which wickedness cannot go, a Lie" (1.2). As with much else we learn in life, often sorrowfully, in truth there is no "yes" without a corresponding "no."

Knowing Truth When We Meet it Depends Greatly upon Already Knowing the One Who is Truth

"What is truth?" When Pilate asked his question he was the one, of course, already under conviction. The prisoner brought before him, bound in fetters, had seared the conscience of his inquisitor with an invisible sword. It divided asunder the thoughts and intentions of Pilate's heart, and he felt the oppressive weight of his own far more heavy (though invisible) shackles. Pilate's kingdom was strictly of this world, and to its temporizing venality he was himself a prisoner. Which is to say, he lived by lies, by the maintenance of politic and fashionable institutional fictions. And yet, when Jesus said to him, "Every one who is of the truth heareth my voice" (John 18:37), his professional composure was evidently pricked. The evidence is not only that he asked his peremptory, skeptical and parrying question, but that he refused to stay for an answer. He did tell the accusers of our Lord: "I find in him no fault at all." What he did not say, unsurprisingly, was whether he was beginning to note fault anywhere else.

A profound irony in Pilate's question to Jesus has often been noted. His evasive skepticism concerning the very possibility of truth in a world where men customarily live by lies had led him to a common category mistake. "What is truth?" he asks, as though truth were a chimerical abstraction. Pilate's question is rhetorical; it presumes the impossibility of a coherent answer. Yet the One of whom it is mockingly asked is, John's Gospel shows us, not less than Truth himself, the only One who has ever been able to say "I am the Way, the Truth, and the Life" (John 14:6). Had Pilate but recognized him, known him for who he is, he would have "heard his voice" and thus at least reformulated his inquisition: "*Who* is Truth?" But that is a question a faithful person alone will ask—"every one who is of the truth." Whoever evades the absolute character of Truth will miss him.

Have you noticed how often it is in Scripture that the mention of God's truth ('*emeth*) is coupled with righteousness (*zedekah*)? In the Song of Moses the prophetic poet sings, "He is the Rock, his Word is perfect: for all his ways are judgment; a God of truth and without iniquity, just and right is he" (Deut 32:4). It is the righteous nation which keeps the truth (Isa 26:2); indeed, "he who speaks the truth," says the book of Proverbs, "exemplifies righteousness" (Prov 12:17). And who among us can read these lines of the Psalmist without being provoked to repentance:

> Lord, who shall abide in thy tabernacle? Who shall dwell in thy holy hill?
> He that walketh uprightly, and worketh righteousness, and speaketh the
> truth in his heart. (Ps 15:2)

If the petitioner after truth is sincere, that is to say, striving after righteousness, then he will not shy away from the persistent connection Scripture makes between truth and judgment, the judgment—we might say the justice—of God. "I have chosen the way of truth," says the Psalmist, and as a consequence, "thy judgments have I laid before me" (Ps 119:30 KJV). "Thy Law is the truth," he writes later in the same poem, "thy commandments are truth" (119:142, 151). If we want to come to a knowledge of the truth, say the writers of Scripture everywhere, then we will have to get into the habit of doing the truth, for that is the only way we can learn to recognize the Author of Truth when he speaks to us or shows us the power of his hand. "These are the things that ye shall do," says the prophet Zechariah, "speak ye every man the truth to his neighbour, execute the judgment of truth and peace in your gates" (8:16 KJV), and St. Paul, echoing him, makes this way of living with each other a demonstrative consequence of our imitating "the truth [as it] is in Jesus," of our putting on the new man "which after God is created in righteousness and true holiness" (Eph 4:21-24 KJV).

When we are careful to speak the truth to our neighbor, our will to truth in principle is strengthened in a manner analogous to the way in which it is strengthened by our carefulness to be honest in our self-examination before God. (The New Testament term is *alêtheia*, both "veracity" and "rectitude.") This is what St. Anselm of Canterbury has in mind in his treatise *On Truth* when he says that truth in the will—"truthfulness in the inward parts" (Ps 51:6)—is, properly speaking, identical to that correctness of the will which we call uprightness (*rectitudo*)" (*De Veritate* 4). It is this reciprocity of rectitude and truth which makes it impossible that anyone should know the truth who does not love Truth, or that anyone should love the truth who does not live it. Doing what truth teaches is "telling the truth," while acting in a way contrary to truth is precisely equivalent to telling a lie (*De Veritate* 9). This is why St. Paul, in Romans 1, can be so categorical when he says that God's judgment falls hard upon those who "hold the truth in unrighteousness" (Rom 1:18). It is entirely possible for someone to mouth the very words of scriptural truth and, in the context of their mouthing, to change the truth of God into a lie (v. 25). And this happens especially when those who, though professing themselves to be wise, in their rejection of revelation and the authority of objective truth, reveal themselves to be fools (Rom 1:22).

I do not pretend that these are not hard words. (I certainly do not find them easy to speak.)

None of us, I think, sets out to become a fool. Foolishness rather comes to us by degrees, as the sodden fruit of a process of self-deception. A lie, repeated often enough, gets to be taken for the truth—first by the one who convinces himself of it, subsequently by others who hear it over and over again and forbear to check on the facts. Conversely, the truth, perhaps repeated often but without being grounded in the love and life of that truth, becomes a living lie in the making. That is what the teaching of Romans 1 makes for the most disastrous of all follies. Yet all the while it too remains correctable by a check for correspondence with the facts of a given life.

This notion of how we may come to know truth pertains most closely both to common sense and to older philosophical theories of truth: there ought to be a correspondence between a proposition (or claim) and a fact or state of affairs that verifies it. The biblical notion of truth bears less relation to the philosophers' more academic notion of verification by coherence (as in the coherence among propositions), simply because the normative character of Scripture grounds all truth in history and revelation. But with the third and now perhaps most common academic definition of truth, that of the pragmatists, biblical truth has nothing in common at all. In pragmatic theory truth is to be defined in terms of its satisfactoriness—i.e., whether in our own social or political circumstances it "works." For William James "true ideas are the ones we can assimilate"[10]—that is to say, the criterion of truth is finally its locatability in the "comfort zone" of the knower. Alas, this is precisely the sort of dissociation from reality which corrupts the idea of objective truth altogether.

Of the three principal definitions of truth propounded by philosophers through the ages—correspondence, coherence, and pragmatic—correspondence is then the one clearly favored by the writers of Scripture. This correspondence is, of course, of words to facts—to the facts of the Gospel, e.g., the atoning death and resurrection of Jesus. It is also in a correspondence of word to life. Scriptural truth is also manifest, therefore, as opposition to falsehood and hypocrisy, as in Jesus' rebuke of the Pharisees, who loved the letter of the law but not its higher purpose, and of the Sadducees, who denied the power of the resurrection. Finally, truth in Scripture is the content of what we believe, guaranteed by the very character of God himself, and of Jesus who is the Truth of God revealed to us. His *troth*, his fidelity to his promises from the beginning of the world, is our guarantee of every other truth, and it is the standard by which, finally, we are able to say what truth is.

In the New Testament, Peter spoke for all of us in the Church when he asked and answered a rhetorical question: "Lord, to whom shall we go? Thou hast the words of eternal life. And we believe and are sure that thou art the Christ, the Son of the living God" (John 6:68–69 KJV). Peter's answer corresponds to what he has come to know personally about Jesus. These phrases become the apostolic words of truth, and, as the substance of holy conversation in the Church (1 Pet 1), they make it possible for the Church to be an oracle which answers still, to be as Paul has it, "the house of God, which is the church of the living God, the pillar and ground of the truth" (1 Tim 3:15 KJV).

When the Church is in love with Jesus, then it knows the ground of Truth: "And hereby do we know that we know him," says St. John in his first pastoral letter, "if we keep his commandments. He that saith, I know him, and keepeth not his commandments, is a liar, and the truth is not in him" (1 John 2:3–4 KJV). Holiness is a matter of practising the truth and a matter of knowing the one who is Truth: "Who is a liar," he continues, "but he that denieth that Jesus is the Christ? He is antichrist, that denieth the Father and the Son" (1 John 2:22 KJV). It is impossible to be holy without a living belief in this Truth. Indeed, it is impossible to be Christian without a living belief in this truth.

Of course, these are unfashionable words. They are not our words. The question is: how can we know their truth in such times? Well, Scripture says, by loving that One who is timeless Truth, and by paying him heed according to his word. His Word is truth, and we will know him in his word, says the beloved disciple, if we live out the truth of his word, not only by a love which is a matter of words, but "in deed and in truth." For, John says, this is the way in which we know that we are of the truth," and "assure our hearts before him" (1 John 3:18–19 KJV).

When we live thus in his truth we are of God, and all those who know God, he says, will give us a hearing. Conversely, we may suppose that whoever does not belong to God will not give us a hearing. Yet even their antagonism is not without value to us with respect to our knowing the truth, for, when we are living in faithful obedience to the One who is Truth, then such antagonism can actually confirm us in our determination to search out and test for truth: "Hereby know we the spirit of truth, and the spirit of error"

(1 John 4:6 KJV). And blessed are we, after all, when men revile us "for his name's sake" (Matt 5:11).

It is crucial to know which spirit is which, since we too shall be judged. Discerning the spirits, as John's first letter encourages, is a necessary task because "many false prophets are gone out into the world" (1 John 4:1) and their falseness is directed above all at a diminishment of Christ. But the purpose of our discernment is not in the first instance to win arguments or political battles with such people. Nor do we seek it as a means of self-justification. It can be, after all, rather easy to identify fault and to name it; and if we are not prayerful, the manner in which we conduct our "trying the spirits, whether they are of God" may open us up to the greater judgment. The trick is to learn to tell the truth which is necessary (not more) without forgetting to live in the light of the Truth while telling it.

When it comes to the extreme case of someone who, while bearing the authority of the Church, willfully misleads others, then we may have little choice but to declare against that lie such truth as we ourselves have been willing to live by. But then we ought to speak only of what we know in that most thorough sense of knowing—the holy conversation of our life in Him who alone is Truth. We will be most true to Him when we speak least for ourselves and perhaps, on some occasions, remain prayerfully silent.

If it is our lot to have to fight the Dragon—and we ought not to presume it to be our lot unless we have unarguably been chosen for it—then we had better be quite sure that we have been equipped for this terrible task. "His truth shall be [our] shield and buckler," says the Psalmist (91:4), and St. Paul adds that against "the rulers of the darkness of this world, against spiritual wickedness in high places" we will need the "whole armor of God." But you and I will want to remember that the foundation of that armor, first on the apostle's list, is that we should have our "loins girt about with truth," and that we should be wearing with it "the breastplate of righteousness" (Eph 6:11–16).

So then, let each of us consider carefully what Augustine says in his commentary on John 14:6: "every true man is true from the Truth [. . .]. The Truth, then, cannot speak contrary to the true man, or the true man contrary to the Truth" (*Tract. Ev. Jo.* 5:1; my translation). That is the "correspondence" for which each of us must daily pray: that we may come to know him who is the ground of all Truth, and so to have, in such measure as is possible for us, more of his mind about all these things.

(1998)

Notes

Chapter 1

1. Hannah Arendt, *Between Past and Future: Eight Exercises in Political Thought* (New York: Viking Press, 1968), 91.
2. Samuel Butler, *The Way of All Flesh* (London: Grant Richards, 1903).
3. Hans-Peter Breuer, *The Notebooks of Samuel Butler.* Vol. 1: 1874–1883 (Lanham and London: University Press of America, 1984).
4. E.g., John Wyclif, *The Truth of Holy Scripture* (trans. Ian Christopher Levy; TEAMS series; Kalamazoo: Medieval Institute Publications, 2001). Michael Treschow, in a translation forthcoming in 2005, opts for "authority."
5. John Bunyan, "The Epistle to Four Sorts of Readers," in *The Holy City* (in *The Miscellaneous Works of John Bunyan*; 11 vols.; ed. Roger Sharrock; Oxford: Oxford University Press, 1976–), 3.71–72.
6. David Lyle Jeffrey, *People of the Book: Christian Identity and Literary Culture* (Grand Rapids: Eerdmans, 1996), 270–74.
7. This most unbiblical notion strikes me as a kind of churchy equivalent of the general tendency in our culture to behave as though personal sexual freedom were the highest possible public good, and it is probably just as pernicious.
8. E.g., Henri de Lubac, *Medieval Exegesis* (2 vols.; Grand Rapids: Eerdmans, 1998, 2002).
9. John Paul II, Pope, *The Splendor of Truth: Veritatis Splendor, Encyclical Letter Addressed to all the Bishops of the Catholic Church Regarding Certain Fundamental Questions of the Church's Moral Teaching* (Vatican translation; Boston: St. Paul Books & Media, 1993), 5.
10. Ibid, 14.
11. It is worthy of note that two of the formative biblical scholars in this group, Jean Daniélou and Henri de Lubac, were elevated to the rank of Cardinal. De Lubac's volumes in particular are an indispensable guide for those who would wish to meet them on the road, so to speak, because they have as their goal the recovery of Scripture's authoritative voice in the life of the Church.
12. Susan Wood, *Spiritual Exegesis and the Church in the Theology of Henri de Lubac* (Grand Rapids: Eerdmans, 1998).
13. Louis Bouyer, "Liturgie et exégèse spirituelle," *La Maison-Dieu* 7 (1946): 27–50. My translation.
14. De Lubac, *Medieval Exegesis*, 2:44.

15. Joseph Lienhard, S.J., publisher's review of Henri de Lubac, *Medieval Exegesis*, vol. 1.

16. Henri de Lubac, *Histoire et Esprit: L'intelligence de l'Écriture d'après Origène* (Paris: Aubier, 1950).

17. De Lubac, *Medieval Exegesis* 1:167.

18. Ibid, 1:19.

19. Hugh of St. Victor, *Didascalicon of Hugh of St. Victor: A Medieval Guide to the Arts* (trans. Jerome Taylor; New York: Columbia University Press, 1961), 140–42.

20. ". . . *capax innumerabilium sententiarum*." Aelred of Riveaulx, *Speculum charitatis* (Migne, PL 195:364A).

21. See U. Milo Kaufmann, *The Pilgrim's Progress and Traditions of Puritan Meditation* (New Haven: Yale University Press, 1966), 61–79, 188–95.

22. John B. Wharey, ed., *John Bunyan's Pilgrim's Progress* (2d ed. Roger Sharrock; Oxford: Clarendon Press, 1960), 29.

Chapter 2

1. Jean François Lyotard, *La condition postmoderne: rapport sur le savoir* (Paris: Les Editions de Minuit, 1979) [Eng. trans. *The Postmodern Condition: A Report on Knowledge* (Minneapolis: University of Minnesota Press, 1984)].

2. This is the territory into which N. T. Wright has taken us so magisterially in his *The New Testament and the People of God* (vol. 1 of *Christian Origins and the Question of God*; Minneapolis: Fortress, 1992), and if what follows here entails something of a qualifier to his superb discussion of grand story and worldview, my interlocution is one prejudiced by largely unadulterated admiration for what he has accomplished in that volume and its sequel.

3. Aziz al Azmeh, *Islam and Modernities* (2d ed.; London: Verso, 1996), 134–37, 163.; quotation from p. 134.

4. Eric Auerbach perhaps most famously demonstrated that style bespeaks a worldview. His examples of worldview starkly contrasted by narrative style were Homeric epic and the biblical story of Abraham, notably in his opening chapter of *Mimesis: The Representation of Reality in Western Literature* (Princeton: Princeton University Press, 1953).

5. Wu Cheng'en, *The Journey to the West by Wu Cheng'en* (3 vols.; trans. W. J. F. Jenner; Beijing: Foreign Languages Press, 1982, 1993, 1997) is the text used here. The translation by Anthony Yu is slightly more recent, and published in 4 volumes (Chicago: University of Chicago Press, 1980–1984).

6. These chapter titles quite accurately reflect the swift recension and sense of religious closure effected by "return" in this text.

7. This is a point much stressed, of course, by structuralists. N. T. Wright cites Vladimir Propp, but Roland Barthes and Northrop Frye are perhaps more accessible proponents of such structure analysis, Frye most notably in his

Anatomy of Criticism (Princeton: Princeton University Press, 1957) and *Secular Scripture: A Study of the Structure of Romance* (Cambridge, Mass.: Harvard University Press, 1976) but also in his *The Great Code: the Bible and Literature* (London: Routledge, 1982).

8. It is of some interest that the greater willingness of Chinese to settle now in other parts of the world—in effect to become permanent emigrants—is related to the Christianization of many of them. See Wang Ling-chi, "On Luodi-shenggen," in *The Chinese Diaspora: Selected Essays* (ed. Wang Ling-chi and Wang Gungwu; 2 vols.; Singapore: Times Academic Press, 1998), 1:x–xi. Cf. Sharon K. Hom, ed. *Chinese Women Traversing Diaspora: Memoirs, Essays and Poetry* (New York: Garland, 1999).

9. See my study, "Journey to the West / Journey to the East: Globalization and the Fate of Masterplots," in *European Literature in the Chinese Context* (ed. Kevin Yan; Beijing: Peking University Press, 2003), 176–184. [Chinese text].

10. This is a point considered thoughtfully by Wright, *New Testament and the People of God*, 67–69, 135–39, etc. With respect to biblical and post-biblical Christian literature in the West it is a theme also in my *People of the Book*.

11. In addition to Auerbach, *Mimesis*, the classic source for *aretê* is Werner Jaeger, *Paideia: The Ideals of Greek Culture* (3 vols.; New York: Oxford University Press, 1965), though a concise and reliable synopsis occurs in C. M. Bowra, *The Greek Experience* (Oxford: Oxford University Press, 1957), 206–15. Dennis R. MacDonald, in *The Homeric Epics and the Gospel of Mark* (New Haven: Yale University Press, 2000) has made the case that parallels in Mark's Gospel with Homeric epic are persistent enough that a conscious or unconscious dependence must be assumed to exist. I think this is to argue too much, but there is enough to suggest that Mark's Greek audience could be expected to see the narrative of Jesus' *aretê* against Homeric epic as a familiar (yet contrastive) background.

12. *Aeneid* 1.480–83: "it was only a picture on a wall, but the sight afforded food for the spirit's need. He saw the Greeks, hard-pressed, in flight, and Trojans coming after [. . .]" (*The Aeneid of Virgil*, trans. Rolfe Humphries; New York: Scribners, 1951).

13. It is of more than passing significance that a poem meant to apostrophize Roman *pietas* should quite literally end with a briefly premeditated revengeful death—as Aeneas slays Turnus.

14. Augustine, *De civitate Dei*. A comment by Michael Walzer in his *Exodus and Revolution* (San Francisco: Harper Collins, 1985) is relevant here. Walzer writes: "In the literature of the ancient world only the *Aeneid* resembles the Exodus in its narrative structure, describing a divinely guided and world-historical journey to something like a promised land. That is why the *Aeneid* was the only rival of the Exodus in the arguments over the American Great Seal" (11). Walzer thinks that "Rome, though it represents for Virgil a 'new order of the

ages' is not, after all, significantly different from Troy; it is only more powerful; while Canaan is the very opposite of Egypt" (11–12). I am inclined to think the comparison more fraught with complexity than Walzer suggests, as the following pages may indicate.

15. Cf. Alan Richardson, *History Sacred and Profane* (London: SCM Press, 1964), 59–60. That the Old Testament stories are deliberately rooted in history and lived out as a reiteration of an ancestral history is of the essence of the literary forms which predominate in biblical narrative: as Alter and others have observed, only Israel amongst the ancient peoples chose to cast its ancestral history in prose—to eschew poetry and the epic genre which they would have known to be normative to other cultures for 'grand narrative' purposes.

16. There are accordingly strong reasons, powerfully expressed in the American grand narrative itself, for the abysmal failure of repeated attempts by educators to overcome the comparatively dismal historical knowledge possessed by American high school and university students. In a context of such overwhelming commitment to "now" and the "new," there is simply not sufficient public will to have it otherwise.

17. Robert Alter, observing differences in the Bible's notion of sacred history from modern historiography, writes: "There is, to begin with, a whole spectrum of relations to history in the sundry biblical narratives but none of these involves the sense of being bound to documentable facts [. . .] that characterizes history in its modern acceptation" (*The Art of Biblical Narrative* [New York: Basic Books, 1981], 24).

18. Anthony Giddens, *The Consequences of Modernity* (Stanford: Stanford University Press, 1990).

19. David Lyle Jeffrey, "C. S. Lewis, The Bible, and its Literary Critics," *Christianity and Literature* 50.1 (2000): 95–110, revised here as ch. 10. This is substantially the argument of Stanley Hauerwas in *Unleashing the Scripture: Freeing the Bible from Captivity to America* (Nashville: Abingdon Press, 1993).

20. One might consider here, for example, Trevor Ross, *The Making of the English Literary Canon: From the Middle Ages to the Late Eighteenth Century* (Montreal: McGill-Queens, 1998); James E. Brenneman, *Canons in Conflict: Negotiating Texts in True and False Prophecy* (Oxford: Oxford University Press, 1997).

21. See, e.g., Lawrence H. Schiffman, *From Text to Tradition: A History of Second Temple and Rabbinic Judaism* (Hoboken, NJ: Ktav, 1991).

22. Wright, *New Testament and the People of God*, 79.

23. Ibid., 216.

24. Ibid., 217.

25. Ibid., 117.

26. Augustine, for example, ties into this understanding also Hebrews 11; 13; 1 Pet 2:11; Ps 28:13 (*Civ. Dei* 1; cf. *Serm.* 14.4.6; 70.7; *Tract. Ev. Jo.*, 40.10); Gregory

the Great in his *Moralia in Job* remarks that "temporal comfort on earth is to the just man what a bed in an inn is to the traveler (*viator*): he will rest in it for awhile bodily, but mentally he is already somewhere else" (*Moral.* 8.54.92; cf. *Ep.* 2.204). But these concepts are already highly visible in the early Church, where Peregrinus and Viator became common baptismal names. *The Epistle to Diognetus* (trans. J. B. Lightfoot and J. R. Harmer, *The Apostolic Father* [London: Macmillan, 1891]) says of the earthly lot of Christians that "they reside in their own fatherlands, but as if they were non-citizens; they partake in all things as if they were citizens and suffer all things as if they were strangers. Every foreign country is thus a fatherland to them, and every fatherland a foreign country. [. . .] They sojourn on earth, but they are citizens in heaven" (5:5, 9).

27. "This World Is not Our Home." For full text and melody see William E. Barton, *Old Plantation Hymns* (Boston: Lamson, Wolffe & Co., 1899), 9.

28. In the interpretative history reflected in n. 17 above, Galatians 4 plays a crucial role, even as it does in Origen, *Contra Celsum* (8.75). It is invoked by Augustine, e.g., in *Civ. Dei* 15.2; likewise by Aquinas, to turn the "inherent gospel principle" of spiritual interpretation, and by Wyclif (*Sermones* 2.33–36); later Protestant commentators such as Matthew Poole in his *Annotations upon the Holy Bible* (1635) emphasize that the spiritual children of Sarah, being obedient through faith, will be true pilgrims, even as Hagar's offspring, carnal by nature, wish to return to a condition of exile.

29. Wright, *New Testament and the People of God*, 135.

30. Ibid.

31. A list here would be long, especially if it were to include not only direct biblical commentary but the sermons of televangelists and "Christian fiction."

32. Wright, *New Testament and the People of God*, 286.

33. Cf. Wright, who says, much as might E. P. Sanders and others, "This Kingdom was not a timeless truth, nor an abstract ethical ideal, nor the coming end of the space-time universe. Nor did the phrase itself *denote* a community, though it would *connote* the birth of a new covenant community. It would denote, rather, the action of the covenant god, within Israel's history, to restore her fortunes, to bring to an end the bitter period of exile, and to defeat through her, the evil that ruled the whole world" (*New Testament and the People of God*, 307). The idea of either Israel (or New Israel) as "chosen arm of God" for the destruction of evil is the volatile element. Here then is an implication of real concern: apocalypticists both Christian and Jewish focus obsessively on the historical Jerusalem in some considerable measure because of their identification with this traditional Jewish eschatological grand narrative expectation.

34. *In omnes S. Pauli apostoli epistolas, commentaria* (2 vols.; Taurini: Petri Marietti, 1924) 2:228. For a fresh and systematic contemporary study of the structure of

Hebrews see George Guthrie, *The Structure of Hebrews: A Text-Linguistic Analysis* (Leiden: E. J. Brill, 1994).

35. See, e.g., Neils-Erik A. Andreason, *Rest and Redemption: A Study of the Biblical Sabbath* (Fife: St. Andrews University Press, 1978), and M. Greenberg, "Sabbath," *EncJud* 14:557–71.

36. See here Guthrie, *Structure of Hebrews*, 3.

37. Richardson, *History Sacred and Profane*.

38. Cf. Augustine, *Civ. Dei* 10.1.

39. It is not without continuing resonance for Augustine, one suspects, that Juno was the civic goddess of Carthage.

40. Cf. Augustine, *Civ. Dei* 2.22.

41. All translations of the *City of God* are from Marcus Dods (vol. 2 of *A Select Library of the Christian Church: The Nicene and Post-Nicene Fathers*. First Series; 14 vols.; ed. Philip Schaff; Peabody, Mass.: Hendrickson, 1999).

42. Cf. John von Heyking, *Augustine and Politics as Longing in the World* (Columbia: University of Missouri Press, 2001), 152–57.

43. See E. A. Gibbs, ed., *Middle English Romances* (Evanston: Northwestern University Press, 1966), 4–7; also David L. Jeffrey, "Literature in an Apocalyptic Age," *Dalhousie Review* 61.3 (1981), 426–46.

44. The *Left Behind* series, now eleven novels and still counting, though sub-literary, almost tabloid in its style and character, affords a kind of gnostic myth of return. See my "*Left Behind* and Getting Ahead," in *Christian Reflections* 2.2 (2002), 70–78, for comment on the series' historicism and neo-dispensationalism.

45. Mather, *Magnalia Christi Americana* 1.44, 46; 2.579.

46. See Jeffrey, *People of the Book*, 320–24, for a fuller account.

47. Herman Melville, *White Jacket: Or, the World in a Man-of-War* (Oxford: Oxford University Press, 1967), 152–53.

48. Wright, *New Testament and the People of God*, 136, cites G. B. Caird (*The Language and Imagery of the Bible* [Philadelphia: Westminster Press, 1980]) to stress his view, shared here, that "the Christian is committed to the belief that certain things are true about the past." It is interesting to see how strongly, in an historical review of the importance to Christian biblical interpretation of allegory, Henri de Lubac, S.J. makes the same point, citing literally dozens of early and medieval commentators to support their insistence that allegory is not, in faithful Christian exegesis, a rejection of history (*Medieval Exegesis*, vol. 2). His seventh chapter, "The Foundation of History" (2:41–82) is a particularly helpful contextualization of the way in which Christian *allegoria* arises from *historia*, both in the biblical text and in more than a millennium of commentary. For de Lubac and the tradition he represents, "Allegory is in truth *the truth* of history" (2:201).

49. *pace* Wright, *New Testament and the People of God*, 136.

50. Georg W. F. Hegel's *Philosophy of History* (New York: Colonial Press, 1899; here cited from Pt. 1, 3.3) has had a pervasive influence since its early reception, even upon biblical criticism. But this is an influence that can distort our understanding not only of the New Testament but of its early Church, medieval, and Reformation commentators. De Lubac's monumental *Ressourcement* study is a welcome caution on this point. It is surely true that for Christians at least (though not for Vergilians) historicism of any kind is alien: "Our ancient exegetes," writes de Lubac, "did not have any idea, thanks be to God, of that 'absolutized History' which is one of the principal idols invented by our age. On the other hand, they did have a sense of biblical history, or even of universal history, because they held on to its principle of discernment in the mystery of Christ" (*Medieval Exegesis*, 2:72).

Chapter 3

1. We know this because he tells us so in his *Retractions*, written in A.D. 427. The earliest existing MS may be Augustine's own: see W. M. Green, "A Fourth-Century Manuscript of St. Augustine?" *Revue bénédictine* 69 (1959): 191–97.
2. These sermons, discovered in 1990 in a just-released catalogue of manuscripts in the city library of Mainz by François Dolbeau and published by him as a recit six years later, are part of a group of twenty-six previously undiscovered sermons by Augustine. See Augustin d'Hippone, *Vingt-six sermons au peuple d'Afrique* (ed. and comm. François Dolbeau; Collection des études augustiniennes, Série Antiquité 147; Paris: Institute d'Etudes augustiniennes, 1996). More recently available is the English translation in *Newly Discovered Sermons* (trans. Edmund Hill, O.P.; pt. 3, vol. 11 of *The Works of Saint Augustine: A Translation for the 21ˢᵗ Century*, ed. John E. Rotelle, O.S.A.; New York: New City Press, 1997). This translation strains at a vernacularity in contemporary idiom to which Augustine's Latin does not descend, and it should be used with care.
3. I refer for convenience to the English translation *On Christian Doctrine* (trans. D. W. Robertson, Jr.; New York: Bobbs-Merrill, 1958). Henceforth, all translations of *De doctrina christiana* are from Robertson.
4. The Donatists were rigorists in the North African community, and split away from Catholics because of their refusal to accept the sacraments from bishops and clergy they felt lacked holiness. Augustine, representatively for Catholics, argued that the office by itself was sufficient to ensure validity of the sacraments, since the true minister was Christ. Converts to Donatism were rebaptized.
5. E.g., in *De utilitate credendi*, 1–4 (written in 391); cf. note 18.
6. See, e.g., the brevity of *Doctr. chr.* 2.5.6.
7. Cf. *Conf.* 1.18.
8. See, e.g., *Doctr. chr.* 2.16.23, in which he acknowledges that "when these names

have been investigated and explained, many figurative expressions in Scripture become clear."

9. See *Serm.* 38.24 (Ben. 88) on Matt. 20:30.

10. Cf. *Contra Faustum* 15.1; 19.7.

11. See here Henry Chadwick, "New Sermons of St. Augustine," *Journal of Theological Studies* 47.1 (1966): 69–91; and François Dolbeau, "Le sermonnaire augustinien de Mayence (Mainz, Stadtbibliothek I 9): analyse et histoire," *Revue Bénédictine* 106 (1996): 5–52. Each offers a useful overview and contextualization.

12. Augustine had begun his near lifelong debate with the Donatists by 393, during which year he wrote a letter (no longer extant) against the rebaptism practices of Donatus the Great, then Bishop of Carthage.

13. See, e.g., *Contra litteras Petiliani* 3.1–3; cf. *Serm.* 3341 (Dolbeau 22) (Mainz 55) on "The Three Ways of Understanding Christ in Scripture Symbolized by Jacob's Three Rods," ed. Hill, 283–309; and *Serm.* 360A (Dolbeau 24) (Mainz 60), "The Testimonies of Scripture against the Donatists and against the Pagans," ed. Hill, 354–65.

14. See Hill, 53, 177, for dating and context. *Serm.* 133 (on John 7:2–10), *Serm.* 89 (on Matt 21:12–19) and the newly discovered *Serm.* 162C (on Gal 2:11) appear to have been preached on three successive days, most likely in Carthage.

15. Peter Brown, *St. Augustine of Hippo: A Biography* (new ed.; Berkeley: University of California Press, 2000), 455: "as a caution to himself and thank-offering to God."

16. Bernard F. Lonergan, *Method in Theology* (Toronto: University of Toronto Press, 1971), 52, 155–61.

17. All translations of the *Confessions* are from R. S. Pine-Coffin, *St. Augustine's Confessions* (London: Penguin, 1961).

18. See Donald Marshall, "Making Letters Speak: Interpreter as Orator in Augustine's *De Doctrina Christiana*," *Religion and Literature* 24.2 (1992): 1–18.

Chapter 4

1. D. W. Robertson, Jr., "The Doctrine of Charity in Medieval Literary Gardens," in *Essays in Medieval Culture* (Princeton: Princeton University Press, 1980), 27.

2. Bernard of Clairvaux, *On Loving God.* Cistercian Fathers series 13B (ed. Emero Steigman; Kalamazoo, MI: Cistercian Publications, Inc., 1973).

3. Aelred of Rievaulx, *The Mirror of Charity.* The *Speculum Caritatis* of St. Aelred of Rievaulx (trans. Geoffrey Webb and Adrian Walker; London: A.R. Mowbray & Co., 1962), 95.

4. Saint Bonaventura. *S. Bonaventurae opera omnia.* Edita studio et cura pp. Collegii a S. Bonaventura, ad plurimus codices mss emendata, anecdotis aucta,

prolegomenis scholiis notisque illustrata. X volumina (Quaracchi: Collegium S. Bonaventurae, 1882–1902).

5. *Thomas Aquinas: Theological Texts* (trans. Thomas Gilby; New York: Oxford University Press, 1955), 228. Henceforth, all translations of *Summa Theologica* are from Gilby.

6. Cf. Dunbar's "Of Luve Erdly and Divine," a similar "progress" poem.

7. See Mark Eccles, ed. *The Macro Plays: The Castle of Perseverence, Wisdom, Mankind.* Early English Text Society 262 (London and New York: Oxford University Press, 1969).

8. Theodor Erbe, ed. *Mirk's Festial: A Collection of Homilies.* Early English Text Society 96 (London: Kegan Paul, Trench, Trübner & Co., 1905).

9. Quoted from David L. Jeffrey, ed., *The Law of Love: English Spirituality in the Age of Wyclif* (Grand Rapids: Eerdmans, 1988), 395.

10. *Speculum Perfectionis* (trans. David L. Jeffrey, *Toward a Perfect Love* (Portland: Multnomah, 1986), 87.

11. F. E. Hutchinson, ed. *The Works of George Herbert* (Oxford: Clarendon Press, 1941; repr. 1972), 66.

12. Quoted from Perry Miller, ed., *The American Puritans: Their Prose and Poetry* (Garden City: Doubleday, 1956), 82.

13. Patrick Grant, *Images and Ideas in Literature of the English Renaissance* (London: MacMillan Press, 1979), 82–83.

14. Ibid., 82; Rosemund Tuve, *Images and Themes in Five Poems by Milton* (Cambridge, Mass.: Harvard University Press, 1957), 130ff., 154.

15. *The Letters of the Rev. John Wesley, A.M.* (5 vols.; ed. John Telford; London: Epworth Press, 1931; repr., 1960).

16. Quoted from David L. Jeffrey, ed., *A Burning and a Shining Light: English Spirituality in the Age of Wesley* (Grand Rapids: Eerdmans, 1987), 302.

17. Ibid.

18. E.g., R. Steele's *The Christian Hero, Spectator,* no. 248; Henry Fielding's "Of True Greatness."

19. "Hymn to the Supreme Being" (1756) in *The Collected Poems of Christopher Smart* (ed. Norman Callan; London: Routledge and Kegan Paul, 1949), 244–48.

20. Charles F. Bahmueller, *The National Charity Company: Jeremy Bentham's Silent Revolution* (Berkeley: University of California Press, 1981).

21. Paul M. Zall, ed. *Literary Criticism of William Wordsworth* (Lincoln: University of Nebraska Press, 1966), 52.

22. M. H. Abrams, *Natural Supernaturalism: Tradition and Revolution in Romantic Literature* (The Norton Library; New York: Norton, 1971), 294–97.

23. Quoted from David Lee Clark, ed., *Shelley's Prose or The Trumpet of a Prophecy* (Albuquerque: University of New Mexico Press, 1954), 277, 282–83.

24. From "On the Manners of the Ancient Greeks," see Clark, *Shelley's Prose*, 220.
25. Abrams, *Natural Supernaturalism*, 297.
26. *The Works of Thomas Carlyle in Thirty Volumes* (New York: AMS Press, 1969), 10:257, 272–74.
27. G. K. Chesterton's book-length study of his friend Shaw continues a debate over the meaning of charity which had been at the core of their testy friendship for many years.
28. John Keble, "Second Sunday after Trinity," in *The Christian Year* (New York: Hurst, 1893), 142–43.

Chapter 5

1. John F. A. Sawyer, *The Fifth Gospel: Isaiah in the History of Christianity* (Cambridge: Cambridge University Press, 1996).
2. Prologue to translation of Isaiah in *Biblia Sacra iuxta Vulgatam versionem* (2d ed.; R. Weber [Stuttgart, 1975]), 12.1096.
3. Sawyer, *Fifth Gospel*, 11.
4. Ibid, 26–28.
5. Cf. Sawyer, *Fifth Gospel*, 126–40.
6. Ibid., 130.
7. *White Jacket*, 152–53.
8. Daniel Berrigan, *Isaiah: Spirit of Courage, Gift of Tears* (Minneapolis: Fortress Press, 1996).
9. Berrigan, *Isaiah*, 12.
10. Ibid., 33.
11. Ibid., 35.
12. Ibid., 14.
13. Ibid., 60.
14. Ibid., 52.
15. Ibid., 109.
16. Ibid., 63.
17. Ibid., 118.
18. Ibid., 66.
19. *The Works of John Newton* (London: Hamilton, Adams, 1820; repr. Edinburgh: Banner of Truth, 1985), 4:68–69.
20. Ibid, 4:208.

Chapter 6

1. The allusion is to Proverbs 14:6. Unless otherwise noted, all Chaucer references are from F. N. Robinson, ed., *The Works of Geoffrey Chaucer* (2d ed.; Cambridge, Mass.: Riverside Press, 1961).

2. The terms are, of course, Northrop Frye's, and inasmuch as the reference is to a kind of "romance" historiography here, I intend the distinction pretty much in his sense. See his *Secular Scripture*.

3. Petrarch had anticipated Chaucer in considering, to the point of preference, Ovid's version: see *Familiares* 9.5 and *Seniles* 1.4; 4.5.

4. Esp. in Benjamin G. Koonce, *Chaucer and the Tradition of Fame: Symbolism in the House of Fame* (Princeton: Princeton University Press, 1966). For an alternate view, compatible with the present hypothesis, see William S. Wilson, "Exegetical Grammar in the *House of Fame*," *English Language Notes* 1 (1964): 244–48.

5. See C. David Benson, *The History of Troy in Middle English Literature* (Woodbridge, Suffolk: D. S. Brewer, 1980). Benson notes the confidence with which historical truth was ascribed to the Troy versions: "The Middle English historians of Troy affirm their common dedication to both history and poetry in their individual prologues. The expressed goal [. . .] is identical: the historical record must be preserved completely" (35). Cf. *Troilus and Creseyde*, however, where he notes an exception; that while Chaucer expects his readers to know the Troy history, he "feels under no obligation to reproduce this history accurately or in full" (134).

6. John Wyclif, *De veritate sacrae scripturae* (ed. R. Buddenseig; 3 pts; vol. 18 of *Wyclif's Latin Works*; London: Wyclif Society, 1905–1907), 1:228–29, 237; cf. 1:51–55.

7. I refer here to Koonce, *Chaucer and the Tradition of Fame*, especially, whose detailed work on the typology of the poem opens up many of the questions pursued here.

8. Esp. Bernardus Silvestris, *Commentum super sex libros Aeneidos Virgilii.*

9. C. S. Lewis, "Historicism," in *Fernseed and Elephants* (Glasgow: Collins, 1975), 59.

10. Cf. also Boethius, *De consolatione philosophiae*, 1.pr.3. The desert could also invoke biblical counterparts, of course: the desert of Moses' canticle (Deut 32:10–12), Ezekiel's desert (Ezek 37:1–14), the desert of Jeremiah (2:6; 17:6–8; 50:12–13), or Isaiah. Cf. Sheila Delany, "Phantom and the *House of Fame*," *Chaucer Review* 2 (1967): 67–74.

11. Cf. W. S. Wilson, "The Eagle's Speech in Chaucer's *House of Fame*," *Quarterly Journal of Speech* 50 (1964): 153–58; Charles P. Tisdale, "The House of Fame: Virgilian Reason and Boethian Wisdom," *Comparative Literature* 25 (1973): 247–61. In *De consolatione* 4.1, Lady Philosophy offers Boethius "swift wings to soar beyond the heavens" to the "host of stars," where "the Lord of kings holds His scepter, governing the reins of the world." Boethius is told that when he arrives at this place he will exclaim "this is my own country"—something which most pointedly does not happen to Chaucer. [Translation of *De consolatione* is from Richard Green, *The Consolation of Philosophy* (New York: Bobbs-Merrill, 1962).]

12. E.g., Augustine, *De consensus evangelistarum*, 1.6.9. Cf. John M. Steadman, "Chaucer's Eagle: A Contemplative Symbol," *Publications of the Modern Language Assocation of America* 75 (1960): 153–59. Chaucer may have in mind Ezekiel's eagle. Pierre Bersuire, in book 15 of his *Reductorium morale*, justifies his moralizing of Ovid by arguing that *fabulae* are used in many passages of Sacred Scripture. One of his two exemplary instances is Ezekiel 17:3, "where we read how the eagle with great wings carried away the branch of the cedar. The *poetae*, inventors of *fabulae*, composed in a similar way; by figments of this kind they wished truths to be understood" (*Reductorium morale, liber XV: De formis figurisquae deorum* [orig. pub. Paris, 1509; Utrecht: Instituut vor Laat Latÿn der Rÿksuniversiteit, 1960], 4). The eagle was also an heraldic symbol for John of Gaunt.

13. Cf. John Leyerle, "Chaucer's Windy Eagle," *University of Toronto Quarterly* 40 (1971): 247–65.

14. Ovid, *Metamorphoses* 11.592ff.

15. "Thus it is said: Awake, you that sleep, and arise from that dead, and Christ shall give you light." (This is the passage, much commented on from Augustine forward, which speaks of "redeeming the time, because the days are evil." See *Confessions*, book 10).

16. Cf. David M. Bevington, "The Obtuse Narrator in Chaucer's *House of Fame*," *Speculum* 36 (1961): 288–98.

17. John H. Fisher, ed., *The Complete Poetry and Prose of Geoffrey Chaucer* (2d ed.; New York: Holt, Rinehart and Winston, 1989).

18. Cf. Dante's *Paradiso* 13–27.

19. Guiseppe Mazzotta, *Dante, Poet of Desert: History and Allegory in the Divine Comedy* (Princeton: Princeton University Press, 1979), writes that for Dante the providential "*opus restaurationis* is also of the temporal order, and [. . .] Dante shows how Roman history is constitutive of the redemptive process" (64). See Mazzotta's fourth chapter, "Vergil and Augustine," and Charles T. Davis, *Dante and the Idea of Rome* (Oxford: Clarendon Press, 1957), where Davis argues that Dante's Vergil becomes "a bridge between the two Romes" (137).

20. See Morton Bloomfield, *Piers Plowman as a Fourteenth Century Apocalypse* (New York: Knopf, 1963), 66–77.

21. John Wyclif, *Sermones* (cd. J. Loserth; 4 pts; vol. 7 of *Wyclif's Latin Works*; London: Wyclif Society, 1887–1890), 4:189–90, 206–7. See also *Select English Works of John Wyclif* (ed. Thomas Arnold; 3 vols.; Oxford: Clarendon Press, 1869–1871), 2:407.

22. Cf. Koonce, *Chaucer and the Tradition of Fame*, 181–85. Koonce itemizes medieval allegorizations of the account in Ezekiel 40:1–2 and 2 Kings 25, which identify the captivity of Jerusalem with the siege and captivity of the Holy Church by the force of Satan in the last days. This typology for the text

may have had some appeal in 1378, the date of Chaucer's poem and the time of the papal Schism.

23. Wyclif, *Comm. In Ezek.*, in Ms. Magdalen Coll., Oxford 117, 176a.

24. Wyclif argues that the prophetic books have a special form, both in his lectures on Isaiah and in his prologue to Isaiah. See *Wycliffite Version of the Holy Bible* (ed. J. Forshall and F. Madden; 4 vols.; Oxford: Oxford University Press, 1850), 3:224–25.

25. Koonce, *Chaucer and the Tradition of Fame*, esp. 105, 106; 178–82.

26. Nicholas of Lyra, in his *Postilla* on Ezekiel (in *Biblia Sacra cum Glossa Ordinaria*, etc. (ed. J. Meursium; Antwerp, 1634), writes: *scilicet idoli zeli quod erat iuxta introitum portae, et illi idolo erat altare constitutum, a quo denominabatur illa porta* and adds the following point by way of moraliter: *Idolatria secunda, est multorum simulacrum, quae tangitur ibi* [. . .] (1129). He observes further, of vv. 14–17, that the women are weeping for Adonis, "which is to say, the love of Venus." He notes that Rabbi Solomon identifies the Hebrew *Thammuz* with the idol, as with the sin *luxuria*, saying that such languishing after Venus is a kind of sickness unto death, a form of idolatry. Wyclif makes points on Ezekiel 8:17: "Sic stulti Christiani delusi detergunt pulverem ymaginum ad ungendum oculos male sanos." Elsewhere he refers to v. 10: "alle idols of the hous of Israel [. . .] peyntid in the wall al aboute in cumpas" (*Wycliffite Version*, 515).

27. The Vulgate is actually: *in abscondito cubilis sui.* Wyclif translates: "ech in the hid place of his couch." (*Wycliffite Version*, 516).

28. Lyra's *Postilla* includes a diagram of the historical temple described in chapter 8, which has three "frames," and a contrasting diagram of the future temple (ch. 40), in which the structure is seen as significantly changed. Here Lyra draws, as before, three "courts" (*atrium immundorum circuitus; atrium mundorum; atrium sacerdotum*), but structures the diagram in such a way that these constitute a series of frames for a fourth entity which may not be explicitated yet, in history, and which is the true inner sanctum, the *templum* to be revealed (1125, 1366). But cf. Helen Rosenau, "The Architecture of Nicolaus de Lyra's Temple Illustrations and the Jewish Tradition," *Journal of Jewish Studies* 25 (1974): 294–304. The Wyclif translation calls the outer porch of the temple "the utmer porche, or *large hous*" (Forshall and Madden, 596). Throughout the prophets the translation regularly employs *hous* to translate "temple bildid of Salomon" (see gloss *Wycliffite Version*, 237).

29. Lyra comments: *dominus ibidem: non solum per essentiam, potentiam, et praesentiam, sicut est, aliis locis: sed etiam per specialem suorum beneficiorum influentiam* (1467). The Wycliffite translations restrain the copula: "The Lord there" (*Wycliffite Version*, 620).

30. E.g., G. A. Cooke, *Ezekiel* (The International Critical Commentary 21; Edinburgh: T. & T. Clark, 1936), xvii; and John B. Taylor, *Ezekiel: An*

Introduction and Commentary (Tyndale Old Testament Commentaries; London: Tyndale Press, 1969).

31. Lyra, *Postilla*, 1365–67; The Wycliffite Bible prologue connects Ezekiel directly to St. John's Apocalypse. The prologue to all the prophetic books argues that the first intention of the prophets is to capitulate in their discourse the whole history of salvation.

32. Cf. Sheila Delaney, "Chaucer's *House of Fame*: The Poetics of Skeptical Fideism," *Dissertation Abstracts* 28 (1967): 178A–83A (Columbia), and her "Phantom and the *House of Fame*," *Chaucer Review* 2 (1967): 67–74.

33. Paul Ricoeur, *History and Truth* (Evanston, Ill.: Northwestern University Press, 1965), 21.

34. In this his line of reflection anticipates early modernity in general and the Reformation in particular, and his way of getting at this aspect of the question of authority is akin to Wyclif. For a general contextualization regarding the latter, see Joan Lockwood O'Donovan, *Theology of Law and Authority in the English Reformation* (Atlanta: Scholars Press, 1991). Cf. Owen Barfield, *Saving the Appearances: A Study in Idolatry* (London: Faber and Faber, 1957), 126–33; Owen Barfield, *History in English Words* (Grand Rapids: Eerdmans, 1967), 172; and Ricoeur, *History and Truth*, 35.

35. Ricoeur, *History and Truth*, 38.

36. Ibid., 29, 36–40. For a fuller development of this point see my *People of the Book*.

37. It is surely one of the poem's nicer ironies that its ending should carry us back to the occasion of its primary question, the plight of Dido. It was she who said: "O, soth ys, every thing ys wist / though hit be kevered with the myst" (351–52), so echoing the Gospel, "there is nothing covered that shall not be revealed; neither hid, that shall not be known" (Luke 12:2 KJV).

38. Mazzotta, *Dante, Poet of the Desert*, 256.

39. Ibid.

40. Cf. Walter Benjamin, *Illuminations* (ed. Hannah Arendt; London: Jonathan Cape, 1970), who argues that in a good traditional storyteller, the product is a kind of wisdom literature in which "counsel is less an answer to a question than a proposal concerning the continuation of a story which is just unfolding" (86).

41. My own imagination suggests to me St. John of the Cross:

> The Father utters one Word and that Word is his Son,
> and he utters him forever in everlasting silence
> and in silence the soul has to hear him.

R. J. Schoeck has offered plausible evidence, on the other hand, to suggest that the poem may have been recited for members of the Inns of Court during an Advent celebration, about the time of the literal December tenth date, which often connected, in fact, readings from Ezekiel with the Advent liturgy. See his "A Legal Reading of Chaucer's *House of Fame*," *University of Toronto Quarterly* 23 (1953): 185–92. Schoeck's reading seems to me to add another conceivable context for that implied here. I am less content with his identification of the "man of gret auctorite" as the Master of Revels. (At least in the literal sense!) One can imagine in such a setting, however, what might come after the unfinished last sentence of the poem. From the Advent liturgy, and originally occasioned by the oppression of that very historicism to which Vergil gave "fame," it might be: "Fear not, for behold I bring you good tydings, of great joy, which shall be to all people."

Chapter 7

1. Description of the Friar in the General Prologue.
2. Arnold Williams, "Chaucer and the Friars," *Speculum* 28 (1953): 506. Williams is not alone in this reading: see also Edwin A. Greenlaw, "A Note on Chaucer's *Prologue*," *Modern Language Notes* 23 (1908): 144; and G. L. Kittredge, "Chaucer's *Prologue 256*," *Modern Language Notes* 23 (1908): 200; Walter W. Skeat, *Notes to the Canterbury Tales* (vol. 5 of *The Complete Works of Geoffrey Chaucer*, ed. Walter W. Skeat; Oxford: Clarendon Press, 1900), 28; and Robinson, ed., *The Works of Geoffrey Chaucer*.
3. See Frederick Pollock, *The Land Laws* (2d ed.; London: Macmillan, 1887), 136. Also Thomas Hahn and Richard W. Kaueper, "Text and Context: Chaucer's *Friar's Tale*," *Studies in the Age of Chaucer: The Yearbook of the New Chaucer Society* 5 (1983): 67–101.
4. Marc Bloch, *Feudal Society* (Chicago: University of Chicago Press, 1961), 231.
5. Ibid., 145–243. See also H. G. Richardson and G. O. Sayles, *The Governance of Medieval England from the Conquest to Magna Carta* (Edinburgh: Edinburgh University Press, 1963), ch. 4, esp. 105–11. Cf. Daniel T. Kline, "'Myne by Right': Oath Making and Intent in the Friar's Tale," *Philological Quarterly* 77 (1998): 271–93.
6. Bloch, *Feudal Society*, 228, 231–34.
7. See Mortimer J. Donovan, "The *Moralitee* of the Nun's Priest's Sermon," *Journal of English and Germanic Philology* 52 (1953): 498ff. The ordination of bishops followed the same conventionalized form of oath and ceremony, a form which has been altered little. See Michel Andrieu, *Les Ordains Romains du Haut Moyen Age* (Louvain: "Spicilegium sacrum lovaniense" bureaux, 1931), vol. 1; *Ordinale Sarum sive Directorium Sacerdotum* (ed. C. Wordsworth; Henry Bradshaw Society; London: Henry Bradshaw Society, 1900), vol. 20.
8. Bloch, *Feudal Society*, 115, plate III. See also David Williams, "From Grammar's Pan to Logic's Fire: Intentionality in Chaucer's *Friar's Tale*," in

Literature and Ethics (ed. Gary Wihl and David Williams; Kingston: McGill-Queens University Press, 1988), 77–95.

9. In addition to the passages quoted, see *Friar's Tale*, 1373–75, 1389–91, 1448–53; *Romaunt of the Rose*, 2255; see also 6832–38, where *rente* is involved as a pun. In addition to these and the quotation from the Wakefield *Coliphizacio* (n. 22, below), some other notable examples of *rente* with the explicitly spiritual meaning here suggested are to be found in *Piers the Plowman* (ed. Walter W. Skeat; 2 vols.; Oxford, repr. 1961), vol. 1, "B," Passus VI, 88–92; in John Skelton, *Magnyficence* (ed. R. L. Ramsay; Early English Text Society, Extra Series 98 (Oxford: Oxford University Press, 1925; repr., 1958), 71; John Donne, *The Sermons of John Donne* (ed. Evelyn M. Simpson and George R. Potter; 10 vols.; Berkeley: University of California Press, 1962), 8:2.61–62.

10. St. Augustine, *Sermones in Lectionibus, Novae Testimentae* 87 (Migne, PL 38:531); for St. Bernard, see his *Sermones in Cantica Canticorum* 58 (Migne, PL 183:1056–57). Cf. Athanasius, *Letters* 6 (*NPNF*² 4:521).

11. Johannes Amundesham, *Annales Monasterii S. Albani* (ed. Henry Thomas Riley; Rerum britannicarum medii ævi scriptores 28, 5; London: Longmans, Green, 1870–71), 457. Cf. the similar formula quoted in Mary Caroline Spalding, *Charters of Christ* (Bryn Mawr College Monograph Series 15; Bryn Mawr, Penn.; Bryn Mawr College, 1914), 4.

12. Pierre Bursuire (Berchorius), notable fourteenth-century lexicographer, illustrates the reciprocality of our relationship to God when defining rent (*reddere*): *Nota quae reddere presupponit promissione, receptionem, vel aliqualem obligatione. Et quia homo obligator et tenetur deo, proximo, sibi et prelato, quia etiam deus tenetur homini sicut creator creature, factor facture, genitore geneturae, hinc et quod aliqua reddit deus, aliqua reddit homo, et aliqua sunt reddeda deo, et aliqua homini* (*Dictionarii sev repertorii moralis* [Cologne, 1517]).

13. *The Orcherd of Syon* (ed. Phyllis Hodgson and Gabriel M. Liegey; Early English Text Series 258; Oxford: Oxford University Press, 1966), 64–65.

14. See *Thomas de Eccleston De adventu fratrum minorum in Angliam* (in *Monumenta Franciscanum*; ed. J. S. Brewer; Britannicarum medii ævi scriptores 4, 1; London: Longmans, Green, 1858), 61. Franciscan Friar Thomas Docking, explicitly connecting the duty of the brothers with the vineyard parable, goes on to say that "A clerk who accepts the goods of a church and neglects his duties is as much a thief as a labourer, who takes his wages and does not do his work" (*Franciscan Papers, Lists, and Documents* [ed. A. G. Little; Manchester: Manchester University Press, 1943], 107, see also 106–8).

15. *Cursor mundi* (ed. R. Morris; Early English Text Society, Original Series 66; London: K. Paul, Trench, Trübner & Co., 1887).

16. St. Augustine makes this clear in his commentary on the vineyard parables in *Sermones in Lectionibus, Novae Testimentae* 87 (Migne, PL 38:530). The *Bible*

Moralisée illustrates the vineyard parable with a parallel picture showing the homage investiture of friars as laborers in God's vineyard. See *La Bible moralisée* (5 vols.; ed. A. Laborde; Paris: Pour les membres de la Société, 1913), 3:512.

17. *The Glossa Ordinaria* (Migne, PL 114), commenting on Matthew 21:38, calls the wicked husbandmen *principes sacerdotum* ("chief priests"), who were trying to obliterate the inheritance of Christ, attempting to "persuade people of a justice which is the letter of the law" *(dum fide ejus existencia justitiam quae ex lege est, gentibus persuadere conabantur).* In Chaucer, for Pharisees and Sadducees read "Friars" and "Summoners." Cf. *The Romance of the Rose* (trans. H. W. Robbins; [New York: Dutton, 1962], 238, lines 140–41) where False-Seeming connects himself with this group, and lines 110–11, for which Chaucer borrows the attribute of the Friar which he translates in the lines initially quoted. Cf. V. A. Kolve, "'Man in the Middle': Art and Religion in Chaucer's *Friar's Tale*," *Studies in the Age of Chaucer* 12 (1990): 3–46.

18. In *Piers the Plowman,* "B," Passus X, 306–7, Learning described the contemporary state of religious orders in the following terms:

> Ac now is Religioun a ryder • a rowmer bi stretes,
> A leder of louedayes • and a londe-bugger.

See also the devil's "rentals" in *The Towneley Plays,* 30 (*The Judgment*) (ed. George England and Alfred W. Pollard; Early English Text Society, Extra Series 71; London: K. Paul, Trench, Trübner & Co, 1897), 133ff.

19. Bersuire further says of *reddere: Adverte tamen quae quidam sunt similes sangui* sugae, *quae sanguinem bene bibit et recepit, ipsum tamen non nisi per violentiam reddit, sic sunt multi qui semper solunt recipere, et nihil reddere* (see n. 12). On "entente" see Richard H. Passon, "'Entente' in Chaucer's *Friar's Tale*," *Chaucer Review* 2 (1968): 166–71.

20. *Old English Dictionary*—it is associated also with concubinage. Cf. *Romaunt of the Rose,* 6840. This usage had dropped out of the language by 1825.

21. *Encyclopaedia Britannica,* 11th ed., 23:102.

22. *The Wakefield Pageants in the Towneley Cycle* (ed. A. C. Cawley; Old and Middle English Texts 1; Manchester: Manchester University Press, 1958).

23. Presumption is the basic element in the "unpardonable sin" (Ps 18:13—*Douai*), the unhappy fault of the Friar's Summoner.

Chapter 8

1. See Alfred Harbage and Samuel Schoenbaum, eds., *Annals of English Drama, 975–1700* (Philadelphia: University of Pennsylvania Press, 1964). The plays, including *Herod's Slaughter of the Innocents,* and an imperfect fragment of the morality *Wisdom, Who is Christ,* have been edited by Frederick James Furnivall,

The Digby Plays (Early English Text Society, Extra Series 70; London: K. Paul, Trench, Trübner & Co., 1896). Cf. E. Catherine Dunn, "The Origin of the Middle English Saints' Plays," in *The Medieval Drama and Its Claudelian Revival: Papers from the 3rd Symposium in Comparative Literature, 1968* (ed. E. Catherine Dunn, Tatiana Zurnitch Fotitch, and Bernard Mann Peebles; Washington D.C.: Catholic University of America Press, 1970), 1–15.

2. Cf. Darryll Grantley, "The Source of the Digby Mary Magdalen," *Notes and Queries* 31 (1984): 457–59.

3. Harold C. Gardiner, S.J. *Mysteries' End: An Investigation of the Last Days of the Medieval Religious Stage* (New Haven: Yale University Press, 1946), 54–57.

4. Documents reproduced by Glynne Wickham, *Early English Stages 1300–1600* (London and Henley: Routledge & Kegan Paul, 1980), vol. II (i), 62–63.

5. *Monumenta Franciscana* (ed. John Sherren Brewer and Richard Howlett; 2 vols.; Rerum britannicarum medii ævi scriptores 4; 1858, 1882; repr. Wiesbaden: Kraus Reprint Co., 1965), 1:606ff.

6. *Reliquae Antiquae* (ed. Thomas Wright and J. O. Halliwell; London, 1841) 2:42–57.

7. *The Vita Sancti Malchi of Reginald of Canterbury* (ed. Levi R. Lind; Urbana, Ill.: The University of Illinois Press, 1942), 40–41.

8. *Gregorii Eps. Turoniensis Liber Vitae Patrum* (in T. Mommsen et al., *Monumenta Germaniae Historica,* Scriptores Rerum Merovingicarum, I), 662–63.

9. Furnivall, *The Digby Plays.*

10. A good conservative example of a legendary life is afforded by Carl Horstmann, ed. *The Early South English Legendary; or Lives of the Saints.* Ms. Laud, 108 in the Bodleian Library (London: N. Trübner & Co., 1887; repr., New York: Kraus Reprint Co., 1973), 462–80.

11. Charles W. Jones, *Saints' Lives and Chronicles in Early England* (Ithaca: Cornell University Press, 1947), 52.

12. See here Theresa Coletti, "Paupertas est Donum Dei: Hagiography, Lay Religion and the Economics of Salvation in the Digby Mary Magdalene," *Speculum* 76 (2001): 337–78. Cf. Scott Boehnen, "The Aesthetics of 'Sprawling' Drama: the Digby Mary Magdalene as Pilgrim's Play," *Journal of English and Germanic Philology* 98 (1999): 325–52.

13. Jones, *Saints' Lives and Chronicles in Early England,* 96.

14. St. Augustine, *De doctrina christiana* 1.8. See here Coletti, "Paupertas est Donum Dei," 337–78.

15. It was Auerbach, *Mimesis,* 136–39, who demonstrated the fusion in the twelfth-century *Jeu d'Adam* of two *styles* in the cycle drama: *sublimitas* and *humilitas*. In the saints' plays, however, what actually occurs is a fusion of genres, whose employment of style, as in *Mary Magdalene,* is much more even. Containing

virtually none of the "grotesquery" which Auerbach feels led to the downfall of the plays, *Mary Magdalene* suggests that the saints' plays problem was their particular expression of the exemplarist view of history itself. The criticisms of even Wyclifite reformists were directed not against grotesquery (cf. passages cited), but against a lack of faithfulness to biblical (or ecclesiastical) history. Cf. Victor Scherb, "Blasphemy and the Grotesque in the Digby Mary Magdalene," *Studies in Philology* 96 (1999): 225–40; also Stefania Maria Maci, "The Language of Mary Magdalene of the Bodleian MS Digby 133," *Linguistica e Filologia* 10 (1999): 105.

16. See Carleton Brown, "An Early Mention of a St. Nicholas Play in England," *Studies in Philology* 28 (1931): 594–601. Most scholars have followed Brown in regarding this reference as sufficient evidence that saints' plays were an established genre here by about 1250.

17. See Arnaldo Fortini, *La Lauda in Assisi e le origini del Teatro Italiano* (Assisi, 1863), 270ff.

18. Ibid., 279; cf. M. D. Anderson, *Drama and Imagery in English Medieval Churches* (Cambridge: Cambridge University Press, 1963), 51ff.

19. I do not mean, of course, that these were necessarily the only styles, nor that they represent the whole range of staging. Saints' plays were performed in fields (as a St. George play at Bassingbourne), on pageant-wagons (as Canterbury's 1504 Thomas à Becket), in a small park (St. Kathcrine at Coventry, 1490), in the round (as *St. Meriasek* in Cornwall), or even in a church (Braintree, Essex, for a play of St. Andrew in 1525).

20. Wickham, *Early English Stages*, vol. 1, 223, records directions for another possible ship, constructed for a tournament pageant in 1501; "a goodly shippe borne up wt men, wt in himself (the hero of the day) ryding in the myddes [. . .] and the sides of the ship covered wt cloth peynted after the colour or likeness of water."

21. *Saint Bonaventure's De reductione artium ad theologiam* (ed. and trans. Sister Emma Thérèse Healy (St. Bonaventure, NY: St. Bonaventure College, 1939), 38.

22. Ibid., 40.

Chapter 9

1. The *Haywain* has been given a variety of modern interpretations. Jaques Combe, *Hieronymus Bosch* (Paris: Pierre Tisné, 1946), placed it in the context of fifteenth-century woodcuts illustrating the metamorphoses of Ulysses's companions, and, like Ludvig von Baldass, *Hieronymus Bosch* (London: Thames and Hudson, 1960) saw in the Hell panel explicit punishment for the Seven Deadly Sins. Baldass (25, 37) also distinguished in the center panel special representa-

tions of the seven sins, here following the very old reading of José de Siguenza, *Tercia parte de la Historia O. S. Jeronimo* (ed. Juan Catalina Garcia López; 2d ed.; 2 vols.; Madrid: Bailly-Bailliére é Hijos, 1907–1909). Charles de Tolnay, *Hieronymus Bosch* (Basel: Les Editions Holbein, 1937) related the wain to a Flemish proverb, "The world is a haystack, and each man grabs from it what he can," a proverb subsequently proved modern by Jan Grauls, "Ter Verklaring van Bosch en Broegel," *Gentsche Bijdragen tot de Kunstgeschiedenis* 6 [1939–1940]: 139–60) who went on to equate the hay with worldly vanity. None of these interpretations, however, integrate more than a few details in the panel, nor speak to its reading as an altarpiece.

Cf. more recently, Walter Bosing, *Hieronymous Bosch, c1450–1516: Between Heaven and Earth* (London: Taschen, 2000), and Thierry Boucquay, "Vessel of Madness: Bosch's *Haywain* as Farcical Intercomposition," *Fifteenth Century Studies* 16 (1990): 43–57. Following his revolutionary interpretation of what has been previously called "The Garden of Earthly Delights," E. H. Gombrich, in "Bosch's '*Garden of Earthly Delights*': A Progress Report," *Journal of the Warburg and Courtald Institute* 32 (1969): 162–70, felt that the painting (*Sicut erat in diebus Noe*) "can be more easily imagined in a chapel or church even than the [. . .] *Haywain*" (167). Given earlier interpretations of the lesser triptych, that must certainly be so. In these pages, however, I wish to place the *Haywain* firmly in the liturgical altarpiece tradition. Professor Gombrich read the first version of this essay in 1970, and expressed doubt that there was anything positive in Bosch's treatment of the musical couple. While I still do, his criticism has caused me to re-examine and revise the interpretation which now follows. Similarly with Kolve, " 'Man in the Middle',": 5–46: Kolve accepts my argument for the pertinence of Thomas à Kempis and the hay/chaff imagery, but has reservations about the concord/discord analogue (esp. 16n, 17n, 21n).

2. See L. Lebeer, "Het Hooi en de Hooiwagen," *Gentsche Bijdragen tot de Kunstgeschiedenis* 5 (1938): 141–77. The American expression, "That's all hooey," is defined as late as M. M. Matthews, *Dictionary of Americanisms on Historical Principles* (Chicago: University of Chicago Press, 1951), 828, as "fanciful." It seems likely, however, that *al hooi* is yet another contribution of the Dutch of New York to American slang, its original meaning certainly fitting contemporary American usage in a more direct way than the currently recorded definition.

3. Charles D. Cutler, *Northern Painting from Pucelle to Bruegel* (New York: Holt, Rinehart, and Winston, 1968), 200.

4. For an excellent discussion of medieval musical theory in the Boethian tradition see David S. Chamberlain, "Philosophy of Music in the *Consolatio* of Boethius," *Speculum* 45 (1970): 80–97. I am also indebted in the following discussion to D. W. Robertson, Jr., *A Preface to Chaucer: Studies in Medieval Perspectives* (Princeton: Princeton University Press, 1963), 114–37, and to

Gretchen L. Finney, "Music: a Book of Knowledge in Renaissance England," *Studies in the Renaissance* 6 (London, 1959): 36–63.

5. Hugh of St. Victor, *Didascalicon* 2.12.3d.

6. This idea had been promulgated by Boethius, *Consolation of Philosophy* 2.m.8.; Cf. D. S. Chamberlain, "Philosophy of Music in the *Consolatio* of Boethius," 83. This relationship constitutes the number eight (octave) as of very special significance for the liturgy, as indeed is suggested even by the prevalence of octagonal shapes for baptismal fonts from the fourth through sixteenth centuries (St. Augustine, *De Trinitate*, 4.3; see E. Tyrell Green, *Baptismal Fonts* [London, Society for Promoting Christian Knowledge, 1928], 30; Richard Krautheimer, *Early Christian and Byzantine Architecture* [Harmondsworth: Penguin, 1965]; Franz Joseph Dölger, *Die Symbolik der Achtzahl* [Berlin, 1934]; Robertson, *Preface to Chaucer*, 124). It is in such contexts that music, when it proceeds according to ratio and harmony, can be seen to reflect the concord of Divine Love.

7. The expression comes from Ovid, *Fasti* 4 invoc.; see E. H. Alton, "The Medieval Commentators on Ovid's *Fasti*," *Hermathena* 44 (1926): 119–35; also John V. Fleming, *The Roman de la Rose: A Study in Allegory and Iconography* (Princeton: Princeton University Press, 1969), 191–92.

8. Albericus of London (Mythographicus Vaticanus Tertius), *Scriptores rerum mythicarum latini tres Romae nuper reperti* (ed. Georg Heinrich Bode; Cellis: E. H. C. Schulze, 1834), 239.

9. Here the sacred and profane Venus are seated on a sarcophagus filled with water, symbolic, according to one critic, of the baptism in which the old Venus gives way to the new and is then clothed in the righteousness of Divine Love: see Erwin Panofsky, *Problems in Titian* (New York: New York University Press, 1969), 110ff.

10. Bernard Sylvestris, *Comm. super sex libros Eneidos Virg.* (ed. Guilielmus Reidel; Griefswald: J. Abel, 1924), 9.

11. *Annotationes in Marcianum* (ed. Cora E. Lutz; Mediaeval Academy of America 34; Cambridge, Mass.: Mediaeval Academy of America, 1939), 13.

12. Robertson, *Preface to Chaucer*, 126. Cf. Folke Nordström, *Virtues and Vices in Fourteenth Century Corbels in the Choir of Uppsula Cathedral* (Stockholm: Almqvist & Wiksell, 1956), 99.

13. A standard introduction to the medieval commonplace of the "two songs" is St. Augustine's sermon *De cantico novo*, though the following excerpt from his popular exposition of Psalm 149 demonstrates the typical opposition: "The old man hath an old song, the new man a new song [. . .] Whoso loveth earthly things singeth and old song: let him that desireth to sing a new song, love the things of eternity. Love itself is new and eternal; therefore is it ever new, because it never groweth old [. . .] And this song is of peace, this song is of charity. Whoso severeth himself from the union of the saints, singeth not a new song; for he hath followed old strife, not new charity. In the new charity what is there?

Peace, the bond of an holy society, a spiritual union, a building of living stones," Augustine, *Expositions on the Book of Psalms* 149.1 (*NPNF*[1] 8:677).

14. Guido Faba, *Summa de viciis* (Paris, Bibliothèque Nationale lat. MS 8652A, folio 51v)—reproduced in Robertson, *Preface to Chaucer,* plate 34.

15. See Robert L. Delevoy, *Bosch: Biographical and Critical Study* (Cleveland: Skira, 1960), 8.

16. A text of the seven-year Brussels cycle is extant, and there are a few shorter plays such as the one-day condensation of sacred history known as *Eerste Bliscap,* which moves from Creation and Fall to the Assumption of the Virgin and warning of Doomsday much in the manner of the English *Ludus Coventriae,* but in only 2100 lines. See Theodoor Weevers, *Poetry of the Netherlands in its European Context, 1170–1930* (London: Athlone Press, 1960), 55–56.

17. See Edmond vander Straeten, *Le théâtre villageois en Flandre* (2 vols.; Brussels: A. Tillot et cie, 1881), 1:15; Laurence Craddock, O.F.M., "Franciscan Influences on Early English Drama," *Franciscan Studies* 10 (1950): 383–417.

18. vander Straeten, *Le théâtre villageois en Flandre,* 1:16.

19. Ibid., 1:25.

20. Ibid., 1:22, 38 ; and 1:23, where he quotes the *Comptes de la ville de Nieuport* for 1488 as follows: "Den rethorisienen van Ghend die t'Aelst speelding in t'ommegaen vander processie, een scoon spel lij kannen van gheliken wijn xl s. vj den." It is apparent that these were nearly always festive occasions, and accounts like the above along with paintings like the one by Pieter Balten in the Rijksmuseum, Amsterdam (included in Phyllis Hartnoll, *Concise History of Theatre* [New York: H. N. Abrams, 1968], pl. 44), make it fairly clear that with plays processional or stationary, community revelry was a condition of their production.

21. For a good recent treatment see V. A. Kolve, *The Play Called Corpus Christi* (Stanford: Stanford University Press, 1966); also Grace Frank, *The Medieval French Drama* (Oxford: Clarendon Press, 1954).

22. See L. M. J. Delaisse, "A la recherche des origines de l'office du Corpus Christi dans les MSS liturgiques," *Scriptorium* 4 (1950): 220–39; P. Browe, S.J., "Die Ausbreitung des Fronleichnams Festes," *Jahrbuch für Liturgiewissenschaft* 8 (1928): 107–44.

23. See *Textus antiqui de festo Corporis Christi* (ed. Peter Browe; Opuscula et textus, fasc. 4; Monasterii: Typis Aschendorff), 31ff; cf. Merle Pierson, "The Relation of the Corpus Christi Procession to the Corpus Play in England," *Transactions of the Wisconsin Academy of Sciences, Arts, and Letters* 18 (1915): 110–65; see also Glynne Wickham, *Early English Stages,* 4 vols. (London: Routledge, 1959), 1:122. (The Wain here in some respects evokes the *carro* [or *plaustra*] of Dante in the *Commedia* [*Inf.* 26.35; *Purg.* 32.95] and, like it, the *plaustrum* of 2 Kings 6, the cart that carries the ark of the covenant on its progress to the promised land, containing the Law, Aaron's rod, and the pot of manna.)

24. "Eenen Hoywagen daer op sittende eenen Sater ghenaempt Bedrieghelijck aen locken, achter volghende alle Natie van volck, treckende aen Het Hoy, als Woekeners, Cassiers, Creemers, etc., midts dat ertsch ghewin als hoy is." See P. de Keyser, "Rhetoricale Toelichting bij het Hooi en den Hooiwagen," *Gentsche Bijdragen tot de Kunstgeschiedenis* 6 (1939–1940): 127–33. (A hay cart with a satyr sitting on it to deceive and entice people of all kinds, such as usurers, money changers, merchants, etc. who follow the wagon, snatching at the hay, which stands for earthly gain); see n. 23; see William Dugdale, *Monasticon anglicanum* (ed. Caley, Ellis, and Bandinell; 8 vols.; London, 1830), 6:1553–54; see Francis Drake, *Eboracum: or, The History and Antiquities of the City of York* (2 vols.; London: W. Browyer, 1736), 2:app. xxix.

25. vander Straeten, *Le théâtre villageois en Flandre*, 1:23.

26. Ibid.; Charles de Tolnay, *Hieronymus Bosch, Kritischer Katalog der Werke* (Baden-Baden: Holle, 1973), 355, accepts 1510 as probable date for the work.

27. Delevoy, *Bosch*, 9–10.

28. Ibid., 10–11.

29. Ibid., 11, 15; see also Joannes Cornelius Antonius Hezenmans, *De Illustre Lieve-Vrouwe Broederschap in den Bosch* (Utrecht: Wed. J. R. Van Rossum, 1877). The relevant records are: Rekeningen van de Lieve-Vrouwe Broederschap, Provenciall Genootschap van Kunsten en wetenschappen in Noord-Brabant, Boisle-Duc; Register der namen en de wapenen der Heeren Beeedigde Broeders soo geestelijke als wereltlijke van de seer doorlugtige Broederschap van Onse Lieve Vrouw firme de Stad s'Hertogenbosch (idem); Registres de la chambre des comptes de Lille, année 1504. Archives du Département du Nord, Ref. F. 190; also Cornelis Rudolphus Hermans, *Bijdragen tot de Geschiedenis, Oudheden, Letteren . . . der Province Noord-Braband* (s'Hertogenbosch, 1845), vol. 1; cf. Père Gerlach, O.F.M. Cap., "Les sources pour l'étude de la vie de Jerome Bosch," *Gazette des Beaux-Arts* 71 (1968): 112–14; and for a discussion of the participation by artists in the mystery plays, see Leopold Schmidt, "Maler-Regisseure des Mittelalters," *Maske und Kothum* 4 (1958): 4ff; see also n. 30.

30. Delevoy, *Bosch*, 11.

31. Writing to his daughter from Lisbon, in 1581, Philip II said: "I regret that you and your brother were not able to see the procession [of Corpus Christi] as it takes place here, although it includes several devils resembling those in Bosch's paintings, [. . .]." (from *The Complete Paintings of Bosch* [ed. Mia Cinotti; London: Weidenfeld and Nicolson, 1969], 10); E. H. Gombrich has considered similarities of presentation in medieval Herod and Magi plays to Bosch's "Epiphany" ("The Evidence of Images," a study of modes of perception in art criticism, in *Interpretation: Theory and Practice* [ed. Charles S. Singleton; Baltimore: Johns Hopkins Press, 1969], 35–104, see esp. 83–87).

32. It is interesting that the figures in the left panel are the most beautifully proportioned (as we might expect of Eden), and that the figures tend to become much

less evenly proportioned as one moves from left to right in the center panel, until from its border into the right panel the degeneration to the utterly grotesque is made complete. The exception to this is the harmonious lovers and good angel, whose wings arched back toward Eden and upward tilted face help to suggest that in prayerful harmony even physical proportion may be restored.

33. The distinction is usually made either in terms of the wheat/chaff metaphor, as in St. Augustine's *On Christian Doctrine* or St. Gregory's introduction to his commentary on the Song of Songs, or in terms of kernel and shell—which amounts to the same image, as in Pseudo-Fulgentius's *De Thebiad,* Alanus de Insulis's *De planctu naturae,* Richard de Bury's *Philobiblion,* and elsewhere. Cf. nn. 33, 34. For a full treatment of this subject see Robertson, *A Preface to Chaucer* and Bernard F. Huppé, *Fruyt and Chaff: Studies in Chaucer's Allegories* (Princeton: Princeton University Press, 1963).

34. Augustine, *Doct. chr.* 3.5.9; St. Gregory, *Super Cantica canticorum* proem. (Migne, PL 79:471ff.); *Glossa ordinaria* (Migne, PL 114:82, etc).

35. *Glossa ordinaria* (Migne, PL 113:2151); cf. Isaiah 65:25 and *Glossa ordinaria* (Migne, PL 113:1311–12).

36. Thomas à Kempis, *The Imitation of Christ* 4.2.279, 4.11.303. Book 4 of *The Imitation of Christ* is entitled "A Devout Exhortation to the Holy Communion." References to *The Imitation of Christ* are from the edition by Leo Sherley-Price (New York: Penguin Books, 1952).

37. The missal quotes Ps 80:17, *Civabit eos ex adipe frumenti, alleluia,* etc.

38. Lebeer, "Het Hooi en de Hooiwagen," 152–55, discusses the connotations of *hooi* which identify it with grass and straw. The Middle Dutch term was somewhat wider of reference than our own word "hay" (see Johannes Franck, *Etymologisch Woordenboek der Nederlandsche taal, supplement* [ed. Nicolaas van Wijk ['s-Gravenhage: M. Nijhoff 1971], 260) as the color of the wain's cargo will suggest. It is straw-yellow. New-mown hay is greenish, old hay brown. Note the smaller snatches under the fallen friar and in the monk's sack, and for color and texture cf. the thatching edges of the stable roof in Bosch's *Madrid Epiphany.*

39. See Albert Hyma, *The Brethren of the Common Life* (Grand Rapids: Eerdmans, 1950); Bosch features Franciscans most prominently in the anticlerical satire of two of his best known paintings, the *Haywain,* and *Ship of Fools.*

40. Quoted in the original in vander Straeten, *Le théâtre villageois en Flandre,* 57–58:

> Qualyc kent men een priester, op strate vry,
> Voor een weerlyke; so moet by gecleet gaen;
> Een huicxken aen't lyf, cort van baten, fy!
> 't Mes aen de side hangt daer gereet aen:
> [. . .]

Van hooghen prelaten dient niet geseit hoe
Dat se sotheit tooghen den gemeenen loop:
't Sot bedryf geven sy haer digiteit toe,
Dat syt doen mogen voor den cleenen hoop;
Dus leggen si den simpelen aen de beenen den knoop,
Daer si over vallen, 't dient niet verswegen.
[. . .]
In 't toogen van sulex noit en was ghehoort,
Als dolende geleerde stellen voort;
Sy ons soberheit onderwysen,
En sy drinken daghelycx at versmoort,
Leerende paeys, en maken selfs discoort.
Oock seggen sy: schoot's overspels afrygsen,
Nochtans sy selve loopen en bysen
Met vrouwen, alsoo men dagelycs siet;
Sy leeren ons den arme spysen,
Selve ne gheven sy een myte niet.

41. Juan de Valdes, *The Christian Alphabet* (trans. Angel M. Mergal; The Library of Christian Classics 25; London: SCM Press, 1953–1966), 370. Valdes was influenced by Erasmus (who in turn had been educated by the Brethren of the Common Life of Bois-de-Duc), was educated by Franciscans—especially renegade and anticlerical Franciscans like Cardinal Cisneros—and was friendly with Franciscan mavericks of the sort who, like Bernardino Ochino, finally broke with the confraternities and brotherhoods and even carried some of them into the Reformation. These are exactly the sorts of anti-Franciscan former brothers to whom I think Bosch might well have looked. Certainly the sentiment of the passage cited suits the *Haywain*. See Hyma, *The Brethren of the Common Life*, passim.

42. *Glossa ordinaria* (Migne, PL 114:38–39).

43. Ibid., 38.

44. Laborde, *La Bible moralisée*, 2:pl. 368, which illuminates Jeremiah 23 with a series of eight illustrations that demonstrate the reasonable orthodoxy of "anticlericalism" in certain cases. In one of these, a cleric and a woman make love, while two other clerics toy with what may be a bowl of sacramental wafers. The series closes with a depiction of Franciscan Friars preaching to simoniac clerics who then give up their money and idols for the Word.

45. Browe, *Textus antiqui de festo Corporis Christi*; the text is Lev 21:6. Chapter 5 of the section on Holy Communion in the *Imitation of Christ* is addressed specifically to priests administering the Sacrament, that their preparation should be most careful.

46. *Glossa ordinaria* (Migne, PL 114:821).

47. Baldass, *Hieronymus Bosch*, 85, has already noticed this.

48. See Prosper Guéranger, *The Liturgical Year* (trans. Dom Laurence Shepherd; 8 vols.; Dublin: Duffy, 1879), 7:230ff. This suggests another avenue of continuity between the panels, since, as F. Oppenheim points out in *Enciclopedia Cattolica* (ed. P. Paschini et. al.; 12 vols.; Città del Vaticano, 1949–1954); 4:612, the Host was usually placed in the chalice for transport by the wagon in the Corpus Christi procession. The antlered hart-grotesques in the right panel near the vainly questing cleric would, in a similar vein, seem to involve the first verse of Psalm 41 from the second nocturn for Corpus Christi: "As the hart pants after the water brooks, so pants my soul after thee, O God" (Latin text repr. in Guéranger 231).

49. For example, St. Paul in 1 Corinthians 9:9–10 (on not muzzling the ox); or Gregory the Great in his *In primum Regnum expositiones* (*Exposition for 1 Kings*) where he also affirms that oxen are types for the *praedicatores ecclesiae* (PL 79.318; cf. PL 113.476).

50. In his commentary on Psalm 9, Augustine connects "the song of the diapsalma" with the "hidden joy [. . .] of the separation which is now made, not in place, but in the affections of the heart, between sinners and the righteous, as of the corn from the chaff, as yet on the floor. And then follows, 'Let the sinners be turned into hell' (v. 17): that is, let them be given into their own hands, when they are spared, and let them be ensnared in deadly delight" (my translation).

51. Isidore of Seville, *Etymologiae* 4.12.3, *Asclepediades quoque medicus phreneticum quendam per symphoniam pristinae sanitati restituit*. Or Apollo, *Etym.* 4.4.1. But see Thomas à Kempis, *Imitation of Christ* 4.11, "How the blessed body of our Lord Jesus Christ is greatly necessary for the health of man's soul."

52. On the identification as gypsies, see Walter Starkie, "Jerome Bosch's 'The Haywain,' " *Journal of the Gypsy Lore Society* 36 (1957): 83–7. Combe, *Hieronymus Bosch*, 80, described the man in the tall hat as a magician, Starkie as a possible gypsy (87). I am not sure whether we are meant to see him as a kind of sixteenth-century Fagin, or perhaps as a gypsy observer to the procession sharing invidious comparisons with more personal caravans.

53. Thomas à Kempis, *Imitation of Christ* 4.284; Hyma, *Brethren of the Common Life* passim.

54. *Didascalicon: A Medieval Guide to the Arts* (trans. Jerome Taylor; New York: Columbia University Press, 1961), 69; St. Augustine, *In Psalmum* 149, says that when men praise God in chorus, in a union of singers in concord the harmony of Christ's community is revealed.

55. For example, St. Augustine, *In Psalmos* 148, 149.

56. *In ipsa quinta feria devote turbe fidelium propter hoc ad ecclesias affectuose concurrant, ut tunc cleri et populi pariter congaudentes in cantica laudis surgant, tunc*

omnium corda et vota, ora et labia ymnos personent letitie salutaris (Browe, *Textus antiqui de festo Corporis Christi*, 32).

57. On salacious bagpipes, see G. Fenwick Jones, "Wittenwiler's *Becki* and the Mediaeval Bagpipe," *Journal of English and German Philology* 48 (1949): 209ff.; also E. A. Block, "Chaucer's Millers and their Bagpipes," *Speculum* 29 (1954): 239–43; Robertson, *Preface to Chaucer*, 128, 130. See also Clifford Davidson and Thomas H. Seiler, *The Iconography of Hell* (Kalamazoo, Mich.: Medieval Institute Publications, 1992).

58. See n. 23 above. 2 Kgs 6; or Thomas à Kempis, who, after many identifications of the ark and its elements with Holy Communion (see quotation following n. 64; from 4.1; 4.11; 4.14, etc.), says, *Et tamen valde magna distantia est inter arcam foederis cum suis reliquiis et mundissimum corpus tuum cum suis ineffabilibus virtutibus; inter legalia illa sacrificia futurorum figuratiua et veram tui corporis hostiam onmium sacrificiorum antiquorum completiuam*, etc. (4.1).

59. Numbers 17:8. See *Biblia pauperum* (ed. Elizabeth Soltész; Budapest: Corvina Press, 1967), pl. 2, which identifies the ark of the covenant with the nativity, and in the representation of which (center panel), the "law," the "rod," and the "pot" are all represented in the crèche scene.

60. For example, at Gloucester, Norwich, Beverley, Anjou, etc. Cf. Louis Réau, *Iconographie de l'art chrétien* (3 vols; Paris: Presses universitaires de France, 1955–1959), 1:126, who points to the association of the owl with Judaism, and this general association seems to be expressed in the Middle English poem "The Owl and the Nightingale," where the owl represents a kind of obtuseness of the Law and blindness to the Light of mercy, or grace. (The little bird attacking the owl seems to be a swallow [*zwaluw*], associated in popular song and contemporary Christian iconography with hope and grace—Ibid., 1:105).

61. "Vessel" in Scripture is often a figure for the body or soul as container of the Holy Spirit; e.g., 2 Tim 2:21, 1 Pet 3:7, Acts 9:15.

62. This poem was translated into numerous medieval vernaculars; see D. L. Jeffrey, "Forms of Spirituality in the Medieval Religious Lyric," in *Imagination and the Spirit* (ed. C. A. Huttar; Grand Rapids: Eerdmans, 1971), 55–85. The intriguing phrase here is *quam vasa figuli*. A check with a standard dictionary (Lewis and Short) reveals that while *figulis* means "potter" or "seal maker," *vas figuli* is a poetic expression found in Juvenal's tenth satire and used also by the Vulgate translation of Psalm 2:9 to allude to the builders of the brick walls of Babylon, whose fate was that "Thou shalt break them with a rod of iron, thou shalt dash them in pieces like a potter's vessel." See also Jeremiah 25:34, which connects the fate of the woeful pastors of Jeremiah 23 (quoted above) to the destruction of a "pleasant vessel."

63. Delevoy, *Bosch*, 217.

64. Ibid., 38.

65. Thomas à Kempis, *Imitation of Christ* 1.1.16–17.

66. As in *Eerste Bliscap* or the *Ludus Coventriae* where we begin with Creation and Fall, move through time present, and project toward the Day of Judgment.

67. It is interesting that he is being harried by a dog, which according to a commonplace medieval bestiary may be associated with the cleric faithful (*fido*): Hugo of St. Victor's *De bestiis et aliis rebus* (*Concerning Beasts and Other Things*) considers hounds and whelps symbolically as representing "priests in their function of curing, both by word and example, sins unwittingly retained in the mind and thus not confessed" (Migne, PL 177:65–66). Is the folded exterior of the *Haywain* a further suggestion that clerics may easily fail of their promise, and harry, rather than lead, the pilgrim toward perfect Community?

Chapter 10

1. But cf. Peter Dronke, *Medieval Latin and the Rise of the European Love-Lyric* (2 vols.; Oxford: Clarendon Press, 1965–66), 1:341–43; and "The Return of Eurydice," *Classica et Medievalia* 23 (1962): 198–212.

2. For echoes of this judgment, first offered by W. P. Ker, *English Literature: Mediæval* (London: Butterworth, 1955), 94, see J. Burke Severs, "The Antecedents of Sir Orfeo," in *Studies in Medieval Literature: In Honor of Professor Albert Croll Baugh* (ed. MacEdward Leach; Philadelphia: University of Pennsylvania Press, 1961), 187; the articles by Kinghorn, Knapp and Gros Louis cited below; and Alan Joseph Bliss, ed., *Sir Orfeo* (2d ed.; Oxford: Clarendon Press, 1966), xli.

3. The story occurs originally in Vergil, *Georgics* 4; Ovid, *Metamorphoses* 10–11; Boethius, *Consolation of Philosophy* 3, m. 12, and has been adapted numerous times. Among the most recent versions are Cocteau's *Orphée*, J. Anouilh's *Eurydice*, Gregory Orr's *Orpheus and Eurydice* and Charles Mikolayeek's *Orpheus*.

4. A. M. Kinghorn, "Human Interest in the Middle English *Sir Orfeo*," *Neophilologus* 50 (1950): 359–69.

5. James F. Knapp, "The Meaning of *Sir Orfeo*," *Modern Language Quarterly* 29 (1968): 263–73; 269.

6. See Winthrop Wetherbee, *Platonism and Poetry in the Twelfth Century: The Literary Influence of the School of Chartres* (Princeton: Princeton University Press, 1972), 78–79, 92–104; cf. n. 1 supra; cf. Jeff Rider, "Receiving Orpheus in the Middle Ages: Allegorization, Remythification and Sir Orfeo," *Sources on Language and Literature* 24 (1988): 343–66.

7. See the discussions by D. W. Robertson, Jr., and Bernard F. Huppé, *Fruyt and Chaf: Studies in Chaucer's Allegories* (Princeton: Princeton University Press, 1963), 32–100; and Russell A. Peck, "Theme and Number in Chaucer's *Book of the Duchess*," in *Silent Poetry: Essays in Numerological Analysis* (ed. Alistair Fowler; London: Routledge & Kegan Paul, 1970), 73–115. See here also Roy

Michael Liuzza, "*Sir Orfeo*: Sources, Traditions, and the Poetics of Performance," *Journal of Medieval and Renaissance Studies* 21 (1991): 269–84; Erik Kooper, "The Twofold Harmony of Middle English Sir Orfeo," in *Companion to Early Middle English Literature* (eds. N. Veldhoen and H. Aertsen; Amsterdam: Vrije Universitat Verlag, 1995), 115–32; cf. James Dean, "Chaucer's Book of the Duchess: A Non-Boethian Interpretation," *Modern Language Quarterly* 46 (1985): 235–49.

8. Translation from John Warrington, *Symposium and other Dialogues* (London: Dent, 1964), 22ff.

9. Robertson, *Fruyt and Chaf,* 89–91.

10. Bliss, "Introduction," xxxv, lv. Cf. C. Bullock-Davies, "Ympe Tre & Nemeton," *Notes and Queries* 9 (1962): 63–83.

11. Cf. Patricia Vicari, "Sparagmos: Orpheus among the Christians," in *Orpheus: The Metamorphoses of a Myth* (ed. John Warden; Toronto: University of Toronto Press, 1982), 63–83.

12. John Block Friedman, "Eurydice, Heurodis, and the Noon Day Demon," *Speculum* 41 (1966): 22–29. See also his *Orpheus in the Middle Ages* (Cambridge, Mass.: Harvard University Press, 1970), 175–94.

13. *Arnolfo d'Orléans: un Cultore di Ovidio nel Secolo XII* (ed. Fausto Ghisalberti; Memorie del Reale Instituto lombardo di scienze e lettere 24; Milano: U. Heopli, 1932), 222; Friedman, "Eurydice," 24. Christ was often portrayed as Orpheus in early Christian art; see Emerson Howland Swift, *Roman Sources of Christian Art* (New York: Columbia University Press, 1951), 51; also Charles Rufus Morey, *Early Christian Art* (Princeton: Princeton University Press, 1953), 64.

14. Quoted and translated in Wetherbee, *Platonism and Poetry in the Twelfth Century*, 102; for a discussion of the poem see 98–104. See also Dronke, *Medieval Latin and the Rise of the European Love-Lyric*; F. J. E. Raby, "Amor and Amicitia; a Medieval Poem," *Speculum* 40 (1965): 599–610; and Brian Stock, "*Parce continuis*: Some Textual and Interpretative Notes," *Medieval Studies* 31 (1969): 164–73. Speaking of the poem's latter version, Wetherbee writes: "The lutanist echoes the lover almost mockingly; his song recovers Eurydice only as any song of any lost love revives that love, and the recovery leads to a still greater loss" (102).

15. For example, *Polychronicon Ranulphi Higden monachi Cestrensis* 1.19 (trans. John de Trevisa; ed. Churchill Babington; 9 pts.; Rerum Britannicarum medii ævi scriptores 41; London: Longman & Co., 1865–1886), 2:375; Anglicus Bartholomaeus, *De proprietatibus rerum* 19.139.l.944 (trans. John Trevisa; ed. M. C. Seymour, *On the Properties of Things*, 3 vols. [Oxford: Clarendon Press, 1975]); Ps 136, etc.; In *Die Pentecosten* 1.25, in *Old English Homilies and Homiletic Treatises* (ed. Richard Morris; 2 pts.; Early English Text Society,

Original series 29, 34; London: N. Trübner & Co., 1867–1868), 1:97; see Henry Holland Carter, *A Dictionary of Middle English Musical Terms* (Bloomington: Indiana University Press, 1961), 193ff. for extensive reference.

16. Carter, *Dictionary of Middle English Musical Terms*, 193ff.

17. In the classical versions (*Metamorphoses* 10.1–111; *Georgics* 4.453–527; and *Consolation of Philosophy* 3.12) the harp is used for obtaining Eurydice's release. In Ovid's version the quieting of the beasts is added, but only after the death of Eurydice, as a prelude to Orpheus's murder (*Metam.* 11.1–65); cf. Penelope Reed Doob, *Nebuchadnezzar's Children: Conventions of Madness in Middle English Literature* (New Haven: Yale University Press, 1974), 164–207.

18. Isidore of Seville, *Etymologiae* 4.11.3: *Asclepiades quoque medicus phreneticum quendam per symphoniam pristinae sanitati restituit*, cf. 4.4.1; also caput XV; *De proprietatibus rerum* 8.28.1.333; 19.131, 939; etc.

19. John Lydgate, *A Seying of the Nightingale* 1.307 (in *The Minor Poems of John Lydgate* [ed. Henry Noble MacCracken; 2 pts.; Early English Text Society, Extra series 107 [part 1], Original Series 192 [part 2]; London: K. Paul, Trench, Trübner & Co., 1911, 1934], 1:232); also *Handlying Synne* (4769), *Cursor Mundi* (7425), Mirk's *Festial*, etc.; the biblical story is from 1 Kgs 16:16–23.

20. *Glossa ordinaria* (Migne, PL 113:555).

21. MacCracken, ed., *The Minor Poems of John Lydgate*, 1:92.

22. Frederick J. Furnivall, ed., *Robert of Brunne's "Handlyng synne"* (2 pts.; Early English Text Society, Original series 119, 123; London: K. Paul, Trench, Trübner & Co., 1901, 1903), 1:158.

23.   'Alas!' quaþ he, 'For lorn icham!
        Whider wiltow go, & to *wham*?
        Whider þou gost ichil wiþ þe,
        Whider y go þou shalt wiþ me.' (127–30)

    Orfeo here attempts to reaffirm the marriage vows.

24. The verb *cling* means both "shrivel" and "to stick to," as a graft "clinge" to a tree (*Middle English Dictionary*, ed. H. Kurath and S. Kuhn) and also can mean both "as" and "as to" (*MED*, 225). Some of this sense may remain in *MacBeth* 5.5.40:

    "Upon the next tree shalt thou hang alive,
    Till famine cling thee."

25. Friedman, "Eurydice," 28–29.

26. Is this deliberately parallel with the removal of Eurydice from the orchard by sixty ladies after her encounter with the king of faëries?

27. That the reader tutored in the old story might not see this immediately makes the point none the less applicable, on reflection, to the poet's construction. For

a compatible viewpoint see L. J. Owen, "The Recognition Scene in *Sir Orfeo*," *Medium Aevum* 40 (1971): 149–52. The reading I have pursued in the previous several pages was, after the first appearance of this essay (*Mosaic* 9 [1976]: 45–60), vigorously contested by A. C. Spearing in *Readings in Medieval Poetry* (Cambridge: Cambridge University Press, 1987), 73. Subsequently, Oren Falk, "The Son of Orfeo: Kingship and Compromise in a Middle English Romance," *Journal of Medieval and Early Modern Studies* 30 (2000): 247–74, has recently defended my reading, contra Spearing (see esp. 270).

28. *Glossa ordinaria* (Migne, PL 113:555–56).

29. Or as Trevisa, *De proprietatibus rerum:* "For alle at ones and acorde of mysyk ben founde amonge sterres of heuens" (13.28.333); "And musyk excyteth and comfortyth bestis and serpents, foules and Delphines, to take hede thereto [. . .] And it is sayd that heuen gooth aboute wyth consonancye and acorde of melody. For musyk meuyth affeccyons and excyteth the wyttes to dyuers dysposycyons [. . .] And musyk abatyth maystry of euyl spyrytes in mankynde." (19.131.939).

30. "Philosophy of Music," 80–97.

31. Translation from Green, *Consolation of Philosophy*, 41; cf. *De proprietatibus rerum* 19.145.947: "Perfyghte Musyk comprehendyth alle thynges." But see Knapp, "The Meaning of *Sir Orfeo*," 273.

32. *Vitis mystica* 7 (Migne, PL 184:655).

33. *Expo. In Psalm.* 56, v. 8 (Migne, PL 152:898).

34. *Commentarium in Apocalypsin* 3, v. 8 (Migne, PL 100:1122): *Apte autem per citharas passiones Christi figurantur [. . .] Sic sic diversa in Christi corpore membra passiones ejus alia plenius, alia minus, imitantur, sed unam concordiae resonant laudem.* (See also Cassiodorus [Migne, PL 70:404]). The negative of this identification is presumably what Bosch portrays in the "Hell" panel of his so-called "Garden of Earthly Delights," where one sinner's torment is to be crucified upon a harp.

35. P. Berchorius, *Dictionari seu repertorii moralis* 105d, where he finds Orpheus a type of the poet and *praedicator* as well as, in *Metamorphosis Ovidiana* (ed. Thomas Wallensis; Paris, 1509), 78, a type of Christ; and see *Gesta Romanorum* (ed. Sidney J. H. Herrtage; Early English Text Society, Extra series 33; London: N. Trübner & Co, 1879), 138; see also the "Crucifixion" by Hans Leonhard Schaufelein (1508) where David plays his harp at the foot of the cross, and cf. pl. 90 of the *Hours of Catherine of Cleves* (ed. John Plummer; London: Barrie and Rockliff, 1966); also see Réau, *Iconographie de l'Art Chrétien*, 2:492; an excellent illustration occurs in the fifteenth century. Franciscan missal, MS Douie 313, where David plays his harp and the "music" is Christ on the cross, suspended in a harp-shaped cloud.

36. Robert of Brunne, "*Handlyng synne*," 4744.

37. Cf. Sharon Coolidge, "The Grafted Tree in Sir Orfeo: A Study of the Iconography of Redemption," *Ball State University Forum* 23 (1982): 62–68.

38. *Gesta Romanorum* 138.35.1; cf. *De proprietatibus rerum* 1.131.939: "For musyk by the whiche acorde and melody is knowe in sowne & in songe (what) is nedeful to know mystyk meanynge of holy wrytte."

39. This and all subsequent translations are from J. R. R. Tolkien, *Sir Gawain and the Green Knight; Pearl; and Sir Orfeo* (Boston: Houghton Mifflin, 1978).

40. Cf. K. R. R. Gros Louis, "The Significance of Orfeo's Self-Exile," *Review of English Studies* 8 (1967): 245–52, esp. 251.

41. Cf. here Psalm 136:1–4: *Super flumina Babylonis, illic sedimus e flevimus; cum recordaremur Sion: In salicibus in medio ejus, suspendimus organa nostra. Quia illic interrogaverunt nos, qui captivos duxerent nos, verba cantionum: Et qui abduxerunt nos: Hymnum cantate nobis de canticus Sion. Quomodo cantabimus canticum Domini in terra aliena?* The *Ordinary Gloss* on this passage identifies the captivity with man's primal exile, and invokes Augustine's "two cities" to suggest that the harp can only praise God as the exile successfully turns to pilgrimage toward the New Jerusalem (Migne, PL 113:1057). While Orfeo's tree is not said to be a willow, it seems that this psalm might conceivably have been in the poet's mind as he composed his version of Orfeo's exile.

42. E.g., *Pearl*, 881–82:

> "As harpore harpen in her harpe,
> þat nwe songe þay songen ful cler,
> In sounande note a gentyl carpe;
> Ful fayre þe mode þay fonge in fere."

The source for this is scriptural, of course (Rev 5:8), but its echoes are everywhere.

43. J. R. R. Tolkien, *Tree and Leaf* (London: Allen & Unwin, 1964), 60.

44. Cf. n. 32, *supra*.

Chapter 11

1. C. S. Lewis, "Membership," in *The Weight of Glory* (Grand Rapids: Eerdmans, 1949), 41.

2. *Weight of Glory*, 6.

3. C. S. Lewis, Introduction to *The Incarnation of the Word of God: Being the Treatise of St. Athanasius, De Incarnatione Verbi Dei* (ed. and trans. Penelope Lawson; New York: Macmillan, 1946, repr. 1961), 10.

4. Ibid., 10; cf. C. S. Lewis, "On the Reading of Old Books," in *Undeceptions: Essays on Theology and Faith* (London: Geoffrey Bles, 1970), 27.

5. C. S. Lewis, *An Experiment in Criticism* (Cambridge: Cambridge University Press, 1961. Repr. 1996), 11, 19.

6. Ibid., 47.
7. Ibid., 93.
8. Ibid., 138.
9. Ibid., 23.
10. C. S. Lewis, "Descriptione De Temporum," in *Selected Literary Essays* (ed. Walter Hooper; Cambridge: Cambridge University Press, 1969), 13.
11. Rudolf Bultmann, among others, had contended that "in an age of electricity" the Gospels could no longer be read as historical accounts.
12. Walter Hooper, ed., *Christian Reflections* (Grand Rapids: Eerdmans, 1967), 154.
13. Lewis, *Weight of Glory*, 50.
14. Ibid.
15. "Historicism," in *Fern-seed and Elephants* (Glasgow: Fontana & Collins, 1975), 44.
16. *They Stand Together: The Letters of C. S. Lewis to Arthur Greeves, 1914–1963* (ed. Walter Hooper; New York: Macmillan Publishing, Co., 1979).
17. From a letter to Arthur Greeves, quoted in Roger Lancelyn Green and Walter Hooper, *C. S. Lewis: A Biography* (Glasgow: Collins, 1979), 121.
18. Austin Farrer, "The Christian Apologist," in *Light on C. S. Lewis* (ed. Jocelyn Gibb; London: Geoffrey Bles, 1965), 26.
19. "Learning in War-time," in *Weight of Glory*, 34.
20. Walter Hooper, ed., *Poems: C. S. Lewis* (New York: Harcourt Brace Jovanovich, 1964), 129.

Chapter 12

1. George Steiner, *George Steiner: A Reader* (New York: Oxford University Press, 1984), 94.
2. Ibid., 95.
3. Donald Marshall, "Making Letters Speak: Interpreter as Orator in Augustine's *De Doctrina Christiana*," *Religion and Literature* 24 (1992): 1–18.
4. Northrop Frye, *Words With Power: Being a Second Study of "The Bible and Literature"* (San Diego: Harcourt Brace Jovanovich, 1990), 241ff.
5. As readers may remember, upon hearing that the first successfully cloned sheep had been spun up from mammary tissue and accordingly named after her, Dolly is reported to have said: "Any publicity is good publicity."
6. Michael J. Christensen, *C. S. Lewis on Scripture* (Waco: Word, 1979), 14; Gary Lee Friesen, "Scripture in the Writings of C. S. Lewis" (MA Thesis, Dallas Theological Seminary, 1973).
7. Clyde S. Kilby, *The Christian World of C. S. Lewis* (Grand Rapids: Eerdmans, 1964), 153.

8. Ibid., 153–54.

9. Hooper, ed. *Christian Reflections*, 118; and C. S. Lewis, *Reflections on the Psalms* (New York: Harcourt Brace Jovanovich, 1958), 20–33.

10. Letter to Corbin Carnell, quoted in Christensen, *C. S. Lewis on Scripture*, 96.

11. C. S. Lewis, *Studies in Words* (Cambridge: Cambridge University Press, 1960), 5.

12. Green and Hooper, *C. S. Lewis: A Biography*, 104.

13. Hooper, ed., *Christian Reflections*, 123–25.

14. Ibid., 129.

15. Ibid.

16. C. S. Lewis, *The Four Loves* (New York: Harcourt Brace Jovanovich, 1960), 148.

17. C. S. Lewis, "Is Theology Poetry?" in *Screwtape Proposes a Toast* (London: Collins, 1965), 42.

18. C. S. Lewis, *The Joyful Christian* (New York: Macmillan, 1974), 106.

19. Robert Alter and Frank Kermode, eds., *The Literary Guide to the Bible* (Cambridge, Mass.: Belknap Press of Harvard University Press, 1987), 2–5.

20. Hooper, ed., *Christian Reflections*, 154.

21. Ibid, 156.

22. Lewis was once (April 18, 1944) provoked with a question about rewriting the Bible for modern times. The exchange is worth reflecting on for reasons other than Lewis's unorthodox answer.

Question 10: The Bible was written thousands of years ago for people in a lower state of mental development than today. Many portions seem preposterous in the light of modern knowledge. In view of this, should not the Bible be rewritten with the object of discarding the fabulous and re-interpreting the remainder?

Lewis: First of all as to the people in a lower state of mental development. I am not so sure what lurks behind that. If it means that people ten thousand years ago didn't know a good many things that we know now, of course, I agree. But if it means that there has been any advance in *intelligence* in that time, I believe there is no evidence for any such thing. The Bible can be divided into two parts—the Old and New Testaments. The Old Testament contains fabulous elements. The New Testament consists mostly of teaching, not of narrative at all: but where it *is* narrative, it is, in my opinion, historical. As to the fabulous element in the Old Testament, I very much doubt if you would be wise to chuck it out. What you get is something *coming gradually into focus.* First you get, scattered through the heathen religions all over the world—but still quite vague and mythical—the idea of a god who is killed and broken and then come to life again. No one knows where he is supposed to have lived and died; he's not historical. Then you get the Old Testament. Religious ideas get a bit more focused. Everything is now connected with a particular nation. And it comes still more into focus as it goes on. Jonah and the Whale, Noah and his Ark, are fabulous; but the Court history of King David is probably as reliable as the Court history of Louis XIV. Then, in the New Testament the *thing really happens.* The dying god really appears—as a historical Person, living in a definite place and time. If we *could* sort out all the fabulous elements in the earlier stages and separate them from the historical ones, I think we might lose an essential part of the whole process. (Lewis, *Undeceptions: Essays,* 33–34).

23. Lewis, *Undeceptions,* 125.
24. Hooper, ed., *Christian Reflections,* 156.
25. Lewis, *Undeceptions,* 126.
26. Lewis often exhibited great sensitivity to evangelicals in his own country as well, among them his boyhood friend Arthur Greeves, who had found *Pilgrim's Regress* too intellectual. In his reply Lewis regrets his complexity, but also defends it:

> You remember we discussed last summer how much more sympathy you had than I with the Puritan simplicity. I doubt if I interpret Our Lord's words quite in the same way as you. I think they mean that the *spirit* of man must become humble and trustful like a child and, like a child, *simple in motive,* i.e. disinterested, not scheming and "on the lookout." I don't think He meant that adult Christians must *think* like children: still less that the processes of thought by wh[ich] people *become* Christians must be childish processes. At any rate the *intellectual* side of my conversion was *not* simple and I can describe only what I know. (Hooper, ed., *They Stand Together,* 447).

Later on, Greeves was to seek Lewis's advice on acquiring a more mature understanding of Scripture. Lewis recommended *A New Commentary on Holy Scripture* (ed. Gore, Goudge and Guillaume; London: Society for Promoting Christian Knowledge, 1928), "a very fat, ugly volume in double columns, but quite readable print" (Hooper, ed., *They Stand Together,* 500). Lewis's copy, in the Wade Collection, is the 1932 edition, and it is underlined and annotated.

27. Lewis, *The Joyful Christian,* 111.
28. Kilby, *The Christian World of C. S. Lewis,* 152.
29. Samuel Taylor Coleridge, *Aids to Reflection and Confessions of an Enquiring Spirit* (London: Bell and Sons, 1890), 126–27.
30. Ibid., 128.
31. Ibid., 320.

32. Ibid., 276.

33. Hooper, ed., *Christian Reflections*, 135.

34. For example, Lewis, *Joyful Christian*, 106.

35. Lewis, *Experiment in Criticism*, 141.

36. Hooper, ed., *Christian Reflections*, 115.

37. Ibid., 116.

38. Lewis, *Joyful Christian*, 105.

39. C. S. Lewis, *The Case for Christianity* (New York: Macmillan, 1974), 36.

40. Ibid., 52.

41. Lewis, *Undeceptions*, 188.

42. C. S. Lewis, *They Asked for a Paper* (London: Geoffrey Bles, 1962), 46–47.

43. Ibid., 48–49.

44. *Times Literary Supplement*, Dec. 2, 1944, 583. In "Religion and Literature," *Selected Prose* (ed. John Hayward; Hammondsworth: Penguin, 1953), 31–42, esp. 32–33, Eliot says, "I could fulminate against the men of letters who have gone into extasies over 'the Bible as literature,' the 'Bible as the noblest monument of English prose'. Those who talk of the Bible as a 'monument of English prose' are merely admiring it as a monument over the grave of Christianity. [. . .] The Bible has had a *literary* influence upon English literature not because it has been considered as literature, but because it has been considered as the report of the Word of God. And the fact that men of letters now discuss it as 'literature' probably indicates the end of its literary influence."

45. Lewis, *Joyful Christian*, 105.

46. Lewis, *Undeceptions*, 189.

47. *Undeceptions*, 188.

48. C. S. Lewis, "Version Vernacular," *The Christian Century* 75 (December 31, 1950): 1515.

49. Lewis, *Undeceptions*, 188.

50. Lewis read with interest W. Schwarz, *Principles and Problems of Biblical Translation: Some Reformation Controversies and Their Background* (Cambridge: Cambridge University Press, 1955). His personal copy, in the Wade Collection, contains useful marginal comments, as well as repeated corrections of the author's Latin. It seems to me entirely characteristic of Lewis's approach that he heavily underlines the sentence (p. 200), "Faith is the most important requirement for any understanding of Scripture." Amusingly, at p. 132 he writes in the margin, "I've given up smoking (again)."

51. Lewis, *The Case for Christianity*, 52–53.

Chapter 13

1. C. L. Wrenn, *Word and Symbol: Studies in English Language* (London: Longmans, 1967), 3.

2. George Steiner puts the relevance of the grammatical issue succinctly, in *In Bluebeard's Castle* (London: Faber and Faber, 1971), 87–88: "The classic speech-construct, the centrality of the word, are informed by and expressive of both a hierarchic value-system, and the trope of transcendence. These nodes of sensibility are interactive and mutually reinforcing at every point. Indo-European syntax is an active mirroring of systems of order, of hierarchic dependence, of active and passive stance, such as have been prominent in the fabric of Western society. The cliché tag regarding the capacity of Latin grammar to reproduce charismatic attitudes in Roman feeling and conduct, is true in a more acute and general sense. An explicit grammar is an acceptance of order: it is a hierarchization, the more penetrating for being enforced so early in the individual life-span, of the forces and valuations prevailing the body politic."

3. See the accessible discussion of this by Fredrick C. Grant, *Translating the Bible* (Greenwich, Conn.: Seabury, 1961), 3–17, 130–66. More fully, see George Steiner, *After Babel: Aspects of Language and Translation* (New York: Oxford University Press, 1975), and the excellent general article by Barry Hoberman, "Translating the Bible: An Endless Task," *The Atlantic* 255 (February 1985): 43–58.

4. Ian Robinson, "The Word of God Now," *PN Review* 6 no. 5 (1980): 26–27.

5. Though the committee stopped short of deleting "God" because it may be construed as a "masculine" term (the feminine being "Goddess"), there is no logical reason why this should not be a next step. Cf. Judith Plaskow, "Why Women Need the Goddess," in *Womanspirit Rising: A Feminist Reader in Religion* (ed. Carol P. Christ and Judith Plaskow; New York: Harper and Row, 1979), 273ff.

6. An example of subtle signification, in a different context and simply as an apparent remark in passing, is afforded by Gail Ramshaw Schmidt in her article "De Divinibus Nominibus: The Gender of God," *Worship* 56 (1982): 117–31, where she writes, " 'It' is used for human persons only for infants and dead bodies . . . ," which casually places infants on a value plane with corpses; the choice of neuter in this case clearly depersonalizes, and involves explicit judgment concerning value.

7. Margaret Doody, "'How Shall We Sing the Lord's Song upon an Alien Soil?': The New Episcopalian Liturgy," in *The State of the Language* (ed. Leonard Michaels and Christopher Ricks; Berkeley: University of California Press, 1980), 113. This well-written article is, along with Ian Robinson, *The Survival of English* (Cambridge: Cambridge University Press, 1973), perhaps the best criticism of "new" liturgies in the Anglican/Episcopal tradition.

8. *The Churchman* 9 no. 8 (October, 1986).

9. Jaroslav Pelikan, *Jesus, Through the Centuries: His Place in the History of Culture* (New Haven: Yale University Press, 1985), 66.

10. See, for example, the article by Gail Ramshaw Schmidt, cited in n. 6 above; also, see Virginia Ramey Mollenkott, *The Divine Feminine: The Biblical Imagery*

of God as Female (New York: Crossroad, 1983); and Nancy A. Hardesty, *Inclusive Language In the Church* (Atlanta: John Knox, 1987).

11. Quoted in Hoberman, "Translating the Bible," 58; also Phyllis Trible, *God and the Rhetoric of Sexuality* (Philadelphia: Fortress, 1978).

12. *Julian of Norwich: Showings* (ed. Edmund Colledge and James Walsh; New York: Paulist Press, 1978); selections translated in David Lyle Jeffrey, *The Law of Love: English Spirituality in the Age of Wyclif* (Grand Rapids: Eerdmans, 1988).

13. Joseph Cardinal Ratzinger, *The Ratzinger Report* (San Francisco: Ignatius Press, 1985), 97.

14. It is also, of course, to deny our creatureliness—that we are derivative beings, something that is emphasized everywhere in Scripture and finds a powerful New Testament summary in Col 1:12–29. When, as Cardinal Ratzinger observes, "certain feminist circles consider it 'unjust' that only the woman is forced to give birth and to suckle" (ibid., 96), it is the predication of creation upon a Creator that is ultimately being resented and opposed; this is consistent in all of these contemporary efforts to "rename" or redefine.

15. The "Self-Blessing Ritual" of Zsuzanna E. Budapest (in Christ and Plaskow, eds., *Womanspirit Rising*, 269–72) and other like statements of value make this less clear than the hard-headed Marxism of feminist Rosemary Radford Ruether. In her chapter, "Motherhood and the Megamachine . . ." from her *Religion and Sexism: Images of Women in the Jewish and Christian Traditions* (New York: Simon and Schuster, 1974), 43–51, she resents that "the bride of Yahweh in the Covenant [. . .] was subordinate and dependent to the male Lord of Hosts" (48). Her conviction is that "women's liberation is [. . .] impossible within the present social system. [. . .] Women simply cannot be persons within the present system of work and the family, and they can only rise to liberated personhood by the most radical and fundamental reshaping of the entire human environment that redefines the very nature of work, family, and the institutional expression of social relations" (44). This rather wooden display of doctrinaire Marxism concludes, predictably, by positing a new and materialist rather than spiritual authority. "It entails literally a global struggle to overthrow and transform the character of power structures and points forward to a new messianic epiphany that will as far transcend the world-rejecting salvation myths of apocalypticism and platonism as these myths transcend the old nature myths of the neolithic villages" (45). Ruether's concern is here neither with theology nor worship life but rather with political power such as would eradicate both.

Chapter 14

1. Salman Rushdie, *Midnight's Children* (London: Jonathan Cape, 1981; repr. Penguin, 1991), 118.

2. Ibid.
3. Anyone reflecting on *An Inclusive Language Lectionary* (3 vols.; Atlanta: John Knox Press, 1983–1985), and service books developed from it, should still consult the review of vol. 1 by Elizabeth Achtemeier in *Interpretation* 38 (1984): 64–66. Arguments attacking Achtemeier typically have not dealt with the substantive hermeneutic and theological issues. Recent examples include Andrew J. Dell'Olio, "Why Not God the Mother?," *Faith and Philosophy* 15 (1998): 193–209, a largely sophistical attempt to argue that "even if Jesus's explicit use of a term may serve as justification for its use by Christians, it does not follow that the absense of the explicit use of a term renders the use of that term by Christians illicit" (198). Cf. Angelo Vigano, *God our father/mother* (London: St. Pauls, 1999). Most feminists put it, nonetheless, in ways that underscore their largely sociological justification. See, e.g., Sandra M. Schneiders' representative preface: "As women have become aware of their inferior status and actual oppression in family, society, and Church, they have also become aware that the gender of God, God's presumed masculinity, has functioned as the ultimate religious legitimization of the unjust structures which victimize women" (*Women and the Word: The Gender of God in the New Testament and the Spirituality of Women* ([New York: Paulist Press, 1986]).
4. Schneiders, earlier in her text, insists that "it is important to be aware that the question of the gender of God is a thoroughly modern issue" (2).
5. *Dialogue* 31 (1998): 31–51.
6. Elisabeth Schüssler Fiorenza, *JESUS: Miriam's Child, Sophia's Prophet: Critical Issues in Feminist Theology* (New York: Continuum, 1994), 76.
7. Schneiders, *Women and the Word*, 7.
8. Ibid., 37.
9. Joachim Jeremias, *Abba: Studien zur neutestamentlichen Theologie und Zeitgeschichte* (Göttingen: Vandenhoeck and Ruprecht, 1966).
10. Charting this territory two decades ago was Anthony C. Thistleton, *The Two Horizons: New Testament Hermeneutics and Philosophical Description with Special Reference to Heidegger, Bultmann, Gadamer, and Wittgenstein* (Grand Rapids: Eerdmans, 1980)—still a useful book.
11. David L. Jeffrey, "Inclusive Language and Worship," in *Best Essays in Theology: 1988* (ed. J. I. Packer; Chicago: CT Publications, 1989), 135–52.
12. Jacob Boas, "The Shrinking World of German Jewry, 1933–1938," *Leo Baeck Institute Yearbook* 31 (1986): 241–44.
13. Franz Rosenzweig, "Scripture and Luther," in Martin Buber and Franz Rosenzweig, *Scripture and Translation* (trans. Lawrence Rosenwald, with Everett Fox; Bloomington: Indiana University Press, 1994), 47–72. See also the subsequent essay by Buber, "On Word Choice in Translating the Bible: in Memoriam Franz Rosenzweig," 73–89.

14. Feuerbach, Nietzsche, and Heidegger were often cited as philosophical authorities who justified such a move. See Adolf Keller, *Religion and the European Mind* (London: Society for Promoting Christian Knowledge, 1934), 103ff. Also the comments by Wolfhart Pannenberg, "Feminine Language About God?" *The Ashbury Theological Journal* 48 (1993): 27–29.

15. Pannenberg, "Feminine Language About God?," 29.

16. See here John W. Miller, *Calling God "Father": Essays on the Bible, Fatherhood, and Culture* (New York: Paulist Press, 1999), esp. chs. 5 and 10, with which I am substantially in agreement.

17. The notion of ex-Catholic theologican and feminist Mary Daly that the emancipation of women requires the emasculation of God ("Since God is male the male is God") certainly misconstrues the Scriptures (*Quest* [Spring 1974], 21). But St. Thomas Aquinas, commenting on the verses in Ephesians (3:14–15) which afford the epigraph for my remarks here, reminds us that the analogy or derivation in St. Paul is central to our sense of the meaning of *human* fatherhood. Aquinas writes: "*Fatherhood* and *generation* are superlative in God, comparative in creatures" (*Sum. Theol.* 1a.33.2). He continues, "Now fatherhood and sonship at full strength are the Father's and the Son's who are one in nature and glory" (1a.33.3). It is not difficult to see that hatred for the one notion of fatherhood may entail hatred for the other.

18. See Donald G. Bloesch, *The Battle for the Trinity: The Debate over Inclusive God-Language* (Ann Arbor: Servant Publications, 1985), who anchors his entire argument on this point. A fine supplement to Bloesch, from a linguistic point of view, is Paul Mankowski, "The Necessary Failure of Inclusive Language Translations: A Linguistic Elucidation," *The Thomist* 62 (1998): 445–68. For another Catholic analysis, relating the Exodus 20 passage to the first article of the historic creeds, see Felix-Alejandro Pastor, " 'Credo in Deum Patrum': sul primo articolo della fede," *Gregorianum* 80 (1999): 469–88.

19. Bloesch, *Battle for the Trinity*; Pannenberg, "Feminine Language About God?;" and Achtemeier, review of *An Inclusive Language Lectionary*; also Donald D. Hook and Alvin A. Kimel, Jr., "The Pronouns of Deity: A Theological Critique of Feminist Proposals," *Scottish Journal of Theology* 46 (1993): 297–323; also Leon J. Podles, *The Church Impotent: The Feminization of Christianity* (Dallas: Spence, 1999).

20. Bloesch, *The Battle for the Trinity*; Achtemeier, review of *An Inclusive Language Lectionary*.

21. See "1992 Synod Summary: Language, Gender, and God," *Year Book of the Diocese of Sydney* (Sydney, Australia, 1993): 446–63; see also Roland Mushat Frye, "Language of God and Feminist Language," *Reports from the Center of Theological Inquiry*, no. 3 (Princeton: Princeton Seminary Publications, 1988),

1–25. From a Catholic perspective, Patrick Henry Reardon, "Father, Glorify Thy Name," *Pro Ecclesia* 7 (1998): 138–51, shows how Aquinas among others utterly rejects the idea that "Father" is metaphor: "[. . .] classifying the Father's proper name as only metaphorical is not in practice at least to explain it; it is rather to explain it away. It makes God's revelation nothing more than a restatement of our ignorance of him, so that we are back where we started, as though there never had been a divine revelation in Jesus Christ" (146). This seems to me to be the decisive point.

22. Bloesch, *Battle for the Trinity*; Frye, "Language of God and Feminist Language," 8.

23. Rom 8–9:8; Gal 4:4–7; Eph 1:5. See here the fine article by Marianne Meye Thompson, " 'Mercy upon All': God as Father in the Epistle to the Romans," in *Romans and the People of God: A Festschrift for Gordon Fee in Honor of his 65th Birthday* (ed. Sven K. Soderlund; Grand Rapids: Eerdmans, 1999), 203–16; also her *The Promise of the Father: Jesus and God in the New Testament* (Louisville, Ky.: Westminster John Knox Press, 2000); also Roch Kereszty, "God the Father," *Communio* 26 (1999): 258–77; also Peter Widdicombe, *The Fatherhood of God from Origen to Athanasius* (Oxford: Clarendon Press, 1994), who shows in ch. 11 how adoption is *the* issue among the early Fathers.

24. Frye, "Language of God and Feminist Language," 8.

25. For Paul Ricoeur, the terms "Father" and "Son" are part of the fundamental symbolism of Christianity. They are performative terms which make possible our being Christian (cf. Rom 8–9). See his *Conflict in Interpretation* (trans. Don Ihde; Evanston, Ill.: Northwestern University Press, 1974), 487–91; cf. Bloesch, *Battle for the Trinity*; Frye, "Language of God and Feminist Language"; Jeffrey, "Inclusive Language and Worship."

26. Some have wanted the text to be much more ambiguous than on any rational construal it is. An example is Elaine Mary Wainwright, *Toward a Feminist Critical Reading of the Gospel* (Berlin: Walter de Gruyter, 1991). Wainwright's strategy is largely to eschew commentary on most of the Matthew texts I have cited (e.g., 336). When she does comment upon one, e.g., Matt 12:50, she simply begs the question (98–99) and defies the integrity of the text attributed to Jesus by reducing it to a mere affirmation of inclusivity. What Jesus is recorded as saying, most evidently, is a description of the adoptive filiation by which obedience to the will of the Father makes those who obey "kin" to Jesus himself.

27. In the powerfully suggestive "theodrammaturgy" of Hans Urs von Balthasar, *The Glory of the Lord* (7 vols.; San Francisco: Ignatius Press, 1989), vol. 7, the Father's omnipotence is revealed dramatically but ironically in his making the expression of his paternal love dependent upon the Son's obedience. In adoption, this Fatherhood "by assent" through a willed acceptance of the Father's

authority is held out to us. See also the good discussion of Balthasar in Margaret M. Turek, "'As the Father has Loved Me' (John 15:9): Balthasar's Theodrammatic Approach to a Theology of God the Father," *Communio* 26 (1999): 295–318.

Chapter 15

1. Translated by Robert Midgley, *Plutarch, Moralia* (London: n.p. 1691, 1704), 9.

2. Jean Daniélou, *The Scandal of Truth* (Baltimore: Helican Press, 1962).

3. Søren Kierkegaard, *The Present Age* and *The Difference between a Genius and an Apostle* (Trans. Alexander Dru; New York and Evanston, Ill.: Harper & Row, 1962), 68–69.

4. *Intentions* (London: McRuen, 1891), 430.

5. Ian Dusby, ed. *The Cambridge Guide to Literature in English* (Cambridge: Cambridge University Press, 1988), 192.

6. Daniélou, *Scandal of Truth*, 8.

7. Ibid, 13.

8. Translated by Howard and Edna Hong (New York: Harper & Row, 1962).

9. Kierkegaard, *Present Age*, 68.

10. William James, *Pragmatism* (Cambridge, Mass.: Harvard University Press, 1978), 6.

"I am a companion of all them that fear Thee, and of them that keep thy precepts."

Psalm 119:63

Index